W9-DAS-912

The Complete Memoirs

The Complete Memoirs

EXPANDED EDITION

PABLO NERUDA

Translated from the Spanish by Hardie St. Martin

and Adrian Nathan West

FARRAR, STRAUS AND GIROUX

NEW YORK

Farrar, Straus and Giroux
120 Broadway, New York 10271

Copyright © 1974 by The Estate of Pablo Neruda
Translation copyright © 1976, 1977 by Farrar, Straus and Giroux
Translation of expanded text copyright © 2021 by Adrian Nathan West
All rights reserved
Printed in the United States of America
Originally published in Spanish in 1974 as *Confieso que he vivido: Memorias*
English translation published in 1977 by Farrar, Straus and Giroux as *Memoirs*
First Farrar, Straus and Giroux expanded edition, 2021

The final editing of Pablo Neruda's memoirs was interrupted by his death.
Matilde Neruda and Miguel Otero Silva prepared the original manuscript for publication
in 1974. An expanded edition was published in Spain in 2017. The English translation
has been revised to conform with this new edition.

Library of Congress Cataloging-in-Publication Data
Names: Neruda, Pablo, 1904–1973, author. | St. Martin, Hardie, translator. | West,
  Adrian Nathan, translator.
Title: The complete memoirs : expanded edition / Pablo Neruda ; translated from the
  Spanish by Hardie St. Martin and Adrian Nathan West.
Other titles: Confieso que he vivido. English
Description: First Farrar, Straus and Giroux expanded edition. | New York : Farrar,
  Straus and Giroux, 2021. | Includes index.
Identifiers: LCCN 2021002270 | ISBN 9780374538125 (paperback)
Subjects: LCSH: Neruda, Pablo, 1904–1973. | Poets, Chilean—20th century—
  Biography.
Classification: LCC PQ8097.N4 Z46 2021 | DDC 861/.62 [B]—dc23
LC record available at https://lccn.loc.gov/2021002270

Designed by Gretchen Achilles

Leaf art by bioraven/shutterstock.com

Our books may be purchased in bulk for promotional, educational,
or business use. Please contact your local bookseller or the Macmillan Corporate
and Premium Sales Department at 1-800-221-7945, extension 5442,
or by email at MacmillanSpecialMarkets@macmillan.com.

www.fsgbooks.com
www.twitter.com/fsgbooks • www.facebook.com/fsgbooks

1   3   5   7   9   10   8   6   4   2

Contents

JOURNEY THROUGH MY POETRY   3

1. THE COUNTRY BOY   7

2. LOST IN THE CITY   41

3. THE ROADS OF THE WORLD   71

4. LUMINOUS SOLITUDE   97

5. SPAIN IN MY HEART   135

6. I WENT OUT TO LOOK FOR THE FALLEN   169

7. MEXICO, BLOSSOMING AND THORNY   191

8. MY COUNTRY IN DARKNESS   209

9. BEGINNING AND END OF EXILE   243

10. VOYAGE AND HOMECOMING   277

11. POETRY IS AN OCCUPATION   315

12. CRUEL, BELOVED HOMELAND   423

FAREWELL   449

Editorial Note: Texts Added to This Edition   451

Chronology   457

Index   481

The Complete Memoirs

Journey Through My Poetry

Today I bring you something of the voracious essences of my poetry, of the cold and fire that have joined me on my way, often walking ahead of me, suffusing themselves with all they found open, striking against the sealed wombs of the world in its extension.

I am aware of the many objections and debates that flare up and burn out from one day to the next concerning my words: we will revisit none of that on this journey: in these moments, I wish to be for you nothing more than a kind companion who will accompany you through a region that at times not even I will recognize.

What is my poetry? I don't know. It would be easier to ask my poetry who am I. She has been my guide amid the dark night of the soul, has chained and unchained me, driven me through solitudes, through love, through people.

I regret terribly that today, I should be my voice's theme. Accept me among you as just another man, a common man, sometimes wounded, sometimes full of cheer, a man who goes out with you into library and forest, to meetings of the people, to the secret redoubts of the heart.

To the south of my poetry is solitude; to the north, the people. Solitude is the mother of my first verses. In its gulfs and labyrinths I cast the nets of the young and solitary fisherman, the man who wants to shatter the mysteries of the night. In that comic, impassioned, sidereal age of my life, the questions rise up in great bitter flight, in crepuscular indecision, in the solitude of the world . . .

Then, like a blaze in the depths of the forest, the lights of love appear, the disordered flames of first tenderness, the discovery of joy and delight. The dark wind of solitude still echoes in the interstices of pleasure, and love's calls bear deep inside them the distillation of desperate experience. The man lost in the sea of the origin grasps at the thorns of love with the anxiety of a small creature drowning in the waters of the abysmal night.

PABLO NERUDA, "Journey Through My Poetry"

In these memoirs or recollections there are gaps here and there, and sometimes they are also forgetful, because life is like that. Intervals of dreaming help us to stand up under days of work. Many of the things I remember have blurred as I recalled them, they have crumbled to dust, like irreparably shattered glass.

What the memoir writer remembers is not the same thing the poet remembers. He may have lived less, but he photographed much more, and he re-creates for us with special attention to detail. The poet gives us a gallery full of ghosts shaken by the fire and darkness of his time.

Perhaps I didn't live just in my self, perhaps I lived the lives of others.

From what I have left in writing on these pages there will always fall—as in the autumn grove or during the harvesting of the vineyards—yellow leaves on their way to death, and grapes that will find new life in the sacred wine.

My life is a life put together from all those lives: the lives of the poet.

The Country Boy

THE CHILEAN FOREST

Under the volcanoes, beside the snow-capped mountains, among the huge lakes, the fragrant, the silent, the tangled Chilean forest ... My feet sink down into the dead leaves, a fragile twig crackles, the giant rauli trees rise in all their bristling height, a bird from the cold jungle passes over, flaps its wings, and stops in the sunless branches. And then, from its hideaway, it sings like an oboe ... The wild scent of the laurel, the dark scent of the boldo herb enter my nostrils and flood my whole being ... The cypress of the Guaitecas blocks my way ... This is a vertical world: a nation of birds, a plenitude of leaves ... I stumble over a rock, dig up the uncovered hollow, an enormous spider covered with red hair stares up at me, motionless, as huge as a crab ... A golden carabus beetle blows its mephitic breath at me, as its brilliant rainbow disappears like lightning ... Going on, I pass through a forest of ferns much taller than I am: from their cold green eyes sixty tears splash down on my face and, behind me, their fans go on quivering for a long time ... A decaying tree trunk: what a treasure! ... Black and blue mushrooms have given it ears, red parasite plants have covered it with rubies, other lazy plants have let it borrow their beards, and a snake springs out of the rotted body like a sudden breath, as if the spirit of the dead trunk were slipping away from it ... Farther along, each tree stands away from its fellows . . . They soar up over the carpet of the secretive forest, and the foliage of each has its own style, linear, bristling, ramulose, lanceolate, as if cut by shears moving in infinite ways . . . A gorge; below, the crystal water slides over granite and jasper . . . A butterfly goes past, bright as a lemon, dancing between the water and the sunlight . . . Close by, innumerable calceolarias nod their little yellow heads in greeting . . . High up, red copihues (Lapageria rosea) dangle like drops from the magic forest's arteries . . . The red copihue is the blood flower, the white copihue is the snow flower . . . A fox cuts through the silence like a flash, sending a shiver through the leaves, but silence is the law of the plant kingdom . . . The barely audible cry of some bewildered animal far off . . . The piercing interruption of a hidden bird . . . The vegetable world keeps up its low rustle until a storm churns up all the music of the earth.

Anyone who hasn't been in the Chilean forest doesn't know this planet.

I have come out of that landscape, that mud, that silence, to roam, to go singing through the world.

CHILDHOOD AND POETRY

I'll start out by saying this about the days and the years of my childhood: the rain was the one unforgettable presence for me then. The great southern rain, coming down like a waterfall from the Pole, from the skies of Cape Horn to the frontier. On this frontier, my country's Wild West, I first opened my eyes to life, the land, poetry, and the rain.

I have traveled a lot, and it seems to me that the art of raining, practiced with a terrible but subtle power in my native Araucanía, has now been lost. Sometimes it rained for a whole month, for a whole year. Threads of rain fell, like long needles of glass snapping off on the roofs or coming up against the windows in transparent waves, and each house was a ship struggling to make port in the ocean of winter.

This cold rain from the south of the Americas is not the sudden squall of hot rain that comes down like a whip and goes on, leaving a blue sky in its wake. The southern rain is patient and keeps falling endlessly from the gray sky.

The street in front of my house has turned into a huge sea of mud. Out the window, through the rain, I watch a cart stuck in the middle of the street. A peasant wearing a heavy black woolen cloak beats his oxen; the rain and the mud are too much for them.

We used to walk to school, along the unpaved sidewalks, stepping from stone to stone, despite the cold and the rain. The wind carried off our umbrellas. Raincoats were expensive, I didn't like gloves, my shoes got soaked through. I'll always remember the wet socks hanging next to the brazier, and lots of shoes, steaming like toy locomotives. Then the floods would come and wash away the settlements along the river, where the poor lived. The earth shook and trembled. At other times, a crest of terrifying light appeared on the sierras: Mt. Llaima, the volcano, was stirring.

Temuco was the farthest outpost of Chilean life in the southern territories, and therefore it had a long bloody history behind it.

When the Spanish conquistadors pushed them back, after three hundred years of fighting, the Araucanian Indians retreated to those cold regions. But the Chileans continued what they called "the pacification of Araucanía," their war of blood and fire to turn our countrymen out of their own lands. Every kind of weapon was used against the Indians, unsparingly: carbine blasts, the burning of villages, and later, a more fatherly method, alcohol and the law. The lawyer became a specialist at stripping them of their fields, the judge sentenced them when they protested, the priest threatened them with eternal fire. And hard spirits finally consummated the annihilation of a superb race whose deeds, valor, and beauty Don Alonso de Ercilla carved in stanzas of jade and iron in his *Araucana*.

My parents had come from Parral, where I was born. There, in central Chile, vineyards thrive and wine is plentiful. My mother,

Doña Rosa Basoalto, died before I could have a memory of her, before I knew it was she my eyes gazed upon. I was born on July 12, 1904, and a month later, in August, wasted away by tuberculosis, my mother was gone.

Life was difficult for small farmers in the central part of the country. My grandfather Don José Angel Reyes had little land and many children. To me, my uncles' names were like the names of princes from far-off kingdoms. Amós, Oseas, Joel, Abadías. My father's name was simply José del Carmen. He left his father's farm while he was still very young and worked as a laborer at the dry docks in the port of Talcahuano, eventually becoming a railroad man in Temuco.

He was a conductor on a ballast train. Few people know what a ballast train is. In the southern region, with its violent gales, the rains would wash away the rails if gravel wasn't poured in between the ties. The ballast had to be taken out of the quarries in hods and this coarse gravel dumped onto flatcars. Forty years ago, the crew on this type of train had to be made of iron. They came from the fields, from the suburbs, from jails, and were huge, muscular laborers. The company paid miserable wages and no references were asked of those looking for work on these trains. My father, the conductor, had grown used to giving and taking orders. Sometimes he took me along. We quarried rocks in Boroa, savage heart of the frontier, scene of the terrible battles between the Spaniards and the Araucanians.

There, nature made me euphoric. Birds, beetles, partridge eggs fascinated me. What a miracle it was, finding them in the ravines, blue, dark, and shiny, the color of a shotgun barrel. I marveled at the perfection of the insects. I collected "snake mothers." This was the grotesque name given to the largest beetle, black, glistening, and tough, the titan of insects in Chile. He gives you quite a turn when you come upon him suddenly, on the trunk of a ginger, wild-apple, or coihue tree, and I knew he was so strong that I could stand on him and he wouldn't even crack. With his mighty shield to protect him, he had no need of venomous pincers.

My expeditions filled the workers with curiosity. Before long, they started taking an active interest in my discoveries. The moment my father's back was turned, they slipped off into the jungle, and with more skill, strength, and intelligence than I, they found fantastic treasures for me. There was one fellow called Monge. According to my father, he was a dangerous man with a knife. He had two huge incisions on his swarthy face. One was the vertical scar left by a knife, and the other his white, horizontal grin, full of charm and deviltry. This fellow, Monge, would bring me white copihues, furry spiders, sucking ringdoves, and once he found for me the most dazzling of all, the beetle of the coihue and the luma trees. I don't know if you have ever seen one. That was the only time I ever did. It was a streak of lightning dressed in the colors of the rainbow. Red and violet and green and yellow glittered on its shell. It escaped from my hands with the speed of lightning and went back into the forest again. Monge wasn't there to catch it for me. I have never quite recovered from that dazzling apparition. Nor have I forgotten my friend. My father told me about his death. He fell from a train and tumbled down a precipice. The convoy was stopped, but by then, my father told me, he was just a sack of bones.

It's difficult to describe a house like ours, a typical frontier house of sixty years ago.

In the first place, these homes intercommunicated. Through the patio of the Reyeses, and the Ortegas, of the Candia and the Mason families, tools and books, birthday cakes, liniments, umbrellas, tables and chairs changed hands. These pioneer homes formed the hub of all the activities of the village.

Don Carlos Mason, a North American with a white mane of hair, who looked like Emerson, was the patriarch of this particular family. The Mason children were true creoles. Don Carlos respected the law and the Bible. He was not an empire builder but one of the original settlers. No one had money, and yet printing presses, hotels, slaughterhouses burgeoned in this family. Some of the sons were newspaper editors and others just worked for them. In time, everything crumbled and everyone was left as poor as before. Only the Germans kept a stubborn hold on their assets, and that singled them out in the hinterlands.

Our houses, then, had something of a settlers' temporary camp about them. Or of an explorers' supply base. Anyone who came in saw kegs, tools, saddles, and all kinds of indescribable objects.

There were always rooms that weren't finished, and half-completed stairways. There was, forever, talk of going on with the building. Parents were already beginning to think of a university education for their children.

In Don Carlos Mason's home, the most important holidays were observed. For every birthday dinner there was turkey with celery, lamb barbecued on a wooden spit, and floating island for dessert. It has been many years since I last tasted this custard. The white-haired patriarch sat at the head of the interminable table with his wife, Doña Micaela Candia. Behind him, there was a huge Chilean flag with a tiny American one pinned onto it. Those were also the proportions of their blood. Chile's lone star predominated.

In the Mason house there was also a living room that we children were not allowed to go into. I never knew what color its furniture was, because it was kept under white covers, until a fire swept it away. There was an album in there with photographs of the family, finer and more delicate than the horrid colored blowups that invaded the frontier later on.

There was a picture of my mother. She was a lady dressed in black, slender, with a faraway look. I have been told that she wrote poems, but I have never seen them, only the lovely portrait.

My father had married again; his second wife was Doña Trinidad Candia Marverde, my stepmother. I find it hard to believe that this is what I must call the guardian angel of my childhood. She was devoted and loving, and had a countrywoman's sense of humor and a diligent, inexhaustible kindness.

As soon as my father came in, she would turn into a quiet shadow, as did all the women there in those days.

I saw mazurkas and quadrilles danced in that living room.

At home we had a trunk filled with fascinating things. A marvelous parrot preened on a calendar at the bottom of the chest. One day, while my mother was going through that sacred ark, I reached for the parrot and fell in, head first. As I got older, I used to open the trunk on the sly. There were some lovely fragile fans in it.

I recall something else in that trunk. The first love story that intrigued me passionately. It consisted of hundreds of postcards sent by someone who signed himself Enrique or Alberto, I don't remember which, all addressed to María Thielman. These cards were marvelous. They were photographs of the great actresses of the day, embossed with little chips of glass and sometimes with real hair pasted on the heads. There were also castles, cities, and foreign landscapes. For years I found pleasure only in the pictures. But, as I grew older, I read those love notes written in a flawless hand. I always imagined the suitor as a man with a derby, a cane, and a diamond stickpin. His messages, sent from all corners of the globe, were filled with reckless passion expressed in dazzling phrases, with love that threw caution to the winds. I, too, began to fall in love with María Thielman. I imagined her as a haughty actress diademed, covered with pearls. But how did these letters come to be in my mother's trunk? I never found out.

The year 1910 came to Temuco. That memorable year I started school, in a rambling mansion with sparsely furnished rooms and a gloomy basement. In the spring we could see from the school the graceful Cautín River winding its way down below, its shores bordered with wild-apple trees. We used to sneak out of class to dip our feet in the cold water running over the white stones.

The school opened infinite vistas for this six-year-old. Anything might contain a mystery. The physics lab, which I was not allowed to enter—filled with glistening instruments, retorts, and test tubes. The library, forever closed. The sons of settlers had no love of book learning. Still, the cellar was the most fascinating place of all. There was a deep silence, a deep darkness, but with candles to light it up for us, we used to play war games there. The victors would tie their prisoners to some ancient columns. The odor of dampness, of a hideaway, a tomb, given off by the school basement in Temuco, still haunts my memory.

I grew older. Books began to interest me. Buffalo Bill's adventures and Salgari's voyages carried me far into the world of dreams. My first loves, the purest ones, found expression in letters to Blanca Wilson, the blacksmith's daughter. One of the boys had fallen head over heels in love with her and asked me to write his love letters. I don't remember what these letters were like exactly, but they may have been my first literary achievement, because one day, when I ran into this schoolgirl, she asked if I was the author of the letters her sweetheart brought her. I couldn't deny my work and I said yes, very embarrassed. Then she handed me a quince, which of course I would not eat and put away like a treasure. Having thus replaced my friend in the girl's heart, I went on writing endless love letters to her and receiving quinces.

The boys in school didn't know I was a poet and wouldn't have respected me for it. The frontier still had its marvelous quality of a Wild West without prejudices. My companions' names were Schnake, Schler, Hauser, Smith, Taito, Seranis. All of us, including the Aracenas and the Ramírezes and the Reyeses, were equal. There were no Basque family names. There were Sephardim: Albalas, Francos. And Irish: McGintys. Poles: Yanichewskys. The Araucanian names gave off a mysterious light, an aroma of wood and water: Melivilus, Catrileos.

Sometimes we would fight with acorns in the huge closed-in shed. Anyone who has never been hit by an acorn doesn't know how much it really hurts. Before reaching school, we would stuff our pockets with ammunition. I had little skill, no strength, and not much cunning. I

always got the worst of it. While I was busy examining the marvelous acorn, green and polished, with its gray, wrinkled hood, or while
I was still trying clumsily to make one of those pipes they eventually
would grab away from me, a downpour of acorns would pelt my head.
During my second year, I decided to wear a bright green rain hat. It
belonged to my father, like the heavy woolen cape, the red and green
signal lanterns, which I found so fascinating and took to school as
soon as I got the chance, to strut around with them . . . This time it
was pouring and there was nothing so fantastic as the green oilskin
hat that looked like a parrot. The moment I reached the shed, where
three hundred roughnecks were chasing around like madmen, my
hat flew off like a parrot. I ran after it, and each time I was about to
catch it, off it flew, followed by the most deafening howls I have ever
heard. I never laid eyes on it again.

Among these memories I can't see clearly the precise order of
time. I confuse insignificant events that were very special to me, and
this one coming back to my mind now seems to have been my first
erotic adventure, strangely mixed in with natural history. Perhaps
love and nature were, very early on, the source of my poems.

Across from my house lived two girls who were always giving me
looks that made my face turn red. They were as precocious and diabolical as I was timid and quiet. This time I stood in my doorway
trying not to look at them; they were holding something that fascinated me. I went closer, gingerly, and they showed me a wild bird's
nest, woven together with moss and tiny feathers; in it were several
marvelous little turquoise-blue eggs. When I reached for it, one of the
girls told me that they would have to feel through my clothes first. I
was so scared I started to tremble and scurried away, pursued by the
young nymphs holding the exciting treasure over their heads. During the chase, I went into an alley leading to a vacant bakery owned
by my father. My assailants managed to catch me and had started to
strip off my trousers, when we heard my father's footsteps coming
down the passage. That was the end of the nest. The marvelous little

eggs were left shattered, while under a counter we, the attacked and the attackers, held our breath.

I also recall that one day, while hunting behind my house for the tiny objects and minuscule beings of my world, I discovered a hole in one of the fence boards. I looked through the opening and saw a patch of land just like ours, untended and wild. I drew back a few steps, because I had a vague feeling that something was about to happen. Suddenly a hand came through. It was the small hand of a boy my own age. When I moved closer, the hand was gone and in its place was a little white sheep.

It was a sheep made of wool that had faded. The wheels on which it had glided were gone. I had never seen such a lovely sheep. I went into my house and came back with a gift, which I left in the same place: a pine cone, partly open, fragrant and resinous, and very precious to me.

I never saw the boy's hand again. I have never again seen a little sheep like that one. I lost it in a fire. And even today, when I go past a toy shop, I look in the windows furtively. But it's no use. A sheep like that one was never made again.

ART AND THE RAIN

Just as the cold, the rain, the mud in the streets—that is, the nagging and crumbling winter of the southern part of America—came down on us, so, too, the yellow, scorching summer visited these regions. We were surrounded by unexplored mountains, but I wanted to know the sea. Providentially, my obliging father was loaned a house by one of his numerous railroad friends. In total darkness, at four o'clock in the night (I have never found out why they say four in the morning), my father woke up the whole house with his conductor's whistle. From that moment on, there was no rest, or any light either,

and surrounded by candles whose tiny flames were battered by the
drafts filtering in everywhere, my mother; my brother and sister, Rodolfo and Laura; and the cook ran to and fro, doing up mattresses
into enormous balls wrapped in burlap that were hastily rolled out
of the way by the women. The beds had to be put aboard the train.
The mattresses were still warm when they left for the nearby station.
Sickly and weak by nature, and startled out of sleep, I felt nauseated
and chilled to the bone. All the while, the fuss around the house went
on, never ending. Everything was taken along on that month-long
poor man's vacation. Even the wicker dryers that were laid over the lit
braziers to dry the sheets and clothes ever damp in that climate were
tagged and bundled into the cart waiting outside for the luggage.

The train's run was the stretch of that cold province between
Temuco and Carahue. It crossed immense, unpopulated, unculti-
vated terrain, crossed virgin forests, rumbled through tunnels and
over bridges, like an earthquake. The way stations were isolated in
that wide countryside, among mimosas and flowering apple trees. In
their ritual dress and ancestral majesty, Araucanian Indians waited
at the stations to sell lambs, chickens, eggs, and textiles to the passengers. My father always bought something, after endless bargaining.
His blond goatee was something to watch as he picked up a hen in
front of some inscrutable Araucanian woman who would not lower
the price of her merchandise by half a cent.

Each station had a lovelier name, almost all of them inherited
from the ancient Araucanian. This was the region of the bloodiest
battles between the invading Spaniards and the first Chileans, deep-
rooted sons of the land.

Labranza was the first station. Boroa and Ranquilco followed.
Names with the fragrance of wild plants, the sound of their syllables
captivated me. These Araucanian names always signified something
delicious: buried honey, lagoons or a river beside a forest, or a wood-
land with the name of a bird. We passed the hamlet of Imperial,

where the poet Don Alonso de Ercilla was nearly executed by the Spanish governor. This was the capital of the conquistadors in the fifteenth and sixteenth centuries. During their war of independence the Araucanians invented the tactic of "scorched earth." They did not leave one building standing in the city described by Ercilla as beautiful and proud.

And then we came to the city on the river. The train whistled cheerfully, darkening the countryside and the station with giant plumes of coal smoke, bells clanged, and you could now smell the wide, sky-blue, and tranquil Imperial River as it ran to the ocean. Taking down the countless pieces of luggage, getting the small family organized, and going in the oxcart to the boat that would ride down the Imperial River was quite a production, directed, of course, by my father's blue eyes and his railwayman's whistle. We squeezed both the luggage and ourselves into the small boat that would take us to the sea. There were no berths. I sat near the bow. The wheels churned the river currents with their paddles, the small vessel's engines snorted and whined, and the taciturn southerners were spread about on the deck like motionless pieces of furniture.

An accordion broke into its romantic plea, its love call. Nothing can flood a fifteen-year-old's heart with feeling like a voyage down a strange, wide river, between steep banks, on the way to the mysterious sea.

Bajo Imperial was only a string of houses with red roofs. It was situated on the river's brow. From the house that had been awaiting us and, even before, from the rickety piers where the little steamer tied up, I heard the ocean thundering in the distance, a commotion far away. The sea swells were coming into my life.

The house belonged to Don Horacio Pacheco, a giant of a farmer who, all during the month we took over his house, went up and down the hills and impassable roads driving his tractor and thresher. With his machine he harvested the wheat of the Indians and those peasants cut off from coastal towns. He was a huge man who would suddenly burst in upon our railwayman's family with a booming voice, his body covered with cereal dust and straw. Then he would return just as noisily to his work in the mountains. For me he was one more example of the hard life in our southern region.

I found everything mysterious in that house, in the neglected streets, in the unknown lives around me, in the deep roar of the sea far off. The house had what seemed to me a huge, straggly garden and, in the center of this, a summerhouse battered by the rain, a summerhouse of white slats covered with vines. No one except me, a mere nobody, ever penetrated this gray solitude, where the ivy, the honeysuckle, and my poetry thrived. And there was another fascinating thing in that strange garden: a huge lifeboat, orphaned in some great shipwreck and now stranded in this garden without waves or storms, a castaway among the poppies.

The strange thing about this unkempt garden was that, by design or through neglect, only poppies grew there. The other plants had disappeared from this gloomy corner. Some were huge and white like doves, some scarlet like drops of blood, some purple or black, like widows forgotten there. I had never seen such a wilderness of poppies, and I have never seen another like it. And though I had a deep respect for them, and a superstitious dread only they, of all flowers, inspire in me, that did not stop me from snapping one off, now and again, the broken stem leaving sticky milk on my hands and a whiff of unearthly perfume. Then I would stroke its sumptuous petals lovingly and put them into a book to keep. To me they were the wings of huge butterflies that couldn't fly.

The first time I stood before the sea, I was overwhelmed. The great ocean unleashed its fury there between two big hills, Huilque and Maule. It wasn't just the immense snow-crested swells, rising many meters above our heads, but the loud pounding of a gigantic heart, the heartbeat of the universe.

The family laid out its table linen and tea things in that spot. The food reached my mouth sprinkled with sand, but I didn't care. What terrified me was the apocalyptic moment when my father ordered us to take our daily swim. Far back from the giant rollers, my sister, Laura, and I were splashed by the water's icy lash. And we trembled, believing that some wave's finger would hook us into the mountains of the sea. When, our teeth chattering and our ribs blue, my sister and I prepared to die, hand in hand, the railwayman's whistle blew and my father's voice freed us from martyrdom.

I'll tell you about other mysteries in that place. One of these was the Percherons, and another the house of the three enchanted sisters.

Several big buildings stood at the end of the small village. They may have been tanneries, owned by French Basques, who almost always ran the leather industry in southern Chile. I don't really know what they were used for. All I was interested in was watching the huge horses that came out of the front gates toward sundown and crossed the town.

They were Percherons, gigantic colts and mares. Their long manes fell down their very tall backs like human hair. They had enormous legs, also covered with tufts of hair that waved like huge plumes when they galloped off. They were deep red, white, roan, powerful. That's how volcanoes would have moved, if they had been able to trot and gallop like those colossal horses. They would go down the dusty, rocky streets like the violent shock of an earthquake. They whinnied huskily, producing subterranean sounds that sent a shudder through the quiet air. I have never again in my life seen such arrogant, massive, and statuesque horses, except perhaps for those I saw in China carved in stone for the tombs of the Ming dynasty. But even the most venerable stone cannot provide a sight like those huge animals that seemed, in my childish eyes, to emerge from the darkness of dreams, headed for some other-world of giants.

In fact, that untamed world was filled with horses. Chilean, German, and Araucanian riders, all wearing ponchos of black Castilian wool, mounted and dismounted in the streets. Scrawny or well fed, shabby or sleek, the horses stayed where the riders left them, munching on the grass, with steam coming out of their nostrils. They were accustomed to their masters and to the lonely life of the settlement. Later they would return, loaded down with sacks of food or farm implements, to the labyrinthine highlands, climbing up dreadful roads or endlessly galloping over the sand by the sea. From time to time an Araucanian rider would come out of a pawnshop or a dim tavern, mount his unperturbed horse with difficulty, and take the road back to his home in the hills, swaying from side to side, drunk to the point of unconsciousness. As I watched him start off on his journey, it seemed to me that the tipsy centaur was about to fall every time he lurched dangerously, but I was wrong: he always righted himself, only to double over again, swaying toward the other side and always recovering, glued to the saddle. He covered mile after mile, sitting on his horse like that, until he merged into the wild world of nature like an animal unsure of its way but mysteriously protected.

We returned many other summers, with the same household ceremonies, to that fascinating region. With the passing of time, between the bitter winters in Temuco and the wonder-filled summers on the coast, I was growing up, reading, falling in love, and writing.

I got used to riding on horseback. My world expanded upward and outward along the towering mud trails, over roads with sudden curves. I encountered the tangled vegetation, the silence or the sounds of wild birds, the sudden outburst of a flowering tree dressed in scarlet robes like a gigantic archbishop of the mountains, or snowed under by a riot of blossoms I had never seen before. Or from time to time, when least expected, the copihue bellflower, wild, untamable, indestructible, dangling from the thickets like a drop of fresh blood. Slowly I got used to the horse, the saddle, the stiff, complicated riding gear, the cruel spurs jangling at my heels. Along endless beaches or thicketed hills, a communion was started between my spirit—that is, my poetry—and the loneliest land in the world. This was many years ago, but that communion, that revelation, that pact with the wilderness, is still a part of my life.

MY FIRST POEM

Now I am going to tell you a story about birds. In Lake Budi, swans were brutally hunted. They were stalked quietly in boats and then, rowing faster, faster . . . Swans, like the albatross, take to the air clumsily, they have to make a run, skimming the water. They lift their huge wings heavily, and so were easily caught, and finished off with sticks.

Someone brought me a swan that was half dead. It was one of those magnificent birds I have not seen again anywhere in the world, a black-necked swan. A snowy vessel with its slender neck looking as if squeezed into a black silk stocking, its beak an orange color and its eyes red.

This happened at the seaside, in Puerto Saavedra, Imperial del Sur.

It was almost dead when they gave it to me. I bathed its wounds and stuffed bits of bread and fish down its throat. It threw up everything. But it recovered from its injuries gradually and began to realize that I was its friend. And I began to realize that homesickness was killing it. So I went down the streets to the river, with the heavy bird in my arms. It swam a little way, close by. I wanted it to fish and showed it the pebbles on the bottom, the sand the silver fish of the south went gliding over. But its sad eyes wandered off into the distance.

I carried it to the river and back to my house every day for more than twenty days. The swan was almost as tall as I. One afternoon it seemed dreamier; it swam near me but wasn't entertained by my ruses for trying to teach it how to fish again. It was very still and I picked it up in my arms to take it home. But when I held it up to my breast, I felt a ribbon unrolling, and something like a black arm brushed my face. It was the long, sinuous neck falling. That's how I found out that swans don't sing when they die.

Summer is like fire in Cautín. It scorches the sky and the wheat. The land would like to shake off its lethargy. The houses are not prepared for summer, just as they were not prepared for winter. I wander off into the countryside and I walk, walk, walk. I become lost on Nielol Hill. I am alone, my pocket filled with beetles. In a box I carry a hairy spider I just caught. Overhead, the sky can't be seen. The forest is always damp, my feet slip. Suddenly a bird cries out, it's the ghostly cry of the chucao bird. A chill of warning creeps upward from my feet. The copihues, drops of blood, can barely be made out. I am only a tiny creature under the giant ferns. A ringdove flies right past my mouth, with a snapping sound of wings. Higher up, other birds laugh harshly, mocking me. I have trouble finding my way back. It's late now.

My father is not here yet. He will be back at three or four in the morning. I go upstairs to my room. I read Salgari. The rain pours down like a waterfall. In less than no time, night and the rain cover the whole world. I am alone, writing poems in my math notebook. I am up very early the next morning. The plums are green. I charge up the slopes. I carry a little packet of salt with me. I climb a tree, make myself comfortable, bite a little chunk out of a plum carefully, and dip the plum into the salt. I eat it. And I repeat this, up to one hundred plums. I know I'm overdoing it.

Our other house burned down, and this new one is filled with mystery. I climb up on the fence and I watch for the neighbors. There is no one around. I lift up some logs. Nothing but a few measly spiders. The toilet is at the back of the place. The trees next to it have caterpillars. The almond trees display their fruit covered with white down. I know how to catch bumblebees without harming them, with a handkerchief. I keep them captive for a little while and hold them up to my ears. What a beautiful buzz!

How lonely a small boy poet, dressed in black, feels on the vast and terrifying frontier wilderness! Little by little, life and books give me glimpses of overwhelming mysteries.

I can't forget what I read last night: in faraway Malaysia, Sandokan and his friends survived on breadfruit.

I don't like Buffalo Bill, because he kills Indians. But he's such a good cowpuncher! The plains and the cone-shaped tepees of the redskins are so beautiful!

I have often been asked when I wrote my first poem, when poetry was born in me.

I'll try to remember. Once, far back in my childhood, when I had barely learned to read, I felt an intense emotion and set down a few words, half rhymed but strange to me, different from everyday language. Overcome by a deep anxiety, something I had not experienced before, a kind of anguish and sadness, I wrote them neatly on a piece of paper. It was a poem to my mother, that is, to the one I knew, the angelic stepmother whose gentle shadow watched over my childhood. I had no way at all of judging my first composition, which I took to my parents. They were in the dining room, immersed in one of those hushed conversations that, more than a river, separate the world of children and the world of grownups. Still trembling after this first visit from the muse, I held out to them the paper with the lines of verse. My father took it absentmindedly, read it absentmindedly, and returned it to me absentmindedly, saying: "Where did you copy this from?" Then he went on talking to my mother in a lowered voice about his important and remote affairs.

That, I seem to remember, was how my first poem was born, and that was how I had my first sample of irresponsible literary criticism.

And all the while I was moving in the world of knowing, on the turbulent river of books, like a solitary navigator. My appetite for reading did not let up day or night. On the coast, in the tiny town of Puerto Saavedra, I found a public library and an old poet, Don Augusto Winter, who was impressed by my literary voracity. "Have you read them already?" he would say to me, handing me a new Vargas

Vila, an Ibsen, a Rocambole. I gobbled up everything, indiscriminately, like an ostrich.

Around this time, a tall lady who wore long, long dresses and flat shoes came to Temuco. She was the new principal of the girls' school. She was from our southernmost city, from Magellan's snows. Her name was Gabriela Mistral.

I used to watch her passing through the streets of my home town, with her sweeping dresses, and I was scared of her. But when I was taken to visit her, I found her to be very gracious. In her dark face, as Indian as a lovely Araucanian pitcher, her very white teeth flashed in a full, generous smile that lit up the room.

I was too young to be her friend, and too shy and taken up with myself. I saw her only a few times, but I always went away with some books she gave me. They were invariably Russian novels, which she considered the most extraordinary thing in world literature. I can say that Gabriela introduced me to the dark and terrifying vision of the Russian novelists and that Tolstoy, Dostoevsky, and Chekhov soon occupied a special place deep within me. They are with me still.

THE HOUSE OF THE THREE WIDOWS

One time I was invited to a threshing; it was to be done in the old way, with mares. The place was high up in the mountains and pretty far from town. I liked the adventure of going off by myself, figuring out the right route in that mountainous country. I thought if I got lost, somebody would help me out. On my horse, I left Bajo Imperial behind and narrowly made it across the sand bar of the river. There the Pacific breaks loose and attacks, again and again, the rocks and the clumps of bushes on Maule Hill, the last height, standing very tall. Then I turned off along the shore of Lake Budi. The surf pounded the foot of the hill with savage blows. I had to take advantage of the few minutes that elapsed when a wave smashed and pulled itself in to regain its strength. We would hurry across the strip between the hill and the water, before a new wave could crush us, my horse and me, against the rugged hillside.

The danger past, the smooth blue sheet of the lake opened out to the west. The sandy coast ran on endlessly toward the mouth of Lake Toltén, a long way off. These coasts of Chile, often rugged and craggy, suddenly turn into endless ribbons and you can go for days and nights over the sand, close to the sea's foam.

The beaches seem infinite, forming, along the length of Chile, something like a planet's ring, a winding band, pursued relentlessly by the roar of the southern seas: a trail that appears to go around the coast of Chile and beyond the South Pole.

On the forested side, hazel trees with shining dark green branches waved to me, some trimmed with clusters of fruit, hazelnuts that seemed to be painted vermilion, so red are they at that time of year. The giant ferns of southern Chile were so tall that we could pass under their branches without touching them, my horse and I. Whenever my head brushed against their green, a shower of dew would drench us. Lake Budi spread out on my right: a steady blue sheet bordered by far-off woods.

It was only at the end of the lake that I saw some people. They were strange fishermen. In that strip where the ocean and the lake join, or embrace, or clash, between the two waters, there were some salt-water fish, cast out by the rough waves. The huge loaches were specially coveted, broad silver fish, strays thrashing about on those shoals. One, two, three, four, five fishermen, erect, concentrating, watched for the wake of the lost fish and suddenly brought a long trident down on the water with a terrific blow. Then they lifted high the oval-shaped silver fish, shuddering and gleaming in the sun before dying in the fishermen's baskets. It was growing late. I had left the banks of the lake and moved inland looking for the road along the jagged spurs of the hills. Darkness was inching in. Suddenly the wail of a strange wild bird passed overhead like a hoarse moan. An eagle or a condor high up in the twilight sky seemed to halt its black wings, as a signal that I was there, following me in its heavy flight. Red-tailed foxes howled or barked or streaked across the road, and small predatory animals of the secret forest that were unknown to me.

I realized that I had lost my way. The night and the forest which had made me so happy became menacing now, they filled me with terror. One solitary traveler appeared unexpectedly in front of me, in the darkening loneliness of the road. As we approached each other, I stopped and saw that he was just one more of those rough peasants, with cheap poncho and scrawny horse, who emerged from the silence every now and then.

I told him what had happened to me.

He answered that I couldn't get to the threshing that night. He knew each and every corner of that terrain. He knew the exact spot where they were threshing. I told him I didn't want to spend the night outdoors and asked if he could tell me where I might find shelter till daybreak. He instructed me, in a few words, to go two leagues down a small trail that branched off from the road.

"You'll see the lights of a big two-story frame house in the distance," he told me.

"Is it a hotel?" I asked him.

"No, young man. But you'll be welcomed. They're three French ladies, in the lumber business, who've been living there thirty years now. They're nice to everybody. They'll put you up."

I thanked the horseman for his meager counsel and he trotted off on his rickety nag. I continued along the narrow trail, like a lost soul. A virgin moon, curved and white like a fragment of fingernail newly clipped off, was starting its climb up the sky.

About nine o'clock that night, I made out lights that could only be a house. I spurred my horse on before bolts and crossbars could block my way to that God-sent haven. I went in the gate of the property and, dodging logs and hills of sawdust, I reached the entrance, or white portico, of that house lost so far out of the way in the wilderness. I rapped on the door, softly at first, and then harder. Some minutes passed, the dreadful thought that no one was there running through my head, before a slender white-haired lady dressed in black appeared. She examined me with stern eyes, opening the door partway to question so late a traveler.

"Who are you? What do you want?" a quiet, ghostly voice asked.

"I've lost my way in the forest. I'm a student. I was invited to the threshing at the Hernándezes'. I'm very tired. Someone told me you and your sisters are very hospitable. I'd just like a corner to sleep in, and I'll be on my way at daybreak."

"Do come in," she said. "Please feel at home."

She led me to a dark parlor and lit two or three paraffin lamps. I noticed that they were lovely art-nouveau lamps, opaline and gilt bronze. The room had a dank smell. Long, red draperies shielded the tall windows. The armchairs were under white slipcovers to protect them. From what?

It was a room from some other century, hard to place and as disquieting as a dream. The white-haired lady, wistful, in black, moved about on feet I couldn't see, with steps I couldn't hear, her hands touching first this, then that, an album, a fan, here, there, in the silence.

I felt as if I had fallen to the bottom of a lake and lived on, exhausted, dreaming down there. Suddenly two ladies, just like the one who had received me, came in. It was late and it was cold. They sat close to me, one with the vague smile of someone flirting just a little, the other with the melancholy eyes of the one who had opened the door.

Suddenly the conversation wandered very far from that out-of-the-way countryside, far also from the night drilled through by thousands of insects, the croaking of frogs, and the songs of night birds. They wanted to know all about my studies. I happened to mention Baudelaire, and told them I had started to translate his poems.

It was like an electric spark. The three dim ladies lit up. Their lifeless eyes and their stiff faces were transfigured, as if three ancient masks had dropped from their ancient features.

"Baudelaire!" they exclaimed. "This is probably the first time since the beginning of the world that anyone has spoken his name in this lonely place. We have his *Fleurs du mal* here. We're the only ones, for five hundred kilometers around, who can read his marvelous pages. No one in these mountains knows any French."

Two of the sisters had been born in Avignon. The youngest, also of French blood, was Chilean by birth. Their grandparents, their parents, all their relatives, had died a long time ago. The three had grown accustomed to the rain, to the wind, to the sawdust from the mill, to having contact with only a very few primitive peasants and country servants. They had decided to remain there, the only house in those shaggy mountains.

An Indian servant girl came in and whispered something into the ear of the eldest lady. We went out then, down chilly hallways, until we came to the dining room. I was stunned. In the center of the room, a round table with a trailing white tablecloth was illuminated by two silver candelabras with many burning candles. Silver and crystal glittered on that amazing table.

I was overcome by great timidity, as if Queen Victoria had invited me to dine at her palace. I had arrived disheveled, exhausted, and covered with dust, and this was a table fit for a prince. I was far from being one. And to them I must have looked more like a sweaty mule driver who had left his drove at their door.

I have seldom eaten so well. My hostesses were masters of the art of cooking and had as a legacy from their grandparents the recipes of their beloved France. Each dish was a surprise, tasty and aromatic. From their cellars they brought out vintage wines, aged by them in the special French way.

Although weariness would suddenly close my eyes, I listened to them speaking of strange wonders. The sisters' greatest pride was the fine points of cookery. For them, the table was the preservation of a sacred heritage, of a culture to which they, separated from their country by time and great oceans, would never return. Laughing a little at themselves, they showed me a curious card file.

"We're just crazy old women," the youngest said.

Over the past thirty years they had been visited by twenty-seven travelers who had come as far as this remote house, some on business, others out of mere curiosity, still others, like myself, by chance. The incredible thing was that they had a personal file for every one of them, with the date of the visit and the menu they had prepared on each occasion.

"We save the menu so as not to repeat even a single dish, if those friends should ever return."

I went off to sleep and dropped into bed like a sack of onions in a market. At dawn I lit a candle, washed up, and got dressed. It was already getting light when one of the stable boys saddled my horse. I didn't have the heart to say goodbye to the kind ladies in black. Deep in me, something told me it had all been a strange, magical dream, and that, to keep from breaking the spell, I must try not to wake up.

All this happened forty-five years ago, when I was just entering adolescence. What became of those three ladies exiled with their *Fleurs du mal* in the heart of the virgin forest? What happened to their bottles of old wine, their resplendent table lit by twenty wax candles? What was the fate of the sawmill and the white house lost among the trees?

The simplest fate: death and oblivion. Perhaps the forest devoured those lives and those rooms that took me in, one unforgettable night. Yet they live on in my memory as in the clear bed of a lake of dreams. Honor to those three melancholy women who struggled in that wild solitude, with no practical purpose, to maintain an old-world elegance. They defended what their ancestors had forged with their own hands, the last traces of an exquisite culture, far off in the wilderness, at the last boundaries of the most impenetrable and lonely mountains in the world.

LOVE IN THE WHEAT

I reached the Hernández camp before noon, fresh and cheerful. My solitary ride over empty roads, and a good night's sleep, had given my reticent young face a certain glow.

The threshing of wheat, oats, barley was still done with mares. There is nothing gayer in the world than the sight of mares circling, trotting around a heap of grain, under the goading shouts of the riders. There was a splendid sun, and the air, an uncut diamond, made the mountains glitter. The threshing is a golden feast. The yellow straw piles up into golden hills; there's noise and activity everywhere; sacks rushing to get filled; women cooking; runaway horses; dogs barking; children who are constantly having to be plucked—like fruit borne by the straw—from under the horses' hoofs.

The Hernándezes were a unique tribe. The men were unkempt and unshaven, in shirtsleeves, with revolvers in their belts, and almost always splattered with grease, with dust from the grain, with mud, or soaked to the bone by rain. Fathers, sons, nephews, cousins all looked alike. They spent hours on end working under a motor, on a roof, perched on a threshing machine. They never had anything to talk about. They joked about everything, except when they got into a brawl. Then they fought, with the fury of a tornado, knocking down anything that stood in their way. They were always the first to get to the beef barbecues out in the open fields, to the red wine and the brooding guitars. They were frontiersmen, the kind of people I liked. Studious-looking and pale, I felt puny next to those vigorous brutes; and I don't know why, but they treated me with a deference they generally didn't show anyone.

After the barbecue, the guitars, the blinding fatigue brought on by the sun and the threshing, we had to find a makeshift bed for the night. Married couples and women who were alone bedded down on the ground, inside the camp walls put up with freshly cut boards. We males had to sleep on the threshing floor. This rose into a mountain of straw and a whole hamlet could have settled into its yellow softness.

All this lack of comfort was new to me. I didn't know how to go about spreading out. I put my shoes carefully under a layer of wheat straw, and this was to serve as my pillow. I took off my clothes, bundled myself up in my poncho, and sank into the mountain of straw. I lagged far behind all the others, who gave themselves up to their snoring at once, as one man.

I lay stretched out on my back for a long while, with my eyes open, my face and arms covered with straw. The night was clear, cold, and penetrating. There was no moon, but the stars looked as if they had recently been watered by the rain and, high above the unseeing sleep of all the others, they twinkled in the sky's lap just for me. Then I fell asleep. But I woke up suddenly, because something was coming toward me, a stranger's body was moving through the straw and coming closer to mine. I was afraid. The thing was slowly drawing closer. I could hear the wisps of straw snapping, crushed by the unknown shape that kept moving toward me. My whole body stiffened, waiting. Maybe I ought to get up and yell. I remained stock-still. I could hear breathing right next to my head.

Suddenly a hand slid over me, a large, calloused hand, but it was a woman's. It ran over my brow, my eyes, my whole face, tenderly. Then an avid mouth clung to mine and I felt a woman's body pressing against mine, all the way down to my feet.

Little by little my fear turned into intense pleasure. My hand slid over braided hair, a smooth brow, eyes with closed lids soft as poppies, and went on exploring. I felt two breasts that were full and firm, broad, rounded buttocks, legs that locked around me, and I sank my fingers into pubic hair like mountain moss. Not a word came from that anonymous mouth.

How difficult it is to make love, without making noise, in a mountain of straw burrowed by the bodies of seven or eight other men, sleeping men who must not be awakened for anything in the world. And yet we can do anything, though it may require infinite care. A little while later, the stranger suddenly fell asleep next to me, and worked into a fever by the situation, I started to get panicky. It would soon be daybreak, I thought, and the first workers would discover the naked woman stretched out beside me on the threshing floor. But I also fell asleep. When I woke up, I put out a startled hand and found only a warm hollow, a warm absence. Soon a bird began to sing and then the whole forest filled with warbling. There was a long blast from a motor horn, and men and women began moving about and turning to their chores. A new day of threshing was getting underway.

At midday all of us had lunch together around a makeshift table of long planks. I looked out of the corners of my eyes as I ate, trying to find which of the women could have been my night visitor. But some were too old, others too skinny, and many were merely young girls as thin as sardines. And I was looking for a well-built woman with full breasts and long, braided hair. Suddenly a woman came in with a piece of roast for her husband, one of the Hernández men. This certainly could be the one. As I watched her from the other end of the table, I was sure I caught this attractive woman in long braids throwing me a quick glance and the slightest of smiles. And I felt as if the smile was growing broader and deeper, opening up inside my whole being.

THE GIRL FROM THE JOURNEY BACK

Days later, I had to go back, taking another road to keep from getting lost. I was joined by a family that was also returning from the mountains to the village on the coast. Two horses followed behind me, women, children, and baskets. There were too many travelers, and they asked me to let one of the girls from the family ride along on the back of my horse. Once I was settled into the saddle, they helped the girl in question straddle him behind me. She must have been around twenty, and all I saw of her were her bare, tanned legs and her cheeks red like wild apples framing her giggling lips. She must have been laughing at my inept handling of my mount. My vanity was stung: after my solitary expeditions, I'd come to think of myself as king of the roads.

Rounding the lake, we rode toward the coast, where Lake Toltén meets the river. On the shore, we would change course and follow the beach until we were back to Bajo Imperial.

We traveled at a slow trot through a uniform landscape of mountains, amid the ominous trees, black-necked swans, and red flamingos of the meandering lakeside terrain: three horses loaded down with people. We had left very early. Before midday, the distant thundering of the restive sea told us we would soon veer away.

We stopped by the sea foam, stayed on our horses, ate bread and cheese, and drank a sip of wine.

Once on our new route, we proceeded more quickly, and without noticing, my passenger and I pulled away from my escorts. Soon we had left them far behind. The sun's naked rays beat down on our heads, and my poor horse was sweating under the weight of my adolescent self and my robust companion. We slowed to let the others catch up. It was beautiful to gaze at the unpeopled expanse, the whorls of sea foam, the wet beaches with their infinite, sun-caressed sand glimmering like salt or crystals. To the right, far off, were hints of the mountains. On our path were no shadows, not a single tree, nothing but the sand flats by the sea.

Through the jolting gallop, my companion gripped the saddle, my waist, or my hips, but soon I noticed that her hands had grown more curious. I felt them, cool and determined, brushing me as if by chance, determined to scrutinize my anatomy. I turned my head and looked at her, and heard nothing but her laughter, a hearty, joyful cackle, like the whinny of a young mare.

Holding the bridle in my left hand, I undertook an investigation of my own with the right, feeling for those parts of her body I could reach. She offered me a leg, a tense, febrile surface, squeezing me tighter and tighter. Slowly these caresses grew more intense. Rashly, I reached farther back. From me she encountered no resistance, and managed to grasp the most sensitive objective of my youth.

The situation had to be dealt with. The sand of the shore was the perfect bed. But where would we hitch the horse? There were no branches, no tree trunks thrown up by the sea, not even a miserable bush. We had to find something. Otherwise there would be no celebration. The horse, half-wild, like all those in the region, would hurry off in search of water and grass in the distant mountains, and she and I would be left there, naked and abandoned, like Adam and Eve expelled from Paradise. But the wave of desire she had conveyed to me was welling now in my veins. In the meanwhile, nothing changed: the sun, the beach, and not a single godforsaken branch where we could tie the horse and consummate our pleasure.

Night began falling. The stragglers caught up. By now we could see the hillsides holding vigil over the village. We returned to the path between the waves and rocks. The red roof and belfry of the church came into view. It was hopeless. All I could do was curse the sands of the sea and the disobliging barrenness of the coastal vegetation.

More than fifty years later, I still remember this with a smile. I believe that day was one of the most frustrated and desperate of my entire life.

THE HORSE FROM THE SADDLER'S

Temuco, that city in the south of my country that I now see before me again, meant the whole of the world's reality and its mystery throughout my long childhood. Long, because the ages are static in the cold and rainy regions.

The trees in the south of Chile need centuries to grow. That is why, on my return, I see nearly the entire landscape ravaged. The landowners are ruthlessly incinerating the marvelous and ancient forests. This immense destruction is the fruit of greed. They need trees that grow quickly. That is what the wood trade demands.

Little is left of the city of the dreams of my youth. Of course, hardly a single human face. Different children, different old people, different people with unfamiliar eyes.

I found only one face I recognized immediately, and that seemed to recognize me. It was the head of a large wooden horse at the old saddler's shop in the village. There it was, among the same wares as always, saddles, leather lassos for roping the cattle, giant spurs to harry the horses, broad belts for the boorish riders.

But from all that array of fascinating backwoods curios, only the glass eyes of the large wooden horse recaptured my imagination. They looked at me with infinite sadness, recognizing the boy who'd taken more than one journey round the world and now had returned to greet him. We were older now, he and I. Surely we had much to tell each other.

In the Temuco of fifty years before, the vendors would advertise their wares with some large symbol dangling over the door. From afar, the Araucanian Indians who came from their mysterious, secluded redoubts could know right away where to buy their oil, their nails, their shoes. A huge hammer on a corner told them this was a place that sold tools. Otherwise they could buy them in the hardware store, El Candado, which announced its presence with a big blue lock. The cobblers drew people in with giant boots posted over their shoe shops. Wooden keys and spoons, three meters high, left no doubt as to where rice, coffee, and sugar could be purchased.

I walked in short pants beneath those colossal insignia, filled with extraordinary respect. They seemed to me part of an outsize world, strange and hostile, like the enormous ferns of the nearby forest or the

vines hanging high in the trees. They were akin to the tempestuous wind
that shook the humble wooden houses and the volcanoes that sang songs
of fire no sooner than they came into view.

But the horse from the saddler's shop was something else. Every day
on my walk to school, I would stop a moment at the display window to
see if he was still there. He never made it up over the door. Lined in real
leather, with real hoofs, mane, and tail, he was too precious to be abandoned to the wind and freezing rain of the southern hemisphere. No, he
stayed inside, very still and proud, with lustrous skin and costly tack.
Once I was sure he was still there, that he hadn't galloped off or even flown
away toward the mountains, I would go inside, stretch out my small hand,
and pass it over his soft muzzle. Rain or shine, the big wooden horse knew
the young schoolboy would come by to pet him. I sensed that many times
from the look in his glassy eyes.

The city is so changed, it seems as if all it was before has vanished. The
wood houses with their wintertide colors have been replaced by large do-
miciles of disconsolate cement. More people are walking the streets. Fewer
horses, fewer carriages stop at the doors of the hardware stores. This is the
only city in Chile with Araucanians on the streets. I'm glad that hasn't
changed. The Indian women with their colorful blankets, the Indian men
in black ponchos with white fretwork patterns repeating like lightning
strikes. There was a time when they only came down to buy and sell their
scant merchandise: fabrics, eggs, and chickens. Now there's something
else. I will tell you of my surprise.

The whole town came to the venue to hear my poetry. It was a Sunday morning, and the room was ringing with the shouts and laughter
of children. Children are master interrupters, and no poetry can stand
its ground against the shout of a child who's suddenly remembered it's
breakfast time. I walked onstage to the public's applause and felt that
vague Herodian inclination that can strike even the most paternally inclined. Then I heard the silence settle. And amid that silence rose up the
strangest, most primordial, ancient, grating music on the planet, coming
from a group in the back.

It was Araucanians playing their instruments and chanting their plaintive melodies for me. Never in history had such a thing been seen: my reclusive compatriots were offering their ritual art to accompany a political and poetic ceremony. I never thought I would see it, and it moved me even more that I was the object of this missive. My eyes misted over as their old leather drums and gigantic flutes played a scale that antedated all music. Muffled and sharp all at once, monotonous and rending like windblown rain or the roar of a primeval animal in torment beneath the earth's crust.

All this to recount how the Araucanians' culture, what remains of it, anyway, seems to emerge from a dream immemorial to move you, and longs to take part in a world that up till now has been denied it.

The fields' physiognomy has changed. Brutally burned, what the mountains were has largely disappeared. On the peaks, you can see their charred scalp, the bony structure of the earth. Erosion proceeds without pity. And then, many houses and buildings in the towns and villages of the south were shaken and destroyed by the earthquake. Time passes, and they only rebuild in the city centers, in the luxury neighborhoods or the administrative zones. In some of the new townships, recently rebuilt and painted in attractive colors, black letters on white backgrounds proclaim the following: "This area was reconstructed thanks to money from the North American people."

Many countries, untold assistance, came to Chile's rescue after its most recent and terrifying calamity. But only the North Americans flaunt their little clusters of neatly painted houses. Naturally, they don't say that the money they make from copper mining alone could rebuild every city, every road and rail line, every bridge and factory, everything man has built in my entire country through the course of its history.

As the old, immobile horse that has witnessed so many changes looks at me, I ought to tell him that I, too, have changed, more than a little.

Old friend: when I left this city, I was writing verses about love and the night, pensive songs that welled in me like the slow seeds of grains or the secret waters flowing beneath these mountains. Let me tell you, old horse, *my poetry changed many times. It was stained by the smoke of the cities, it has spoken up in meetings, it has been a weapon and a flag.*

I'm happy, old friend.

But I don't want to be cataloged, not definitively, shoved into a drawer with the dogmas of our era. I want to perpetually change, be perpetually born, perpetually grow. I want to sing with my erstwhile intimacy with the rain and with the earth. I've come back to you, old friend, to tell you I've changed as no one can change and that still, I am the same.

I said these words with my eyes, as my lips were unable utter them, and I went to say goodbye, stroking his wooden muzzle once more, and there, where I placed my hand, the leather of his face, of his handsome muzzle, was worn, and I could feel the wood beneath it. It was like touching the old horse's soul.

Before now, I'd always thought I was the only child who'd had that habit of caressing the horse in the saddler's shop, but that hollow showed that many, many others had done as I had. Many, many children, I saw, continued to take that road on their walks from home to school and back.

And I grasped that even an old wooden horse lost in the immensity of the world could hope for tenderness. The tenderness of children passing often over that long road that leads us to become men.

Lost in the City

ROOMING HOUSES

After many years of school, and the struggle through the math exam each December, I was outwardly prepared to face the university in Santiago. I say outwardly because my head was filled with books, dreams, and poems buzzing around like bees.

Carrying a metal trunk, wearing the requisite black suit of the poet, all skin and bones, thin-featured as a knife, I boarded the third-class section of a night train that took an interminable day and night to reach Santiago.

This long train crossed different zones and climates; I took it so many times and it still holds a strange fascination for me. Peasants with wet ponchos and baskets filled with chickens, uncommunicative Indians—an entire life unfolded in the third-class coach. Quite a number of people traveled without paying, under the seats. Whenever the ticket collector came around, a metamorphosis took place. Many disappeared, and others might hide under a poncho on which two passengers immediately pretended to play a game of cards, to keep the conductor from noticing the improvised table.

Meanwhile, the train passed from the countryside covered with oaks and araucaria trees and frame houses with sodden walls to the poplars and the dusty adobe buildings of central Chile. I made the round trip between the capital and the provinces many times, but I always felt myself stifling as soon as I left the great forests, the timberland that drew me back like a mother. To me, the adobe houses, the cities with a past, seemed to be filled with cobwebs and silence. Even now I am still a poet of the great outdoors, of the cold forest that was lost to me after that.

I brought my references to a rooming house at 513 Maruri Street. Nothing can make me forget this number. I forget all kinds of dates, even years, but the number 513 is still in my mind, where I engraved it so many years ago, fearing I would never find that rooming house and would lose my way in the strange, awe-inspiring city. On the street just mentioned I used to sit out on the balcony and watch the dying afternoon, the sky with its green and crimson banners, the desolation of the rooftops on the edge of town threatened by the burning sky.

At that time, living in a rooming house for students meant starvation. I wrote a lot more than I had up until then, but I ate a lot less. Some of the poets I knew in those days broke down under the strict diet of poverty. Among them, I remember Romeo Murga, a poet my own age but much taller and gawkier than I, whose subtle lyric poetry was filled with emanations that lingered wherever it was heard.

Romeo Murga and I went to read our poetry together in the city of San Bernardo, near the capital. Before we took the stage, everyone had been in a festive mood, watching the queen of the Floral Games—fair and blond—with her court, and enjoying the speeches of the town dignitaries, and the so-called local bands; but when I went on and began reciting my poems in the most wretched voice in the world, everything changed. The audience coughed, joked about me, and had a good time laughing at my melancholy poems. Seeing this reaction from the barbarians, I rushed through my reading and left the stage to my companion, Romeo Murga. It was something to remember. When this Quixote, over six feet tall, with dark, frayed clothes, came on and began reading in a voice that was even more wretched than mine, no one in the audience could hold back his indignation and they all began to shout: You starving poets! Get out! Don't spoil the celebration.

I moved out of the Maruri Street rooming house like a mollusk leaving its shell. I said goodbye to that shell and went out to explore the sea—that is, the world. The unknown sea was the streets of Santiago, which I had seen almost nothing of, as I walked back and forth between the university and the room I was now leaving for good.

I knew that during this adventure there would be more of the old hunger to face. At least my former landladies, remotely linked to my part of the country, mercifully doled out a potato or an onion from time to time. But I could not help it: life, love, glory, freedom called to me. Or so it seemed.

I rented the first room where I was completely on my own, over on Argüelles Street, near the Teachers Institute. A sign peered through a window on that gray street: "Rooms for rent." The landlord lived in the front rooms. He was a man with graying hair, a noble bearing, and eyes that seemed odd to me. He was talkative and quite eloquent, and he earned a living as a ladies' hairdresser, an occupation he shrugged off. He explained that he was more interested in the invisible world, the world of the beyond.

I unpacked my books and the few clothes I possessed, from the trunk that had traveled with me from Temuco, and I stretched out in bed to read and sleep, filled with pride at my independence and my idleness.

The house had no patio, only a gallery lined with innumerable closed rooms. The next morning, as I explored the nooks and crannies of the lonely mansion, I noticed that all the walls, including the toilet's, displayed signs saying more or less the same thing: "Resign yourself. You cannot get in touch with us. You are dead." Alarming notices that cropped up in every room, in the dining room, in the corridors, in the tiny parlors.

It was during one of Santiago's harsh winters. From colonial Spain my country had inherited a vulnerability to the rigors of nature as well as a disregard for them. (Fifty years after the events I am recounting now, Ilya Ehrenburg, who had just come from the snowy streets of Moscow, told me he had never felt so cold as he had in Chile.) Winter had turned the glass windows blue. The trees on my street shivered with cold. The horses pulling the old carriages blew clouds of steam through their nostrils. It was the worst possible time to be in that house, among sinister intimations of the beyond.

Coiffeur pour dames and occultist, the landlord stared straight through me with the eyes of a madman, and calmly explained: "My wife, Charito, died four months ago. This is a trying moment for the dead. They go on visiting the old places where they lived. We can't see them, but they don't know that we can't see them. We have to let them know this so they won't suffer, thinking we're indifferent. That's why I've put up those signs for Charito, they will make it easier for her to understand that she is dead now."

But the gray-headed man must have thought that I was much too clever. He started to watch my comings and goings, to make rules about female visitors, to pry into my books and my letters. I would enter my room without warning, to find the occultist going over my scanty furniture, investigating my poor belongings.

I had to look for new lodgings to shelter my threatened independence, so I made the rounds of the unfriendly streets in the dead of winter. I found a place a short distance away, in a laundry. It was obvious to me that here the landlady had nothing to do with the world beyond. Run-down gardens straggled through chilly patios with fountains whose stagnant water the algae covered with solid green rugs. There was a back room with a very high ceiling, and transoms over tall doors; in my eyes, this increased the distance between the floor and the ceiling. I stayed in that house, in that room.

We student poets led a wild life. I kept up my country ways, working in my room, writing several poems every day, and forever drinking cups of tea I prepared for myself. But, away from my room and my street, the turbulent life of writers in those days had its special fascination. They didn't go to the cafés but to the beer taverns and the regular bars. Conversations and poems were passed around till daybreak. My studies were suffering from all this.

The railroad company supplied my father with a cape of thick gray felt for his outdoor work, but he never wore it. I made it a feature of the poet. Three or four other poets also started wearing similar capes, and these constantly changed hands. This garment used to stir up the fury of good people and of others who were not so good. It was the heyday of the tango, which came to Chile not only with its heavy beat and its thrumming "tijera," its accordions and its rhythm, but also with its entourage of toughs who invaded our night life and the out-of-the-way places where we got together. These underworld characters—dancers and troublemakers—sniggered at our capes and our way of life. We poets fought back hard.

Around that time I unexpectedly struck up a friendship with a widow who is stamped forever on my mind. She had big blue eyes that became misty with tenderness whenever she remembered her late beloved husband. He had been a young novelist, noted for his handsome physique. Together they had made a striking couple, she with her wheat-colored hair, her irreproachable figure, and her deep blue eyes, and he very tall and athletic. The novelist had been destroyed by what used to be called galloping consumption. Later I've felt sure that his blond consort also contributed her share as galloping Venus, and that together the pre-penicillin age and the spirited widow carried off the monumental husband in a couple of months.

The lovely widow had not yet peeled off her dark clothing for me, the black and purple silks that made her look like a snow-white fruit covered with a rind of mourning. That skin slipped off one afternoon in my room, at the rear of the laundry, and I was able to fondle and explore all that fruit of fiery snow. The natural rapture was about to be consummated, when I noticed her eyes closing below mine, as she cried out, sighing and sobbing, "Oh, Roberto, Roberto!" (It seemed to be a ritual performance. The vestal virgin calling on the vanished god before surrendering to a new rite.)

However, in spite of my youth and need, this widow seemed too much for me. Her invocations became more and more urgent and her spirited heart was slowly leading me to a premature destruction. Love, in such doses, is not good for malnutrition. And my malnutrition was becoming more dramatic every day.

SHYNESS

I really lived many of the first years of my life, and perhaps many of the next ones and the ones after that, as a kind of deaf-mute.

Dressed in ritual black since I had been a young boy, like the true poets of the last century, I had the vague impression that I didn't look bad at all. But, instead of going after girls, since I knew I would stutter or turn red in front of them, I preferred to pass them up and go on my way, showing a total lack of interest I was very far from feeling. They were all a deep mystery to me. I would have liked to burn at the stake in that secret fire, to drown in the inscrutable depth of that well, but I lacked the courage to throw myself into the fire or the water. And since I could find no one to give me a push, I walked along the fascinating edge, without even a side glance, much less a smile.

The same thing happened to me in front of grownups, insignificant persons, railroad or post-office employees with their "señoras esposas," their lady wives, so referred to because the petite bourgeoisie is shocked, intimidated, by the word "mujer," woman or wife. I listened to the conversations at my father's table. But the next day, if I ran into those who had dined at my home the evening before, I didn't dare greet them, I even crossed over to the other side of the street to avoid embarrassment.

Shyness is a kink in the soul, a special category, a dimension that opens out into solitude. Moreover, it is an inherent suffering, as if we had two epidermises and the one underneath rebelled and shrank back from life. Of the things that make up a man, this quality, this damaging thing, is a part of the alloy that lays the foundation, in the long run, for the perpetuity of the self.

My rain-haunted backwardness, my long-drawn-out retreat into myself, lasted longer than it should have. When I came to the capital, I slowly acquired new friends of both sexes. The less attention people paid to me, the easier it was for me to make friends. I was not particularly curious about mankind then. I can't get to know all the people in this world, I said to myself. Still and all, a faint curiosity was stirred up in certain circles by this new poet, just over sixteen, a reticent boy, a loner, whom they saw come and go without so much as a good morning or goodbye. Aside from the fact that I'd be wearing a long Spanish cape that made me look like a scarecrow. No one suspected that my striking attire was made-to-order for my poverty.

Among the people who sought my company were two big snobs of the day: Pilo Yáñez and his wife, Mina. They were the perfect embodiment of the beautiful idle life I would have loved to live, more remote than a dream. It was my first time in a house with heat, soft lighting, pleasant furniture, walls covered with books whose multicolored spines were like a springtime that was inaccessible to me. Kindly and discreet, overlooking my various layers of silence and withdrawal, the Yáñezes often invited me to their home. I used to leave their house in a happy mood, and they noticed and invited me again.

I saw cubist paintings for the first time in that house, a Juan Gris among them. They told me that Juan Gris had been a friend of the family's in Paris. But what intrigued me most was my friend's pajamas.

Whenever I could, I examined them out of the corner of my eye with intense admiration. It was winter, and the pajamas were made of a heavy material, like the baize on billiard tables, but a deep-sea blue. In those days I couldn't imagine any kind of pajamas except striped ones, like prison uniforms. Pilo Yáñez's were like nothing I had ever seen. Their heavy fabric, their resplendent blue, aroused the envy of the poor poet who lived in the Santiago suburbs. And in fifty years I have not come across any pajamas quite like those.

I lost sight of the Yáñezes for many years. She gave up her husband, and she also gave up the soft lighting and excellent armchairs, for an acrobat in a Russian circus that passed through Santiago. Later on, she sold tickets, all the way from Australia to the British Isles, to help out the acrobat who had swept her off her feet. She ended up as a Rosicrucian or something like that, with a group of mystics in the South of France.

As for Pilo Yáñez, the husband, he changed his name to Juan Emar and in time became a powerful, though still undiscovered writer. We were lifelong friends. Silent and kindly but poor, that's how he died. His many books have yet to be published, but they are sure to take root and blossom someday.

I'll leave Pilo Yáñez, or Juan Emar, and take up my shyness again, recalling that during my student days my friend Pilo was set on introducing me to his father. "I'm sure he'll get you a trip to Europe," he told me. At that moment, all Latin American poets and painters had their eyes riveted on Paris. Pilo's father was a very important man, a senator. He lived in one of those enormous ugly houses on a street near the Plaza de Armas and the presidential palace—where no doubt he would have preferred to live.

My friends stayed in the anteroom, after stripping off my cape to make me look more normal. They opened the door to the senator's study for me and shut it behind me. It was an immense room, and may have been a great reception hall at one time, but it was just about empty now, except deep inside, at the far end, where I could make out an armchair, with the senator in it under a floor lamp. The pages of the newspaper he was reading hid him completely, like a screen.

Taking my first step on the murderously waxed and buffed parquet, I slid like a skier. I picked up speed dizzily. I tried to brake myself, only to lose my footing and fall several times. My last spill was right at the feet of the senator, who was observing me now with cold eyes, without letting go of his paper.

I managed to sit down in a small chair next to him. The great man inspected me with the eye of a bored entomologist to whom someone brings a specimen that he already knows inside out, a harmless spider. He questioned me vaguely about my projects. After my spill, I was even more timid and less eloquent than ever.

I don't know what I told him. At the end of twenty minutes he put out a tiny hand toward me, as a sign of dismissal. I thought I heard him promise in a very soft voice that I would hear from him. Then he picked up his newspaper again and I started back across the dangerous parquet, taking all the precautions I should have taken when first stepping onto it. Of course the senator, my friend's father, never let me hear from him. On the other hand, sometime later a military revolt, which was actually stupid and reactionary, got him to jump out of his chair with his everlasting paper. I confess that this made me happy.

THE STUDENT FEDERATION

In Temuco I had been a correspondent for the review *Claridad*, the Student Federation's organ, and I used to sell twenty or thirty copies to my schoolmates. One piece of news that reached Temuco in 1920 left bloody scars on my generation. The "golden youth," offspring of the oligarchy, had attacked and destroyed the Student Federation's headquarters. The authorities, who from colonial times to the present have been at the service of the rich, did not jail the assaulters but the assaulted. Domingo Gómez Rojas, the young hope of Chilean poetry, was tortured, and went mad and died in a dungeon. Within the national context of a small country, the repercussions of this crime were as profound and far-reaching as those of Federico García Lorca's assassination in Granada later.

When I arrived in Santiago, in March 1921, to enter the university, the capital of Chile had only five hundred thousand inhabitants. It smelled of gas fumes and coffee. Thousands of buildings housed strangers and bedbugs. Public transportation was handled by small rickety streetcars that struggled along with a loud clanking of iron and bells. The ride from Independencia Avenue to the other end of town, near the Central Station, where my college was located, took forever.

The Student Federation's headquarters was frequented by the most famous figures of the student rebellion, ideologically linked to the powerful anarchist movement of the day. Alfredo Demaría, Daniel Schweitzer, Santiago Labarca, Juan Gandulfo were the best-known leaders. The most formidable was undoubtedly Juan Gandulfo, who was feared for his bold political thinking and his unflagging courage. He treated me as if I was just a boy, which, of course, I was. On one occasion, when I arrived at his office late for a medical appointment, he frowned at me and said, "Why didn't you get here on time? There are other patients waiting." "I didn't know what time it was," I replied. "Take this, so you'll know next time," he said, pulling his watch from his vest pocket and giving it to me.

Juan Gandulfo was short, moonfaced, and prematurely bald, yet he always made his presence felt. Once, a troublemaking army man, who was well known as a bully and a good swordsman, challenged him to a duel. Gandulfo took him up on it, learned fencing in two weeks, and left his rival battered and scared witless. Around that same time, he engraved in wood the cover and all the illustrations for my first book, *Crepusculario*—impressive woodcuts done by a man no one ever associated with art.

The most important figure in the revolutionist literary world was Roberto Meza Fuentes, editor of the magazine *Juventud*, owned also by the Student Federation, but with more contributors, and more carefully prepared than *Claridad*. Outstanding in it was the work of González Vera and Manuel Rojas, who were, for me, from a much older generation. Manuel Rojas had recently come back from Argentina after many years there, and he astonished us with his impressive size and his words, dropped with a kind of condescension, pride, or dignity. He was a linotypist. I had known González Vera in Temuco, where he had fled after the police assault on the Student Federation. He came to see me straight from the railroad station, which was a short distance from my house. His sudden appearance had to impress a sixteen-year-old poet. I had never seen such a pale man. His flesh-less face seemed to be carved in bone or ivory. He wore black, a black frayed at the extremities of trouser legs and sleeves, which, however, did not make him look less elegant. His words sounded ironical and sharp from the very first. On the rainy night that brought him to my house—I had not even known that he existed—I was moved by his presence, just as Sacha Yegulev is moved by the revolutionary nihilist's coming to his home; Andreyev's fictional character Yegulev was looked on by young Latin American rebels as their model.

ALBERTO ROJAS GIMÉNEZ

The review *Claridad*, which I joined as a political and literary militant, was run almost singlehandedly by Alberto Rojas Giménez, who was to become one of the closest friends I would have among my own generation. He wore a cordovan hat and the long mutton-chop whiskers of a grandee. Well groomed and elegant despite his poverty, in the midst of which he seemed to preen like a golden bird, he embodied all the qualities of the new dandy, an attitude of contempt, a quick grasp of our numerous conflicts, as well as a cheerful sophistication and an appetite for everything in life. He knew all about everything—books and girls, bottles and ships, itineraries and archipelagos—and he flaunted this knowledge even in his slightest gestures. He moved about in the literary world with the condescending air of a perpetual idler, someone in the habit of wasting all his talent and charm. His neckties were always magnificent displays of prosperity in the midst of general poverty. He was constantly moving into a new home or to a new city, and thus for a few weeks his natural good humor, his persistent and spontaneous Bohemian ways, delighted incredulous people in Rancagua, Curicó, Valdivia, Concepción, Valparaíso. He always went away as he had come, leaving poems, drawings, neckties, loves, and friendships wherever he had been. Since he was as unpredictable as a storybook prince and unbelievably generous, he gave away everything—his hat, his shirt, his jacket, and even his shoes. When he had no material belongings left, he would jot down a phrase on a scrap of paper, a line from a poem or something amusing that came into his head, and he would offer it to you as he went, with a magnanimous look on his face, as if he were putting a priceless jewel in your hand.

His poems were written in the latest fashion, according to the doctrines of Apollinaire and Spain's ultraist group. He had founded a new school of poetry and called it "Agu," which, he said, was man's first cry, the newborn infant's first poem.

Rojas Giménez set off new fads in the way we dressed, in the way we smoked, in our handwriting. Mimicking me, in gentle fun, he helped me get rid of my melancholy tone. Neither his skeptical attitude nor his wild drinking sprees ever infected me, but I am still deeply moved when I remember his face that made everything light up, that made beauty fly out from every corner, as if he had set a hidden butterfly in motion.

From Don Miguel de Unamuno he had learned how to make little paper birds. He would make one with a long neck and outspread wings, which he would then blow out into the air. He called that giving them their "vital push." He discovered French poets, dark bottles buried away in wine cellars, and wrote love letters to Francis Jammes heroines.

His lovely poems went around all wrinkled in his pockets, without ever, to this day, getting published.

Being generous to a fault, he attracted so much attention that one day, in a café, a stranger came up to him and said, "Sir, I have been listening to you talk and I have taken a great liking to you. May I ask you for something?" "What is it?" Rojas Giménez asked, looking put out. "Let me leap over you," the stranger said. "What?" the poet asked. "Are you so powerful that you can leap over me here, sitting at this table?" "No, sir," the stranger said meekly. "I want to leap over you later, when you are resting in your coffin. It's my way of paying tribute to the interesting people I've met in my life: leaping over them, if they let me, after they're dead. I'm a lonely man and this is my only hobby." And taking out his notebook, he said, "Here's the list of people I've leaped over." Wild with joy, Rojas Giménez accepted the strange proposition. Several years later, during the rainiest winter anyone in Chile can remember, Rojas Giménez died. As usual, he had left his jacket in some bar in downtown Santiago. In the middle of the Antarctic winter, he had walked across the city, in his shirtsleeves, to his sister Rosita's house over in the Quinta Normal neighborhood. Two days later, bronchial pneumonia carried off from this world one of the most fascinating human beings I have ever known. The poet flew away with his little paper birds into the sky, in the rain.

But friends present at his wake that night had an unusual visitor. A torrential rain was falling on the rooftops, with lightning and the wind together illuminating and shaking the huge plantain trees on Quinta Normal, when the door opened and a man all in black, drenched by the rain, walked in. No one knew who he was. Before the curious eyes of the friends keeping vigil, the stranger braced himself and leaped over the coffin. And he left immediately, as suddenly as he had arrived, without uttering a word, vanishing into the night and the rain. And so Alberto Rojas Giménez's amazing life was sealed with a mysterious rite nobody has yet been able to puzzle out.

I had just arrived in Spain when I received the news of his death. Seldom have I felt such intense grief. This was in Barcelona. I immediately began writing my elegy "Alberto Rojas Giménez viene volando" ("Alberto Rojas Giménez Comes Flying"), which *Revista de Occidente* later published.

But I also had to say farewell to him with some kind of ceremony. He had died so far away, in Chile, when days of heavy rain were flooding the cemetery. I could not be near his mortal remains, or be with him on his final voyage, so I had an idea for a ceremony. I went to my friend Isaías Cabezón, the painter, and together we headed for the marvelous basilica of Santa María del Mar. We bought two huge candles, each almost as tall as a man, and with them we entered the shadows of that strange temple. Santa María del Mar was the cathedral of seafarers. Fishermen and sailors built it stone by stone many centuries ago. Then it was embellished with thousands of votive offerings: miniature boats of all sizes and shapes, sailing through eternity, formed a tapestry over the walls and ceilings of the beautiful basilica. It occurred to me that this was the perfect setting for the late poet, this would have been his favorite spot if he had come to know it. My friend the painter and I lit the huge candles in the center of the basilica, near the clouds of the coffered ceiling, and sat in the empty church, each of us with a bottle of white wine, feeling that, despite our agnosticism, the silent ceremony brought us closer to our dead friend in some mysterious way. Burning in the highest part of the empty basilica, the candles were alive and radiant and might have been the two eyes of the mad poet, whose heart had been extinguished forever, looking at us from the shadows, among the votive offerings.

MADMAN IN WINTER

Apropos of Rojas Giménez, I'll say that madness, a certain kind of madness, often goes hand in hand with poetry. It would be very difficult for predominantly rational people to be poets, and perhaps it is just as difficult for poets to be rational. Yet reason gets the upper hand, and it is reason, the mainstay of justice, that must govern the world. Miguel de Unamuno, who loved Chile very much, once said: "The thing I don't like is that motto. What is it all about, *through reason or force?* Through reason and always through reason."

I'll talk about Alberto Valdivia, one of the mad poets I knew in the old days. Alberto Valdivia was one of the skinniest men in the world and so sallow-complexioned that he seemed to be made entirely of bone, with a wild shock of gray hair and a pair of glasses covering his myopic eyes, which always had a faraway look. We called him Valdivia the Corpse.

He went in and out of bars and eating places, cafés and concerts, without ever making a sound and with a mysterious little bundle of newspapers under his arm. "Dear Corpse," his friends used to say, embracing his incorporeal body, with the sensation that we were embracing a gust of air.

He wrote some lovely lines packed with subtle feeling, with intense sweetness. Here are a few:

Everything will go—the afternoon, the sun, life:
evil, which cannot be undone, will prevail.
Only you will stay, inseparable
sister of the twilight of my life.

This poet whom we fondly knew as Valdivia the Corpse was a true poet. We often said to him: "Stay and have dinner with us, Corpse." Our nickname never upset him. Sometimes a smile played on his very thin lips. His phrases were few and far between, but they were always to the point. We made a rite of taking him to the cemetery every year. On the eve of November 1 we used to give a dinner for him, as sumptuous as the miserable pockets of young students and writers would permit. Our "Corpse" occupied the seat of honor. At twelve on the dot, we cleared the table and headed for the cemetery in a lighthearted procession. Someone would make a speech honoring the "late" poet, in the stillness of the night. Then each of us said goodbye solemnly and we marched off, leaving him all alone at the graveyard gate. The "Corpse" had long accepted this traditional rite, and there was no cruelty in it, since he took an active role in the farce all the way to the end. Before leaving, we would hand him some pesos, so he could eat a sandwich in his grave.

Two or three days later, no one was surprised to see the poet-corpse quietly slip back into our small knot of friends and into the cafés. He could count on being left in peace until the following November 1.

In Buenos Aires I met a very eccentric Argentine writer whose name was, or is, Omar Vignole; I don't know if he is still living. He was a giant of a man and carried a heavy walking stick. Once, in a midtown restaurant where he had invited me to dinner, he turned to me at the table, motioning me to a seat, and said in a booming voice that could be heard throughout the room, which was filled with regular customers: "Sit down, Omar Vignole!" I sat down a bit uneasily and promptly asked: "Why do you call me Omar Vignole? You know that you are Omar Vignole and I am Pablo Neruda." "Yes," he replied, "but there are lots of people in this restaurant who only know me by name. And several of them want to thrash the daylights out of me; I'd rather have them do it to you." Vignole had been an agronomist in an Argentine province and had brought back a cow that became his inseparable friend. He used to walk all over Buenos Aires with his cow, leading her by a rope. Around that time, he published some books, all with intriguing titles: *What the Cow Thinks*, *My Cow and I*, etc. When the P.E.N. club had its first world congress in Buenos Aires, the writers, who were headed by Victoria Ocampo, trembled at the thought that Vignole would turn up with his cow. They explained this imminent threat to the authorities, and the police cordoned off the streets around the Plaza Hotel to prevent my eccentric friend from showing up with his ruminant at the luxurious place where the congress was being held. It was all in vain. The festivities were in full swing and the writers were discussing the classical world of the Greeks and its relation to the modern meaning of history, when the great Vignole burst in upon the conference hall with his inseparable cow, which, to top things off, started to moo as if she wanted to join the debate. He had brought her into the heart of the city in an enormous closed van that had somehow eluded the vigilance of the police.

Something else I want to tell about this same Vignole is that he once challenged a wrestler. The pro called his bluff, and on the night of the match my friend showed up at a packed Luna Park right on time with his cow, hitched her to a corner of the ring, shed his super-elegant robe, and faced the Calcutta Strangler.

Well, neither the cow nor the wrestling poet's gorgeous apparel could help him here. The Calcutta Strangler pounced on Vignole and tied him into a helpless knot in double-quick time. What's more, adding insult to injury, he placed one foot on the literary bull's throat, amid tremendous whistles and catcalls from an audience that demanded that the fight continue.

A few months later Vignole brought out a new book: *Conversations with the Cow*. I'll never forget the unique dedication that appeared on the first page. If memory serves me, it read: "I dedicate this philosophical work to the forty thousand sons of bitches who hissed and called for my blood in Luna Park on the night of February 24."

In Paris, before the last war, I met Alvaro Guevara, the painter who was known in Europe as Chile Guevara. One day he called me on the telephone, with an urgent tone in his voice. "It's something very important," he said.

I had come up from Spain, and our struggle then was against Hitler, the Nixon of that era. My house in Madrid had been bombed and I had seen men, women, and children wiped out by the bombings. The world war was in the offing. Other writers and I had started to fight Fascism in our own way: with books urging people to open their eyes to this grave threat.

My countryman had stayed out of the struggle. He was an uncommunicative man, a hard-working painter, and always kept busy. We were sitting on a keg of gunpowder. When the great powers blocked the delivery of arms for the defense of the Spanish Republic, and later, in Munich, when they threw the doors wide open for Hitler's army, the war had arrived.

I complied with Chile Guevara's plea that I go see him. What he wanted to tell me was very important.

"What's it all about?" I asked him.

"There's no time to lose," he answered. "There's no reason for you to be anti-Fascist. No one has to be anti-anything. We must get down to brass tacks, and I have found those brass tacks. I want to tell you about it right away so that you'll drop your anti-Nazi congresses and settle down to serious work. There's no time to lose."

"Well, tell me what it's all about. Alvaro, I really have very little time."

"Pablo, my idea is really expressed in a three-act play. I've brought it along to read to you." And he stared at me hard—his face, with its bushy eyebrows, like an ex-boxer's—as he pulled out a voluminous manuscript.

Panicky, and stressing my lack of time as an excuse, I convinced him to give me a quick rundown of the ideas that he planned to use to save the human race.

"It's like Columbus's egg, easier to crack than it looks," he said. "I'll explain. If you plant one potato, how many potatoes will it yield?"

"Well, maybe four or five," I answered, just to say something.

"Lots more," he answered. "Sometimes as many as forty, sometimes more than one hundred potatoes. Imagine everybody planting one potato in the garden, on the balcony, anywhere. How many people are there in Chile? Eight million. Eight million planted potatoes. Pablo, multiply this by four, by one hundred. That's the end of hunger, the end of war. How many people are there in China? Five hundred million, right? Each Chinese plants one potato. Forty potatoes come from each potato that's been planted. Five hundred million by forty potatoes. Humanity is saved."

When the Nazis marched into Paris, they did not take into account that world-saving idea: Columbus's egg, or rather, Columbus's potato. Alvaro Guevara was arrested at his home in Paris on a cold, foggy night. They dragged him off to a concentration camp and held him prisoner there, marked with a tattoo on his arm, until the end of the war. He came out of that hell a human skeleton, and he never recovered. He came to Chile for the last time, as if to bid his country goodbye, giving it a final kiss, a sleepwalker's kiss, and returned to France, where death completed its work.

Great painter, dear friend, Chile Guevara, I want to tell you one thing: I know you are dead, that your non-aligned potato politics did not help you at all. I know that the Nazis killed you. And yet—last June I went into the National Gallery. I was only going to look at the Turners, but I hadn't reached the main room, when I discovered an impressive painting: a painting as lovely to me as the Turners, a resplendently beautiful work. It was the portrait of a lady, a famous lady: her name, Edith Sitwell. And this painting was your work, the only work by a Latin American painter ever privileged to hang among the masterpieces of the great London museum.

I don't care about the place, or the honor, and, at heart, I also care very little about that lovely canvas. What matters to me is that we did not get to know each other better, to understand each other more, and that we let our lives cross without understanding, all because of a potato.

I have been too simple a man: this has been my honor and my shame. I went along with my friends' shenanigans and envied their brilliant plumage, their Satanic poses, their little paper birds, and even their cows, which, in some unexplained way, may have something to do with literature. Anyway, I believe I was born not to pass judgment but to love. Even the divisionists who attack me, ganging up to gouge out my eyes, after having first nourished themselves on my poetry, deserve my silence if nothing else. I was never afraid I'd contaminate myself circulating among my enemies, because the only enemies I have are the enemies of the people.

Apollinaire said: "Mercy on us who explore the frontiers of the unreal." I quote from memory, thinking of the stories I have just told, stories about people who are no less dear to me because they were eccentric, and no less valorous because I did not know what to make of them.

BIG BUSINESS

We poets have always believed we could come up with brilliant ideas that would make us rich, that we are geniuses at planning business deals, but geniuses no one understands. I recall that in 1924 I was prompted by one of those money-making brainstorms to sell my Chilean publisher the rights to my book *Crepusculario*, not for one edition, but for eternity. I thought this sale would make me rich, and signed the contract before a notary. The fellow paid me five hundred pesos, a little under five dollars in those days. Rojas Giménez, Alvaro Hinojosa, Homero Arce were waiting for me outside the notary public's door, to celebrate this commercial success with a big banquet. And in fact we ate in what was then the best restaurant, La Bahía, with exquisite wines, cigars, and liqueurs. But first we had our shoes shined until they glittered like mirrors. The restaurant, four shoeshine boys, and a publisher profited from this business deal. Prosperity stopped short of the poet.

Alvaro Hinojosa claimed he had an eagle's eye for all kinds of business. We were impressed by those grandiose schemes of his that, put into practice, would make money rain down on our heads. For us down-at-the-heels Bohemians, his command of English, his Virginia-blend cigarettes, his years of study at a university in New York spoke volumes for the pragmatism of his great business brain.

One day he called me aside, very confidentially, to let me in on a fantastic plan aimed at making us rich quick. I could go in fifty-fifty with him, and simply by contributing a few pesos I would get somewhere. He would put up the rest. That day we felt like capitalists beyond God and the law, capable of anything.

"What kind of merchandise is it?" I asked the unappreciated king of finance timidly.

Alvaro closed his eyes, expelled a mouthful of smoke that broke up into small rings, and finally answered in a hushed voice: "Pelts!"

"Pelts?" I echoed in amazement.

"From seals. To be precise, from hair seals all the same color."

I couldn't bring myself to ask for more details. I didn't know that seals, or sea lions, had hair of any color. When I had watched them on a rock, on southern beaches, I had seen a shiny skin that glistened in the sun, had never noticed the slightest hint of hair on their lazy bellies.

I converted everything I owned into ready cash with lightning speed, without paying my rent, or my tailor's installment, or the shoemaker's bill, and I placed my share of the money in my business associate's hands.

We went to look at the pelts. Alvaro had bought them from an aunt of his, a southerner who owned several uninhabited islands. On those desolate rookeries, the sea lions carried out their erotic ceremonies. And they were here now, before my eyes, as huge bundles of yellow pelts riddled by the carbines of the wicked aunt's hirelings. The packs of skins were stacked all the way up to the ceiling in the storehouse rented by Alvaro to impress prospective buyers.

"And what are we going to do with this enormous mass, this mountain of pelts?" I asked sheepishly.

"Everybody needs this kind of pelt. You'll see." And we left the storehouse, Alvaro shooting off sparks of energy, I with lowered head, wordlessly.

Alvaro made the rounds with a portfolio made of our genuine pelts from "hair seals all the same color," a portfolio filled with blank forms to make it look business-like. Our last money went for newspaper ads. Just let one interested and appreciative magnate read them, and that was it. We'd be rich. Alvaro, a very elegant dresser, wanted to have a half dozen suits made out of English cloth. Much more modest, I harbored among my unfulfilled dreams the dream of buying a good shaving brush, now that the one I had was well on its way to turning unacceptably bald.

A buyer showed up at last. He worked in leather goods, a short, robust man with fearless eyes, sparing with words, and with an air of candor which, I thought, verged on rudeness. Alvaro received him with guarded indifference and set a suitable time, three days later, for showing him our fabulous merchandise.

During those three days Alvaro bought some superb English cigarettes and some "Romeo y Julieta" Havana cigars, which he stuck in his breast pocket, in plain sight, just before the client was expected to arrive. We had laid out the better-looking skins on the floor.

The man showed up for our appointment right on time. He did not take off his hat and barely greeted us with a grunt. He glanced scornfully and quickly at the skins spread out on the floor. Then he ran his sharp, stern eyes over the crammed shelves. He raised a pudgy hand, and a suspicious fingernail pointed out a bundle of skins, one of those highest and farthest away. Exactly where I had jammed the worst ones into a corner.

Alvaro made the most of this crucial moment to offer him one of his genuine Havanas. The small-time merchant grabbed it, bit off the end, rammed the cigar into his mouth, and went on calmly pointing to the bundle he wanted to inspect.

There was nothing to do but show it to him. My partner climbed up the ladder and came back down with the thick bundle, smiling like a man sentenced to death. Pausing now and then to draw more and more smoke from Alvaro's cigar, the buyer examined all the skins in the package, one by one.

The man picked up a pelt, rubbed it together, bent it double, tossed it aside scornfully, and immediately went on to the next, which in turn was scratched, rubbed, sniffed, and dropped. When he was finally through with his inspection, he once more ran his vulture's eyes over the shelves brimming with our pelts from hair seals all the same color, and at last halted his gaze on the forehead of my partner, the business expert.

Then, in a hard, dry voice, he uttered words that, for us at least, became immortal: "My dear sirs, I'm not getting hitched to these skins." And he walked out forever, with his hat still on, smoking Alvaro's superb cigar, without saying goodbye, implacable slayer of our millionaire's dreams.

MY FIRST BOOKS

I sought refuge in poetry with the intensity of someone timid. The new literary movements hovered over Santiago. I finished writing my first book at 513 Maruri Street. I used to write two, three, four, five poems each day. In the late afternoon, outside my balcony, there unfolded a spectacle I never missed for anything in the world. It was the sunset with its glorious sheaves of colors, scattered arrays of light, enormous orange and scarlet fans. The middle section of my book is called "Maruri Twilights." No one ever asked me what Maruri is supposed to mean. Maybe a very small number of people know it's only a modest street frequented by the most extraordinary twilights.

In 1923 my first book, *Crepusculario*, appeared. I had setbacks and successes every day, trying to pay for the first printing. I sold the few pieces of furniture I owned. The watch my father had solemnly given me, on which he had had two little crossed flags enameled, soon went off to the pawnbroker's. My black poet's suit followed the watch. The printer was adamant, and in the end, when the edition was all ready and the covers had been pasted on, he said to me, with an evil look, "No. You are not taking a single copy until you pay me for the entire thing." The critic Alone generously contributed the last pesos, which were gobbled up by my printer, and off I went into the street carrying my books on my shoulder, with holes in my shoes, but beside myself with joy.

My first book! *I have always maintained that the writer's task has nothing to do with mystery or magic, and that the poet's, at least, must be a personal effort for the benefit of all. The closest thing to poetry is a loaf of bread or a ceramic dish or a piece of wood lovingly carved, even if by clumsy hands.* And yet I don't believe any craftsman except the poet, still shaken by the confusion of his dreams, ever experiences the ecstasy produced only once in his life, by the first object his hands have created. It's a moment that will never come back. There will be many editions, more elaborate, more beautiful. His words will be poured into the glasses of other languages like a wine, to sing and spread its aroma to other places on this earth. But that moment when the first book appears with its ink fresh and its paper still crisp, that enchanted and ecstatic moment, with the sound of wings beating or the first flower opening on the conquered height, that moment comes only once in the poet's lifetime.

One of my poems seemed to break away from that immature book and go off on its own: "Farewell," which many people, wherever I go, still know by heart. They would recite it to me in the most unlikely places, or ask me to do it. I might find it annoying, but the minute I was introduced at a gathering, some girl would raise her voice with those obsessive lines, and sometimes ministers of state would receive me with a military salute while reciting the first stanza.

Years later in Spain, Federico García Lorca told me how the same thing kept happening to him with his poem "La casada infiel" ("The Faithless Wife"). The greatest proof of friendship Federico could offer anyone was to repeat for him his enormously popular and lovely poem. We become allergic to the unshakable success of just one of our poems. This is a healthy and natural feeling. Such an imposition by readers tends to transfix the poet in a single moment of time, whereas creation is really a steady wheel spinning along with more and more facility and self-confidence, though perhaps with less freshness and spontaneity.

I was now leaving *Crepusculario* behind me. Deep anxieties stirred my poetry. Short trips to the south renewed my powers. In 1923 I had a strange experience. I had returned home to Temuco. It was past midnight. Before going to bed, I opened the windows in my room. The sky dazzled me. The entire sky was alive, swarming with a lively multitude of stars. The night looked freshly washed and the Antarctic stars were spreading out in formation over my head.

I became star-drunk, celestially, cosmically drunk. I rushed to my table and wrote, with heart beating high, as if I were taking dictation, the first poem of a book that would have many titles and would end up as *El hondero entusiasta*. It was smooth going, as if I were swimming in my very own waters.

The following day, filled with happiness, I read my poem. Later, when I got to Santiago, the wizard Aliro Oyarzún listened with admiration to those lines of mine. Then he asked in his deep voice: "Are you sure those lines haven't been influenced by Sabat Ercasty?"

"I'm pretty sure. I wrote them in a fit of inspiration."

Then I decided to send my poem to Sabat Ercasty himself, a great Uruguayan poet unjustly neglected today. In him I had seen realized my ambition to write poetry that would embrace not only man but nature, its hidden forces: an epic poetry that would deal with the great mystery of the universe and with man's potential as well. I started an exchange of letters with him. While I continued my work and mellowed it, I read with great care the letters Sabat Ercasty addressed to me, an unknown young poet.

I sent Sabat Ercasty, in Montevideo, the poem I had written that night and I asked him if it showed any influence from his poetry. A kind letter from him promptly answered my question: "I have seldom seen such a successful, such a magnificent poem, but I have to tell you: Yes, there are echoes of Sabat Ercasty in your lines."

It was a flash of light in the darkness, of clarity, and I am still grateful for it. The letter spent a good many days in my pocket, wrinkling until it fell apart. Many things were at stake. I was particularly obsessed with the fruitless rush of feelings that night. I had fallen into that well of stars in vain, that storm of stars had struck my senses in vain. I had made an error. I must be wary of inspiration. Reason must guide me step by step down the narrow paths. I had to learn humility. I ripped up many manuscripts, I misplaced others. It would be ten years before these last poems would reappear and be published.

Sabat Ercasty's letter ended my recurrent ambition for an expansive poetry. I locked the door on a rhetoric that I could never go on with, and deliberately toned down my style and my expression.

Looking for more unpretentious qualities, for the harmony of my own world, I began to write another book. *Veinte poemas* was the result.

Those *Veinte poemas de amor y una canción desesperada* make a painful book of pastoral poems filled with my most tormented adolescent passions, mingled with the devastating nature of the southern part of my country. It is a book I love because, in spite of its acute melancholy, the joyfulness of being alive is present in it. A river and its mouth helped me to write it: the Imperial River. *Veinte poemas* is my love affair with Santiago, with its student-crowded streets, the university, and the honeysuckle fragrance of requited love.

The Santiago sections were written between Echaurren Street and España Avenue, and inside the old building of the Teachers Institute, but the landscape is always the waters and the trees of the south. The docks in the "Canción desesperada" ("Song of Despair") are the old docks of Carahue and Bajo Imperial: the broken planks and the beams like stumps battered by the wide river: the wingbeat of the gulls was heard and can still be heard at that river's mouth.

In the long, slender-bodied, abandoned lifeboat left over from some shipwreck, I read the whole of *Jean-Christophe*, and I wrote the "Canción desesperada." The sky overhead was the most violent blue I have ever seen. I used to write inside the boat, hidden in the earth. I don't think I have ever again been so exalted or so profound as during those days. Overhead, the impenetrable blue sky. In my hands, *Jean-Christophe* or the nascent lines of my poem. Beside me, everything that existed and continued always to exist in my poetry: the distant sound of the sea, the cries of the wild birds, and love burning, without consuming itself, like an immortal bush.

I am always being asked who the woman in *Veinte poemas* is, a difficult question to answer. The two women who weave in and out of these melancholy and passionate poems correspond, let's say, to Marisol and Marisombra: Sea and Sun, Sea and Shadow. Marisol is love in the enchanted countryside, with stars in bold relief at night, and dark eyes like the wet sky of Temuco. She appears with all her joyfulness and her lively beauty on almost every page, surrounded by the waters of the port and by a half-moon over the mountains. Marisombra is the student in the city. Gray beret, very gentle eyes, the ever-present honeysuckle fragrance of my footloose and fancy-free student days, the physical peace of the passionate meetings in the city's hideaways.

Meanwhile, life was changing in Chile.

The Chilean people's movement was starting up, clamoring, looking for stronger support among students and writers. On the one hand, the great leader of the petite bourgeoisie, Arturo Alessandri Palma, a dynamic and demagogic man, became President of the Republic, but not before he had rocked the country with his fiery and threatening speeches. In spite of his extraordinary personality, once in power he quickly turned into the classic ruler of our Americas; the dominant sector of the oligarchy, whom he had fought, opened its maw and swallowed him and his revolutionary speeches. The country continued to be torn apart by bitter strife.

At the same time, a working-class leader, Luis Emilio Recabarren, was extraordinarily active organizing the proletariat, setting up union centers, establishing nine or ten workers' newspapers throughout the country. An avalanche of unemployment sent the country's institutions staggering. I contributed weekly articles to *Claridad*. We students supported the rights of the people and were beaten up by the police in the streets of Santiago. Thousands of jobless nitrate and copper workers flocked to the capital. The demonstrations and the subsequent repression left a tragic stain on the life of the country.

From that time on, with interruptions now and then, politics became part of my poetry and my life. In my poems I could not shut the door to the street, just as I could not shut the door to love, life, joy, or sadness in my young poet's heart.

THE WORD

. . . You can say anything you want, yessir, but it's the words that sing, they soar and descend . . . I bow to them . . . I love them, I cling to them, I run them down, I bite into them, I melt them down . . . I love words so much . . . The unexpected ones . . . The ones I wait for greedily or stalk until, suddenly, they drop . . . Vowels I love . . . They glitter like colored stones, they leap like silver fish, they are foam, thread, metal, dew . . . I run after certain words . . . They are so beautiful that I want to fit them all into my poem . . . I catch them in mid-flight, as they buzz past, I trap them, clean them, peel them, I set myself in front of the dish, they have a crystalline texture to me, vibrant, ivory, vegetable, oily, like fruit, like algae, like agates, like olives . . . And then I stir them, I shake them, I drink them, I gulp them down, I mash them, I garnish them, I let them go . . . I leave them in my poem like stalactites, like slivers of polished wood, like coals, pickings from a shipwreck, gifts from the waves . . . Everything exists in the word . . . An idea goes through a complete change because one word shifted its place, or because another settled down like a spoiled little thing inside a phrase that was not expecting her but obeys her . . . They have shadow, transparence, weight, feathers, hair, and everything they gathered from so much rolling down the river, from so much wandering from country to country, from being roots so long . . . They are very ancient and very new . . . They live in the bier, hidden away, and in the budding flower . . . What a great language I have, it's a fine language we inherited from the fierce conquistadors . . . They strode over the giant cordilleras, over the rugged Americas, hunting for potatoes, sausages, beans, black tobacco, gold, corn, fried eggs, with a voracious appetite not found in the world since then . . . They swallowed up everything, religions, pyramids, tribes, idolatries just like the ones they brought along in their

huge sacks . . . Wherever they went, they razed the land . . . But words fell like pebbles out of the boots of the barbarians, out of their beards, their helmets, their horseshoes, luminous words that were left glittering here . . . our language. We came up losers . . . We came up winners . . . They carried off the gold and left us the gold . . . They carried everything off and left us everything . . . They left us the words.

The Roads of the World

ROAMING IN VALPARAÍSO

Valparaíso is very close to Santiago. They are separated only by the shaggy mountains on whose peaks tall cacti, hostile but flowering, rise like obelisks. And yet something impossible to define keeps Valparaíso apart from Santiago. Santiago is a captive city behind walls of snow. Valparaíso, on the other hand, throws its doors wide to the infinite sea, to its street cries, to the eyes of children: everything there is different.

At the wildest stage of our young manhood, we would suddenly—always at daybreak, always without having slept, always without a penny in our pockets—board a third-class coach, guided by the star of Valparaíso. We were poets and painters, all of us about twenty years old, brimming over with a precious store of impulsive madness that was dying to be used, to expand, to burst out. Valparaíso beckoned to us with its magnetic pulsebeat.

It wasn't until many years later that I felt this same inexplicable call again. It was during my years in Madrid. In a tavern, coming out of the theater in the small hours, or simply walking the streets, I would suddenly hear the voice of Toledo calling me, the soundless voice of its ghosts and its silence. And at that late hour, with friends as crazy as those of my younger days, I took off for the ancient, ashen, twisted citadel. To sleep in our clothes on the sands of the Tagus, under stone bridges.

I don't know why, but of all the trips to Valparaíso I can picture to myself, one remains fixed in my mind, permeated by an aroma of herbs uprooted from the intimacy of the fields. I will tell the story.

We were going to see a poet and a painter off, they would be traveling to France in a third-class cabin on the P.S.N.C. (Pacific Steam Navigation Company) anchored out in the bay. The ship floated there, resplendent, blowing smoke from its thick chimney: there was no doubt it was set to depart. We did not have enough money between all of us to pay for even the dingiest hotel, so we looked up Novoa, one of our favorite lunatics in wonderful Valparaíso. We knew he was trustworthy, and the door to his house in the hills was always wide open for mayhem. It was late in the evening when we set out. It wasn't easy to get to his house. Scrambling and slipping up and down endless hills, we followed Novoa's undaunted silhouette as he guided us along.

He was an impressive man, with a bushy beard and a thick moustache. His dark coattails flapped like wings on the mysterious slopes of the ridge we were climbing, blindly, worn out.

He wouldn't stop talking. He was a mad saint, canonized by us poets alone. He wasn't interested in that canonization, but only in the secret relations, known only to him, between bodily health and the natural bounties of the earth. He was, naturally, a naturist. He was a vegetal vegetarian. He preached to us as he walked along; he threw his thundering voice back at us, as if we were his disciples. His huge figure advanced like a St. Christopher native to these dark, forsaken suburbs.

At last we reached his house, which turned out to be a cabin with two rooms. Our St. Christopher's bed occupied one of them. The other was mostly taken up by an enormous wicker armchair, lavishly crisscrossed by superfluous rosettes and with quaint little drawers built into its arms. A Victorian masterpiece.

The huge armchair was assigned to me for sleeping that night.

My friends spread the evening papers over the floor and stretched out carefully on news items and editorial columns.

Their breathing and their snores soon told me that they were all sound asleep. Sitting in that monumental piece of furniture, my weary bones found it difficult to coax sleep. My weariness kept me awake.

I could hear a silence coming from the heights, the lonely peaks. Only the occasional barking of the Dog Stars in the darkness, only the faraway whistle of an arriving or departing ship made this night in Valparaíso real for me.

Suddenly I felt a strange, irresistible force flooding through me. It was a mountain fragrance, a smell of the prairie, of vegetation that had grown up with me during my childhood and which I had forgotten in the noisy hubbub of city life. I started to feel drowsy, cradled in the lullaby of the mother soil. Where could this wild breath of the earth, this purest of aromas, be coming from? It suffused me, overwhelmed my senses with an invasive scent composed of the pure virginity of aromas. In the darkness, I felt around for the wicker frame of my colossal chair.

Probing with my fingers into its nooks and crannies, I discovered the innumerable little drawers. And in them, blinded by the darkness, I felt with my hands dry, smooth plants, coarse, rounded sheaves, spear-like, soft or metallic leaves. The entire health-giving arsenal of our vegetarian preacher, the complete record of a life spent by our exuberant wandering St. Christopher gathering wild plants with his huge hands. Once this enigma had been cleared up, I fell asleep peacefully, protected by the fragrance of those guardian herbs.

When I recall it today, on Isla Negra, on this morning in August of 1973, I realize that all my friends from that strange, aromatic night have met their deaths, each fulfilling his own tranquil or tragic fate.

It's been years now since Novoa and his moustache disappeared. The ones who left for Paris the next day are gone as well. A hurricane coming in from the ocean swept away forever the cabin and the armchair that sheltered me and blessed me with sleep on that occasion.

Everything is gone. All that persists, and sometimes comes to torment me at night, is the aroma of dry, wild herbs that steps into my dreams, whose provenance I alone know.

For several weeks I lived across from Don Zoilo Escobar's house on a narrow street in Valparaíso. Our balconies almost touched. My neighbor would come out on his balcony early in the morning to do exercises like a hermit, exposing the harp of his ribs. Invariably dressed in a poor man's overalls or a frayed overcoat, half sailor, half archangel, he had retired long ago from his sea voyages, from the customs house, from the ships' crews. He brushed his Sunday suit every day with the meticulous thoroughness of a perfectionist. It was a distinguished-looking black flannel suit that, over the years, I never saw him wear—an outfit he kept among his treasures in a decrepit old wardrobe.

But his most precious and heart-rending treasure was a Stradivarius, which he watched over with devotion all his life, never playing it or allowing anyone else to. Don Zoilo was thinking of selling it in New York, where he would be given a fortune for the famed instrument. Sometimes he brought it out of the dilapidated wardrobe and let us look at it, reverently. Someday Don Zoilo would go north and return without a violin but loaded with flashy rings and with gold teeth filling the gaps the slow passing of the years had gradually left in his mouth.

One morning he did not come out to his gymnasium balcony. We buried him in the cemetery up on the hill, in his black flannel suit, which covered his small hermit's bones for the first time. The strings of the Stradivarius could not weep over his departure. Nobody knew how to play it. Moreover, the violin was not in the wardrobe when it was opened. Perhaps it had flown out to sea, or to New York, to crown Don Zoilo's dreams.

Valparaíso is secretive, sinuous, winding. Poverty spills over its hills like a waterfall. Everyone knows how much the infinite number of people on the hills eat and how they dress (and also how much they do not eat and how they do not dress). The wash hanging out to dry decks each house with flags and the swarm of bare feet constantly multiplying betrays unquenchable love.

Near the sea, however, on flat ground, there are balconied houses with closed windows, where hardly any footsteps ever enter. The explorer's mansion was one of those houses. I knocked repeatedly with the bronze knocker to make sure I would be heard. At last, soft footfalls approached and a quizzical face suspiciously opened the portal just a crack, wanting to keep me out. It was the old serving woman of the house, a shadow in a square shawl and an apron, whose footsteps were barely a whisper.

The explorer, who was also quite old, and the servant lived all alone in the spacious house with its windows closed. I had come there to see what his collection of idols was like. Corridors and walls were filled with bright red creatures, masks with white and ash-colored stripes, statues representing the vanished anatomies of sea gods, wigs of dried-up Polynesian hair, hostile wooden shields covered with leopard skin, necklaces of fierce-looking teeth, the oars of skiffs that may have cut through the foam of favorable waters. Menacing knives made the walls shudder with silver blades that gleamed through the shadows.

I noticed that the virile wooden gods had been emasculated. Their phalluses had been carefully covered with loincloths, obviously the same cloth used by the servant for her shawl and her apron.

The old explorer moved among his trophies stealthily. In room after room, he supplied me with the explanations, half peremptory and half ironic, of someone who had lived a good deal and continued to live in the afterglow of his images. His white goatee resembled a Samoan idol's. He showed me the muskets and huge pistols he had used to hunt the enemy and make antelopes and tigers bite the dust. He told his adventures without varying his hushed tone. It was as if the sunlight had come in through the closed windows to leave just one tiny ray, a tiny butterfly, alive, flitting among the idols.

On my way out, I mentioned a trip I planned to the Islands, my eagerness to leave very soon for the golden sands. Then, peering all around him, he put his frazzled moustache to my ear and shakily let slip: "Don't let her find out, she mustn't know about it, but I am getting ready for a trip, too."

He stood that way for an instant, one finger on his lips, listening for the possible tread of a tiger in the jungle. And then the door closed on him, dark and abrupt, like night falling over Africa.

I questioned the neighbors: "Are there any new eccentrics around? Is there anything worth coming back to Valparaíso for?"

They answered: "There's almost nothing to speak of. But if you go down that street you'll run into Don Bartolomé."

"And how am I going to know him?"

"There's no way you can make a mistake. He always travels in a grand coach."

A few hours later I was buying some apples in a fruit store when a horse-drawn carriage halted at the door. A tall, ungainly character dressed in black got out of it. He, too, was going to buy apples. On his shoulder he carried an all-green parrot, which immediately flew over to me and perched on my head without even looking where it was going.

"Are you Don Bartolomé?" I asked the gentleman.

"That's right. My name is Bartolomé." And pulling out a long sword he carried under his cape, he handed it to me, while he filled his basket with the apples and grapes he was buying. It was an ancient sword, long and sharp, with a hilt worked by fancy silversmiths, a hilt like a blown rose.

I didn't know him, and I never saw him again. But I accompanied him into the street with due respect, silently opened the carriage door for him and his basket of fruit to get in, and solemnly placed the bird and the sword in his hands.

Small worlds of Valparaíso, unjustly neglected, left behind by time, like crates abandoned in the back of a warehouse, nobody knows when, never claimed, come from nobody knows where, crates that will never go anywhere. Perhaps in these secret realms, in these souls of Valparaíso, was stored forever the lost power of a wave, the storm, the salt, the sea that flickers and hums. The menacing sea locked inside each person: an uncommunicable sound, an isolated movement that turned into the flour and the foam of dreams.

I was amazed that those eccentric lives I discovered were such an inseparable part of the heartbreaking life of the port. Above, on the hills, poverty flourishes in wild spurts of tar and joy. The derricks, the piers, the works of man cover the waist of the coast with a mask painted on by happiness that comes and goes. But others never made it to the hilltops, or down below, to the jobs. They put away their own infinite world, their fragment of the sea, each in his own box.

And they watched over it with whatever they had, while oblivion closed in on them like a mist.

Sometimes Valparaíso twitches like a wounded whale. It flounders in the air, is in agony, dies, and comes back to life.

Every native of the city carries in him the memory of an earthquake. He is a petal of fear clinging all his life to the city's heart. Every native is a hero even before he is born. Because in the memory of the port itself there is defeat, the shudder of the earth as it quakes and the rumble that surfaces from deep down as if a city under the sea, under the land, were tolling the bells in its buried towers to tell man that it's all over.

Sometimes when the walls and the roofs have come crashing down in dust and flames, down into the screams and the silence, when everything seems to have been silenced by death once and for all, there rises out of the sea, like the final apparition, the mountainous wave, the immense green arm that surges, tall and menacing, like a tower of vengeance, to sweep away whatever life remains within its reach.

Sometimes it all begins with a vague stirring, and those who are sleeping wake up. Sleeping fitfully, the soul reaches down to profound roots, to their very depth under the earth. It has always wanted to know it. And knows it now. And then, during the great tremor, there is nowhere to run, because the gods have gone away, the vainglorious churches have been ground up into heaps of rubble.

This is not the terror felt by someone running from a furious bull, a threatening knife, or water that swallows everything. This is a cosmic terror, an instant danger, the universe caving in and crumbling away. And, meanwhile, the earth lets out a muffled sound of thunder, in a voice no one knew it had.

The dust raised by the houses as they came crashing down settles little by little. And we are left alone with our dead, with all the dead, not knowing how we happen to be still alive.

The stairs start out from the bottom and from the top, winding as they climb. They taper off like strands of hair, give you a slight respite, and then go straight up. They become dizzy. Plunge down. Drag out. Turn back. They never end.

How many stairs? How many steps to the stairs? How many feet on the steps? How many centuries of footsteps, of going down and back up with a book, tomatoes, fish, bottles, bread? How many thousands of hours have worn away the steps, making them into little drains where the rain runs down, playing and crying?

Stairways!

No other city has spilled them, shed them like petals into its history, down its own face, fanned them into the air and put them together again, as Valparaíso has. No city has had on its face these furrows where lives come and go, as if they were always going up to heaven or down into the earth.

Stairs that have given birth, in the middle of their climb, to a thistle with purple flowers! Stairs the sailor, back from Asia, went up only to find a new smile or a terrifying absence in his house! Stairs down which a staggering drunk dived like a black meteor! Stairs the sun climbs to go make love to the hills!

If we walk up and down all of Valparaíso's stairs, we will have made a trip around the world.

Valparaíso of my sorrows . . . ! What happened in the solitudes of the South Pacific? Wandering star or battle of glowworms whose phosphorescence survived the disaster?

Night in Valparaíso! A speck on the planet lit up, ever so tiny in the empty universe. Fireflies flickered and a golden horseshoe started burning in the mountains.

What happened then is that the immense deserted night set up its formation of colossal figures that seeded light far and wide. Aldebaran trembled, throbbing far above, Cassiopeia hung her dress on heaven's doors, while the noiseless chariot of the Southern Cross rolled over the night sperm of the Milky Way.

Then the rearing, hairy Sagittarius dropped something, a diamond from his hidden hoofs, a flea from his hide, very far above.

Valparaíso was born, bright with lights, and humming, edged with foam and meretricious.

Night in its narrow streets filled up with black water nymphs. Doors lurked in the darkness, hands pulled you in, the bedsheets in the south led the sailor astray. Polyanta, Tritetonga, Carmela, Flor de Dios, Multicula, Berenice, Baby Sweet packed the beer taverns, they cared for those who had survived the shipwreck of delirium, relieved one another and were replaced, they danced listlessly, with the melancholy of my rain-haunted people.

The sturdiest whaling vessels left port to subdue leviathan. Other ships sailed for the Californias and their gold. The last of them crossed the Seven Seas later to pick up from the Chilean desert cargoes of the nitrate that lies like the limitless dust of a statue crushed under the driest stretches of land in the world.

These were the great adventures.

Valparaíso shimmered across the night of the world. In from the world and out into the world, ships surged, dressed up like fantastic pigeons, sweet-smelling vessels, starved frigates held up overlong by Cape Horn . . . In many instances, men who had just hit port threw themselves down on the grass . . . Fierce and fantastic days when the oceans opened into each other only at the far-off Patagonian strait. Times when Valparaíso paid good money to the crews that spit on her and loved her.

A grand piano arrived on some ship; on another, Flora Tristan, Gauguin's Peruvian grandmother, passed through; and on yet another, on the *Wager*, the original Robinson Crusoe came in, in the flesh, recently picked up at the Juan Fernández Islands . . . Other ships brought pineapples, coffee, black pepper from Sumatra, bananas from Guayaquil, jasmine tea from Assam, anise from Spain . . . The remote bay, the Centaur's rusty horseshoe, filled with intermittent gusts of fragrance: in one street you were overwhelmed by a sweetness of cinnamon; in another, the smell of custard apples shot right through your being like a white arrow; the detritus of seaweed from all over the Chilean sea came out to challenge you.

Valparaíso then would light up and turn a deep gold; it was gradually transformed into an orange tree by the sea, it had leaves, it had coolness and shade, it was resplendent with fruit.

The hills of Valparaíso decided to dislodge their inhabitants, to let go of the houses on top, to let them dangle from cliffs that are red with clay, yellow with gold thimble flowers, and a fleeting green with wild vegetation. But houses and people clung to the heights, writhing, digging in, worrying, their hearts set on staying up there, hanging on, tooth and nail, to each cliff. The port is a tug-of-war between the sea and nature, untamed on the cordilleras. But it was man who won the battle little by little. The hills and the sea's abundance gave the city a pattern, making it uniform, not like a barracks, but with the variety of spring, its clashing colors, its resonant bustle. The houses became colors: a blend of amaranth and yellow, crimson and cobalt, green and purple. And Valparaíso carried out its mission as a true port, a great sailing vessel that has run aground but is still alive, a fleet of ships with their flags to the wind. The wind of the Pacific Ocean deserved a city covered with flags.

I have lived among these fragrant, wounded hills. They are abundant hills, where life touches one's heart with numberless shanties, with unfathomable snaking spirals and the twisting loops of a trumpet. Waiting for you at one of these turns are an orange-colored merry-go-round, a friar walking down, a barefoot girl with her face buried in a watermelon, an eddy of sailors and women, a store in a very rusty tin shack, a tiny circus with a tent just large enough for the animal tamer's moustaches, a ladder rising to the clouds, an elevator going up with a full load of onions, seven donkeys carrying water up, a fire truck on the way back from a fire, a store window and in it a collection of bottles containing life or death.

But these hills have profound names. Traveling through these names is a voyage that never ends, because the voyage through Valparaíso ends neither on earth nor in the word. Merry Hill, Butterfly Hill, Polanco's Hill, Hospital, Little Table, Corner, Sea Lion, Hauling Tackle, Potters', Chaparro's, Fern, Litre, Windmill, Almond Grove, Pequenes, Chercanes, Acevedo's, Straw, Prison, Vixens', Doña Elvira's, St. Stephen's, Astorga, Emerald, Almond Tree, Rodríguez's, Artillery, Milkmen's, Immaculate Conception, Cemetery, Thistle, Leafy Tree, English Hospital, Palm Tree, Queen Victoria's, Caravallo's, St. John of God, Pocuro's, Cove, Goat, Biscayne, Don Elias's, Cape, Sugar Cane, Lookout, Parrasia, Quince, Ox, Flower.

I can't go to so many places. Valparaíso needs a new sea monster, an eight-legged one that will manage to cover all of it. I make the most of its immensity, its familiar immensity, but I can't take in all of its multicolored right flank, the green vegetation on its left, its cliffs or its abyss.

I can only follow it through its bells, its undulations, and its names.

Above all, through its names, because they are taproots and rootlets, they are air and oil, they are history and opera: red blood runs in their syllables.

CHILEAN CONSUL IN A HOLE

A literary prize at school, some popularity my new books enjoyed, and my notorious cape had given me a small aura of respectability beyond artistic circles. But in the twenties, cultural life in our countries depended exclusively on Europe, with a few rare and heroic exceptions. A cosmopolitan elite was active in each of our republics, and the writers who belonged to the ruling class lived in Paris. Our great poet Vicente Huidobro not only wrote in French but even changed his name, making it Vincent instead of Vicente.

In fact, as soon as I had the first little bit of youthful fame, people in the street started asking me: "Well, what are you doing here? You must go to Paris."

A friend spoke to the head of a department in the Foreign Ministry on my behalf, and he saw me right away. He knew my poems.

"I also know your aspirations. Sit down in that comfortable armchair. From here you have a good view of the square, of the carnival in the square. Look at those cars. All is vanity. You are a fortunate young poet. Do you see that palace? It belonged to my family once. And here I am now, in this cubbyhole, up to my neck in bureaucracy. When the things of the spirit are all that matter. Do you like Tchaikovsky?"

Giving me a parting handshake, after an hour-long conversation about the arts, he told me not to worry about a thing, he was the head of the consular service. "You may now consider yourself virtually appointed to a post abroad."

For two years I visited, from time to time, the office of the diplomatic department head, who was more obsequious each time. The moment he saw me appear, he would glumly call one of his secretaries and, arching his brows, would say, "I'm not in for anyone. I want to forget everyday prose. The only spiritual thing about this ministry is this poet's visit. I hope he never forsakes us."

I am sure he spoke with sincerity. Right after that, he would talk without respite about thoroughbred dogs. "Anyone who doesn't love dogs doesn't love children." He would go on to the English novel, then jump to anthropology and spiritism, and end up with questions of heraldry and genealogy. When I took leave of him, he would repeat once more, as if it were a terrifying little secret between the two of us, that my post abroad was guaranteed. Although I didn't have enough money to eat, I would leave in the evening breathing like a diplomat. And when my friends asked me what I was up to, I put on important airs and said, "I'm working on my trip to Europe."

This lasted until I ran into my friend Bianchi. The Bianchi family of Chile is a noble clan. Painters and popular musicians, jurists and writers, explorers and climbers of the Andes give all those with the Bianchi name an aura of restlessness and sharp intelligence. My friend, who had been an ambassador and knew the ins and outs of the ministries, asked me: "Hasn't your appointment come through yet?"

"I'll get it any moment now, I've been assured of it by a high patron of the arts in the Ministry."

He grinned and said: "Let's go see the Minister."

He took me by the arm and we went up the marble steps. Orderlies and employees scurried out of our way. I was dumbstruck. I was about to see my first Foreign Minister. He was quite short, and to disguise this, he swung himself up and sat on his desk. My friend mentioned how much I wanted to leave Chile. The Minister pressed one of his many buzzers, and to top off my confusion, my spiritual protector suddenly appeared.

"What posts are available in the service?" the Minister asked him.

The elegant functionary, who could not bring up Tchaikovsky now, listed various countries scattered over the world, but I managed to catch only one name, which I had never heard or read before: Rangoon.

"Where do you want to go, Pablo?" the Minister said to me.

"To Rangoon," I answered without hesitating.

"Give him the appointment," the Minister ordered my protector, who hustled out and came back in nothing flat with the official order.

There was a globe in the Minister's office. My friend Bianchi and I looked for the unknown city of Rangoon. The old map had a deep dent in a region of Asia and it was in this depression that we discovered it. "Rangoon. Here's Rangoon."

But when I met my poet friends some hours later and they decided to celebrate my appointment, I had completely forgotten the city's name. Bubbling over with joy, I could only explain that I had been named consul to the fabulous Orient and that the place I was being sent to was in a little hole in the map.

MONTPARNASSE

One day in June 1927 we set out for faraway regions. In Buenos Aires we turned in my first-class for two third-class fares and sailed on the *Baden*. This German ship supposedly had just one class, but that must have been fifth class. There were two sittings for meals: one to serve the Portuguese and Spanish immigrants as fast as possible, and another for the remaining sundry passengers, particularly the Germans, who were returning from the mines and factories of Latin America. Alvaro, my companion, immediately classified the female passengers. He was a very active lady-killer. He divided women into two groups: those who prey on man and those who obey the whip. These distinctions did not always apply. He had a whole bag of tricks for winning the affection of the ladies. Whenever a pair of these interesting passengers appeared on deck, he would quickly grab one of my hands and pretend to read my palm, with mysterious looks and gestures. The second time around, the strollers would stop and beg him to read their future. He would take their hands at once, stroking them far too much, and the future he read always indicated a visit to our cabin.

But the voyage soon took a different turn for me and I stopped seeing the passengers, who grumbled noisily about the eternal fare of *Kartoffeln*; I stopped seeing the world and the monotonous Atlantic to feast my eyes only on the enormous dark eyes of a Brazilian, an ever so Brazilian girl, who boarded the ship in Rio de Janeiro with her parents and two brothers.

The carefree Lisbon of those years, with fishermen in the streets and without Salazar on the throne, filled me with wonder. The food at our small hotel was delicious. Huge trays of fruit crowned the table. Houses of various colors; old palaces with arched doorways; cathedrals like

monstrous vaults, which God would have abandoned centuries ago
to go live elsewhere; gambling casinos in former palaces; the crowds
on the avenues with their child-like curiosity; the Duchess of Braganza, out of her mind, walking solemnly down a cobbled street,
trailed by a hundred awestruck street urchins—this was my entry
into Europe.

And then Madrid with its crowded cafés; hail-fellow Primo de Rivera teaching the first lesson in tyranny to a country that would later
learn all the rest. The first poems of my *Residencia en la tierra*, which
the Spaniards were slow to understand and would only understand
later, when the generation of Alberti, Lorca, Aleixandre, and Diego
appeared. And for me Spain was also the interminable train and the
sorriest third-class coach in the world, taking us to Paris.

We disappeared into Montparnasse's swarming crowds, among Argentinians, Brazilians, Chileans. Venezuelans, still buried away under Gómez's reign, did not yet dream of coming. And, over there,
the first Hindus in their full-length robes. And my neighbor at the
next table, with her tiny snake coiled around her neck, drinking a *café
crème* with melancholy languor. Our South American colony drank
cognac and danced the tango, waiting for the slightest chance to start
a battle royal and take on half the world.

Paris, France, Europe, for us small-town Bohemians from South
America, consisted of a stretch of two hundred meters and a couple
of street corners: Montparnasse, La Rotonde, Le Dôme, La Coupole,
and three or four other cafés. *Boîtes* with black singers and musicians
were just beginning to become popular. The Argentinians were the
most numerous of the South Americans, the first to pick a fight, and
the richest. Hell could break loose at any time and an Argentine
would be lifted up by four waiters, and would pass, in the air, over
the tables, to be summarily deposited right out in the street. Our
cousins from Buenos Aires did not care at all for this rough handling

that wrinkled their trousers and, worse still, mussed up their hair. In those days, pomade was an essential part of Argentine culture.

Actually, in those first days in Paris, whose hours flitted past, I did not meet a single Frenchman, a single European, a single Asian, much less anyone from Africa or Oceania. Spanish-speaking Americans, from the Mexicans down to the Patagonians, went about in cliques, picking on one another, disparaging one another, but unable to live without one another. A Guatemalan prefers the company of a Paraguayan bum, with whom he can idle the time away exquisitely, to that of a Pasteur.

Around this time I met César Vallejo, the great *cholo*; a poet whose poetry had a rough surface, as rugged to the touch as a wild animal's skin, but it was magnificent poetry with extraordinary power.

Incidentally, we had a little run-in right after we met. It was in La Rotonde. We were introduced, and in his precise Peruvian accent, he greeted me with: "You are the greatest of all our poets. Only Rubén Darío can compare with you."

"Vallejo," I said, "if you want us to be friends, don't ever say anything like that to me again. I don't know where we'd end up if we started treating each other like writers."

My words appeared to unsettle him. My anti-literary education prompted me to be bad-mannered. On the other hand, he belonged to a race that was older than mine, with viceroyalty and courtesy behind it. When I saw that he was offended, I felt like an unwelcome boor.

But this blew over like a small cloud. We became true friends from that moment on. Years later, when I spent more time in Paris, we saw each other daily. Then I got to know him really well.

Vallejo was shorter than I, thinner, more heavy-boned. He was also more Indian than I, with very dark eyes and a very tall, domed forehead. He had a handsome Inca face, saddened by an air of unmistakable majesty. Vain like all poets, he loved it when people talked to him this way about his Indian features. He would hold his head high to let me admire it and say, "I've got something, haven't I?" And then laugh at himself quietly.

His self-regard was nothing like that sometimes expressed by Vicente Huidobro, a poet who was Vallejo's opposite in so many ways. Huidobro would let a lock of hair hang over his forehead, insert his fingers in his vest, push out his chest, and ask: "Have you noticed how much I look like Napoleon Bonaparte?"

Vallejo was moody but only on the outside, like a man who had been huddling in the shadows a long time. He had a solemn nature and his face resembled a rigid, quasi-hieratic mask. But his inner self was something else again. I often saw him (especially when we managed to pry him away from his domineering wife, a tyrannical, proud Frenchwoman who was a concierge's daughter), yes, I saw him jumping up and down happily, like a schoolboy. Later he would slip back into his moroseness and his submission.

The Maecenas we had been waiting for but who never showed up rose suddenly out of the Paris shadows. He was a Chilean writer, a friend of Rafael Alberti's, of the French, in fact almost everybody's friend. Also, and far more important, he was the son of Chile's biggest shipping magnate. And well-known as a big spender.

This messiah who had just fallen out of the sky wanted to fete me, so he took all of us to a White Russian *boîte* called the Caucasian Wine Cellar. Its walls were decorated with Caucasian costumes and landscapes. We were soon surrounded by Russian or phony Russian girls dressed as peasants from the mountains.

Condon, for that was our host's name, looked like the last of the Russian decadents. A frail-looking blond, he ordered bottle after bottle of champagne and did mad leaps in the air, imitating Cossack dances he had never seen.

"Champagne, more champagne!" And, all of a sudden, our pale

millionaire host collapsed on the ground. He lay there under the table fast asleep, like the bloodless corpse of a Caucasian done in by a bear.

A shiver ran through us. The man would not come to even with ice compresses or bottles of ammonia uncorked under his nose. Seeing our helplessness and confusion, all the dancing girls deserted us, except one. In our host's pockets we found an impressive checkbook that, in his corpse-like condition, he could not use.

The head Cossack demanded immediate payment and closed the exit door to stop us from getting out. We escaped from his custody only by leaving my brand-new diplomatic passport as security.

We departed with our lifeless millionaire on our shoulders. It took a herculean effort to carry him to a taxi, settle him in it, and then unload him at his deluxe hotel. We left him in the arms of two huge doormen in red livery, who carried him off like an admiral fallen on the bridge of his ship.

The one girl from the *boîte* who had not deserted us in our misfortune was waiting for us in the cab. Alvaro and I invited her to Les Halles to enjoy the early-morning onion soup. We bought her flowers in the market, thanked her with a kiss for being a good Samaritan, and noticed that she was rather attractive. She was neither pretty nor homely, but her turned-up nose, so typical of Paris girls, made up for that. Then we invited her to our seedy hotel. She had no objection to coming with us.

She went with Alvaro to his room. I dropped into bed exhausted, but all at once I felt someone shaking me roughly. It was Alvaro. His harmless maniac's face seemed a little odd. "Listen," he said. "This woman is something special, fantastic, I can't explain to you. You've got to try her right away."

A few minutes later the stranger got into my bed, sleepily but obligingly. Making love to her, I received proof of her mysterious gift. It was something I can't pin down with words, something that rushed up from deep within her, something that went back to the very origins of pleasure, to the first upsurge of a wave, to the erotic secrets of Venus. Alvaro was right.

At breakfast the next morning, Alvaro warned me, on the side, in Spanish: "If we don't leave this woman right away, our trip will be doomed. We will be sunk, not at sea but in the unfathomable sacrament of sex."

We decided to shower her with little gifts: flowers, chocolates, and half the francs we had left. She confessed that she didn't work in the Caucasian nightclub; she had gone there the night before for the first and only time. Then we got into a taxi with her. The driver was passing through an unfamiliar neighborhood when we told him to stop. We said goodbye to her with big kisses and left her there, confused but smiling.

We never saw her again.

VOYAGE TO THE EAST

Nor will I ever forget the train that took us to Marseilles, loaded, like a basket of exotic fruit, with a motley crowd of people, country girls, and sailors, with accordions and songs chorused by everyone in the coach. We were heading for the Mediterranean Sea, toward the doors of light . . . This was 1927. I was fascinated by Marseilles, with its commercial romanticism and the Vieux-Port winged with sails seething in their own ominous turbulence. But the Messageries Maritimes ship on which we sailed for Singapore was a piece of France at sea, with its petite bourgeoisie emigrating to occupy posts in the remote colonies. During the trip, when the crew noticed our typewriters and our writers' manuscripts and papers, they asked us to pound out their letters on our machines. We took down the most incredible letters, dictated by the crew for their girls in Marseilles, in Bordeaux, in the provinces. Deep down, they were more interested in their letters being typewritten than in the message. Still, the things they said in them sounded like poems by Tristan Sepúlveda, artless, tender messages, all of them. The Mediterranean, with its ports, its carpets, its traders, its markets, slowly opened before our prow. In the Red Sea I was impressed by the port of Djibouti. The calcined sand, tracked so often by Arthur Rimbaud's comings and goings; Negresses like statues with their baskets of fruit, the miserable huts of the native population; and the ramshackle look of cafés lit by spectral overhead lights . . . They served iced tea with lemon there.

The thing to do was to see what went on at night in Shanghai. Cities with a bad reputation draw you like deadly women. Shanghai opened its night mouth for us, two country boys set adrift in the world, third-class passengers with little money and a joyless curiosity.

We went to the big nightclubs, one after the other. It was a weekday night and they were empty. It was depressing to look at those enormous dance floors, big enough for hundreds of elephants to dance on, and nobody dancing there. Women from the Tsar's Russia, thin as skeletons, came out of dark corners, yawning and asking us to invite them to drink champagne. So we did the rounds of six or seven dens of sin and lost souls, where all we were losing was our time.

It was late to be getting back to the ship we had left a long ways behind, beyond the crisscrossing, narrow streets of the waterfront. We each took a rickshaw. We weren't used to this kind of transportation provided by human horses. In 1927, those Chinese trotted for long distances, pulling the little cart without ever stopping to rest.

Since it had started raining and the rain was coming down harder now, our rickshawmen thoughtfully halted their carriages and carefully covered the fronts of the rickshaws with rainproof cloth so that not one drop should spatter our foreign noses. "They're such a refined and considerate people. Two thousand years of culture have not gone for nothing," Alvaro and I thought, in our mobile seats.

And yet something began to make me feel uneasy. I couldn't see a thing, shut in under the hood considerately put up for our protection, but through the oilskin I could hear my driver's voice sending out a kind of buzz. The sound of his bare feet was soon joined by the rhythmic sounds of other bare feet trotting alongside on the wet pavement. The sounds finally became muffled, it was a sign that the pavement had ended. Apparently, we were now traveling over open ground, outside the city.

All at once my rickshaw halted. The driver skillfully undid the cloth that protected me from the rain. There wasn't the shadow of a ship in those deserted outskirts. The other rickshaw was standing beside mine, and Alvaro climbed down from his seat, obviously alarmed.

"Money! Money!" seven or eight Chinese who circled us kept repeating steadily.

My friend moved as if to reach for a weapon in his trousers pocket, and it was enough to earn each of us a rabbit punch. I fell back, but the Chinese caught my head in mid-air, keeping me from crashing down, and gently laid me out on the wet ground. With lightning speed they went through my pockets, shirt, hat, shoes and socks, and my necktie, like sleight-of-hand artists putting on an extravagant display of skill. Not one inch of clothing remained unaccounted for, not a penny of the little money we had. But one thing: with the traditional consideration of Shanghai thieves, they scrupulously respected our papers and our passports.

Once we were alone, we walked toward the lights we could make out far off. Before long, we ran into hundreds of Chinese who were out at this hour and yet were honest. None of them knew French, or English, or Spanish, but all wanted to help us in our predicament, and somehow we were guided to the yearned-for paradise of our third-class cabin.

We got to Japan. The money we were expecting from Chile was supposed to be at the consulate. In the interim, we had to put up at a seaman's shelter in Yokohama. We slept on dreadful straw mattresses. A glass pane had been knocked out, it was snowing, and the cold went right through our bones. No one noticed us. One morning, at daybreak, an oil tanker split in two off the Japanese coast and the refuge was filled with stranded seamen. Among them was a Basque who could only speak Spanish and his own language. He told us his adventure: for four days and nights he had stayed afloat on a piece of the wreck, surrounded by waves of burning oil. The survivors were supplied with blankets and rations, and the Basque, a big-hearted fellow, became our benefactor.

The Consul General of Chile, on the other hand—I think his name was De la Marina or De la Rivera—received us in a high-handed manner, letting us know our place as lowly castaways. He had no time to spare. He was dining with Countess Yufu San that evening. The Imperial Court had invited him to tea. Or else he was immersed in profound studies of the reigning dynasty. "The emperor is such a refined man"—and so on.

No. He didn't have a telephone. Why have a telephone in Yokohama? They would only call him up in Japanese. As for news about our money, the manager of the bank, a close friend of his, hadn't mentioned it. He was very sorry but he must leave. He was expected at a gala reception. See you tomorrow.

The same story, day after day. We would leave the consulate shivering, since the robbery had reduced our wardrobe and all we had were some bedraggled sweaters given to us castaways. On the last day, we found out that our funds had arrived in Yokohama ahead of us. The bank had sent the consul three notices, and the pompous mannequin, the high-and-mighty functionary, had overlooked this minor point, so far beneath his station. (Whenever I read in the papers about consuls murdered by their crazed countrymen, I think longingly of that distinguished, bemedaled official.)

That night we went to the best café in Tokyo, the Koraku, on the Ginza. There was excellent food in Tokyo in those days; besides, our week of hunger gave the delicacies an added flavor. In the pleasant company of lovely Japanese girls, we drank toasts to all the unfortunate travelers neglected by perverse consuls all over the world.

Singapore. We thought we were next door to Rangoon. What a bitter letdown! What had only been a few millimeters on the map had become a gaping abyss. Ahead of us we had several days on board a ship, and what's more, the one making the regular run had left for Rangoon the previous day. We had no money to pay the hotel or our fares. More funds were waiting for us in Rangoon.

Ah, but my colleague the Chilean consul in Singapore was there for a purpose. Señor Mansilla hurried in. His smile dwindled little by little until it disappeared completely, giving way to a wry grimace. "I can't do a thing for you. Get in touch with the Ministry."

I suggested that we consuls must stick together, but it was no use. The man had the face of a heartless jailer. He grabbed his hat and was already making a dash for the door when a Machiavellian thought struck me: "Señor Mansilla, I'll be forced to give some lectures on our country, with paid attendance, to put together enough money for our fares. Please get me a hall, an interpreter, and the necessary permit."

The man went white. "Lectures on Chile, in Singapore? I won't allow it. I am in charge and I am the only one who can give lectures on Chile here."

"Calm down, Señor Mansilla," I said. "The more people like us there are talking about our remote country, the better. I don't see why you are so upset."

In the end, this crazy proposition that boiled down to patriotic blackmail led to a compromise. Shaking with anger, he made us sign receipts and handed us the money. When we counted it, we remarked that the receipts were made out for a larger amount.

"That's the interest," he explained.

(Ten days later I sent him a check from Rangoon, but without the interest, of course.)

From the deck, as the ship drew into Rangoon, I saw looming ahead the gold funnel of the great pagoda Shwe Dagon. A multitude of strange costumes clashed their vibrant colors on the pier. A broad dirty river's mouth emptied there, into the Gulf of Martaban. This river has the most beautiful name of all the rivers in the world: Irrawaddy.

Beside its waters, my new life was about to begin.

ALVARO

...A hell of a guy, Alvaro... His name is now Alvaro de Silva... He lives in New York... He has spent most of his life in the New York jungle... I imagine him eating oranges at outlandish hours, burning cigarette paper with a match, asking a lot of people annoying questions... He was always an undisciplined teacher, had a brilliant intelligence, an inquisitive intelligence that seemed to lead nowhere but to New York. It was 1925... Between the violets that almost slipped from his hands as he rushed them to some passing stranger he wanted to go to bed with right away, without even finding out her name or where she came from, between this and his interminable lectures on Joyce, he revealed to me, and to many others, unsuspected opinions, viewpoints of the man of the world who lives in the city, in his lair, and goes out to investigate the latest in music, painting, books, the dance... Forever eating oranges, paring apples, impossible in his eating habits, amusingly up on everything, in him we finally saw the urbane model of our dreams, what all of us provincials wanted to be, no labels pasted on suitcases, but carried within, an assortment of countries and concerts, cafés in the small hours, universities with snow-covered roofs... He reached a point where he made life impossible for

me . . . Wherever I go, I settle into a vegetable dream, I set my mind on one spot and try to put down roots, so as to think, to go on existing . . . Alvaro was always jumping from one wild enthusiasm to another, fascinated by any film we could work in, immediately dressing up as Moslems to go to the studio . . . There are pictures around somewhere of me in a Bengalese costume (I went into a cigarette shop in Calcutta and did not speak, and they took me for a member of Tagore's family) when we used to go to the Dum-Dum studios to see if they would hire us . . And then we'd have to leave the Y.M.C.A. on the sly because we hadn't paid our bill . . . And the nurses who loved us . . . Alvaro got tangled up in fabulous business ventures . . . He wanted us to sell tea from Assam, cloth from Kashmir, clocks, ancient treasures . . . Everything fizzled out quickly . . . He left samples from Kashmir, his little tea bags, on the tables, on the beds . . . He had already grabbed another suitcase and was somewhere else . . . In Munich . . . In New York . . .

I have seen many writers, steady, inexhaustible, and prolific, but he is the greatest . . . He almost never publishes anything . . . I don't understand . . . In the morning, without getting out of bed, with glasses mounted on the little hump of his nose, he's already at it, banging away at the typewriter, consuming reams of every kind of paper, of all the paper he can get his hands on . . . And yet his mobility, his criticism, his oranges, his periodic communications, his lair in New York, his violets, his muddle that appears to be so clear, his lucidity that is so muddled up . . . He never turns out the work everyone's always expected of him . . . Maybe it's because he doesn't feel like it . . . Maybe it's because he can't do it . . . Because he's doing too many things at once . . . Or because he's not doing anything . . . But he knows everything, he sees everything across continents with those impulsive blue eyes, with that fine sensibility, nevertheless letting the sands of time sift through his fingers . . .

Luminous Solitude

FOREST IMAGES

Immersed in these memories, I suddenly have to wake up. It's the sound of the sea. I am writing in Isla Negra, on the coast, near Valparaíso. The powerful winds that whipped the shore have just blown themselves out. The ocean—rather than my watching it from my window, it watches me with a thousand eyes of foam—still shows signs, in its surf, of the terrible persistence of the storm.

Years that are so far away! Reconstructing them, it's as if the sound of the waves I hear now touched something inside me again and again, sometimes lulling me to sleep, then with the abrupt flash of a sword. I shall take up those images without attention to chronological order, just like these waves that come and go.

Nineteen twenty-nine. Night. I see the crowd pressing together. It's a Moslem holiday. They have made a long trough in the middle of the street and filled it with burning coals. I move closer. My face is flushed by the powerful heat of the coals heaped, under a thin sheet of ashes, on the scarlet ribbon of living fire. All at once, a fantastic personage appears. With his face smeared red and white, he comes on the shoulders of four men dressed in red. They set him down, he starts to walk drunkenly over the coals, shrieking as he walks: "Allah! Allah!"

The huge crowd devours the scene, stunned. The magician has now walked unharmed over the long ribbon of coals. Then one man breaks away from the multitude, kicks his sandals off, and goes over the same span on naked feet. Volunteers keep coming forward interminably. Some pause midway along the trough to stomp on the fire, crying out, "Allah! Allah!," howling, with hair-raising grimaces, rolling their eyes to heaven. Others pass over with children in their arms. No one is burned, or maybe they are, but I'm not sure.

Beside the sacred river looms the temple of Kali, goddess of death. We enter, mingling with hundreds of pilgrims who have come from deep in Hindu country to win her grace. Terrified, in rags, they are shoved along by the Brahmins who demand money for something or other, every step of the way. The Brahmins lift one of the execrable goddess's seven veils, and as they lift it, there is the blast of a gong loud enough to wake up the dead. The pilgrims fall to their knees, make their obeisance with joined hands, touch their foreheads to the ground, and move on to the next veil. The priests drive them into a courtyard, where they chop off the heads of goats with one blow from an ax and collect new tributes. The bleating of wounded animals is drowned out by the blasts of the gong. The filthy whitewashed walls are splashed right up to the roof with blood. The goddess is a statue with a swarthy face and white eyes. A scarlet tongue two meters long hangs from her mouth to the ground. Necklaces of skulls and emblems of death weigh down her ears and her neck. The pilgrims contribute their last coins before being swept out into the street.

The poets who surrounded me to chant their songs and their poems were nothing like these abject pilgrims. Dressed in their trailing white garments, squatting on the grass, accompanying themselves with their tambourines, each let out a low-pitched, broken cry, and from his lips rose up a song he had composed in the same form and meter as the ancient, millennial songs. But the songs' emphasis had changed. These were not sensual or joyful songs but songs of protest, songs against hunger, songs written in prison. Many of these young poets I met all over India, whose brooding eyes I'll never be able to drive out of my mind, had just come out of jail and would perhaps return to their cells tomorrow. For they sought to rise up against misery and against the gods as well. This is the time we have been destined to live in. And this is the golden age of world poetry. While the new songs are hunted down, a million men sleep by the roadside, on the outskirts of Bombay, night after night. They sleep. They are born and they die. There is no housing, no bread, no medicines. Civilized, proud England left her colonial empire like this. She parted from her former subjects without leaving them schools, or industries, or housing, or hospitals, only prisons and mountains of empty whiskey bottles.

The memory of Rango the orangutan is another tender image that comes back in with the waves. In Medan, Sumatra, I knocked at the gate of the run-down Botanical Gardens on more than one occasion. To my amazement, he came to open it for me each time. We used to go down a path hand in hand, to sit down at a table on which he banged with both hands and both feet. A waiter would then appear, and he would serve us our pitcher of beer, not too small, not too large, just right for the orangutan and the poet.

In the Singapore zoo we saw a lyrebird in a cage, glittering, enraged, with the resplendent beauty of a bird who has just flown out of Eden. And farther along, a black female panther, with the smell of the jungle still fresh on her, was pacing in her cage. She was a strange patch of starry night, a magnetic ribbon in constant motion, a lithe black volcano ready to destroy the world, a dynamo of pure, undulating power, and two yellow eyes, two unerring knives, probing with their fire, unable to understand her imprisonment or the human race.

We came to the strange Snake Temple on the outskirts of the city of Penang, in what used to be called Indochina.

This temple has been described over and over by travelers and journalists. So many wars, such repeated destruction, and so much time and rain have come down on the streets of Penang that I wonder if it is still there. Under the tiled roof, a low, blackish building, eaten away by the tropical rains, in a thick wilderness of huge plantain leaves. A dank smell. A scent of frangipani. When we first enter the temple, we see nothing in the dimness. A strong odor of incense, and something moving over there. It's a snake stretching out lazily. Little by little we notice others. Then we see that there may be dozens. Later we realize that there are hundreds or thousands of snakes. There are tiny ones coiled around the candelabras, there are some that are dark, metallic, and slender, they all look drowsy and sated. Sure enough, fine porcelain bowls can be seen everywhere, some brimming with milk, others filled with eggs. The snakes don't notice us. We pass down the narrow labyrinths of the temple, brushing against them. They are over our heads, hanging from the golden architecture; they are sleeping on the stonework, or curled up on the altars. Over there is the dreaded Russell's viper; it's swallowing an egg, near a dozen lethal coral snakes, whose scarlet rings advertise their instant poison. I made out the fer-de-lance, several enormous pythons, the coluber de rusi, and the coluber noya. Green, gray, blue, black serpents filled the hall. A dead silence everywhere. From time to time, a bonze dressed in saffron robes crosses the shadows. The brilliant color of his tunic makes him look like one more snake, stirring lazily in quest of an egg or a bowl of milk.

Were these snakes brought here? How did they adjust? Our questions are answered with a smile, we are told that they came on their own, and will go on their own when they feel like it. The doors, in fact, are open and there is no grating or glass or anything forcing them to stay in the temple.

The bus was to leave Penang and cross the forest country and villages of Indochina to get to Saigon. No one understood my language, nor did I understand theirs. We made stops along the interminable road at out-of-the-way places in the jungle, and passengers got off, peasants in unusual clothes, slant-eyed and quietly dignified. By now, only three or four remained in the undaunted old rattletrap that whined and threatened to come apart in the sweltering night.

All of a sudden, I was seized with panic. Where was I? Where was I going? Why was I spending this endless night among these strangers? We were crossing from Laos into Cambodia. I took in the inscrutable faces of the last of my fellow travelers. Their eyes were wide open. They looked like robbers. No doubt about it, I was among the sort of bandits usually found in Oriental stories.

They exchanged knowing glances and watched me out of the corner of their eyes. Just then, the bus came to a dead stop right in the middle of the jungle. I picked the spot where I would die. I wouldn't let them carry me off to be sacrificed under those unfamiliar trees whose dark shadows cut off the sky. I would die here, on this bench in the rickety bus, trapped among baskets full of vegetables and chickens in crates, the only friendly things around at that terrible moment. I looked about me, ready to face the fury of my killers, and I noticed that they, too, had vanished.

I waited a long while, alone, with my spirit completely crushed by the intense darkness of the alien night. I was going to die and no one would hear about it. So far from my small, beloved country! So far away from my books and from all those I loved!

Suddenly a light appeared, and then another. The road came alive with lights. There was the sound of a drum; an outburst of shrill notes of Cambodian music. Flutes, tambourines, and torches filled the road with music and patches of light. A man got on and told me in English: "The bus has broken down. Since there will be a long wait, perhaps till daybreak, and there is no place to sleep here, the passengers went out to look for a troupe of musicians and dancers to entertain you."

For hours, under those trees that were no longer intimidating, I watched the lovely ritual dances of a noble and ancient culture and listened, till sunup, to its delightful music flooding the road.

The poet cannot be afraid of the people. Life seemed to be handing me a warning and teaching me a lesson I would never forget: the lesson of hidden honor, of fraternity we know nothing about, of beauty that blossoms in the dark.

A CONGRESS IN INDIA

This is a glorious day. We are present at the congress of the Indian National Congress Party. A nation in the thick of its fight for liberation. Thousands of delegates pack the galleries. I meet Gandhi. And Pandit Motilal Nehru, another patriarch of the movement. And his son, the elegant young Jawaharlal, recently back from England. Nehru is all for independence, while Gandhi favors simple autonomy as a necessary first step. Gandhi: the sharp profile of a very cunning fox; a practical man; a politician along the lines of our early creole leaders; a mastermind at committees; a shrewd tactician, indefatigable. As the multitude passes by in an endless stream, touching the hem of his white tunic worshipfully and crying, "Gandhiji! Gandhiji!," he gives them a perfunctory salute and smiles without taking off his glasses. He receives messages and reads them; he answers telegrams; all this without effort; he is a saint who never wears himself out. Nehru: the intelligent promulgator of their revolution.

One of the great figures at the congress was Subhas Chandra Bose, impetuous demagogue, violent anti-imperialist, fascinating political figure of his country. In the war of 1914, during the Japanese invasion, he sided with the invaders against the British Empire. Many years later, here in India, one of his friends tells me how the fortress of Singapore fell. "Our weapons were trained on the Japanese besiegers. Suddenly we began asking ourselves why. We had our soldiers do an about-face and we pointed our guns at the English troops. It was quite simple. The Japanese invaders were just passing through. The English seemed to be here for all eternity."

Subhas Bose was arrested, tried, found guilty of high treason, and sentenced to death by the British courts in India. The protests triggered off by the independence movement multiplied. At last, after many legal battles, his lawyer—Nehru himself—won amnesty for him. He became a popular hero from that moment on.

THE RECLINING GODS

... *Statues of Buddha everywhere, of Lord Buddha* ... *The severe, upright, worm-eaten statues, with a golden patina like an animal's sheen, deteriorating as if the air were wearing them away* ... *In their cheeks, in the folds of their tunics, at elbows and navel and mouth and smile, tiny blemishes: fungi, pockmarks, traces of jungle excrement* ... *Or the recumbent, the immense, recumbent statues, forty meters of stone, of sand granite, pale, stretched out among the rustling fronds, emerging suddenly from some corner of the jungle, from its surrounding site* ... *Asleep or not asleep, they have been there a hundred years, a thousand, one thousand times a thousand years* ... *Yet there is something soft about them and they are known for an other-worldly air of indecision, longing to stay or go away* ... *And that very soft stone smile, that imponderable majesty which is nevertheless made of hard, everlasting stone—at whom, at how many, on the bloodstained planet are they smiling* ... ? *The fleeing peasant women passed, the men from the fire, the visored warriors, the false high priests, the tourists who devour everything* ... *And the statue remained in place, the immense stone with knees, with folds in its stone tunic, with a look lost in the distance and yet really here, thoroughly inhuman and also in some way human, in some form or contradiction a statue, god and not god, stone and not stone, under the screeching of black birds, surrounded by the wingbeats of red birds, of the birds of the forest ... We are reminded of the terrible Spanish Christs we inherited wounds and all, pustules and all, scars and all, with that odor given off by churches, of wax candles, of mustiness, of a closed room ... Those Christs had second thoughts about being men or gods ... To make them human beings, to bring them closer to those who suffer, midwives and beheaded men, cripples and avaricious men, the inner circles of churches and those outside the churches, to make them human, the sculptors gave them the most gruesome wounds, and all this ended up as the religion of suffering, as sin and you'll suffer, don't sin and you'll suffer, live and you'll suffer, leaving you no possible way out ... Not here, here the stone found peace ... The sculptors rebelled against the canons of pain, and these colossal Buddhas, with the feet of giant gods, have a smile on their stone faces that is beatifically human, without all that pain ... And they give off an odor, not of a dead room, not of sacristies and cobwebs, but an odor of vegetable space, of sudden gusts of wind swooping down in wild swirls of feathers, leaves, pollen from the infinite forest ...*

HAPLESS HUMAN FAMILY

In several essays on my poetry I have read that my stay in the Far East influenced it in some ways, especially *Residencia en la tierra*. As it happens, the poems of *Residencia en la tierra* are the only ones I wrote at that time, but without going so far as to defend my statement categorically, I say that this business of influence is mistaken.

All the esoteric philosophy of the Oriental countries, when confronted with real life, turned out to be a by-product of the anxiety, neurosis, confusion, and opportunism of the West; that is, of the crisis in the guiding principles of capitalism. In the India of those years there was little room for deep contemplation of one's navel.

An existence that made brutal physical demands, a colonial position based on the most cold-blooded degradation, thousands dying every day of cholera, smallpox, fever, and hunger, a feudal society thrown into chaos by India's immense population and industrial poverty, stamped such great ferocity on life that all semblance of mysticism disappeared.

The theosophic centers were generally run by adventurers from the West, including North and South Americans. Of course, there were people among them who acted in good faith, but the majority exploited a cheap market where exotic amulets and fetishes wrapped in metaphysical sales talk were sold wholesale. These people were always spouting Dharma and Yoga. They reveled in religious acrobatics, all empty show and high-sounding words.

For these reasons, the Orient struck me as a large, hapless human family, leaving no room in my conscience for its rites and gods. I don't believe, then, that my poetry during this period reflected anything but the loneliness of an outsider transplanted to a violent, alien world.

I recall one of those tourists of the occult, a vegetarian and a lecturer. He was a little middle-aged character named Powers, with a shiny bald dome and very light blue eyes, whose cynical look pierced right through you. He came from North America, from California, was a Buddhist, and he always closed his lectures with the following dietetic prescription: "As Rockefeller used to say, eat an orange every day."

Powers's cheerful openness appealed to me. He spoke Spanish. After his lectures we used to go off together and feast on huge bellyfuls of roast lamb with onions. He was a Buddhist theologian— whether or not he was the real thing, I don't know—but his voracious appetite was more authentic than the contents of his lectures.

He soon fell in love, first with a half-caste who was crazy about his tuxedo and his theories; she was an anemic young lady with long-suffering eyes who believed he was a god, a living Buddha. That's how religions are born.

After several months with this woman, he came to see me one day about attending a new marriage of his. On his motorcycle, provided by the commercial concern for which he was a refrigerator salesman, we quickly left groves, monasteries, and rice paddies behind us, finally coming to a small village with Chinese houses and Chinese inhabitants. Powers was received with fireworks and music, while the young bride, looking like an idol in her white make-up, remained seated on a chair that was higher than any of the others. Music was played while we sipped refreshments of all colors. Not once did Powers and his new wife say a word to each other.

We returned to the city. Powers explained that only the bride took part in this wedding ritual. The ceremonies would go on without his having to be there. Later he would go back to live with her.

"You realize you're a polygamist, don't you?"

"My other wife knows about it and will be very happy," he said.

This statement had as much truth in it as his story about an orange a day. When we got to his house, his first wife's home, we found her, the long-suffering half-caste, almost dead, with her cup of poison and a farewell note on the night table. Her dark body lay completely naked and motionless under the mosquito net. Her agony lasted several hours.

Although I was now beginning to find him repulsive, I stood by Powers because his suffering was obviously sincere. The cynic in him had gone to pieces. I went to the funeral with him. We placed the cheap coffin on a pile of firewood, on the bank of a river. Powers lit some kindling with a match, muttering ritual phrases in Sanskrit.

A few musicians dressed in orange-colored tunics chanted or blew on some very sad-sounding instruments. The pyre kept burning a little, then going out, and the fire had to be revived with matches. The river flowed on between its banks indifferently. The eternal blue sky of the Orient also displayed absolute unconcern, infinite disregard for the pitiful and lonely funeral of a poor forsaken creature.

My official duties demanded my attention only once every three months, when a ship arrived from Calcutta bound for Chile with hard paraffin and large cases of tea. I had to stamp and sign documents with feverish speed. Then three months of doing nothing followed, of solitary contemplation in markets and temples. This was the most painful period for my poetry.

The street became my religion. The Burmese street, the Chinese quarter with its open-air theaters and its paper dragons and its brilliant lanterns. The Hindu street, the humblest of them, with its temples operated as a business by one caste, and the poor people prostrate in the mud outside. Markets where the betel leaves rose in green pyramids like mountains of malachite. The stalls and pens where they sold wild animals and birds. The winding streets where supple Burmese women walked with long cheroots in their mouths. All this engrossed me and drew me gradually under the spell of real life.

The caste system had the Indian people arranged like an amphitheater of parallelepiped galleries superimposed one above the other, with the gods sitting at the top. The English, in turn, maintained their own caste system, starting with the small shop clerks, going on to professionals and intellectuals, then to exporters, and culminating on the system's garden roof, where the aristocrats of the Civil Service and the bankers of the Empire lounged in comfort.

These two worlds never touched. The natives were not allowed in the places reserved for the English, and the English lived away from the throbbing pulse of the country. This situation created problems for me. My British friends saw me in a gharry, a little horse-drawn cab used mainly for ephemeral trysts in transit, and offered me the kindly advice that a consul should never use these vehicles for any purpose. They also suggested that I should not frequent a lively Persian restaurant, where I drank the best tea in the world in little translucent cups. These were final warnings. After that, they stopped greeting me.

This boycott couldn't have pleased me more. Those intolerant Europeans were not really interesting, and after all, I had not come to the Orient to spend my life with transient colonizers but with the ancient spirit of that world, with that large hapless human family. I went so deep into the soul and the life of the people that I lost my heart to a native girl. In the street she dressed like an Englishwoman and used the name Josie Bliss, but in the privacy of her home, which I soon shared, she shed those clothes and that name to wear her dazzling sarong and her secret Burmese name.

WIDOWER'S TANGO

I had a troubled home life. Sweet Josie Bliss gradually became so brooding and possessive that her jealous tantrums turned into an illness. Except for this, perhaps I would have stayed at her side forever. I loved her naked feet, the white flowers brightening her dark hair. But her temper drove her to savage paroxysms. The letters I received from abroad made her jealous and furious; she hid my telegrams without opening them, she glowered at the air I breathed.

Sometimes a light would wake me up, a ghost moving on the other side of the mosquito net. It was she, dressed in white, brandishing her long, sharpened native knife. It was she, walking around and around my bed for hours at a time, without quite making up her mind to kill me. When you die, she used to say to me, my fears will end. The next day she would carry out mysterious rituals to make me remain faithful.

She would have ended up by killing me. Fortunately, I received official notice of my transfer to Ceylon. I made secret preparations for my departure and one day, abandoning my clothes and my books, I left the house as usual and boarded the ship that was to carry me far away.

I was leaving Josie Bliss, a kind of Burmese panther, with the deepest sorrow. The ship had barely started pitching and rolling in the Gulf of Bengal, when I started to write "Tango del viudo" ("Widower's Tango"), a tragic poem dedicated to the woman I lost and who lost me, because a volcano of anger boiled constantly in her blood. The night looked so vast, the earth so lonely!

OPIUM

... *Entire streets were set aside for opium* ... *The smokers stretched out on low benches* ... *They were in the true holy places of India* ... *These contained no signs of luxury, no upholstery, no silk cushions* ... *Nothing but unpainted planks, bamboo pipes, and pillows of Chinese porcelain* ... *An air of decorum and austerity prevailed which was not to be found in the temples* ... *The dreamers never stirred or made any sound* ... *I smoked one pipe* ... *There was nothing to it* ... *Just a haze of smoke, warm and milky* ... *I smoked four pipes and was sick for five days, with a nausea that rose from my spinal cord, that descended from my brain* ... *And hatred for the sunlight, for life itself* ... *Opium's revenge* ... *There had to be more to it than this* ... *So much had been said, so much had been written, there had been so much poking into briefcases and bags, in attempts to intercept the poison in customs, the famed, sacred poison* ... *I would have to overcome my queasiness* ... *Become familiar with opium, experience it, before I could pass judgment* ... *I smoked many pipefuls, until I knew* ... *There are no dreams, no images, there is no paroxysm* ... *There is a melodious draining of strength, as if an infinitely soft note lingered in the air* ... *A blacking out, a hollow feeling inside oneself* ... *The slightest movement, an elbow, the neck, any far-off sound of a carriage, a horn, or a street cry, became part of the oneness, a delicious, sleepy sensation* ... *I understood why hired hands from plantations, day laborers, rickshaw-men who pull and pull the rickshaw all day long, would lay there dazed, motionless* ... *Opium was not, as painted to me, the paradise of the exotic, but an escape for the exploited ... All those in the opium dens were poor devils ... There was no embroidered cushion, not the slightest hint of luxury ... Not a flicker of light in the place, not even in the half-closed eyes of the smokers ... Were they resting, were they sleeping ...? I was never able to find out ... No one spoke ... No one ever spoke ... No furnishings, no rugs, nothing ... On the worn benches, smoothed by so much contact, a few small wooden bolsters could be seen ... Nothing else, except silence and the aroma of opium, strangely repellent yet powerful ... No doubt, here was a path to destruction ... The opium of the magnates, of the colonizers, was reserved for the colonized ... At the entrance, the smokers found their authorized ration, their number, and their permit ready for them ... Inside, a vast, smoky silence reigned, an immobility that eased away unhappiness and sweetened fatigue ... A hazy silence, the dregs of many broken dreams, found a placid retreat here ... The dreamers with their half-closed eyes were living an hour submerged in the sea, an entire night on a hilltop, delighting in a subtle and delicious repose ...*

After that, I did not go back to the smoking dens ... I already knew ... I had experienced ... I had touched the untouchable ... hidden far back behind the smoke ...

CEYLON

In 1929, Ceylon, the most beautiful of the world's large islands, had the same colonial structure as Burma and India. The English had entrenched themselves in their neighborhoods and their clubs, hemmed in by a vast multitude of musicians, potters, weavers, plantation slaves, monks in yellow, and immense gods carved into the stone mountains.

Caught between the Englishmen dressed every evening in dinner jackets and the Hindus I couldn't hope to reach in their fabulous immensity, I had only solitude open to me, and so that time was the loneliest in my life. Yet I also recall it as the most luminous, as if a lightning flash of extraordinary brightness had stopped at my window to throw light on my destiny inside and out.

I went to live in a small bungalow recently built in the suburb of Wellawatte, near the sea. It was a sparsely populated area, with the surf breaking on the reefs nearby. The music of the sea swelled into the evening.

In the morning, the miracle of this newly washed nature was overwhelming. I joined the fishermen very early. Equipped with long floats, the boats looked like sea spiders. The men pulled out fish of vivid colors, fish like birds from the teeming forest, some with the deep blue phosphorescence of intense living velvet, others shaped like prickly balloons that shriveled up into sorry little sacs of thorns.

With horror I watched the massacre of those jewels of the sea. The fish were sold in segments to the poor. The machetes hacked to pieces the God-sent sustenance from the deep, turning it into blood-drenched merchandise.

Strolling up the shore, I would come to the elephants' bathing hole. With my dog alongside, I couldn't get lost. Out of the smooth water surged a perfectly still, gray mushroom: soon it turned into a serpent, then into an enormous head, and finally into a mountain with tusks. No other country in the world had, or has even now, so many elephants doing work on its roads. They were an amazing sight, far from any circus or the bars of any zoo, trudging up and down with their loads of timber, like hard-working giant journeymen.

My dog and my mongoose were my sole companions. Fresh from the jungle, the latter grew up at my side, slept in my bed, and ate at my table. No one can imagine the affectionate nature of a mongoose. My little pet was familiar with every minute of my day-to-day life, she tramped all over my papers, and raced after me all day long. She curled up between my shoulder and my head at siesta time and slept there the fitful, electric sleep of wild animals.

My tame mongoose became famous in the neighborhood. The constant battles mongooses wage so courageously against the deadly cobras have earned them a kind of mythological prestige. I believe in this, having often seen them fight these snakes, whom they defeat through sheer agility and because of their thick salt-and-pepper coat of hair, which deceives and confuses the reptiles. The country people believe that, after battling its poisonous enemy, the mongoose goes in search of antidotal herbs.

Anyway, the fame of my mongoose, who accompanied me every day on my long walks by the seashore, brought all the neighborhood kids to my house one afternoon in an impressive procession. An enormous snake had appeared in the streets, and they had come to ask for Kiria, my celebrated mongoose, whose sure victory they were ready to cheer on. Followed by my admirers—entire bands of Tamils and Singhalese youngsters wearing nothing but loincloths—I led the fight-bound parade, with my mongoose in my arms.

The ophidian was the dreaded black polonga, or Russell's viper, which has a deadly bite. It was sunning itself in the weeds on top of a white water main, silhouetted like a whip on snow.

My followers dropped behind silently. I followed the pipe and released my mongoose about two meters from the viper. Kiria sniffed danger and crawled slowly toward the serpent. My small friends and I held our breaths. The great battle was about to begin. The snake coiled, raised its head, opened its gullet, and fixed its hypnotic eyes on the small animal. The mongoose kept edging forward. Only a few centimeters from the monster's mouth, however, she realized exactly what was about to happen. Then, with a great leap, she streaked wildly in the opposite direction, leaving serpent and spectators behind, and did not stop running until she reached my bedroom.

That's how I lost caste, more than thirty years ago, in the suburb of Wellawatte.

The other day, my sister brought me a notebook containing my earliest poems, written in 1918 and 1919. Reading them over, I had to smile at their childish and adolescent melancholy, that literary sense of solitude given off by all my youthful work. The young writer cannot write without that shudder of loneliness, even when it is only imaginary, any more than the mature writer will be able to produce anything without a flavor of human companionship, of society.

I learned what true loneliness was, in those days and years in Wellawatte. During all that time I slept on a field cot like a soldier, an explorer. All I had for company were a table and two chairs, my work, my dog, my mongoose, and the "boy" who did the housework and returned to his village at night. This man was not, properly speaking, a companion; his status as an Oriental servant forced him to be quieter than a shadow. His name was, or still is, Bhrampy. There was no need to give him any orders, since he always had everything ready: my meal on the table, my freshly ironed clothes, the bottle of whiskey on the verandah. He seemed to have forgotten how to speak. The only thing he knew how to do was smile, with huge equine teeth.

Solitude, in this case, was not a formula for building up a writing mood but something as hard as a prison wall; you could smash your head against the wall and nobody came, no matter how you screamed or wept.

Across the blue air, across the yellow sand, past the primordial forest, past the vipers and the elephants, I realized, there were hundreds, thousands of human beings who worked and sang by the waterside, who lit fires and molded pitchers; and passionate women also, sleeping naked on thin mats, under the light of the immense stars. But how was I to get close to that throbbing world without being looked upon as an enemy?

Step by step, I became familiar with the island. One night I crossed all the dark neighborhoods of Colombo to attend a gala dinner. From a darkened house came the voice of a boy or a woman singing. I had the rickshaw stop. At the humble door, I was overwhelmed by a strong scent, Ceylon's unmistakable odor: a mixture of jasmine, sweat, coconut oil, frangipani, and magnolia. Dark faces, which blended in with the color and the odor of the night, invited me in. I sat down quietly on a mat, while the mysterious human voice that had made me stop sang on in the dark; the voice of a boy or a woman, tremulous and sobbing, rose to an unbelievable pitch, was suddenly cut off, and sank so low it became as dark as the shadows, clinging to the fragrance of the frangipani, looping itself in arabesques and suddenly dropping with all its crystalline weight, as if its highest jet had touched the sky, only to spill back quickly in among the jasmines.

I stayed there a long while, caught in the magic spell of the drums and fascinated by the voice, and then I went on my way, drunk with the enigma of an emotion I can't describe, of a rhythm whose mystery issued from the whole earth. An earth filled with music and wrapped in fragrance and shadows.

The English were already seated at the table, dressed in black and white.

"Forgive me. I stopped along the way to listen to some music," I told them.

They, who had lived in Ceylon for twenty-five years, reacted with elegant disbelief. Music? The natives had musicians? No one had known about it. This was news to them.

This terrible gap between the British masters and the vast world of the Asians was never closed. And it ensured an inhuman isolation, a total ignorance of the values and the life of the Asians.

There were exceptions within this narrow colonialism, I found out later. Suddenly an Englishman from the Service Club would go off the deep end about some Indian beauty. He was immediately fired and cut off like a leper by his countrymen. Something else happened at about this time: the colonists ordered the burning of a Singhalese peasant's hut, to rout him out in order to expropriate his land. The Englishman ordered to burn the hut to the ground was a modest official named Leonard Woolf. He refused and was dismissed from his post. Shipped back to England, he wrote one of the best books ever published about the Orient: *The Village in the Jungle*. A masterpiece true both to life and to literature, it was virtually eclipsed by the fame of his wife, none other than Virginia Woolf, the great subjective novelist of world renown.

Little by little the impenetrable crust began to crack open and I struck up a few good friendships. At the same time, I discovered the younger generation, steeped in colonialist culture, who talked only about books just out in England. I found out that the pianist, photographer, critic, and cinematographer Lionel Wendt was the central figure of a cultural life torn between the death rattles of the Empire and a human appraisal of the untapped values of Ceylon.

Lionel Wendt, who owned an extensive library and received all the latest books from England, got into the extravagant and generous habit of every week sending to my house, which was a good distance from the city, a cyclist loaded down with a sack of books. Thus, for some time, I read kilometers of English novels, among them the first edition of *Lady Chatterley's Lover*, published privately in Florence. Lawrence's works impressed me because of their poetic quality and a certain vital magnetism focused on the hidden relationships between human beings. However, it soon became clear to me that, for all his genius, he was frustrated by his passion for instructing the reader, like so many other great English writers. D. H. Lawrence sets up a course in sexual education that has almost nothing to do with what we learn spontaneously from love and life. He ended up boring me stiff, but this did not lessen my admiration for his tortured mystico-sexual search, all the more painful because it was so useless.

One of the things I remember from my Ceylon days is a great elephant hunt.

The elephants had grown much too numerous in one district, where they made constant raids, damaging houses and farmlands. For over a month, all along the banks of a wide river, the peasants had gradually rounded up the wild herds—with grass fires, bonfires, and tom-toms—and driven them back toward one spot in the jungle. Night and day, the fires and the noise excited the huge beasts, drifting now like a slow river toward the northwestern part of the island.

On this particular day, the kraal was all set. A stockade penned off a part of the forest. I saw how the first elephant went in through a narrow passage and sensed itself trapped. It was too late. Hundreds more followed into this dead-end passage. Almost five hundred strong, the immense herd of elephants could neither advance nor retrace their steps.

The most powerful males charged the palisades, trying to knock them down, but innumerable spears surged up on the other side and halted them. Then they regrouped in the center of the enclosure, determined to protect the females and the young. Their organization and their protectiveness made them a touching sight. They let out an anguished call, a kind of neigh or trumpet blast, and in their despair uprooted the weakest trees.

Suddenly the tamers went in, mounted on two huge trained elephants. The domesticated pair acted like common policemen. They took their places on either side of the captive animal, pummeled him with their trunks, and helped reduce him to immobility. Next, with thick ropes, the hunters secured one of his hind legs to a strong tree. One by one, the creatures were rendered helpless in this same way.

The captive elephant turns down his food for a good many days. But the hunters know his weaknesses. They let the animals fast awhile and then bring them the sprouts and tender stalks of their favorite plants, those they would forage for on their long forest treks when they were still free to roam at will. At last, the elephant breaks down and eats. He has been tamed and begins to learn his heavy chores.

LIFE IN COLOMBO

In Colombo there seemed to be no visible symptoms of revolution. Its political climate was different from India's. Everything was engulfed by an oppressive calm. The country supplied England with the finest tea in the world.

The country was split into sectors, or compartments. The English, who occupied the tip of the pyramid and lived in large residences with gardens, were followed by a middle class much like that in South American countries. They were and may still be called burghers and were descendants of the former Boers, the Dutch settlers of South Africa exiled to Ceylon during the colonial war of the last century.

Below them was the Buddhist and Moslem population of Ceylon, which numbered many millions. And still further down, making up the worst-paid working ranks, and also running into the millions, were the Indian immigrants, all from the southern part of that country; they spoke Tamil and professed the Hindu religion.

In the so-called "polite society," which paraded its finest clothes and jewels in Colombo's exclusive clubs, two famous snobs competed for leadership. One was a phony French nobleman, Count de Mauny, who had a group of devotees. The other was an elegant and devil-may-care Pole, my friend Winzer, who dominated the few fashionable salons there were. This man was extremely witty, quite cynical, and a source of knowledge about everything in the world. He had a strange profession—"preserver of the cultural and archaeological treasure"—and going along with him on one of his official expeditions was an eye-opening experience to me.

Excavations had brought to light two magnificent cities the jungle had swallowed up: Anuradhapura and Polonnaruwa. Pillars and corridors gleamed once again in the brilliant Singhalese sun. Naturally, everything that could be shipped was carefully packed and went on its way to the British Museum in London.

My friend Winzer was pretty good at his work. He went to remote monasteries and, to the enormous satisfaction of the Buddhist monks, he loaded the official van with marvelous stone sculptures, thousands of years old, that would end up in England's museums. The look of contentment on the faces of the saffron-garbed monks was something to see, when Winzer would leave them some painted-up celluloid Buddhist images, made in Japan, as replacements for their own antiques. They would look them over with reverent eyes and set them up on the same altars from which the jasper and granite statues had smiled for centuries.

My friend Winzer was an excellent product of the Empire; that is, an elegant short-change artist.

Something came to throw a cloud over those days literally burned away by the sun. Without warning, my Burmese love, the tempestuous Josie Bliss, pitched camp in front of my house. She had come all the way from her far-off country. Believing that rice was not grown anywhere except in Rangoon, she arrived with a sack of it on her back, with our favorite Paul Robeson records, and a long, rolled-up mat. She spent all her time posted at the front door, looking out for anyone who came to visit me, and she would pounce on them and insult them. I can see her now, consumed by her overwhelming jealousy, threatening to burn down my house, and attacking a sweet Eurasian girl who had come to pay a call.

The colonial police considered her uncontrollable behavior a focus of disruption in the quiet street, and I was warned that she would be thrown out of the country if I didn't take her in. I felt wretched for days, racked between the tenderness her unhappy love stirred in me and the terror I had of her. I didn't dare let her set foot in my house. She was a love-smitten terrorist, capable of anything.

One day, at last, she made up her mind to go away. She begged me to go with her to the ship. When it was time to weigh anchor and I had to go ashore, she wrenched away from the passengers around her, and seized by a gust of grief and love, she covered my face with kisses and bathed me with her tears. She kissed my arms, my suit, in a kind of ritual, and suddenly slipped down to my shoes, before I could stop her. When she stood up again, the chalk polish of my white shoes was smeared like flour all over her face. I couldn't ask her to give up her trip, to leave the ship with me instead of going away forever. My better judgment prevented me from doing that, but my heart received a great scar which is still part of me. That unrestrained grief, those terrible tears rolling down her chalky face, are still fresh in my memory.

I had almost finished writing the first part of *Residencia en la tierra*. But my work was progressing very slowly. Distance and a deep silence separated me from my world, and I could not bring myself to enter wholeheartedly the alien world around me.

Things that happened in my life, which was suspended in a vacuum, were brought together in my book as if they were natural events: "Closer to life's blood than to the ink." I tried to purify my style, but relied more and more on a wild melancholy. I insisted on truth and effective rhetoric (because they are the ingredients for the bread of poetry) in a bitter style that worked systematically toward my own destruction. The style is not only the man. It is also everything around him, and if the very air he breathes does not enter into the poem, the poem is dead: dead because it has not had a chance to breathe.

I have never read with so much pleasure or so voluminously as I did in that suburb of Colombo where I lived all alone for so long. From time to time I would return to Rimbaud, Quevedo, or Proust. *Swann's Way* made me experience all over again the torments, the loves and jealousies of my adolescence. And I realized that in the phrase from the Vinteuil Sonata, a musical phrase Proust referred to as "aerial and fragrant," one savors not only the most exquisite description of sensuous sound but also a desperate measure of passion itself.

My problem, in those solitary surroundings, was to find this music so that I might listen to it. With the help of my friend the musician and musicologist, we pursued the matter until we learned that Proust's Vinteuil was probably a combination of Schubert and Wagner and Saint-Saëns and Fauré and d'Indy and César Franck. My shamefully skimpy musical curriculum had omitted almost all those composers. Their works were boxes that were missing, or sealed to me. My ear could never recognize any but the most obvious melodies and, even then, with difficulty.

Making further headway in the investigation, more literary than musical, I finally got hold of a three-record album of César Franck's Sonata for Piano and Violin. No doubt about it, Vinteuil's phrase was there. There was absolutely no room for doubt.

For me its attraction had been purely literary. In his sharp-sighted narrative about a dying society he loved and hated, Proust, the greatest exponent of poetic realism, lingered with passionate indulgence over many works of art, paintings and cathedrals, actresses and books. But although his insight illuminated whatever it touched, he often went back to the enchantment of this sonata and its renascent phrase with an intensity that he probably did not give to any other descriptive passages. His words led me to relive my own life, to recover the hidden sentiments I had almost lost within myself in my long absence. I wanted to see in that musical phrase Proust's magical narrative and I was swept away on music's wings.

The phrase loses itself in the depths of the shadows, falling in pitch, prolonging, enhancing its agony. It appears to build up in anguish like a Gothic structure, volutes repeated on and on, swayed by the rhythm that lifts a slender spire endlessly upward.

The element born of pain looks for a triumphal way out that, in its rise, will not deny its origin transmuted by sadness. It curls seemingly into a melancholy spiral, while the dark notes of the piano accompany time and again the death and renascence of the sound. The heart-rending intimacy of the piano repeats, time and again, the serpentine birth, until love and pain come together in death and victory.

There could be no doubt for me that this was the phrase and this the sonata.

Savage darkness came down like a fist on my house lost among the coconut trees of Wellawatte, but each night the sonata lived with me, leading me on, welling around me, filling me with its everlasting sadness, its victorious melancholy.

Until now, the critics who have scrutinized my work have not detected this secret influence I am confessing here. For I wrote a large part of *Residencia en la tierra* there, in Wellawatte. Although my poetry is not "fragrant or aerial" but sadly earth-bound, I think those qualities, so often clad in mourning, have something to do with my deep feelings for this music that lived within me.

Years later, back in Chile once more, I met the big three of Chilean music—young, gathered together at a party. It was 1932, I believe, in Marta Brunet's home. Claudio Arrau was chatting in a corner with Domingo Santa Cruz and Armando Carvajal. I sauntered over, but they hardly spared me a glance. They went on talking imperturbably about music and composers. So I tried to show off a little, bringing up that sonata, the only one I knew. They looked at me with a distracted air and spoke down to me: "César Franck? Why César Franck? Verdi is what you should get to know." And they went on with their conversation, burying me under my own ignorance, from which I still haven't been able to escape.

SINGAPORE

Solitude in Colombo was not only dull but indolent. I had a few friends on the street where I lived. Girls of various colorings visited my campaign cot, leaving no record but the lightning spasm of the flesh. My body was a lonely bonfire burning night and day on that tropical coast. One friend, Patsy, showed up frequently with some of her friends, dusky and golden, girls of Boer, English, Dravidian blood. They went to bed with me sportingly, asking for nothing in return.

One of them told me all about her visits to the "chummeries." That's what they called the bungalows where young Englishmen, clerks in shops or firms, lived together in groups to save on money and food. Without a trace of cynicism in her voice, as if it were the most natural thing in the world, the girl told me that she had once had sex with fourteen of them.

"And why did you do it?" I asked her.

"They were having a party one night and I was alone with them. They turned on a gramophone, I danced a few steps with each of them, and as we danced, we'd lose our way into one bedroom or another. That way, everyone was happy."

She was not a prostitute. No, she was just another product of colonialism, a candid and generous fruit off its tree. Her story impressed me, and from then on, I had a soft spot for her in my heart.

My solitary bungalow was far from any urban development. When I rented it, I tried to find out where the toilet was; I couldn't see it anywhere. Actually, it was nowhere near the shower, it was at the back of the house. I inspected it with curiosity. It was a wooden box with a hole in the middle, very much like the artifact I had known as a child in the Chilean countryside. But our toilets were set over a deep well or over running water. Here the receptacle was a simple metal pail under the round hole.

The pail was clean every morning, but I had no idea how its contents disappeared. One morning I rose earlier than usual, and I was amazed when I saw what had been happening.

Into the back of the house, walking like a dusky statue, came the most beautiful woman I had yet seen in Ceylon, a Tamil of the pariah caste. She was wearing a red-and-gold sari of the cheapest kind of cloth. She had heavy bangles on her bare ankles. Two tiny red dots glittered on either side of her nose. They must have been ordinary glass, but on her they were rubies.

She walked solemnly toward the latrine, without so much as a side glance at me, not bothering to acknowledge my existence, and vanished with the disgusting receptacle on her head, moving away with the steps of a goddess.

She was so lovely that, regardless of her humble job, I couldn't get her off my mind. Like a shy jungle animal she belonged to another kind of existence, a different world. I called to her, but it was no use. After that, I sometimes put a gift in her path, a piece of silk or some fruit. She would go past without hearing or looking. That ignoble routine had been transformed by her dark beauty into the dutiful ceremony of an indifferent queen.

One morning, I decided to go all the way. I got a strong grip on her wrist and stared into her eyes. There was no language I could talk with her. Unsmiling, she let herself be led away and was soon naked in my bed. Her waist, so very slim, her full hips, the brimming cups of her breasts made her like one of the thousand-year-old sculptures from the south of India. It was the coming together of a man and a statue. She kept her eyes wide open all the while, completely un-responsive. She was right to despise me. The experience was never repeated.

I hardly believed it when I read the cable. The Minister of Foreign Relations was notifying me of my new appointment. I would end my term as consul in Colombo and go on to carry out the same func-tion in Singapore and Batavia. This raised me from the first circle of poverty into the second. In Colombo I had the right to retain (if it was taken in) the sum of $166.66. Now, as consul in two colonies at once, I could retain (if it was taken in) twice $166.66; namely, the sum of $333.32 (if it was taken in). This meant that, for the present anyway, I would stop sleeping on a field cot. My material aspirations were not too high.

But what was I going to do with Kiria, my mongoose? Give her to the impudent neighborhood kids, who no longer believed in her power against serpents? I wouldn't dream of it. They would neglect her; they would not let her eat at the table, as she was used to with me. Set her loose in the forest to revert to her primitive state? Never. She had doubtless lost her defensive instincts and the birds of prey would devour her in an unguarded moment. But how could I take her with me? Such a singular passenger would never be allowed on board ship.

So I decided to have Bhrampy, my Singhalese "boy," make the trip with me. It was a millionaire's luxury, and it was also madness; we were going to countries—Malaya, Indonesia—whose languages Bhrampy couldn't speak a word of. The mongoose, on the other hand, could travel incognito in a basket on deck. Bhrampy knew her as well as I did. Customs was a problem, but crafty Bhrampy would be sure to get around it.

And that's how, with sadness, joy, and the mongoose, we left the island of Ceylon, headed for another, unknown world.

It must be difficult to understand why Chile had consulates scattered all over the world. It surely would seem odd that a small republic tucked down in a corner near the South Pole should post and maintain official representatives on archipelagos, coasts, and reefs on the other side of the globe.

In truth—as I see it—these consulates are evidence of the flights of fancy and self-importance we South Americans generally indulge in. But also, as I have already mentioned, from these far-flung places Chile got jute, and paraffin to manufacture candles, and, above all, tea, enormous quantities of tea. In Chile we drink tea four times a day. And we can't grow it. Once we had a widespread strike among the nitrate workers because of a shortage of this exotic product. I recall that one day, after a few whiskeys, some English exporters asked me what we did in Chile with such exorbitant quantities of tea.

"We drink it," I told them.

(If they expected to pump out of me some secret industrial exploitation of tea in Chile, I was sorry to disappoint them.)

The consulate in Singapore had already been in existence for ten years. I went ashore, then, with the confidence instilled in me by my twenty-three years, with Bhrampy and my mongoose in tow. We went straight to the Raffles Hotel. There I sent out my laundry, of which I had quite a bit, and then I sat down on the verandah. I stretched out lazily in an easy chair and ordered one, two, perhaps three *gin pahits*.

It was all very much like something in Somerset Maugham, until I decided to look in the telephone book for my consulate's headquarters. It wasn't listed, dammit! I immediately put an urgent call through to the British government offices. They replied, after checking, that there was no Chilean consulate there. I made inquiries about the consul, Señor Mansilla. They knew nothing of him.

I was crushed. I barely had enough money to pay for one day at the hotel and for my laundry. Then it struck me that the phantom consulate must have its headquarters in Batavia, and I decided to get back on the ship I had come on, since Batavia was where it was going and it was still in port. I ordered my laundry removed from the tub where it was soaking, Bhrampy rolled it up into a wet bundle, and we set out for the docks at breakneck speed.

They were drawing up the ship's ladder. I puffed up the steps. My ex–traveling companions and the ship's officers stared at me incredulously. I moved back into the cabin I had left that morning, and lying on my back on the bunk, I closed my eyes as the ship pulled away from that unlucky port.

I had met a Jewish girl on the ship. Her name was Kruzi. A blonde, on the plump side, she had orange-colored eyes and was bubbling over with good spirits. She told me she had a good job in Batavia. I stayed close to her during the cruise's farewell party. She kept dragging me out to dance, between drinks, and I followed her clumsily in the slow contortions that were popular at the time. We spent that last night making love in my cabin, in a friendly way, knowing that chance had brought us together for this brief time only. I told her about my misadventures. She comforted me gently and her light-hearted tenderness touched me.

Kruzi, in turn, confided the real nature of the job waiting for her in Batavia. There was an organization, more or less international, which placed European girls in the beds of respectable Asians. She had been given a choice between a maharaja, a prince of Siam, and a wealthy Chinese merchant. She picked the last, a young but mild-mannered man.

When we landed, the following day, I got a look at the Chinese magnate's Rolls-Royce as well as its owner's profile through the automobile's flowered curtains. Kruzi vanished among the crowd and luggage.

I settled into the Nederlanden Hotel and was getting ready for lunch, when I saw Kruzi come in. She flung herself into my arms, choked by sobs.

"They're throwing me out of here. I have to leave tomorrow."

"But who is throwing you out, why are they throwing you out?"

She sobbed out her unhappy story. She was about to get into the Rolls-Royce when the immigration officers stopped her and subjected her to a brutal interrogation. She had to confess everything. The Dutch authorities considered it a grave offense for her to live as the concubine of a Chinese. They finally let her go, on her promise not to visit her gallant and to get back on the ship she had arrived in, which was returning to the West the next day.

What hurt her most was to disappoint the man who had been waiting for her, a sentiment the imposing Rolls-Royce may have had some bearing on. Still, Kruzi was sentimental at heart. There was much more to her tears than her frustrated interests: she felt humili-ated and deeply offended.

"Do you know his address? Do you have his telephone number?" I asked.

"Yes," she said. "But I'm afraid they'll arrest me. They threatened to throw me in jail."

"You have nothing to lose. Go see the man whose dreams must have been full of you, though he did not even know you. You owe him at least a few words. Why worry about the Dutch police at this point? Get even with them. Go see your Chinese. Take care, give them the slip, and you'll feel better. I'm sure you'll leave this country feeling happier then."

Late that night she returned. She had seen her mail-order suitor, and she told me all about their meeting. The Oriental was a literate man who affected French manners and spoke French quite well. He was married, observed the mores and practices of honorable Chinese matrimony, and led a very boring life.

The yellow-skinned suitor had prepared for his white, Western sweetheart a bungalow with a garden, mosquito screens, Louis XVI furniture, and a huge bed, which they tried out that night. The house's owner sadly showed her the little refinements he had been preparing for her, the silver knives and forks (he himself used only chopsticks), the bar stocked with European drinks, the refrigerator filled with fruit.

Then he stopped before a huge locked chest. He took a key from his pants pocket and opened the trunk, revealing the strangest of treasures to Kruzi's eyes: hundreds of ladies' undergarments, soft, silken panties, the scantiest of briefs—intimate women's dainties, hundreds, thousands of them stuffed into that piece of furniture sanctified by the pungent aroma of sandalwood. Every kind of silk, every color, was there. From violet to yellow, from every shade of pink to the mystic greens, from strident reds to shimmering blacks, from electric sky-blues to nuptial white. The entire rainbow of male concupiscence put together by a fetishist who obviously had collected the items for his own sensual pleasure.

"I was stunned," Kruzi said, beginning to sob again. "I grabbed a handful at random and here they are."

I, too, was touched by this mystery of human behavior. Our Chinese, a serious businessman, importer and exporter, amassed ladies' panties as if he were collecting butterflies. Who would have dreamed it?

"Let me have one of them," I said to my friend.

She picked out a white and green garment and stroked it softly before handing it to me.

"Write something on it for me, Kruzi, please."

She smoothed it out with care and wrote my name and hers on its silky surface, which she also sprinkled with a few tears.

She left the next day without my seeing her, and I have never seen her again. Those sheerest of panties, with her words of dedication and her tears, traveled around in my suitcases among my clothes and my books for a good many years. I never knew when or how some cheeky lady visitor walked out of my house with them on.

BATAVIA

In those days, when motels had not yet come into the world, the Nederlanden was a rarity. It had a large central building, for dining room service and offices, and then individual bungalows for the guests, separated by tiny gardens and robust trees. In the high tops of these trees lived an infinitude of birds, flying squirrels that flitted from branch to branch, and insects that chirred just as if in the jungle. Bhrampy outdid himself at his job of looking after the mongoose, which was more and more restive in her new home.

There really was a Chilean consulate here. At least it was listed in the telephone book. I set out for its offices on the following day, rested and more appropriately dressed. The consular coat of arms of Chile hung on the façade of a huge building occupied by a steamship line. One of its numerous personnel took me to the office of the manager, a florid, corpulent Dutchman who looked more like a long-shoreman than like the manager of a shipping firm.

"I am the new Chilean consul," I introduced myself. "First, let me thank you for your help, and then I'd be obliged if you would brief me on the running of the consulate. I propose to take over my post right away."

"I am the only consul here!" he said angrily.

"How's that?"

"Start off by paying me what you people owe me!" he shouted.

The man may have known something about shipping, but he had no idea what good manners were, in any language. Phrase after phrase tumbled out, while he chewed furiously on an awful cheroot that was polluting the air.

The wild man hardly let me get a word in edgewise. His indignation and his cheroot threw him into deafening coughing fits, or else into gargles that turned into gobs of spit. I was finally able to get in a word in self-defense: "Sir, I don't owe you a thing, and I don't have to pay you a thing. It is my understanding that you are consul *ad honorem*, honorary consul, that is. And if this seems open to question, I hardly see how it can be settled with all this shouting, which I don't intend to put up with."

Later I learned that the nasty Dutchman had every argument on his side. The fellow had been the victim of a swindle that, of course, could not be blamed either on the government of Chile or on me. Mansilla was the crook at the source of the Dutchman's rage. I discovered that Mansilla, the so-and-so, had never assumed his duties as consul in Batavia; he had been living in Paris for some time. He had made a deal with the Dutchman to have him perform the consular duties and send him, Mansilla, the papers and fees he took in every month. Mansilla pledged to pay him a monthly stipend, which he never paid. Thence the indignation of this naive Dutchman, who came down on my head like a collapsing roof.

———

I felt miserable the next day. Malignant fever, flu, loneliness, and hemorrhaging. I was burning hot and perspiring profusely. My nose began to bleed as it had in my childhood in Temuco's cold climate.

Mustering all my strength, I headed for the government offices. They were located in Buitenzorg, in the magnificent Botanical Gardens. The bureaucrats raised their blue eyes from their white papers with difficulty. They took out their pens, which were also dripping with perspiration, and wrote down my name with a few drops of sweat.

I came out feeling worse than when I had gone in. I walked down the avenues and finally sat down under an enormous tree. Here everything was healthy and cool, life breathed calm and powerful. Before me, the giant trees lifted their trunks straight, smooth, and silvery, a hundred meters into the air. I read the enameled nameplates identifying them. They were varieties of eucalyptus I was not familiar with. A chill perfume drifted down to my nostrils from the immense height. That emperor of trees had taken pity on me, and a gust of its scent restored my strength.

Or perhaps it was the green solemnity of the Botanical Gardens, the infinite variety of leaves, the crisscrossing vines, the orchids flashing like sea stars in the foliage, the undersea depth of that forest-like enclosure, the shrieks of the macaws, the squeals of the monkeys— all of it restored my confidence in the future and returned my zest for living, which had been flickering like the stub of a candle.

I got back to the hotel in better spirits and sat down on the verandah of my bungalow, with writing paper and my mongoose on my table; I had decided to send a cable to the Chilean government. I needed ink. So I called a boy from the hotel and asked him in English for some ink, hoping he'd bring me an inkwell. He didn't show the slightest glimmer of understanding. He just called another boy, also dressed in white and barefoot, to help interpret my baffling request.

It was no use. Whenever I said "Ink" and moved my pen, dipping it into an imaginary inkwell, the seven or eight boys who had by now congregated to advise the first repeated my motion as one man, with pens they had drawn out of their pockets, exclaiming vigorously, "Ink, ink," and nearly dying with laughter. They thought it was a new ritual they were learning. I rushed desperately into the bungalow across the way, followed by the string of servants in white.

From the solitary table I took an inkwell that by sheer luck was there, and waving it in front of their astonished eyes, I screamed at them: "This! This!"

They all smiled and sang out together: *"Tinta! Tinta!"*

In time I regained the right to take up my duties as consul. My disputed patrimony consisted of a moth-eaten rubber stamp, an ink pad, and a few folders with records of profits and losses. The profits had ended up in the pockets of the wily consul operating from Paris. His swindled Dutch surrogate handed me the insignificant sheaf of papers with the cold smile of a frustrated mastodon, and never stopped chewing on his cheroot.

From time to time I signed consular invoices and put the dilapidated official stamp on them. That's how I obtained the dollars that, converted into guilders, made it possible for me to eke out a living: food and lodging for me, Bhrampy's wages, and the upkeep of my mongoose, Kiria, who was growing noticeably and consumed three or four eggs a day. Besides, I had to buy myself a white dinner jacket and tails, which I undertook to pay for by the month. Sometimes I would sit, almost always alone, in a crowded open-air café alongside a wide canal, to have a beer or a *gin pahit*. That is, I resumed my desperately uneventful life.

The rice table of the hotel restaurant was fit for a king. A procession of ten or fifteen serving boys would come into the dining room, filing past with their respective platters held high. Each platter was divided into sections, and each section held a mysterious, magnificent delicacy. Each item of this endless variety of food was mounted on a rice base. I have always been a hearty eater, and I had been undereating for such a long time; I would choose something from the platter offered by each of the fifteen or eighteen serving boys, until my plate became a small mountain where exotic fish, indescribable eggs, astonishing vegetables, incredible chickens, the choicest, rarest meats covered the summit of my lunch like a flag. The Chinese say that food must excel in three things: taste, aroma, and color. The rice table at my hotel had those three virtues and one more: abundance.

At about this time I lost my mongoose. Kiria had the dangerous habit of tagging after me wherever I went, with quick, imperceptible steps. Following me meant plunging into streets traveled by cars, trucks, rickshaws, and Dutch, Chinese, and Malay pedestrians. A turbulent life for a trusting mongoose who knew only two persons in the whole world.

The inevitable happened. On my return to the hotel one day, I saw the tragedy written all over Bhrampy's face. I didn't ask him anything. But when I sat down on the verandah, she did not come to jump on my knees or brush her furry tail against my head.

I placed an ad in the papers: "Lost: mongoose, answers to the name of Kiria." There was no reply. None of the neighbors had seen her. Maybe she was already dead. She had disappeared forever.

Bhrampy, her guardian, felt so disgraced that he stayed out of sight. My clothes, my shoes were taken care of by a phantom. Sometimes I thought I heard Kiria squeal, calling me from a tree during the night. I would turn on the light, open the windows and doors, peer into the coconut trees. It wasn't she. The world Kiria knew had betrayed her; her trustfulness had shattered in the city's dangerous jungle. I was grief-stricken for a long time.

Overcome with shame, Bhrampy decided to go back to his native country. I was not happy about it, but the mongoose had really been the only thing we had in common. One afternoon he came in to show me the new suit he had bought so that he could return well dressed to his home town in Ceylon. He showed up suddenly, dressed in white and buttoned all the way up to his neck. The most surprising thing was the huge chef's cap he had settled on his jet-black head. I burst out laughing, in spite of myself. Bhrampy was not insulted. On the contrary, he smiled at me sweetly, with a smile of understanding for my ignorance.

My new home in Batavia was on a street called Probolinggo. It had a living room, a bedroom, a kitchen, a bathroom. I never owned a car, but I did have a garage that was always empty. I had more than enough space in this tiny house. I took on a Javanese cook, an old peasant woman, charming and egalitarian. A "boy," also Javanese, served table and looked after my clothes. There I finished *Residencia en la tierra*.

My solitude became even deeper. I decided to get married. I had met a creole—to be exact, a Dutch girl with a few drops of Malay blood—and I became very fond of her. She was a tall, gentle girl and knew nothing of the world of arts and letters. (About this marriage of mine, my friend and biographer Margarita Aguirre was to write several years later: "Neruda returned to Chile in 1932. Two years earlier, in Batavia, he had married María Antonieta Hagenaar, a young Dutch woman who lived in Java. She is quite proud of being a consul's wife and has a most exotic opinion of America. She doesn't know any Spanish, but she's learning it. However, there is no doubt that it is not just the language that she has had trouble learning. In spite of all this, she's very much attached to Neruda, and they are always together. Maruca, that's what Pablo calls her, is tall, stately, hieratic.")

My life was very simple. I was soon meeting other amiable people. Linked by our common language, the Cuban consul and his wife became my friends as a matter of course. Capablanca's country-man talked nonstop, like a self-winding machine. Officially he was representing Machado, the Cuban tyrant. Yet he would tell me how items belonging to political prisoners—watches, rings, sometimes even gold teeth—would turn up in the bellies of sharks caught in Havana's bay.

The German consul, Hertz, was a great admirer of the modern plastic arts, Franz Marc's blue horses, Wilhelm Lehmbruck's elongated figures. He was a sensitive person, romantic in temperament, a Jew with a centuries-old cultural heritage.

I once asked him: "And this Hitler whose name appears from time to time in the newspapers, this anti-Semite, anti-Communist leader, don't you think he can assume power?"

"Impossible," he told me.

"Why impossible, when history is full of the most absurd incidents?"

"But you don't know Germany," he stated flatly. "That's the one place where it is absolutely impossible for a mad agitator like him to run even a village."

My poor friend, poor Consul Hertz! That mad agitator barely missed running the world. And the ingenuous Hertz, with all his culture and his noble romanticism, must have ended up in some monstrous, anonymous gas chamber.

5

Spain in My Heart

WHAT FEDERICO WAS LIKE

A long sea voyage of two months brought me back to Chile in 1932. There I published *El hondero entusiasta*, which had been mislaid among my papers, and *Residencia en la tierra*, which I had written in the Orient. In 1933 I was appointed consul of Chile in Buenos Aires, and there I arrived in the month of August.

Federico García Lorca arrived in that city almost at the same time, to direct his tragedy *Blood Wedding*, performed by Lola Membrives's troupe. We hadn't known each other, but we met in Buenos Aires and were often feted together by writers and friends. Of course, we had our share of incidents. Federico had his detractors. So did I, and I still have them. These detractors are driven by a desire to snuff out the lights, to keep us from being seen. That's what happened this time. Because there was a lot of interest in attending the banquet the P.E.N. club was holding for Federico and me at the Plaza Hotel, someone kept the phones busy all day long spreading the word that the dinner in our honor had been called off. They were so persistent that they even called the hotel manager, the telephone operators, and the chef to make sure no reservations were accepted and no dinner was prepared. But the maneuver fell through and in the end Federico García Lorca and I got together with a hundred Argentine writers.

We came up with a big surprise. We had prepared a talk *al alimón*. You probably don't know what that means, and neither did I. Federico, who always had some invention or idea up his sleeve, explained: "Two bullfighters can fight the same bull at the same time, using only one cape between them. This is one of the most perilous feats in bullfighting. That's why it is so seldom seen. Not more than twice or three times in a century, and it can be done only by two bullfighters who are brothers, or at least blood relations. This is called fighting a bull *al alimón*. And that's the way we'll do our talk."

And that is what we did. But no one knew about it beforehand. When we got up to thank the president of the P.E.N. club for honoring us with the banquet, we did it together, like two bullfighters, to make our single speech. The diners sat at small, separate tables, and Federico was at one end of the room, I at the other. People on my side tugged at my jacket to make me sit down, believing there was a mix-up, and the same thing happened to Federico on the other side of the room. Well, we set out speaking together, with me saying "Ladies" and he continuing with "and gentlemen," twining our phrases throughout, so that they flowed like a single speech, right to the end. The oration was dedicated to Rubén Darío, because, though no one could accuse us of being modernists, both García Lorca and I regarded Rubén Darío as one of the most creative poets in the Spanish language.

Here is the text of the speech:

NERUDA: Ladies . . .

LORCA: . . . and gentlemen: In bullfighting there is what is known as "bullfighting *al alimón*," in which two toreros, holding one cape between them, outwit the bull together.

NERUDA: Linked as if by an electrical impulse, Federico and I will together thank you for this prestigious reception.

LORCA: At these gatherings it is customary for a poet to bring forth his living word, be it of silver or wood, and hail his companions and friends with his own voice.

NERUDA: We, however, are going to seat a dead man among you, to bring you a table companion who is widowed, obscured by the darkness of a death greater than other deaths, widowed of life, whose dazzling spouse he was, in his shining hour. We shall stand in his fiery shadow, we shall call out his name until his powers leap back from oblivion.

LORCA: First, a symbolic embrace, with our penguin-like tenderness, to that exquisite poet Amado Villar. Then we offer a great name upon the festal board, in the knowledge that wineglasses will shatter, forks fly in search of the eye they hunger for, and a tidal wave stain the table linen. We give you the poet of America and Spain: Rubén . . .

NERUDA: Darío. Because, ladies . . .

LORCA: and gentlemen . . .

NERUDA: Where, in Bueno Aires, is there a Rubén Darío Plaza?

LORCA: Where is Rubén Darío's statue?

NERUDA: He loved parks. Where is Rubén Darío Park?

LORCA: What florist carries Rubén Darío roses?

NERUDA: Where are Rubén Darío apple trees? Rubén Darío apples?

LORCA: Where is the cast of Rubén Darío's hand?

NERUDA: Where?

LORCA: Rubén Darío sleeps in the Nicaragua of his birth under a ghastly lion made of plaster like those the rich set at their gates.

NERUDA: A mail-order lion for him who was a founder of lions, a lion without stars for him who dedicated the stars to others.

LORCA: In an adjective he gave us the sounds of the forest.

Like Fray Luis de Granada, a master of words, he created constellations with the lemon, and the stag's foot, and mollusks filled with terror and infinity: he sent us to sea with frigates and shadows in the pupils of our eyes, and he built a limitless esplanade of gin across the grayest afternoon the sky has ever known, and he talked to the south wind in familiar terms, all heart, like the romantic poet he was, and his hand rested on the Corinthian capital, skeptical about all the ages, ironic and sorrowing.

NERUDA: His luminous name should be remembered in its every essence, with the terrible griefs of his heart, his incandescent incertitude, his descent into the deepest circles of hell, his rise to the castles of fame, his greatness as a poet, then and forever and unequaled.

LORCA: As a Spanish poet, he was teacher in Spain to the older masters as well as to the children, with a sense of universality and a generosity present-day poets do not possess. He was teacher to Valle-Inclán and Juan Ramón Jiménez and the Machado brothers, and his voice was water and nitrate in the furrows of our time-honored language. From Rodrigo Caro to the Argensolas and Don Juan del Arguijo, the Spanish language had not had such a festival of words, such clashing of consonants, such fire and such form as in Rubén Darío. From Velázquez's landscape and Goya's campfire, from Quevedo's melancholy to the precious apple cheeks of Majorcan peasant girls, Darío traveled over the land of Spain as if it were his own land.

NERUDA: The tide brought him to Chile, the warm sea of the north, and the sea left him there, abandoned on the rugged, rock-toothed coast, and the ocean pounded him with foam and bells, and Valparaíso's black wind covered him with songs of salt. Tonight let us make him a statue of air and let smoke, voices, circumstances, and life flow through it,

like his magnificent poetry with dreams and sounds flowing through it.

LORCA: But I want to give this statue of air blood like a coral
branch stirred by the sea; nerves like a cluster of lightning
in a photograph; the head of a minotaur with Góngora's
snow painted on by a flight of hummingbirds; the wandering and absent eyes of a millionaire of tears; and also his
failings. Shelving eaten away by hedge mustard, where the
empty spaces are echoes of a flute; the cognac bottles of
his spectacular drunken sprees; his charming lack of taste;
and the barefaced verbal stunts that make the vast majority
of his poems so human. The fertile substance of his great
poetry stands outside norms, forms, or schools.

NERUDA: Federico García Lorca, a Spaniard, and I, a Chilean, turn over the honor of this evening among friends
to that great shadow who sang more loftily than we and
hailed with his unique voice the Argentine soil on which
we stand.

LORCA: Pablo Neruda, a Chilean, and I, a Spaniard, linked by
our language and by the person of the great Nicaraguan,
Argentine, Chilean, and Spanish poet Rubén Darío.

NERUDA AND LORCA: In whose honor and glory we raise
our glasses!

MIGUEL HERNÁNDEZ

I was not at the consulate in Buenos Aires very long. At the start of
1934, I was transferred to Barcelona in the same capacity. Don Tulio
Maqueira, the Consul General of Chile in Spain, was my boss. He
was, incidentally, the most dedicated official in the Chilean consular
service I have come across. A severe man, with a reputation for reticence, he was extremely kind, understanding, and cordial to me.

Don Tulio Maqueira quickly learned that I was very bad at subtracting and multiplying, and that I didn't know how to divide (I have never been able to learn). So he said to me: "Pablo, you should go live in Madrid. That's where the poetry is. All we have here in Barcelona is that terrible multiplication and division that certainly doesn't need you around. I can handle it."

In Madrid, turned overnight, as if by magic, into a Chilean consul in the capital of Spain, I met García Lorca's and Alberti's friends. They were many. And within a few days I was one with the Spanish poets. Spaniards and Latin Americans are different, of course—a difference that is borne with pride, or in error, by either side.

The young poet Miguel Hernández was one of Federico's and Alberti's friends. I met him when he came up, in espadrilles and the typical corduroy trousers peasants wear, from his native Orihuela, where he had been a goatherd. I published his poems in my review *Caballo verde* (Green Horse), and I was enthusiastic about the radiance and vigor of his exuberant poetry.

Miguel was a peasant with an aura of earthiness about him. He had a face like a clod of earth or a potato that has just been pulled up from among the roots and still has its subterranean freshness. He was living and writing in my house. My American poetry, with other horizons and plains, had its impact and gradually made changes in him.

He told me earthy stories about animals and birds. He was the kind of writer who emerges from nature like an uncut stone, with the freshness of the forest and an irresistible vitality. He would tell me how exciting it was to put your ear against the belly of a sleeping she-goat. You could hear the milk coursing down to the udders, a secret sound no one but that poet of goats has been able to listen to.

At other times he would talk to me about the nightingale's song. Eastern Spain, where he came from, swarmed with blossoming orange trees and nightingales. Since that bird, that sublime singer, does not exist in my country, crazy Miguel liked to give me the most vivid imitation of what it could do. He would shinny up one of the trees in the street and from its highest branches would whistle or warble like his beloved native birds.

Since he had nothing to live on, I tried to get him a job. It was hard to find work for a poet in Spain. At last a viscount, a high official in the Ministry of Foreign Relations, took an interest in his case and replied that yes, he was all for it, he had read Miguel's poems, admired them, and Miguel just had to indicate what position he preferred and he would be given the appointment.

I was jubilant and said: "Miguel Hernández, your future is all set, at last. The viscount has a job for you. You'll be a high-ranking employee. Tell me what kind of work you want, and your appointment will go through."

Miguel gave it some thought. His face, with its deep, premature lines, clouded up with anxiety. Hours went by and it was not until late in the afternoon that he gave me his answer. With the radiant look of someone who has found the solution to his whole life, he said to me: "Could the viscount put me in charge of a flock of goats somewhere near Madrid?"

The memory of Miguel Hernández can never be rooted out of my heart. The song of the Levantine nightingales, their spires of sound soaring between the darkness and the orange blossoms, was an obsession with him. They were in his blood, in his earthy and wild poetry, where all the extravagances of color, of perfume, and of the voice of the Spanish Levant came together, with the exuberance and the fragrance of a powerful and virile youth.

His face was the face of Spain. Chiseled by the light, rutted like a planted field, it had some of the roundness of bread or of earth. Filled with fire, burning in that surface scorched and made leathery by the wind, his eyes were two beams of strength and tenderness.

I saw the very elements of poetry rise out of his words, altered now by a new greatness, by a savage light, by the miracle that converts old blood into an infant son. In all my years as poet, as wandering poet, I can say that life has not given me the privilege of setting eyes on anyone with a vocation and an electrical knowledge of words like his.

GREEN HORSE

Federico and Alberti, who lived near my house in an apartment overlooking an avenue of trees, his lost grove; the sculptor Alberto, a baker from Toledo who was master of abstract sculpture; Altolaguirre and Bergamín; the great poet Luis Cernuda; Vicente Aleixandre, poet of limitless dimension; Luis Lacasa, the architect—all of us, singly or in groups, would get together every day in someone's home or in a café.

From Castellana Avenue or from the Correos tavern we would go to my house, the "House of Flowers," in the Argüelles sector. Down from the upper deck of one of the double-decker buses that my countryman the great Cotapos called "bombardones" we would come in boisterous groups to eat, drink, and sing. Among my young companions in poetry and merriment, I recall Arturo Serrano Plaja, poet; José Caballero, a painter of dazzling talent and a very amusing fellow; Antonio Aparicio, who came from Andalusia straight to my house; and so many others who are no longer near or no longer alive, but whose friendship I miss as keenly as some part of my body or the substance of my soul.

Ah, Madrid in those days! I would make the rounds of the working-class neighborhoods with Maruja Mallo, the Galician painter, looking for the places where esparto grass and mats were sold, looking for the streets of the barrelmakers, of the ropemakers, streets where they deal in all the dry goods of Spain, goods that entangle and choke her heart. Spain is dry and rocky, and the high sun beats down on it hard, drawing sparks from the flatlands, building castles of light out of clouds of dust. The only true rivers of Spain are its poets: Quevedo, with his profound green waters and black foam; Calderón, with his syllables that sing; the crystalline Argensolas; Góngora, river of rubies.

I saw Valle-Inclán only once. Very thin, with an endless white beard and a complexion like a yellowing page, he seemed to have walked out of one of his own books, which had pressed him flat.

I met Ramón Gómez de la Serna in his crypt, the Pombo café, and later on I saw him at home. I can never forget Ramón's booming voice guiding, from his spot in the café, the conversation and the laughter, the trends of thought and the smoke. Ramón Gómez de la Serna is for me one of the finest writers in our language, and his genius has some of the variegated greatness of Quevedo and Picasso. Every page of Ramón Gómez de la Serna pries like a ferret into the physical and the metaphysical, into the truth and the spectrum, and what he knows and has written about Spain has been said by him and no one else. He has put together a secret universe. He has changed the syntax of the language with his own hands, leaving his fingerprints so embedded in it that no one can wipe them off.

I saw Don Antonio Machado several times, sitting in his favorite café dressed in his black notary's suit, silent and withdrawn, as sweet and austere as an old Spanish tree. Incidentally, mean-tongued Juan Ramón Jiménez, diabolical old brat of poetry, said of him, of Don Antonio, that he went around covered in ashes and that cigarette butts were all he carried in his pockets.

It was Juan Ramón Jiménez, poet of great splendor, who took it upon himself to teach me all about that legendary Spanish envy. This poet who had no need to envy anyone, since his work is a resplendent beam flashing on the dark beginnings of the century, affected the life of a hermit, lashing out from his hideaway at anything he thought might overshadow him.

The younger generation—García Lorca and Alberti, as well as Jorge Guillén and Pedro Salinas—were doggedly needled by Juan Ramón, a bearded demon who dug his knife daily into one or another. He said unfavorable things about me every week in the elaborate critical commentaries he published Sunday after Sunday in the newspaper *El sol*. But I made up my mind to live and let live. I never answered back. I never replied to literary attacks, and I still don't.

The poet Manuel Altolaguirre, who had a printing press and the vocation of printer, came by my house one day to tell me that he was going to bring out a handsome poetry review, in the finest format and with the best work in Spain.

"There's only one person who can edit it," he said to me, "and you're that person."

I had been a heroic founder of magazines who quickly dropped them or was dropped by them. In 1925 I started *Caballo de bastos* (Jack of Clubs). In those days we wrote without punctuation and were discovering Dublin by way of the streets in Joyce. Humberto Díaz Casanueva sported a turtleneck sweater, a very daring thing for a poet at that time. His poetry was lovely and immaculate, as it has continued to be. Rosamel del Valle always dressed in black from head to toe, as poets should. I remember these two distinguished friends as my active collaborators. I have forgotten some of the others. At any rate, our galloping horse jolted the times.

"Yes, Manolito, I'll edit the review."

Manuel Altolaguirre was an excellent printer whose own hands arrayed the cases with magnificent Bodoni characters. Manolito honored poetry with his poems and with his hands, a hard-working archangel's hands. He also printed Pedro de Espinosa's *Fábula del Genil* (Fable of the Genil River). What brilliance flashed from the lustrous golden verses of the poem in that majestic typography that made the words stand out as if they had been recast in the smelting furnace.

Five fine, handsome issues of my *Caballo verde* appeared on the bookstands. I liked to watch Manolito, always full of laughter and smiles, pick out the type, set the characters in the cases, and then activate the small letterpress with his foot. Sometimes he would set off with the copies of the review in his daughter Paloma's baby carriage. People in the streets made much of this: "What a wonderful father! Going out even in this hellish traffic with his baby!"

The baby was Poetry, riding her Green Horse. The review published Miguel Hernández's first new poem and of course the poems of Federico, Cernuda, Aleixandre, Guillén (the good one, the Spaniard). Neurotic, turn-of-the-century Juan Ramón Jiménez went on aiming his Sunday darts at me. Rafael Alberti didn't like the title: "Why a green horse? 'Red Horse' is what it should be called."

I did not change its color. And Rafael and I didn't bicker over it. We never bickered over anything. There is plenty of room in the world for horses and poets of all the colors of the rainbow.

The sixth number of *Caballo verde* was left on Viriato Street, the pages not yet collated and sewn. It was dedicated to Julio Herrera y Reissig—a second Lautréamont, produced by Montevideo—and the texts written in his honor by the poets of Spain were silenced in all their beauty, stillborn, having nowhere to go. The magazine was to have come out on July 19, 1936, but on that day the streets were filled with shooting. In his African garrison an obscure general, Francisco Franco, had risen against the Republic.

THE CRIME WAS IN GRANADA

Right now, as I write these lines, Spain is officially celebrating many—so many—years of successful insurrection. In Madrid at this very moment, dressed in blue and gold, surrounded by his Moorish guards, and at his side the ambassadors of the United States, England, and several other countries, the Supreme Commander is reviewing his troops. Troops made up mostly of boys who did not see that war.

But I saw it. A million dead Spaniards. A million exiles. It seemed as if that thorn covered with blood would never be plucked from the conscience of mankind. And yet, perhaps the boys who are now passing in review before the Moorish guards don't know the truth about the terrible history of that war.

For me, it started on the evening of July 19, 1936. A resourceful and pleasant Chilean, Bobby Deglané, was the wrestling promoter in Madrid's huge Circo Price arena. I had expressed my reservations about the seriousness of that "sport" and he convinced me to go to the arena that evening with García Lorca to see how authentic the show really was. I talked García Lorca into it and we agreed to meet there at a certain time. We were going to have great fun watching the truculence of the Masked Troglodyte, the Abyssinian Strangler, and the Sinister Orangutan.

Federico did not show up. He was at that hour already on his way to death. We never saw each other again: he had an appointment with another strangler. And so the Spanish war, which changed my poetry, began for me with a poet's disappearance.

What a poet! I have never seen grace and genius, a winged heart and a crystalline waterfall, come together in anyone else as they did in him. Federico García Lorca was the extravagant "duende," his was a magnetic joyfulness that generated a zest for life in his heart and radiated it like a planet. Openhearted and comical, worldly and provincial, an extraordinary musical talent, a splendid mime, easily alarmed and superstitious, radiant and noble, he was the epitome of Spain through the ages, of her popular tradition. Of Arabic-Andalusian roots, he brightened and perfumed like jasmine the stage set of a Spain that, alas, is gone forever.

García Lorca's monumental command of metaphor seduced me, and everything he wrote attracted me. For his part, he would sometimes ask me to read him my latest poems, and halfway through the reading he would break in, shouting: "Stop, stop, I'm letting myself be influenced by you!"

In the theater and in a silence, in a crowd and in a small group, he generated beauty. I have never known anyone else with such magical hands, I never had a brother who loved laughter more. He laughed, sang, played the piano, leaped, invented, he sparkled. Poor friend, he had all the natural gifts, and he was a goldsmith, a drone in the hive of great poetry, but he also wasted his creative talent sometimes.

"Listen," he would say, taking hold of my arm, "do you see that window? Don't you think it's chorpatelic?"

"And what does 'chorpatelic' mean?"

"I don't know either, but one must know what is and what's not chorpatelic. Otherwise, you're lost. Look at that dog, he's really chorpatelic!"

Or he would tell me that he had been invited to a ceremony commemorating *Don Quixote* at a school for boys, and that when he walked into the classroom the children, led by the headmistress, sang:

This book, which was explicated
by F. Rodríguez Marín (Ph.D.),
will be everywhere celebrated
forever and ever. Amen.

Once I gave a talk on García Lorca, years after his death, and someone in the audience asked me: "In your 'Oda a Federico García Lorca,' why do you say that they paint hospitals blue for him?"

"Look, my friend," I replied, "asking a poet that kind of question is like asking a woman her age. Poetry is not static matter but a flowing current that quite often escapes from the hands of the creator himself. His raw material consists of elements that are and at the same time are not, of things that exist and do not exist. Anyway, I'll try to give you an honest answer. For me, blue is the most beautiful color. It suggests space as man sees it, like the dome of the sky, rising toward liberty and joy. Federico's presence, his personal magic, instilled a mood of joy around him. My line probably means that even hospitals, even the sadness of hospitals, could be transformed by the magic spell of his influence and suddenly changed into beautiful blue buildings."

Federico had a premonition of his death. Once, shortly after returning from a theatrical tour, he called me up to tell me about a strange incident. He had arrived with the La Barraca troupe at some out-of-the-way village in Castile and camped on the edge of town. Overtired because of the pressures of the trip, Federico could not sleep. He got up at dawn and went out to wander around alone. It was cold, the knife-like cold that Castile reserves for the traveler, the outsider. The mist separated into white masses, giving everything a ghostly dimension.

A huge rusted iron grating. Broken statues and pillars fallen among decaying leaves. He had stopped at the gate of an old estate, the entrance to the immense park of a feudal manor. Its state of abandonment, the hour, and the cold made the solitude even more penetrating. Suddenly Federico felt oppressed as if by something about to come out of the dawn, something about to happen. He sat down on the broken-off capital of a pillar lying toppled there.

A tiny lamb came out to browse in the weeds among the ruins, appearing like an angel of mist, out of nowhere, to turn solitude into something human, dropping like a gentle petal on the solitude of the place. The poet no longer felt alone. Suddenly a herd of swine also came into the area. There were four or five dark animals, half-wild pigs with a savage hunger and hoofs like rocks. Then Federico witnessed a bloodcurdling scene: the swine fell on the lamb and, to the great horror of the poet, tore it to pieces and devoured it.

This bloody scene in that lonely place made Federico take his touring company back on the road immediately. Three months before the civil war, when he told me this chilling story, Federico was still haunted by the horror of it. Later on I saw, more and more clearly, that the incident had been a vision of his own death, the premonition of his incredible tragedy.

Federico García Lorca was not merely shot; he was assassinated. It would never have crossed anyone's mind that they would kill him one day. He was the most loved, the most cherished, of all Spanish poets, and he was the closest to being a child, because of his marvelous happy temperament. Who could have believed there were monsters on this earth, in his own Granada, capable of such an inconceivable crime?

This criminal act was for me the most painful in the course of a long struggle. Spain was always a battleground of gladiators, a country where much blood has flowed. The bullring, with its sacrifice and its cruel elegance, repeats—glamorized in a flamboyant spectacle—the age-old struggle to the death between darkness and light.

The Inquisition incarcerated Fray Luis de León; Quevedo suffered torments in a dungeon; Columbus hobbled with irons on his ankles. And the great showplace was the charnel house of El Escorial, just as the Monument to the Fallen is today, with its cross standing over a million dead and numberless dark prisons.

THE *SONNETS OF DARK LOVE*

In his romances and his impassioned or descriptive poems about human love, Lorca very rarely offers the keys to certain deep feelings.

Perhaps his love life passed through a number of different cycles. I know too little of those problems to illuminate them.

But there is an old sonnet in which, at a certain point, he seems to reveal himself. Indeed, it is one of Federico's best. I always asked him to recite it, and one time he wrote it down for me with a pencil and paper when the two of us were seated in a restaurant. After repeating it aloud from memory, he slid it over to me, saying: "I am truly giving this to you. What I mean is no one else has a copy."

One of the verses says:

An Apollo of bone sweeps the inhuman riverbed
Where my blood weaves rushes in spring . . .

And ends:

Oh lithe brunette with the slender waist!
Oh metal and melancholy Peru!
Oh Spain, oh dead moon on hard stone!

The poet wrote these verses for a Peruvian friend, Carmen, the wife of the Chilean Alfredo Condon.

I also cannot forget those verses he uttered once from memory, a few weeks before they killed him, in the home of Manuel Altolaguirre, with the title *Sonnets of Dark Love*. They struck me as very beautiful, and must have been dedicated to his last, his true love.

They say the book remained intact among the papers of the murdered poet. If this is true, and if, from a false sense of morality, the García Lorca family has barred its publication, this is an unpardonable sin. But I am not certain it is true. When I met Francisco García Lorca some years back in São Paolo, I didn't have the chance to clarify this matter.

THE LAST LOVE OF THE POET FEDERICO

There are those who treat with a kind of obscurantism the homosexuality of García Lorca, a subject that to me seems unavoidable. This is the way in Spain and Latin America: scrupulously concealing Federico's personal inclinations. In many ways, this attitude shows respect for the murdered poet. But there is also a sexual taboo there, the ecclesiastical legacy of imperialism and Spanish colonialism, nineteenth-century hypocrisy.

Then there are those scandal-mongers, almost always reactionaries, who, to suppress this horrendous political crime, have proffered García Lorca's erotic proclivities as a probable reason of his death. This is a smoke screen. Fascism in Spain, as in Germany and Italy, specialized in the extermination of intellectuals.

In the occupied territories, the Nazis massacred writers, professionals, artists, men of science. In Poland, their hope was to let live no more than a few thousand Poles with rudimentary skills who could serve as amanuenses in their decimated nation.

The Spanish didn't do badly, either. The persecution of teachers, professionals, masons, university graduates, reached the peak of its ferocity in Galicia. They would round people up at night, searching for intellectuals they would gather in the bullring in Badajoz or else shoot at dawn wherever they were. The Galician painter Maruja Mallo told me she used to sleep out in the open in the fields, dying from cold. She spent three months like that, terrified that they might find her. In the morning, she would sneak into her house. On her way home, she would come across a half dozen bodies, those executed that day at sunup.

García Lorca's execution was surely no different than Alberti's or Machado's would have been, had they been caught. In his only declaration concerning the poet's death, Franco blamed it on the reigning disorder of the early days of the civil war. But the long captivity, martyrdom, and death of the imprisoned poet Miguel Hernández disprove his words. There were many chances to free him. Embassies, cardinals, and writers intervened against the fascist authorities, and all they could do was prolong Miguel Hernández's incarceration. His death, like Federico's, was a repellent political assassination.

Returning to García Lorca's intimate disposition: I will say I have known and dealt with a great number of homosexuals, but even after seeing the poet nearly every day in Buenos Aires in 1933, I never saw this side of him, and I couldn't say he exuded any sort of feminine charm. He emanated a splendid intelligence the way a precious stone refracts rays of light. His dark, fleshy face was not effeminate in the least, his seductiveness was natural and intellectual. His homosexuality has been confirmed, and I saw proof of it eventually. But perhaps there are also happy and doomed homosexuals, and the visible becomes more so in sorrow. Federico radiated happiness and in that overflowing cup there must have been something of his satisfied loves.

In Buenos Aires I began to suspect the nature of his amorous inclinations. One time, he told me his hotel room was filled with girls, almost all of them budding poetesses, and they gave him no room to breathe. He told me this amid a series of jokes about his situation. This gave me some sense of his panic when besieged by women, and immediately I offered my assistance. We agreed that in moments of authentic alarm, he would call me on the phone, and I would rush quick as lightning to the hotel and take charge, one way or another, of the agreeable mission of dragging off one or another of his admirers.

We sealed our pact gladly, and with a certain degree of success: my collaboration brought me more than one unexpectedly exquisite reward. Several of those little doves, dazzled by Federico's brilliance, wound up falling into my arms.

Incidentally, he once aided me in an erotic-cosmic adventure, an episode of juvenile urgency that still makes me smile when it surfaces in my memory.

We had been invited one night by one of those millionaire big shots of a kind only to be found in Argentina or the U.S.A. He was a headstrong, self-taught man who had made a spectacular fortune with his sensationalist news rag. His house, surrounded by an enormous park, was the very incarnation of the dreams of a vigorous nouveau riche. Hundreds of cages lined the walkway with pheasants of all colors from all possible countries. The bookshelves were lined with antique books my host bought by cable at bibliophile auctions in Europe: his library was extensive and the shelves were bursting. But most extraordinary of all was the floor of this enormous room, covered entirely in panther skins sewn together to form a single, gigantic tapestry. I found out the man had had agents in Africa, Asia, and the Amazon whose sole function was to gather pelts of leopards, ocelots, and other great cats, whose spots now glimmered beneath my feet in the library of this capricious capitalist.

Such was the lay of the land at the home of the famous Natalio Botana, redoubtable nouveau riche, master of Buenos Aires. Federico and I sat at the table next to the man of the house and across from a tall, blond, wispy poetess whose eyes were more on me than on Federico during our meal: an entire grilled ox brought out still roasting over coals and ashes on a kind of colossal litter borne on the shoulders of eight or ten gauchos. The night was a starred and furious blue. The aroma of the roasted meat in its skin, a sublime invention of the Argentines, mingled with the air of the pampa, with the fragrance of clover and mint, with the murmur of thousands of crickets and toads.

I got up after dining with the poetess and Federico, who rejoiced at everything and laughed at everything, and walked to the illuminated pool. García Lorca went ahead of me and laughed and talked the whole time. He was happy. That was typical. Happiness was his skin.

A tall tower rose up over the brightly lit pool. Its whiteness, like limewash, glowed phosphorescent in the nocturnal lights.

The three of us were alone, and we climbed slowly up to the lookout at the top of the tower. Once there, the three of us, three different sorts of poet, were all cut off from the world. The blue eye of the pool glimmered below. Farther off, guitars and singing from the party could be heard. The night above was so near and starry that it seemed to envelop our heads, to submerge them in its depths.

I took the tall, golden girl in my arms, and when I kissed her, I realized she was a compact, carnal woman through and through.

To Federico's surprise, we lay down on the floor of the lookout, and I had already started to undress her and myself when I saw Federico's bulging eyes pinned to us, watching without daring to believe what was happening or was going to happen.

I shouted: "Get out! Go away, and make sure no one comes upstairs!"

And so, while we were consummating the sacrifice to the starry sky and nocturnal Aphrodite in the tower's heights, Federico, pleased with his mission of matchmaker and citadel, hurried so quickly down the dark steps of the tower that he stumbled on several of them. My new friend and I had to lower him, with great difficulty, the rest of the way. He limped for fifteen days.

When I arrived in Madrid in 1934, I met all García Lorca's and Alberti's friends. There were many of them, and in a few days I was just one more Spanish poet. Naturally the Spanish are very different from us Latin Americans, and this inevitably leads to pridefulness on one or the other side, however misplaced that may be.

I found that the Spanish of my generation showed far more solidarity and kindness than my colleagues back in Latin America. At the same time, I saw we were more universal, more familiar with other languages and cultures. Few people in Spain spoke foreign languages. When Desnos and Crevel came to Madrid, I had to translate for them so they could be understood. Federico didn't even know four words in French. Naturally, there were exceptions: Alberti, Guillén, Salinas had traveled, and the world was broader for them. But generally, the Spanish struck me as the provincials of Europe. At first, I liked that a great deal. Later I came to grasp that Spain's principle strength, its spiritual purpose or lack thereof, lay in its geographical limitations, and that its tragedy, perhaps, had its roots there as well.

In Federico's circle, which I frequented every day during my life in Spain, there were hardly any homosexuals. Perhaps Federico, who was flamboyant as a championship bullfighter, conducted his affairs elsewhere. Later, when we met to drink and chat, he always brought along the same stout, manly, handsome young man. Little by little, I realized the boy was Federico's longstanding love, his last one. His name was Rafael Rapín [Rafael Rodríguez Rapún]. He was from working-class stock. Timid, with long, curly hair, neither tall nor thin, he had that simplicity typical of the popular classes in Spain and struck me as completely normal. He and the guys who accompanied him to the café looked sexually forlorn, so one day, like a loving father, I took two or three, including Federico's friend, to a brothel near the tavern where we used to meet. For me, a precocious boy from the Americas, it was inconceivable that these kids had still never been with a woman.

Sexual hunger in Spain was ravenous. One afternoon we were passing through the suburbs on our way to La Bombilla, a classic neighborhood for those out for a good time. We drove down toward the Manzanares River on a dusty road that stretched on forever, hemmed in by walls that ran for kilometers on both sides. I noticed the white walls were covered end to end with graffiti, to the point that they were almost black.

I got out of the car to examine the curious inscriptions. All of them spelled out the same legend, in clumsy letters of all shapes and sizes: "Pepe was here and wanted to fuck!!" "Antonio, Alberto, and José María were here and wanted to fuck!!!" "On July 3, P.S. and R. were here and wanted to fuck!!"

This rabid eroticism forms a part of Spain, its silence, its iron suit of armor. For me, this was scandalous. Little more than a teenager, I had already been in and out of women's beds and bodies. Even if colonial chastity had been imposed on Spanish America, everyone had still found a way to flout it.

I didn't think much of having taken the kids for an adventure, and Federico, whom I must have been cagey with, laughed the whole thing off. I retell the story now to give some sense of how little the poet's deviance mattered.

Because it seems to me that, just as he lambasted fiercely the perversion of vice in his poems about New York, he was a pure human creature. He doled out his tenderness eccentrically, following a sacred order of nature that he was incapable of disobeying.

During the war, the armed insurrection of the reactionary forces ended the life of that happy poet.

A few weeks after his death, Rafael Rapín, the protagonist of that strange idyll, paid his tribute to death in turn.

He fell in the heart of Teruel. He was manning an antiaircraft gun. The enemy's machine guns fired straight into his post.

Nothing was left of that handsome young man. His bones and blood were scattered in minuscule fragments, almost invisible mottles on the Spanish soil, which every day swallowed thousands of other anonymous dead.

MY BOOK ON SPAIN

Time passed. We were beginning to lose the war. The poets sided with the Spanish people: Federico had been murdered in Granada. Miguel Hernández had been transformed from a goatherd into a fighting word. In soldier's uniform, he read his poems on the front lines. Manuel Altolaguirre kept his printing presses going. He set one up on the eastern front, near Gerona, in an old monastery. My book *España en el corazón* was printed there in a unique way. I believe few books, in the extraordinary history of so many books, have had such a curious birth and fate.

The soldiers at the front learned to set type. But there was no paper. They found an old mill and decided to make it there. A strange mixture was concocted, between one falling bomb and the next, in the middle of the fighting. They threw everything they could get their hands on into the mill, from an enemy flag to a Moorish soldier's bloodstained tunic. And in spite of the unusual materials used and the total inexperience of its manufacturers, the paper turned out to be very beautiful. The few copies of that book still in existence produce astonishment at its typography and at its mysteriously manufactured pages. Years later I saw a copy in the Library of Congress in Washington, D.C., displayed in a showcase as one of the rarest books of our time.

My book had just been printed and bound when the Republic's defeat was suddenly upon us. Hundreds of thousands of refugees glutted the roads leading out of Spain. It was the exodus, the most painful event in the history of that country.

Among those lines of people going into exile were the survivors of the eastern front, and with them Manuel Altolaguirre and the soldiers who had made the paper and printed *España en el corazón*. My book was the pride of these men who had worked to bring out my poetry in the face of death. I learned that many carried copies of the book in their sacks, instead of their own food and clothing. With those sacks over their shoulders, they set out on the long march to France.

The endless column walking to exile was bombed hundreds of times. Soldiers fell and the books were spilled on the highway. Others continued their interminable flight. On the other side of the border, the Spaniards who reached exile met with brutal treatment. The last copies of this impassioned book that was born and perished in the midst of fierce fighting were immolated in a bonfire.

Miguel Hernández sought refuge in the Chilean Embassy, which during the war had granted asylum to four thousand Franco followers. Carlos Morla Lynch, the ambassador, claimed to be his friend but denied the great poet his protection. A few days after, he was arrested and thrown into prison. He died of tuberculosis in jail three years later. The nightingale could not survive in captivity.

My consular duties had come to an end. Because I had taken part in the defense of the Spanish Republic, the Chilean government decided to remove me from my post.

THE WAR AND PARIS

We reached Paris. I took an apartment together with Rafael Alberti and his wife, María Teresa León, on the Quai de l'Horloge, a quiet, marvelous neighborhood. From our place I could see the Pont-Neuf, the statue of Henri IV, and the fishermen dangling over the banks of the Seine. Nerval's Place Dauphine, with its smell of leaves and restaurants, was behind us. The "French" writer Alejo Carpentier, one of the most uncommitted men I have known, lived there. He didn't dare voice an opinion on anything, not even on the Nazis, who were about to fall upon Paris like famished wolves.

From my balcony, to the right, I could make out the black towers of the Conciergerie. Its big gold clock was, for me, the neighborhood's final boundary.

In France then, and for many years after, I had the good fortune to count as dear friends the two foremost figures of her literature, Paul Eluard and Aragon. They were and are extraordinary classic examples of naturalness, with a vital authenticity that gives them a place in the most resonant part of the forest of France. At the same time, they are unshakable and intrinsic adherents of historical morality. Few human beings were as different from each other as these two. I often enjoyed the poetic pleasure of wasting time with Paul Eluard. If poets answered public-opinion polls truthfully, they would give the secret away: There is nothing as beautiful as wasting time. Everyone has his own style for this pastime, as old as time itself. With Paul, I would lose all sense of the passing of day or night, and I never cared if what we were talking about was important or not. Aragon is an electronic machine of intelligence, learning, virulence, high-speed eloquence. I always left Eluard's home smiling without even knowing why. I come out of a few hours spent with Aragon completely worn out, because this demon of a man has forced me to think. Both men have been my stalwart friends, and perhaps what attracts me most about them is the tremendous difference in the nature of their great talents.

NANCY CUNARD

Nancy Cunard and I decided to put out a poetry review which I titled *Les poètes du monde défendent le peuple espagnol* (The Poets of the World Defend the Spanish People).

Nancy had a small printing press in her country house, in the French provinces. I don't remember the name of the place, but it was far from Paris. When we got to her house, it was night and the moon was out. The snow and the moonlight fluttered like a curtain around the estate. I went for a walk, filled with excitement. On my way back, the snowflakes swirled around my head with chilly insistence. I lost my bearings completely and had to grope my way through the whiteness of the night for half an hour.

Nancy had printing experience. During her close relationship with Aragon, she had published the translation of "The Hunting of the Snark" done by Aragon and herself. This Lewis Carroll poem is really untranslatable and only in Góngora, I believe, can we find a parallel to its insane mosaic.

I started setting type for the first time and I am sure there has never been a worse typesetter. I printed *p*'s upside down and they turned into *d*'s through my typographical clumsiness. A line in which the word "párpados" (eyelids) appeared twice ended up with two "dardapos." For years after, Nancy punished me by calling me that. "My dear Dardapo . . . ," she would begin her letters from London. But it turned out to be an attractive publication and we managed to print six or seven issues. Besides militant poets like González Tuñón or Alberti, and some French ones, we published impassioned poems by W. H. Auden, Spender, etc. These English gentlemen will never know how much my lazy fingers suffered setting their poems.

From time to time, poets would come over from England, friends of Nancy's, dandies with a white flower in their lapel, who also wrote anti-Franco verses. In the history of the intellect there has not been a subject as fertile for poets as the Spanish war. The blood spilled in Spain was a magnet that sent shudders through the poetry of a great period.

I don't know if the publication was a success or not, because the war in Spain came to its disastrous end at this time and a second world war had its disastrous beginning. In spite of its magnitude, its immeasurable cruelty, and all the heroic blood it spilled, that war did not manage to grip the collective heart of poetry as the one in Spain had.

A short time later I would have to leave Europe to return to my country. Nancy would also be going to Chile soon, with a bullfighter who then left her and the bulls in Santiago to set up a business in sausages and cold cuts. But my dear friend, who was a high-class snob, was not one to give up easily. In Chile she took a poet as her lover, a slovenly vagrant, a Chilean of Basque descent with some talent but no teeth. What's more, Nancy's new lover was a hopeless drunk and gave the aristocratic Englishwoman nightly beatings that forced her to appear in public wearing enormous dark glasses.

Quixotic, unalterable, fearless, and pathetic, Nancy was one of the strangest persons I have ever known. The sole heir to the Cunard Line, Nancy, daughter of Lady Cunard, had scandalized London in 1930 by running away with a black man, a musician in one of the first jazz bands imported by the Savoy Hotel.

When Lady Cunard found her daughter's bed empty and a letter proudly informing her of her black future, the noblewoman went to her lawyer and proceeded to cut her off without a cent. And that was how this young woman I met roaming the world had been disinherited from the British nobility. Her mother's salons were frequented by George Moore (who, gossip had it, was Nancy's real father), Sir Thomas Beecham, young Aldous Huxley, and the future Duke of Windsor, still Prince of Wales at the time.

Nancy Cunard struck back. In December of the year in which her mother excommunicated her, the English aristocracy received as a Christmas present a pamphlet bound in red, entitled "Negro Man and White Ladyship." I have never seen anything more vitriolic. It is as trenchant as Swift, in some passages.

Her arguments in defense of blacks came down like clubs on the heads of Lady Cunard and English society. I recall that she said—I am quoting from memory, and her words were more eloquent—"Suppose you, your white ladyship, or rather your people, had been kidnapped, beaten, and chained by a more powerful tribe and then shipped far from England to be sold as slaves, displayed as ludicrous specimens of human ugliness, forced to work under the whip and fed poorly. What would be left of your race? The blacks suffered all this violence and cruelty and much more besides. After centuries of suffering, however, they are still the best and most graceful athletes, and they have created a new music that is more universal than any other. Could you, and whites like you, have emerged victorious from so much iniquity? Who is better, then?"

And so on, for thirty pages.

Nancy was never able to live in England after that, and from then on, she embraced the cause of the persecuted black race. During the invasion of Ethiopia she went to Addis Ababa. Then she traveled to the United States to make common cause with the black boys of Scottsboro who were accused of infamous crimes they had not committed. The young blacks were sentenced by racist U.S. justice, and Nancy Cunard was deported by the democratic North American police.

My friend Nancy Cunard would die in 1969 in Paris. A sudden turn in her death agony made her go downstairs in the hotel elevator all but naked. There she collapsed on the floor and closed her lovely sky-blue eyes forever.

She weighed thirty-five kilos at the time of her death. She was a mere skeleton. Her body had wasted away in a long battle against injustice in the world. Her reward was a life that became progressively lonelier, and a godforsaken death.

A CONGRESS IN MADRID

The war in Spain was going from bad to worse, but the Spanish people's spirit of resistance had captivated the whole world. International brigades were already fighting in Spain. I saw them arrive in Madrid, in 1936, in uniform. They were a magnificent group of people of different ages, coloring, hair.

Now it was 1937 and we were in Paris, and the main thing was to organize an anti-Fascist congress of writers from all over the world. The congress would be held in Madrid. That's when I began to know Aragon better. The first thing about him that surprised me was his incredible capacity for work and organization. He dictated all his letters, corrected and remembered them. Not even the slightest detail escaped him. He worked long, steady hours in our small office. Yet, as everyone knows, he writes thick volumes of prose, and his poetry is the most beautiful in the French language. I saw him correcting the galleys of translations he had done of Russian and English writers, and I saw him redo them right on the printer's proofs. He is really an extraordinary man, and that's when I began to appreciate that fact.

I had been left without a consulship and consequently without a penny. I went to work, for four hundred (old) francs, in an organization for the defense of culture, managed by Aragon. Delia del Carril, my wife then and for many years to come, was reputed to be a rich landowner, but she was actually poorer than I. We lived in a dubious, run-down hotel whose first floor was reserved for transient couples that came and went. For months we ate very little and badly. But the congress of anti-Fascist writers became a reality. Priceless replies poured in from all over. One was from Yeats, Ireland's national poet; another, from Selma Lagerlöf, the notable Swedish writer. They were both too old to travel to a beleaguered city like Madrid, which was being steadily pounded by bombs, but they rallied to the defense of the Spanish Republic.

I have always considered myself a man of few qualifications, especially in practical matters or for high-minded missions. I stared open-mouthed, therefore, when I received a bank draft from the Spanish government, for a considerable sum, to cover expenses for the congress, including fares for delegates from other continents. Dozens of writers were flocking to Paris.

I was at a complete loss. What was I to do with the money? I decided to endorse the funds to the organization that was behind the congress. "I haven't laid eyes on the money, and I wouldn't know what to do with it, anyway," I told Rafael Alberti, who was passing through Paris.

"You're a big fool," Rafael said. "You've lost your consular post defending the Spanish cause, you're walking around with holes in your shoes, and you won't even set aside a few thousand francs for your work and your minimum needs."

I glanced at my shoes, and in fact they did have holes. Alberti made me a gift of a new pair.

We were leaving for Madrid in a few hours, with all the delegates. Delia and Amparo González Tuñón and I were swamped with paperwork to clear the way for the writers who were planning to attend. The French exit visas presented us with endless problems, so we practically took over the Paris police headquarters, where the formal acknowledgments jocularly referred to as *recipissé* were issued.

Sometimes we ourselves stamped the passports with that supreme French contrivance called *tampon*.

Along with the Norwegians, the Italians, the Argentines, the poet Octavio Paz arrived from Mexico, after a thousand adventures and misadventures. I was proud of having brought him. He had published just one book, which I had received two months before and which seemed to contain genuine promise. No one knew him yet.

My old friend César Vallejo came to see me with a scowl on his face. He was angry because his wife, whom the rest of us found unbearable, had not been issued a ticket. I got one for her quickly. We gave it to Vallejo and he left, as surly as when he had come in. Something was bothering him and it took me several months to discover what it was.

At the bottom of it was this: My countryman Vicente Huidobro had come to Paris to attend the congress. Huidobro and I had had a falling out and were not speaking. But he was a close friend of Vallejo's and used his few days in Paris to fill my trusting friend's head with stories about me. Everything was cleared up later in a heated conversation I had with Vallejo.

Never had a train left Paris packed with so many writers. We recognized or ignored one another in the corridors. Some slept. Others chain-smoked. For many, Spain was both the enigma and the key to that moment of history.

Vallejo and Huidobro were somewhere on the train. André Malraux stopped to talk to me for a moment, with his facial tics, his raincoat tossed over his shoulders. This time he was traveling alone. I had always seen him before with the flier Corniglion-Molinier, who was his right-hand man in his adventures through the skies of Spain: cities lost and discovered, or a vital delivery of planes to the Republic.

I remember that the train was held up a long time at the border. Apparently Huidobro had lost a suitcase. Everyone was occupied, or preoccupied, with the delay and no one was in a mood to listen to him. The Chilean poet picked the wrong moment to come looking for his bag out on the platform, where Malraux, the leader of the expedition, was. Nervous by nature, and with a lot of problems accumulating around him, Malraux was at the end of his tether. Maybe he didn't know Huidobro by sight or by name. When he came up to complain about losing his suitcase, Malraux lost the little patience he had left. I heard him shout: "Is this the time to be pestering anyone? Get away! *Je vous enmerde!*"

It's too bad that I had to be the one to witness this incident which deflated the Chilean's vanity. I wish I had been a thousand miles away at that moment. But life is fickle. I was the one person Huidobro detested on that train. And to make matters worse, I, his countryman, and not any of the hundred other writers traveling with us, had to be the sole spectator of this incident.

When we got underway again, with the night far advanced and the train rolling through the Spanish countryside, I thought of Huidobro, his suitcase, the unpleasant moment he had been through. So I said to some young Central American writers who had come to my compartment: "Go see Huidobro, too, he must be alone and depressed."

They were back in twenty minutes, their faces beaming. Huidobro had said to them: "Don't talk to me about the lost bag; that's not important. What really matters is that although the universities of Chicago, Berlin, Copenhagen, and Prague have conferred honorary titles on me, the small university in the small country you come from insists on ignoring me. I haven't even been asked to give a lecture on creationism."

My countryman the great poet was definitely a hopeless case.

We finally reached Madrid. While the visitors were being welcomed and assigned a place to stay, I decided to visit the home I had left almost a year before. My books and my things, everything had been left behind in it. It was an apartment in a building called the "House of Flowers," near the entrance to the university campus. Franco's advance lines had reached it and the block of apartments had changed hands several times.

Miguel Hernández, who was wearing his militia uniform and carrying his rifle, got a van to transport the books and the belongings I was most interested in taking with me.

We went up to the fifth floor and opened the apartment door expectantly. Flak had knocked in the windows and chunks of the walls. The books had toppled off the shelves. It was impossible to find one's way in the rubble. I searched for things haphazardly. Oddly enough, the most useless, superfluous things had vanished, carried off by invading or defending forces. The pots and pans, the sewing machine, the dishes were there: they were scattered all over, but they had survived, yet there was not a trace of my consul's tail coat, my Polynesian masks, my Oriental knives.

"War is as whimsical as dreams, Miguel."

Miguel found some manuscripts of mine somewhere among the strewn papers. That chaos was a final door closing on my life. I said to Miguel, "I don't want to take anything with me."

"Nothing? Not even one book?"

"Not even one book."

And we went back with the van empty.

THE MASKS AND THE WAR

... My house was caught between the two fronts ... On one side, Moors and Italians advanced ... On the other, Madrid's defenders advanced, fell back, or were halted ... The artillery had crashed through the walls ... The windows were smashed to smithereens ... On the floor, among my books, I found shrapnel ... But my masks were gone ... Masks collected

in Siam, Bali, Sumatra, the Malay Archipelago, Bandung . . . Gilded, ashen, tomato-red, with silver eyebrows, blue, demonic eyebrows, lost in thought, my masks had been my sole keepsakes from the Orient I had gone to alone that first time, which had received me with its odor of tea, dung, opium, sweat, the intensest jasmine, frangipani, fruit rotting in the streets . . . Those masks, a reminder of the purest dances, of the dancing before the temple . . . Wooden drops colored by myth, the residue of a mythology of flowers that sketched dreams in the air, customs, demons, mysteries alien to my American nature . . . And then . . . Perhaps the militiamen had leaned out the windows of my house between shots with the masks on to strike terror into the Moors . . . Many masks had been left there smashed, spattered with blood . . . Others had rolled down from my fifth-floor apartment, wrenched off by a bullet . . . Franco's advance lines had taken up their positions in front of them . . . The horde of illiterate mercenaries had screeched past before them . . . Thirty masks of Asian gods rising from my house in their last dance, the dance of death . . . A moment of respite . . . The positions had reversed . . . I sat looking at the debris, the bloodstains on the mat . . . And through the new windows, the gaping holes left by the gunfire . . . I stared far off, beyond the campus, toward flatlands, toward ancient castles . . . Spain looked empty to me . . . It looked as if my last guests had gone off forever . . . With masks or without, in the middle of the shooting and the war chants, the mad rejoicing, the incredible defense, death or life, all that was over for me . . . It was the last silence after the feasting . . . After the last feasting . . . With the masks that had gone, with the masks that had fallen, with those soldiers I had not invited in, Spain had gone for me . . .

6

I Went Out to Look for the Fallen

I PICKED A ROAD

I received my activist's card much later in Chile, when I enrolled in the party officially, but I believe I had looked upon myself as a Communist during the war in Spain. Many things had contributed to my deep conviction.

My contradictory friend the Nietzschean poet León Felipe was a very likable man whose most attractive quality was his anarchist's proclivity to indiscipline and his mocking rebelliousness. At the height of the civil war he fell easily for the blustery propaganda of the FAI (Iberian Anarchist Federation). He was often at the anarchist fronts, where he lectured on his theories and read his iconoclastic poems. These reflected an ideology that was vaguely libertarian, anti-clerical, capped with invocations and blasphemies. His words captivated the anarchist groups that blossomed like hothouse flowers in Madrid while the rest of the people were at the battlefront, which was coming closer and closer. These lawless groups had painted the trolleys and buses half red and half yellow. With their long hair and beards, wearing bullets strung into necklaces and bracelets, they played a leading role in Spain's carnival of death. I saw several of them in symbolic leather shoes, half red and half black, which must have put the shoemakers to a lot of trouble. And don't let anyone think it was all innocent show. They carried knives, revolvers, rifles, and carbines. Groups of them would park themselves at the main entrances of buildings, smoking and spitting, showing off their hardware. Their main concern was to collect rents from terrorized tenants or make them hand over their jewels, rings, and watches.

León Felipe was on his way back from one of his pro-anarchist lectures late one night when we ran into each other at the café on the corner of my house. The poet was wearing a Spanish cape that went very well with his Nazarene beard. On the way out, the elegant folds of his romantic attire brushed against one of his touchy religiosos. I don't know if León Felipe's bearing, that of an old-time hidalgo, annoyed that "hero" of the rear guard, but I do know that we were stopped a few steps farther on by a bunch of anarchists headed by the man who had considered himself offended at the café. They wanted to check our papers, and after they had glanced at them, the Spanish poet was taken away between two armed men.

As he was being led off to a place of execution near my house, where firing squads often kept me awake at night, I saw two armed militiamen coming back from the front. I explained who León Felipe was, the offense he had been accused of, and was able to get my friend's attackers to release them.

This ideological, if gratuitous instruction gave me much to think about. I heard of the exploits of an Austrian anarchist, a nearsighted man with a long black beard, who specialized in taking people "for a walk." He had formed a squad which he called ... because it went into action at daybreak.

"Haven't you ever had a toothache?" he would ask.

"Yes, of course, comrade."

"Well, I'm trying to administer an excellent remedy," he would say, pointing his revolver at the victim and pulling the trigger.

in Siam, Bali, Sumatra, the Malay Archipelago, Bandung . . . Gilded, ashen, tomato-red, with silver eyebrows, blue, demonic eyebrows, lost in thought, my masks had been my sole keepsakes from the Orient I had gone to alone that first time, which had received me with its odor of tea, dung, opium, sweat, the intensest jasmine, frangipani, fruit rotting in the streets . . . Those masks, a reminder of the purest dances, of the dancing before the temple . . . Wooden drops colored by myth, the residue of a mythology of flowers that sketched dreams in the air, customs, demons, mysteries alien to my American nature . . . And then . . . Perhaps the militiamen had leaned out the windows of my house between shots with the masks on to strike terror into the Moors . . . Many masks had been left there smashed, spattered with blood . . . Others had rolled down from my fifth-floor apartment, wrenched off by a bullet . . . Franco's advance lines had taken up their positions in front of them . . . The horde of illiterate mercenaries had screeched past before them . . . Thirty masks of Asian gods rising from my house in their last dance, the dance of death . . . A moment of respite . . . The positions had reversed . . . I sat looking at the debris, the bloodstains on the mat . . . And through the new windows, the gaping holes left by the gunfire . . . I stared far off, beyond the campus, toward flatlands, toward ancient castles . . . Spain looked empty to me . . . It looked as if my last guests had gone off forever . . . With masks or without, in the middle of the shooting and the war chants, the mad rejoicing, the incredible defense, death or life, all that was over for me . . . It was the last silence after the feasting . . . After the last feasting . . . With the masks that had gone, with the masks that had fallen, with those soldiers I had not invited in, Spain had gone for me . . .

Gangs like these roamed Madrid's pitch-black nights. The Communists were the only organized group and had put together an army to confront Italians, Germans, Moors, and Falangists. They were also the moral force that kept the resistance and the anti-Fascist struggle going. It boiled down to this: you had to pick the road you would take. That is what I did and I have never had reason to regret the choice I made between darkness and hope in that tragic time.

RAFAEL ALBERTI

Poetry is an act of peace. Peace goes into the making of a poet as flour goes into the making of bread.

Arsonists, warmongers, wolves hunt down the poet to burn, kill, sink their teeth into him. A swordsman left Pushkin mortally wounded under the trees in a dark and gloomy park. The fiery horses of war charged over Petöfi's lifeless body. Byron died in Greece, fighting against war. The Spanish Fascists started off the war in Spain by assassinating its greatest poet.

Rafael Alberti is a kind of survivor. He was marked for death a thousand times. One of those times, in Granada, like Lorca. Another time death waited for him in Badajoz. They looked for him in sun-drenched Seville and in Cádiz and Puerto de Santa María in his home province, to kill him, to hang him, and so deal poetry another death blow.

But poetry has not died, it has a cat's nine lives. They harass it, they drag it through the streets, they spit on it and make it the butt of their jokes, they try to strangle it, drive it into exile, throw it into prison, pump lead into it, and it survives every attempt with a clear face and a smile as bright as grains of rice.

I knew Alberti when he walked through the streets of Madrid in a blue shirt and a red tie. I knew him fighting in the ranks of the people when not too many poets were following that difficult course. The bells had not yet tolled for Spain, but he knew what might be coming. He is a man from the south, born near the singing sea and cellars filled with wine as golden yellow as topaz. There his heart took fire from the grape and song from the wave. He was always a poet, but he himself did not know this in his early years. Later all Spain would know it, and still later, the world.

For those of us who have the good fortune to speak and know the language of Castile, Rafael Alberti embodies all the resplendent qualities of Spanish poetry. He is not only a born poet but also a master craftsman. Like a red rose blooming miraculously in winter, his poetry contains a flake of Góngora's snow, a root from Jorge Manrique, a petal from Garcilaso, a fragrance of mourning from Gustavo Adolfo Bécquer. The true essences of Spanish poetry come together in his crystalline wineglass.

His red rose threw its brilliance over the road for those who tried to stop Fascism in Spain. The world knows this heroic and tragic story. Alberti wrote epic sonnets, he read them in barracks and at the front, and he invented poetry's guerrilla warfare, poetry's war against war. He invented songs that grew wings under the thunder of artillery fire, songs that later soared over the entire planet.

A consummate poet, he showed how useful poetry could be at a moment that was critical for the whole world. In this, he resembles Mayakovsky. This application of poetry for the benefit of the majority is based on strength, tenderness, joy, on man's true nature. Without it, poetry gives off sound, but it doesn't sing. Alberti's poems always sing.

THE GIFT OF MIST

In Madrid, not long before the war, I gave a dog to Rafael Alberti, I never really knew if it was male or female.

This is all I ever gave to a person who gave me so much.

I will speak first of my gift, and then of his gifts.

One night, I walked from Casa de las Flores toward Rafael's building, some ways off on a steep elevation overlooking the Calle Marqués de Urquijo and the foliage of the tree-lined, sonorous park. At the entry to his home, which had belonged to a ferocious general, a slayer of freedom fighters in the colonies, was a gigantic shell from the genus *Tridacna*, the biggest I have ever seen, brought over, perhaps, from the Philippines.

I liked to cover the six or seven blocks that separated us on foot, then climb the hill to Alberti's lovely home. I used to always leave behind some keepsake to gall the memory of that colonel from the colonies, and I almost always placed it in that giant shell, which had once been filled with holy water. After mounting the spiral staircase in silence and semidarkness, one arrived at that light that Rafael signified, along with María Teresa, the brilliant blond Castilian, who made a powerful contribution to brightening that ample space. Rafael, like me, revels every night because he works like a mule during the day.

I arrived there with the dog—a boy or girl. Its sex, its breed, the language it barked in were unknowable, so disheveled, so tangled, so thick-browed and bearded was that puff of fog that had followed me from home.

It was deep winter and, unusually for Madrid, the fog had settled over the city with a typically Spanish consistency, serious and compact. And the fog hardly let me walk and made it nearly impossible to see. But it did let me hear, and I noticed along the way that something was following me. Something, maybe a specter, a crow, a never-again. Severely alone, half-lost in the fog, I was a walker in absolute solitude at that hour, no one passed and nothing was audible but that strange tic-tac, like the footfalls of a ghost, trailing behind me. When I stopped, that solicitous sound did, too. And as soon as I set off again, something, whatever it was, began to walk with me. And with this in the midst of all that fog, I grew exasperated. Only when

I reached Alberti's thick door did a fluffy dog emerge from the mist and climb with me up the stairway. A dog from the slums, half fog and half dream, the color of asphalt all over, it looked at us through its crisscrossing thicket of silvery hairs, recollecting in a way a sheep strayed off into the city, but conserving in its eyes the purity of a wild beast.

When I entered with the dog, Rafael immediately christened it "Mist" because it looked to be steeped in that mysterious substance. Down it sat in the middle of the room, object of the poets' adoration, that strange dog that was natural and necessary from that point forward, there amid the arbitrary, abstract sculptures in stone and iron by Alberto Sánchez that filled the Alberti León household.

Mist, with that name and that sylvatic hair, became Rafael's unforgettable dog and abiding companion, helping him on his strolls through the street and even when he wrote his poems, because a dog like that, which materializes out of the night, is good for everything. They only separated with the coming of the war, which took so much away from us and left Rafael bereft of his Spain and his dog named Mist.

It may be that was all I ever gave, my whole life long, to Rafael Alberti, poet of the shores of Puerto de Santa María, of heroic Madrid, of fertile exile.

What Rafael gave me in those long, long years, and what I owe him, is another matter. I have spoken of it occasionally, in more than one poem.

Is it possible that this is everything? It is already a lot. And yet I could have owed him much more. And that is what I would have wished for.

Now that he is turning seventy, ahead of me, but not by much, as age is nipping at our heels, it should be said that when they emigrated, and I brought him and his beloved to American soil, I had arranged for them to go to my country, but they got lost amid the brilliance of Buenos Aires.

All these long years would have indebted me deeply to Rafael and to her. They both have the gift of light, and of bringing happiness as no others can.

Rafael is radiant. I would have owed him for these years of friendship and that joy he knows how to provoke. I am a territorial type, imbued with the black light of the regions of my birth, the Antarctic south, the rain of the great forests, the volcanoes that form the cold diadem of my fatherland. For me, Rafael is a window opening onto honey, onto the open space of his florid origins.

With no one else do I enjoy myself so much as with Rafael. Perhaps Federico García Lorca, our brother in common, made me laugh as Rafael does. Laugh with pure laughter, with that laughter as needful as bread and fruit. The two of them, so different, have never lived far from my heart. Until one of them was murdered by the other's enemies.

But now I am speaking of the one still alive, of Rafael Alberti, who remains resplendent, jubilant, and combative. Because his perfect personality, like the grave combat that has been his life, continues and shall continue to be joined to the exemplary transparency of his immortal poetry.

NAZIS IN CHILE

Once again I returned to my country, third-class. In Latin America there were no eminent writers, like Céline, Drieu La Rochelle, or Ezra Pound, who turned traitor to serve Fascism, but there was a strong Fascist movement nurtured, with or without financial aid, by Hitlerism. Groups sprang up everywhere whose members dressed like storm troopers and raised their arm in the Fascist salute. And they weren't just small groups. The old feudal oligarchies of the continent sided, and still side, with anti-Communism of any kind, whether it came from Germany or the creole ultra-left. What's more, let's remember that people of German descent make up the bulk of the population in some parts of Chile, Brazil, and Mexico. Those areas were easily seduced by Hitler's meteoric rise and by the fabled millennium of German greatness.

More than once, in those days of Hitler's resounding victories, I literally had to walk through a street, in some small village or town in the south of Chile, under forests of flags bearing the swastika. Once, in a small southern town, I was forced to pay an involuntary tribute to the Führer in order to use the telephone. The German owner of the establishment, which had the only telephone in town, had managed to place the instrument so that, to take the receiver off the hook, you had to raise your arm to a portrait of Hitler, whose arm was also raised.

I was editor of the magazine *Aurora de Chile*. All its literary weapons (we had no others) were aimed at the Nazis, who were swallowing country after country. Hitler's ambassador to Chile donated books, by authors of the so-called neo-German culture, to the National Library. We countered by asking our readers to send us German books that were faithful to the real Germany, the Germany banned by Hitler. It was a momentous experience. I received death threats. And many neatly wrapped packages arrived with books smeared with filth. We also received whole collections of *Der Stürmer*, a pornographic periodical that was sadistic and anti-Semitic, edited by Julius Streicher, deservedly hanged in Nuremberg years later. German-language editions of Heinrich Heine, Thomas Mann, Anna Seghers, Einstein, Arnold Zweig also trickled in. And when we had nearly five hundred volumes, we took them to the National Library.

We were in for a surprise. The National Library had padlocked its doors to us.

Then we organized a march and entered the university's hall of honor carrying pictures of the Reverend Niemöller and Carl von Ossietzky. Some kind of ceremonial act was taking place, presided over by Don Miguel Cruchaga Tocornal, the Foreign Minister. We set the books and portraits down carefully on the speakers' dais. The battle was won. The books were accepted.

ISLA NEGRA

I made up my mind to throw myself into my writing with more devotion and energy. My visit to Spain had given me added strength and maturity. The bitterness in my poetry had to end. The brooding subjectivity of my *Veinte poemas de amor*, the painful moodiness of my *Residencia en la tierra* were coming to a close. In them, I now believed, I had struck a vein, not in rocks underground, but in the pages of books. Can poetry serve our fellow men? Can it find a place in man's struggles? I had already done enough tramping over the irrational and the negative. I had to pause and find the road to humanism, outlawed from contemporary literature but deeply rooted in the aspirations of mankind.

I started work on my *Canto general*.

For this, I needed a place to work. I found a stone house facing the ocean, in a place nobody knew about, Isla Negra. Its owner, a Spanish socialist of long standing, a sea captain, Don Eladio Sobrino, was building it for his family but agreed to sell it to me. How could I buy it? I submitted a projected *Canto general*, but it was turned down by Editorial Ercilla, my publisher at the time. In 1939, with the help of another publisher, who reimbursed the owner of the house directly, I was finally able to get my house on Isla Negra to work in.

I felt a pressing need to write a central poem that would bring together the historical events, the geographical situations, the life and struggles of our peoples. Isla Negra's wild coastal strip, with its turbulent ocean, was the place to give myself passionately to the writing of my new song.

"BRING ME SPANIARDS"

But life wrested me away almost at once.

The chilling news of the Spanish exodus reached Chile. More than five hundred thousand men and women, combatants and civilians, had crossed the French border. In France, under pressure from reactionary forces, Léon Blum's government herded them into concentration camps, dispersed them to fortresses and prisons, massed them together in its African possessions near the Sahara.

In Chile the government had changed. The vicissitudes of the Spanish people had brought fresh strength to Chile's popular forces and we had a progressive government now.

Chile's Popular Front government decided to send me to France on the noblest mission I have ever undertaken: to get Spaniards out of their French prisons and send them to my country. And so, like a radiant light from America, my poetry would spread among throngs of human beings burdened with suffering and heroic like no other people. My poetry would become one with material assistance from America, which, by taking in the Spaniards, would be paying an age-old debt.

Virtually an invalid, just recovering from an operation and with one leg in a cast—such was my health at the time—I left my haven and went to see the President of the Republic. Don Pedro Aguirre Cerda received me warmly. "Yes, bring me thousands of Spaniards. We have work for all of them. Bring me fishermen; bring me Basques, Castilians, people from Extremadura."

A few days later I left for France, still in my cast, to fetch Spaniards to Chile. I had a specific mission. My appointment papers stated that I was consul in charge of the immigration of the Spaniards. I showed up at the Chilean Embassy in Paris flashing my credentials.

My country's government and political situation were not what they had been, but the Embassy in Paris was still the same. The idea of sending Spaniards to Chile infuriated our smartly dressed diplomats.

They set me up in an office next to the kitchen, they harassed me in every way they could, even going so far as to deny me writing paper. The wave of undesirables was already beginning to reach the doors of the Embassy: wounded veterans, jurists and writers, professionals who had lost their practice, all kinds of skilled workers.

They had to make their way against hell and high water to get to my office, and since it was on the fourth floor, our Embassy people thought up a fiendish scheme: they cut off elevator service. Many of the Spaniards had war wounds and were survivors of the African concentration camps; it broke my heart to see them come up to the fourth floor with such painful effort, while the cruel officials gloated over my difficulties.

A DIABOLICAL CHARACTER

To complicate my life, the Popular Front government sent me word of the arrival of a chargé d'affaires. This made me very happy, because a new department head at the Embassy would be able to rid me of the many stumbling blocks the old diplomatic personnel had put in my way to impede the immigration of the Spaniards. A slender youngster with a pince-nez that gave him the air of an old bookworm came out of the Gare Saint-Lazare. He must have been twenty-four or twenty-five. In a high-pitched, effeminate voice broken by emotion, he told me that he accepted me as his boss and that the sole purpose of his coming was to act as my helper in the great task of sending to Chile "the glorious vanquished of the war." My satisfaction at having a new assistant continued, but this character made me uncomfortable. In spite of the adulation and excessive attention he lavished on me, something about him did not ring true. I found out later that, with the triumph of the Popular Front in Chile, he had done an abrupt about-face, leaving the Knights of Columbus, that Jesuit organization, to become a member of the Communist youth movement, which was avidly recruiting members and was delighted with his intellectual qualifications. Arellano Marín wrote plays and articles, was an erudite lecturer, and seemed to know everything.

World War II was almost upon us. Paris waited every night for the German bombings, and every home had instructions on how to protect itself from the aerial attacks. I went home to Villennes-sur-Seine every evening, to a small house facing the river, which I left with a heavy heart every morning to return to the Embassy.

Within a few days the new arrival, Arellano Marín, had assumed an importance I had never attained. I had introduced him to Negrín, Alvarez del Vayo, and a few leaders of the Spanish parties. A week later the new functionary was on familiar terms with almost all of them. Spanish leaders whom I didn't know went in and out of his office. Their extensive conversations were a mystery to me. From time to time he called me over to show me a diamond or an emerald he had bought for his mother, or to confide in me about a very cute blonde who made him spend more than he should in the Paris cabarets. Arellano Marín became a close friend of the Aragons', especially of Elsa, when the Embassy took them in to protect them from anti-Communist repression; he regaled them with attentions and little presents. This person's psychology must have intrigued Elsa Triolet, for she mentions him in one or two of her novels.

I gradually realized that his greed for luxury and wealth was growing before my very eyes, which have never been too wide-awake. He slipped easily from one make of automobile to another and rented luxurious homes. And each day the cute blonde seemed to be driving him more and more out of his mind with her demands.

I had to go to Brussels to attend to a critical problem involving the emigrants. As I was leaving the unpretentious hotel where I was staying, I literally ran into my new assistant, the elegant Arellano Marín. He made a loud fuss over me and invited me to dine that same day.

We met at his hotel, the most expensive in Brussels. He had had orchids placed on our table. Naturally, he ordered caviar and champagne. During the meal I was silent and preoccupied, listening to my host rave on about his lavish plans, his upcoming pleasure trips, the jewels he had bought. I was listening, I felt, to a nouveau riche with certain symptoms of insanity; his penetrating eyes, his cocksure pronouncements—all of it made me sick. I decided to take a drastic step and tell him openly what was on my mind. I suggested that we have coffee in his room, because I had something to say to him.

As we were on our way upstairs, two strangers walked up to him at the foot of the grand staircase. He told them in Spanish to wait for him, he would be down in a few minutes.

Once we were in his room, I thought no more about the coffee. Ours was a strained conversation. "I believe you're heading down the wrong road," I said to him. "You are becoming money-mad. Maybe you're still too young to understand this, but our political obligations are a very serious matter. The fate of thousands of immigrants is in our hands, and this can't be taken lightly. I don't want to know anything about your affairs, but I do want to give you a piece of advice. There are a lot of people who say, at the end of an unhappy life: 'Nobody gave me advice, nobody warned me.' That's something you won't be able to say. I've made my speech. And now I am leaving."

I looked at him as I said goodbye. Tears rolled down his eyes to his mouth. I could have bitten my tongue. Had I gone too far? I went to him and put my hand on his shoulder. "Don't cry!"

"It's just that I'm furious," he said.

I left without another word. I returned to Paris and never saw him again. When they saw me coming down, the two strangers who had been waiting for him hurried up to his room.

The conclusion of this story came much later, in Mexico, when I was Chilean Consul General there. One day I was invited to lunch by a group of Spanish refugees and two of them recognized me.

"Where do you know me from?" I asked.

"We are the two fellows who went up to speak to your countryman Arellano Marín when you came down from his room in Brussels."

"Oh, and what happened then? I've always been curious about it."

They told me something extraordinary. They had found him swimming in tears, hysterical, and he had sobbed out: "I've just had the biggest shock of my life. Neruda has gone to turn you in to the Gestapo as dangerous Spanish Communists. I couldn't talk him into waiting even a few hours. You have only minutes to get away. Leave your suitcases with me, I'll watch them for you and send them on later."

"The bastard!" I exclaimed. "Thank heavens you managed to escape from the Germans, anyway."

"Yes, but the suitcases contained ninety thousand dollars that belonged to the Spanish workers' unions, and we never set eyes on that money again."

Still later, I heard that this diabolical character had made an extended pleasure tour of the Near East with his Parisian lover. Incidentally, the cute blonde who had been so demanding turned out to be a blond male student from the Sorbonne.

Sometime afterward, his resignation from the Communist Party made news in Chile. "Strong ideological differences compel me to make this decision," he said in his letter to the newspapers.

A GENERAL AND A POET

Each man who emerged from the defeat or from captivity was a novel with chapters, tears, laughter, loneliness, and idylls. Some of these stories really amazed me.

I met an air force general, tall and lean, a military-academy man with all kinds of titles. There he was, roaming the Paris streets, a quixotic shadow from the Spanish soil, old and straight as the poplars of Castile. When Franco's army split the Republican zone in two, this general, Herrera, had to go the rounds in pitch darkness, inspect defenses, give orders right and left. On the blackest nights, he flew his airplane, with all its lights out, over enemy territory. Every now and again, gunfire from the Franco side barely missed his craft. But the general became bored with flying in the dark. So he learned Braille. Once he had mastered this writing for the blind, he went on his dangerous missions reading with his fingers, while below him the fire and the pain of the civil war raged on. The general told me that he had read *The Count of Monte Cristo* and was just getting into *The Three Musketeers*, when his night reading in Braille was interrupted by defeat and exile.

Another story I recall with deep feeling is the story of the Andalusian poet Pedro Garfias, who ended up in exile in Scotland at the castle of some lord. The castle was always empty, and Garfias, a restless Andalusian, went to the local tavern every day; speaking no English, only a gypsy Spanish that even I could not always understand, he drank his solitary beer in silence. This wordless customer attracted the tavernkeeper's interest, and one night, when the other drinkers had left, the tavernkeeper begged him to stay and they went on drinking silently next to the hearth, whose fire sputtered, doing the talking for the two of them.

This invitation became a ritual. Each night, Garfias was welcomed by the bartender, lonely like him, with no wife or family. Little by little their tongues loosened up. Garfias told him about the Spanish war, with exclamations, oaths, and curses that were typically Andalusian. The other man listened in religious silence, not understanding a word, of course.

The Scotsman, in turn, poured out his miseries, probably the story of a wife who had deserted him, the exploits of his sons, whose pictures in military uniform decorated the fireplace. I say "probably," because during the long months that these strange conversations lasted, Garfias did not understand a word either.

Still, the bond of fellowship grew stronger and stronger between the two lonely men, each speaking with deep feeling about his own affairs in his own language, inaccessible to the other. Seeing each other every night and talking into the small hours became a necessity for both.

When Garfias had to leave for Mexico, they said goodbye, drinking and talking, embracing and weeping. The feeling that bound them so deeply was the sundering of their two solitudes.

"Pedro," I often said to the poet, "what do you think he was telling you?"

"I never understood a word, Pablo, but when I listened to him I always felt, I was always sure, that I knew what he meant. And when I talked, I was sure that he also knew what I meant."

THE *WINNIPEG*

One morning when I got to the Embassy, I was handed a pretty long cable by the officials. Everyone was smiling, which was odd, since they no longer even greeted me. There had to be something in the message that delighted them.

It was a cable from Chile, signed by the President himself, Don Pedro Aguirre Cerda, from whom I had received clear instructions to put the Spanish exiles on a ship bound for Chile.

I was shocked to read that our good President, Don Pedro, had learned that very morning, much to his surprise, that I was arranging for the Spanish emigrants to go to Chile. He asked me to deny this outlandish news immediately.

What was outlandish to me was the President's cable. The job of organizing, screening, selecting the immigrants had been hard, lonely work. Fortunately, Spain's government-in-exile had understood the importance of my mission. Yet new and unexpected obstacles presented themselves daily. Meanwhile, hundreds of refugees were leaving or preparing to leave the concentration camps in France and Africa, where thousands of them were crowded together, and go to Chile.

The Republican government-in-exile had succeeded in buying a ship, the *Winnipeg*. It had been converted to increase its passenger capacity and was waiting, tied up at the pier at Trompe-loup, a little port near Bordeaux.

What should I do? This time-consuming and vital work, on the brink of the Second World War, was the crowning point of my life. The hand I held out to the persecuted meant their salvation, and showed them the true nature of my country, which welcomed and championed them. The President's cable was about to collapse all these dreams.

I decided to talk things over with Negrín. I had had the good luck to make friends with President Juan Negrín, Minister Alvarez del Vayo, and some of the other members of the Spanish Republican government. Negrín was the most interesting. Spanish high politics had always seemed to me a bit parochial, provincial, shortsighted. Negrín was cosmopolitan, or European, anyway. He had studied in Leipzig and had university standing. In Paris he kept alive, with all dignity, the flimsy shadow that a government-in-exile is.

We talked. I explained the situation, the President's strange cable, which in fact made me look like an impostor, a charlatan offering a people in exile a pipe dream asylum. There were three possible ways out. The first, a revolting one, was simply to announce that the immigration of Spaniards to Chile had been called off. The second, a dramatic one, was to air publicly my objections, consider my mission ended, and put a bullet through my head. The third, a defiant one, was to fill the ship with immigrants, go aboard with them, and set out for Valparaíso without authorization, come what may.

Negrín leaned back in his armchair, puffing on his huge cigar. Then a melancholy smile crossed his lips and he said: "Can't you use the telephone?"

In those days, telephone communication between Europe and America was intolerably difficult, with hours of waiting. Between deafening noises and abrupt interruptions, I managed to hear the

Foreign Minister's voice far away. In a broken conversation, with phrases having to be repeated twenty times, without knowing whether we were getting through to each other, screaming our heads off and hearing only the ocean's trumpet blasts in reply, I thought I made it clear to Minister Ortega that I wasn't obeying the President's countermand. I also felt sure I had heard him ask me to wait until the following day.

Naturally, I spent a troubled night in my tiny Paris hotel. The next afternoon, I learned that the Foreign Minister had resigned that morning. He would not accept the withdrawal of my authority, either. The Cabinet tottered, and our fine President, after a temporary disruption due to pressures beyond his control, recovered his authority. I received a fresh cable with instructions to go ahead with the immigration.

We finally put them aboard the *Winnipeg*. Husbands and wives, parents and children who had been separated for a long time and were coming from one or the other end of Europe or Africa were reunited at the embarkation point. The waiting crowd surged forward as each train came in. Rushing up and down, weeping and shouting, they would recognize their dear ones among those putting their heads out the windows in clusters. Everyone eventually got aboard ship. There were fishermen, peasants, laborers, intellectuals, a cross section of strength, heroism, and hard work. My poetry, in its struggle, had succeeded in finding them a country. And I was filled with pride.

I bought a newspaper. I was strolling down a street in Villennes-sur-Seine. I was passing by the ancient castle whose ruins, scarlet with vines, lifted small slate towers skyward. That ancient castle where Ronsard and the Pléiade poets met centuries ago captured my imagination with its stone and marble, its hendecasyllables set down in ancient gold characters. I opened the newspaper. The Second World War had broken out that day. The newspaper which my hands dropped in that old, lost village said so in bold characters in smudgy black ink.

Everyone had been expecting it. Hitler had been gobbling up territories, while English and French statesmen scurried with their umbrellas to offer him more cities, kingdoms, human beings.

A great smoke drift of confusion filled people's consciences. From my window in Paris I looked out on Les Invalides and I saw the first contingents leaving, youngsters who had not yet learned how to wear their soldier's uniforms but were marching straight into death's gaping mouth.

Their going was sad, and nothing could disguise that. It was like a war lost beforehand, something inexpressible. Chauvinist groups prowled the streets, hunting down progressive intellectuals. To them, the enemy was not Hitler's disciples, the Lavals, but the flower of French thought. At the Embassy, which had undergone a significant change, we received the great poet Louis Aragon. He spent four days there, writing day and night, while the hordes searched for him to take his life. In the Chilean Embassy he finished his novel *Passengers of Destiny*. The fifth day, he left for the front, in uniform. It was his second war against the Germans.

In those twilight days, I grew accustomed to the European lack of resolve, which does not permit continual revolutions or earthquakes yet allows the deadly poison of war to permeate the air we breathe and the bread we eat. In constant fear of bombings, the great metropolis blacked out every night, and this darkness shared by seven million people, a thick darkness in the heart of the city of light, still clings to my memory.

At the end of this era, I am alone once more in newly discovered lands, as if this whole long voyage had been a waste. I go into an agony, into a second solitude, just as in the throes of birth, in the alarming beginning, filled with the metaphysical terror from which the spring of my early poems flowed, in the new twilight my own creation has provoked. Where am I to go? Which way should I return, aim for, which way to silence or a breathing space? I turn the light and the darkness upside down and inside out, and I find nothing but the emptiness my hands built with such deadly care.

And yet what has always been closest to me, the most fundamental, the most extensive, the completely unexpected, would appear in my path for the first time now. I had thought hard about all the world, but not about man. Cruelly and painfully, I had probed man's heart; without a thought for mankind, I had seen cities, but empty cities; I had seen factories whose very presence was a tragedy, but I had not really seen the suffering under those roofs, on the streets, at every way station, in the cities and the countryside.

As the first bullets ripped into the guitars of Spain, when blood instead of music gushed out of them, my poetry stopped dead like a ghost in the streets of human anguish and a rush of roots and blood surged up through it. From then on, my road meets everyman's road. And suddenly I see that from the south of solitude I have moved to the north, which is the people, the people whose sword, whose handkerchief my humble poetry wants to be, to dry the sweat of its vast sorrows and give it a weapon in its struggle for bread.

Then space opens out, makes itself deep and permanent. We are now standing squarely on the earth. We want to take infinite possession of everything that exists. We are not looking for any mystery, we are the mystery. My poetry is becoming a material part of an atmosphere that extends infinitely, that runs under the sea and under the earth both, it begins to enter galleries of startling vegetation, to speak in broad daylight with the specters of the sun, to explore pits of minerals hidden deep in the secretive earth, to establish forgotten links between autumn and man. The air dims and at intervals thunderbolts of phosphorescence and terror light it up; a new structure that is far from the evident, from trite words, looms on the horizon; a new continent rises from the innermost substance of my poetry. I have spent years settling these lands, classifying this kingdom, touching its many mysterious shorelines, soothing its foam, going over its zoology and the length of its geography; in this I have spent dark, solitary, remote years.

Mexico, Blossoming and Thorny

My government sent me to Mexico. Oppressed to the breaking point by the memory of so many painful experiences and such chaos, in 1940 I came to the Anáhuac plateau, to breathe what Alfonso Reyes hailed as the most transparent region of the air.

Mexico with its prickly pear and its serpent; Mexico, blossoming and thorny, dry and lashed by hurricane winds, violent in outline and color, violent in eruption and creation, surrounded me with its magic and its extraordinary light.

I traveled through it for years, from market to market. Because Mexico is to be found in its markets. Not in the guttural songs of the movies or in the false image of the Mexican in sombrero, with moustache and pistol. Mexico is a land of crimson and phosphorescent turquoise shawls. Mexico is a land of earthen bowls and pitchers, and fruit lying open to a swarm of insects. Mexico is an infinite countryside of steel-blue century plants with yellow thorns.

The most beautiful markets in the world have all this to offer. Fruit and wool, clay and weaving looms, give evidence of the incredible skill of the fertile and timeless fingers of the Mexicans.

I drifted through Mexico, I roamed over all its coasts, along its steep coastlines set ablaze by uninterrupted flares of shimmering lightning. I came down from Topolobampo in Sinaloa, past names indigenous to this hemisphere, harsh names willed to Mexico by the gods, when men less cruel than those gods came to rule its lands. I traveled through all those mysterious and majestic syllables from the dawn of time. Sonora and Yucatán; Anáhuac, rising like a cold brazier that draws to itself the mixed aromas of the land, from Nayarit to Michoacán, from where you can make out smoke from the islet of Janitzio, and the odor of corn and maguey drifting up from Jalisco, and sulphur from the new volcano, Paricutín, blending in with the wet fragrance of fish from Lake Pátzcuaro. Mexico, the last of the magic countries, because of its age and its history, its music and its geography. Working my way like a tramp over those rocks forever scourged by blood, rocks crisscrossed by a wide ribbon of blood and moss, I felt mighty and ancient, worthy to walk among such timeless things. Abrupt valleys partitioned off by immense walls of rock; tall hills that looked as if cut level with a knife; immense tropical forests teeming with timber and serpents, birds and legends. In that vast land made habitable as far as the eye can see by man's struggle through the ages, in its huge spaces, I found that we, Chile and Mexico, are the two countries most unlike each other in all America. I have never been moved by the conventional niceties of protocol that lead the ambassador of Japan, looking at Chile's cherry trees, to find that we are alike; or the Englishman experiencing the fog along our coast, or the Argentine or German seeing our snow, to find that we are much like all other countries. I delight in the diversity of landscapes on this planet, the varied products of the earth in every latitude. I don't mean to detract in any way from Mexico, a place I love, by describing it as not even remotely resembling our ocean-washed and grain-rich land. I only hold up its differences so that our America may be seen on all its levels, its great heights, and its depths. And in America, perhaps on the whole planet, no country is more profoundly human than Mexico and its people. In its brilliant achievements, as well as its gigantic errors, one sees the same chain of grand generosity, deep-rooted vitality, inexhaustible history, and limitless growth.

We made a turnoff one day—into fishing villages whose nets are so diaphanous they look like huge butterflies returning to the waters to pick up the silver scales they are missing; through mining centers whose metal turns from hard ingot to resplendent geometric forms almost as soon as it is out of the depths; over roads where Catholic convents loom, thick and thorny like giant cactus plants; through markets where the rich colors and flavors of vegetables displayed like flowers make you dizzy—and crossing Mexico like this, we reached Yucatán, the submerged cradle of the oldest race in the world, the idolatrous Maya. There the earth has been shaken by history and by the germinating seed. Side by side with the century plant, the ruins steeped in human intelligence and sacrifices are still growing.

Having crossed the last roads, we come to the vast territory where the ancient peoples of Mexico left their embroidered history hidden away in the jungle. There we find a new water, the most mysterious water on earth. It is not sea, stream, river, or any of the waters we know. In Yucatán the water is all under the ground, which may crack open suddenly, producing enormous jungle pools whose sides, overgrown with tropical vegetation, leave open to view, down below, a very deep water, deep as the sky, and green. The Mayas discovered those fissures in the earth called *cenotes* and deified them with their strange rites. Like all religions, in the beginning theirs consecrated necessity and fertility, and the land's aridity was vanquished by those hidden waters, for which the earth had opened.

Then for thousands of years on the rims of the sacred pools, first the indigenous and then the invaders' religion increased the mystery of the waters. From the banks of the *cenote*, after nuptial ceremonies, hundreds of virgins decked with flowers and gold and laden with jewels were hurled into the whirling, bottomless waters. Garlands and golden crowns would float up from the depths to the surface, but the maidens stayed in the mud of the bottom, held fast by their gold chains.

Thousands of years later, only a tiny portion of the jewels has been recovered and they are in the display cases of Mexican and U.S. museums. I went into that wilderness, not in search of gold, but seeking the cries of the drowned maidens. In the shrieks of the birds I seemed to hear the hoarse anguish of the virgins; and in their swift flight, as they swept over the gloomy deeps of the timeless waters, I saw the yellow hands of the dead young girls.

Once I watched a dove light on a statue that stretches its bright stone hand over the eternal waters and the air. An eagle may have been after it. It did not belong in that place whose only birds—the roadrunner with its stammer, the quetzal with its fabulous plumes, the turquoise hummingbird, and the birds of prey—conquered the jungle for their rapine, for their splendor. The dove lighted on the statue's hand, like a white snowflake among tropical rocks. I gazed at her because she came from another world, from a measured and harmonious world, from a Pythagorean column or a Mediterranean round number. She had stopped on the edge of the darkness, she respected my silence, for I had become part of this original American, bloodstained, ancient world, and my eyes followed her flight until they lost her in the sky.

THE MEXICAN PAINTERS

Mexico's intellectual life was dominated by painting. Mexican painters covered the city with history and geography, with civil strife, with fierce controversies. José Clemente Orozco, lean, one-armed titan, has his place on an elevated peak, a sort of Goya in his phantasmagorical country. I talked to him often. The violence that haunted his work seemed alien to his personality. He had the gentleness of a potter who has lost his hand at the potter's wheel but feels he must go on creating worlds with his other hand. His soldiers and their women, his peasants gunned down by overseers, his sarcophagi with horrible crucified bodies, are immortal in our native American painting, bearing witness to our cruelty.

By this time Diego Rivera had done so much work, and so much squabbling with everyone, that this burly painter was a legend. Looking at him, it seemed strange to me that he didn't have scaly fishtails or cloven hoofs. Diego Rivera had always been a fabricator. In Paris, before the First World War, Ilya Ehrenburg had published a book about his exploits and hoaxes: *The Extraordinary Adventures of Julio Jurenito*. Thirty years later Diego Rivera was still a great master as painter and teller of tall stories. He used to recommend the eating of human flesh as a healthy diet much favored by the greatest gourmets. He gave out recipes for cooking people of all ages. At other times he went to great lengths theorizing on lesbian love, maintaining that it was the only normal relationship, as proved by the oldest historical remains found in excavations he himself had directed.

Sometimes he would ramble on for hours, working his hooded Indian eyes and telling me all about his Jewish background. At other times, forgetting the previous conversations, he swore to me that he was General Rommel's father, but this confidence must be kept very secret, as its disclosure could have grave international consequences. His extraordinarily persuasive tone and his serene way of delineating the minutest and most incredible details made him a marvelous charlatan whose charm can never be forgotten by anyone who knew him.

David Alfaro Siqueiros was in jail then. Someone had sent him on an armed raid of Trotsky's home. I met him in prison, and outside as well, because we used to go out with Commandant Pérez Rulfo, the warden, to have a drink somewhere where we wouldn't be noticed too much. We would return late at night and I would bid David goodbye with an embrace, and he would stay there behind bars.

On one of those trips back from the streets to the prison with Siqueiros, I met his brother, Jesús Siqueiros, a most unusual man. "Crafty," in the good sense of the word, comes closest to describing him. He glided alongside the walls without making a sound or any perceptible movement. Suddenly you noticed him right behind or beside you. He seldom spoke, and when he did speak, it was barely above a whisper. Which did not prevent him from hauling around, just as quietly, forty or fifty pistols in a small bag. It was just my luck to open the bag once, absentmindedly, and discover with a shock the arsenal of black, pearl, and silver handles.

It all meant nothing, because Jesús Siqueiros was as peace-loving as his brother, David, was tempestuous. Jesús was also a gifted artist and actor, a mime. Without moving his body or his hands, without letting out the slightest sound, acting only with his face, whose lines he changed at will, turning it into a series of masks, he gave vivid impressions of terror, anguish, joy, tenderness. He bore that pale, ghostly face through the labyrinth of his life, emerging, from time to time, with all those pistols that he never used.

Those volcanic painters kept the public in line. Sometimes they got into tremendous debates. During one of these, having run out of arguments, Diego Rivera and Siqueiros drew huge pistols and fired almost as one man, not at each other, but at the wings of the plaster-of-Paris angels on the theater's ceiling. When the heavy plaster wings started falling on the heads of the people in the audience, the theater emptied out and the discussion ended with a powerful smell of gunpowder in a deserted hall.

Rufino Tamayo was not living in Mexico at this time. Complex and passionate, as Mexican as the fruit or the woven goods in the markets, his paintings came to us from New York.

No parallel can be drawn between the painting of Diego Rivera and that of David Alfaro Siqueiros. Diego has a classicist's feeling for line; with that infinitely undulating line, a kind of historian's calligraphy, he gradually tied together Mexico's history and brought out in high relief its events, traditions, and tragedies. Siqueiros is the explosion of a volcanic temperament that combines an amazing technique and painstaking research.

During clandestine sorties from jail and conversations on every topic, Siqueiros and I planned his final deliverance. On a visa I personally affixed to his passport, he traveled to Chile with his wife, Angélica Arenales. The people of Mexico had built a school in the Chilean city of Chillán, which had been destroyed by earthquakes, and in that "Mexico School" Siqueiros painted one of his extraordinary murals. The government of Chile repaid me for that service to our nation's culture by suspending me from my consular duties for two months.

NAPOLEON UBICO

I decided to visit Guatemala and set out by car. We passed through the isthmus of Tehuantepec, Mexico's golden region, with its women dressed like butterflies and a scent of honey and sugar in the air. Next we went into the great forest of Chiapas. We would stop the car at night, intimidated by the noises, the jungle's telegraph messages. Here, there, and everywhere, thousands of cicadas transmitted a deafening sound. Enigmatic Mexico spread its green shadows over ancient structures, remote paintings, jewels and monuments, colossal heads, stone animals. All this lay about in the forest, the untold riches of fabulous Mexico. Across the border, on the highest ridges of Central America, the narrow Guatemalan road dazzled me with its lianas and mammoth vegetation; and later with its placid lakes, high up in the mountains, like eyes forgotten by wasteful gods; and finally with its pine forests and broad primordial rivers where manatees peered out of the water like human beings.

I stayed for a week with Miguel Angel Asturias, who had not yet become known for his successful novels. We realized we were born brothers and spent almost every day together. In the evening we would plan visits to faraway places on mountains shrouded in mist or to United Fruit's tropical ports.

Guatemalans did not have the right of free speech, and no one talked politics. The walls had ears and could turn you in. Sometimes we would stop the car on a high plateau and make sure nobody was lurking behind some tree, and we would discuss the situation avidly. The despot's name was Ubico and he had been running the country for a good many years. He was a corpulent man, with cold, cruel eyes. His word was law, and nothing in Guatemala was done without his explicit approval. I met one of his secretaries, now my friend, a revolutionary. For arguing back about something, some petty detail, he had been bound on the spot to a column in the presidential office and whipped mercilessly by Ubico himself.

The young poets asked me to give a poetry reading. They sent Ubico a telegram requesting permission. All my friends and many young students filled the auditorium. I was happy to read my poems, they seemed to open a tiny crack in the window of a vast prison. The chief of police sat conspicuously in the front row. Later I found out that four machine guns had been trained on me and the audience, ready to burst into action if the chief of police interrupted the reading by leaving his seat in a huff.

But nothing of the kind happened, the man stayed and listened to my poems to the end.

Later someone wanted to introduce me to the dictator, a man with a Napoleon complex. He liked to wear a lock of hair on his forehead, and had his photograph taken a number of times in Bonaparte's famous pose. I was told that it was dangerous to turn down the offer, but I preferred not to shake his hand and went back to Mexico as fast as I could.

ANTHOLOGY OF PISTOLS

Mexico in those days was more gun-toting than gunfighter. There was a cult of the revolver, a fetishism of the .45. Colts were whipped out at the drop of a pin. Parliamentary candidates and newspapers would start their "depistolization" campaigns, but would quickly realize that it was easier to pull a Mexican's tooth then wrest his beloved gun from him.

Once, a group of poets entertained me with an outing in a flower-laden boat. Fifteen or twenty bards met at Lake Xochimilco and took me on this ride, hemmed in by water and blossoms, over canals and through a maze of everglades used for flowery rides since the time of the Aztecs. Every inch of the boat is decorated with flowers, overflowing with marvelous patterns and colors. The hands of the Mexicans, like the hands of the Chinese, are incapable of creating anything ugly, whether they work in stone, silver, clay, or carnations.

Well, during the ride, after a good many tequilas, one of the poets insisted that, as a special honor of a different kind, I should fire into the sky his beautiful pistol, whose grip was decorated with silver and gold designs. The colleague nearest to him whipped out his own pistol and, carried away with enthusiasm, slapped aside the first man's weapon and invited me to do the shooting with his. Each of the other rhapsodists unsheathed his pistol on the instant, and a free-for-all ensued: they all raised their guns over my head, each insisting I choose his instead of one of the others. As the precarious panoply of pistols being waved in front of my nose or passed under my arms became more and more dangerous, it occurred to me to take a huge, typical sombrero and gather all the firearms into it, asking the battalion of poets for their guns in the name of poetry and peace. Everyone obeyed and I was able to confiscate the weapons and keep them safe in my house for several days. I am the only poet, I believe, in whose honor an anthology of pistols has been put together.

WHY NERUDA

The salt of the earth had gathered in Mexico: exiled writers of every nationality had rallied to the camp of Mexican freedom, while the war dragged on in Europe, with victory upon victory going to Hitler's forces, which already occupied France and Italy. Among those present were Anna Seghers and the Czech humorist Egon Erwin Kisch, who has since died. Kisch left some fascinating books and I greatly admired his wonderful talent, his child-like curiosity, and his dexterity at legerdemain. No sooner had he entered my house than he would pull an egg out of his ear or swallow, one by one, as many as seven coins, which this very fine, impoverished exile could well use for himself. We had known each other in Spain, and when he showed incessant curiosity about my reason for using the name Neruda, which I was not born with, I kidded him: "Great Kisch, you may have uncovered the secret of Colonel Redl"—the famous Austrian spy case of 1914—"but you will never clear up the mystery of my name."

And so it was. He died in Prague, having been accorded every honor his liberated country could give him, but this professional interloper was never able to find out why Neruda called himself Neruda. The answer was so simple and so lacking in glamour that I was careful not to give the secret away. When I was fourteen, my father was always at me about my literary endeavors. He didn't like the idea of having a son who was a poet. To cover up the publication of my first poems, I looked for a last name that would throw him completely off the scent. I took the Czech name from a magazine, without knowing it was the name of a great writer loved by a whole nation, the author of elegant ballads and narrative poems, whose monument stood in Prague's Mala Strana quarter. Many years later, the first thing I did when I got to Czechoslovakia was to place a flower at the foot of the bearded statue.

THE EVE OF PEARL HARBOR

Wenceslao Roces, from Salamanca, and Constancia de la Mora, a Republican as well as a relative of the Duke of Maura, and the author of the book *In Place of Splendor*, which was a bestseller in North America, and the poets León Felipe, Juan Rejano, Moreno Villa, Herrera Petere, and the painters Miguel Prieto and Rodríguez Luna used to come to my house. They were all Spaniards. Vittorio Vidali, the famed Commandant Carlos of the Fifth Regiment, and Mario Montagnana, Italian exiles, full of memories, amazing stories, and possessed of a culture always in flux. Jacques Soustelle and Gilbert Medioni were also there. They were Gaullist leaders, representatives of Free France. Mexico also swarmed with voluntary or forced exiles from Central America: Guatemalans, Salvadorians, Hondurans. All this gave it an international flavor, and sometimes my home, an old villa in the San Angel neighborhood, pulsated as if it were the heart of the world.

In connection with Soustelle, who was then a left-wing socialist and who years later, as political leader of the attempted rebel coup in Algiers, would cause President de Gaulle so much trouble, something happened to me that I must tell about. We were far into the year 1941. The Nazis had laid siege to Leningrad and were penetrating farther into Soviet territory. The foxy Japanese military leaders, committed to the Berlin–Rome–Tokyo axis, were in a spot: Germany might win the war, and they would be deprived of their share of the spoils. Various rumors were circulating around the globe. Zero hour, when the mighty Japanese forces would be unleashed in the East, loomed closer. Meanwhile, in Washington, a Japanese peace mission was curtsying and bowing to the United States government. There wasn't the slightest room for doubt that the Japanese would launch a surprise attack, for blitzkrieg was the bloody order of the day.

To make my story clear, I must mention that an old Nipponese steamship line linked Japan to Chile. I traveled on those ships more than once and I knew them very well. They called at our ports and their captains spent their time buying scrap iron and taking photographs. They touched shore at points along the coastline of Chile,

Peru, and Ecuador, going as far as the Mexican port of Manzanillo, where they pointed their bows toward Yokohama, across the Pacific.

Well, one day, while I was still Consul General of Chile in Mexico, I received a visit from seven Japanese who were in a rush to obtain a Chilean visa. They had come from San Francisco, Los Angeles, and other ports on the North American west coast. A certain uneasiness was written across their faces. They were dressed well and their papers were in order; they could have been engineers or business executives.

I asked them, of course, why they wanted to take the very first plane to Chile, having just arrived in Mexico. They replied that they intended to catch a Japanese ship in Tocopilla, a nitrate-shipping port in northern Chile. I countered that there was no need to travel to Chile, at the other end of the continent, for this, because that same Japanese line called at Manzanillo, which they could reach even on foot, if they wished, with time to spare.

They exchanged embarrassed glances and smiles, and talked among themselves in their own language. They consulted the secretary of the Japanese Embassy, who was with them. He decided to be open with me and said, "Look, colleague, this ship happens to have changed its itinerary and won't be coming to Manzanillo any more. And, therefore, these distinguished specialists must catch it at the Chilean port."

A confused vision flashed across my mind: this was something very important. I asked for their passports, photographs, for data about their work in the United States, etc., and told them to return the next day. They objected. They had to have the visas immediately and would be willing to pay any price. I was playing for time. I explained that I did not have the authority to issue visas on the spot, we would discuss it the next day.

I was left to myself.

Little by little, the puzzle unraveled in my mind. Why the hasty flight from North America and the pressing need for the visas? And why was the Japanese ship changing its route for the first time in thirty years? What could it mean?

Then it dawned on me. Of course, this was an important, well-informed group, Japanese spies beating a hasty retreat from the United States because something critical was about to happen. And that could be nothing but Japan's entry into the war. The Japanese in my story were in on the secret.

The conclusion I had reached left me in an extremely nervous state. What could I do? I did not know the English or the North American representatives of the Allied nations in Mexico. I was in direct contact only with those officially accredited as General de Gaulle's delegates, who had access to the Mexican government. I got in touch with them at once and explained the situation. We had at hand the names of the Japanese and vital information about them. Should the French decide to take steps, the Japanese would be trapped. I presented my arguments eagerly at first, and then impatiently, before the indifferent Gaullists. "Young diplomats," I told them, "here is your chance to cover yourselves with glory. Find out the secret of these Japanese spies. As for me, I won't give them the visa. But you have to make a quick decision."

This fast and loose game lasted two days longer. Soustelle took no interest in the matter. They would do nothing, and I, a Chilean consul, could take it no further. Since I refused to grant them a visa, the Japanese immediately obtained diplomatic passports, went to the Chilean Embassy, and made it in time to take the ship in Tocopilla. One week later, the world would wake up to the news of the bombing of Pearl Harbor.

MYSELF AS MALACOLOGIST

Years ago a newspaper in Chile printed a story about my good friend the celebrated Professor Julian Huxley, who arrived in Santiago and asked for me at the airport. "Neruda the poet?" the newsmen questioned him.

"No. I don't know any poet by the name of Neruda. I want to speak to Neruda the malacologist."

That Greek word means "specialist in mollusks."

I was delighted by this story, which was intended to nettle me. It could not possibly be true, because Huxley and I had known each other for years and he is a sharp fellow, much more quick-witted and genuine than his well-known brother, Aldous.

In Mexico I roamed the beaches, dived into the clear, temperate waters, and collected magnificent seashells. Later, in Cuba and elsewhere, I swapped and bought, received as gifts and filched (there's no such thing as an honest collector), gradually swelling my sea treasure until it filled room after room in my house.

I owned the rarest specimens from the China Sea and the Philippines, from Japan and the Baltic; Antarctic conches and *Polymitas* from Cuba; painter shells dressed in red and saffron, blue and purple like Caribbean dancers. One of the few specimens I did not have, I admit, was a land snail from Brazil's Mato Grosso. I saw one once but couldn't buy it, and I was not able to travel into the jungle to get one. It was all green, as beautiful as a new emerald.

I became such an avid collector that I visited the most remote seas. Friends also began to hunt for conches, to become snail-crazed.

When I had gathered together fifteen thousand shells, they filled every last shelf and began to spill from tables and chairs. Books on conchology or malacology—call it what you will—overflowed my library. So one day I took my whole collection and carried it to the university in huge crates, making my first donation to my alma mater. It was a famous collection by then. Like any good South American institution, my university received it with praises and panegyrics, and buried it away in a basement. No one has seen it since.

ARAUCANÍA

While I was far away, at my post on the islands of the remote archipelago, the sea hummed to me and the silent world was filled with things that spoke to my solitude. But cold and hot wars corrupted the consular service and eventually made each consul an automaton, without personality, unable to make any decisions for himself, and his work became suspiciously close to that of the police. The Ministry insisted on my checking the ethnic origins of immigrants; Africans, Asians, and Jews could not enter my country.

This stupidity reached such extremes that I, too, became its victim when I started a handsome magazine (without a subsidy from the national treasury) and named it *Araucanía*. On the cover I used the picture of a lovely Araucanian wearing a toothy smile. That's all the Foreign Minister needed to give me a severe dressing down for what he considered something debasing, even though Don Pedro Aguirre Cerda, whose pleasant and noble face had all the features of our mixed race, was President of the Republic.

It is common knowledge that the Araucanians were crushed and, finally, forgotten or conquered. What's more, history is written by the conquerors or by those who reap the spoils of victory. There are few races worthier than the Araucanian. Someday we'll see Araucanian universities, books printed in Araucanian, and we'll realize how much we have lost with their clarity, their purity and volcanic energy.

The absurd "racial" pretensions of some South American countries, which are themselves the results of many national origins and mixed breeding, are a colonialist vice. They want to set up a dais where a handful of snobs, scrupulously white or light-skinned, can appear in society, posturing in front of pure Aryans or pretentious tourists. Fortunately, all this is becoming a thing of the past and the UN is filling up with black and Mongolian representatives; in short, as the sap of intelligence rises, the foliage of all the races is gradually displaying all the colors of its leaves.

I ended by getting fed up and one day I resigned from my career as Consul General forever.

MAGIC AND MYSTERY

Furthermore, I realized that the Mexican world—repressed, violent, and nationalistic, cloaked in its pre-Columbian civility—would get along without my presence or approval. When I decided to return to my country, I understood less about Mexican life than when I came to Mexico. Arts and letters thrived in rival circles, but God help any outsider who sided with or against any individual or group: everyone came down on him.

When I was almost ready to leave, I was honored with a monstrous public demonstration: a dinner for almost three thousand persons, not counting hundreds who couldn't even get in. Several presidents sent congratulations. Still, Mexico is the touchstone of America, and it was not an accident that the solar calendar of ancient America, the node of irradiation, wisdom, and mystery, was carved there.

Everything could happen, everything did happen there. The only opposition newspaper was subsidized by the government. It was the most dictatorial democracy anyone can imagine.

I recall a tragic event that left me badly shaken. A strike was dragging on in a factory, with no solution in sight. The strikers' wives got together and agreed to try to see the President and tell him perhaps of their privations and their distress. Of course, they had no weapons. Along the way they got some flowers to present to the head of state and his wife. A guard halted the women as they were entering the palace, and they were allowed no farther. The President would not receive them; they would have to go to the appropriate government bureau. Anyway, they must vacate the premises. It was an ultimatum.

The women pleaded their cause. They wouldn't be any trouble. They just wanted to deliver the flowers to the President and ask if he could do something to settle the strike soon. Their children had no food; they couldn't go on like that. The officer of the guard refused to relay any message. And the women would not go.

Then a volley of shots from the direction of the palace guard splintered the air. Six or seven women were killed on the spot, and many others wounded.

A hasty funeral took place on the following day. I had believed an immense procession would follow the caskets of the assassinated women, but only a few people showed up. Oh, yes, the union leader made a speech. He was known as a prominent revolutionary. His speech at the cemetery was in an irreproachable style. I read the entire text the next day in the newspapers. It did not contain a single line of protest, not a single angry word or any demand that those responsible for such an atrocity be put on trial. Two weeks later, no one even spoke of the massacre. And I have never seen it mentioned in writing by anyone.

The President was an Aztec ruler, a thousand times more untouchable than England's royal family. No newspaper could criticize the exalted functionary, either in jest or seriously, without suffering immediate consequences.

Mexican dramas are so clothed in the picturesque that one comes away astounded by all the allegory—allegory that is every day more remote from the essential throb of life, the blood-spattered skeleton. The philosophers have become euphuistic and launch into existentialist dissertations that seem foolish under a volcano. Civilian action is intermittent and difficult. Submission takes on varying aspects that stratify around the throne.

But every kind of magic is always appearing and reappearing in Mexico: from the volcano born before a peasant's eyes in his humble orchard, while he was planting beans, to the wild search for the skeleton of Cortés, who, rumor has it, rests in Mexican soil with his gold helmet protecting the conquistador's skull these many centuries, and the no less intense hunt for the remains of the Aztec emperor Cuauhtémoc. Lost four centuries ago, they keep showing up here and there, safeguarded by secretive Indians, only to sink back time and again into unfathomable darkness.

Mexico lives on in me like a small stray eagle circulating through my veins. Only death will fold its wings over my sleeping soldier's heart.

8

My Country in Darkness

MACCHU PICCHU

The Ministry lost no time in accepting the voluntary end to my career.

My diplomatic suicide gave me the infinite pleasure of being able to return to Chile. I believe a man should live in his own country and I think the deracination of human beings leads to frustration, in one way or another obstructing the light of the soul. I can live only in my own country. I cannot live without having my feet and my hands on it and my ear against it, without feeling the movement of its waters and its shadows, without feeling my roots reach down into its soil for maternal nourishment.

But, before getting back to Chile, I made another discovery that was to add a new layer of growth to my poetry.

I stopped in Peru and made a trip to the ruins of Macchu Picchu. There was no highway then and we rode up on horseback. At the top I saw the ancient stone structures hedged in by the tall peaks of the verdant Andes. Torrents hurtled down from the citadel, eaten away and weathered by the passage of the centuries. White fog drifted up in masses from the Willkamayu River. I felt infinitely small in the center of that navel of rocks, the navel of a deserted world, proud, towering high, to which I somehow belonged. I felt that my own hands had labored there at some remote point in time, digging furrows, polishing the rocks.

I felt Chilean, Peruvian, American. On those difficult heights, among those glorious, scattered ruins, I had found the principles of faith I needed to continue my poetry.

My poem *Alturas de Macchu Picchu* was born there.

THE NITRATE PAMPA

At the end of 1943 I arrived in Santiago once more. I settled down in a house I bought on the installment plan. I piled all my books into this house surrounded by huge trees, and took up the hard life again.

Once more I sought my country's beauty, the loveliness of its women, nature's overpowering splendor, the work of my fellows, the intelligence of my countrymen. The country had not changed. Fields and sleeping villages, heartbreaking poverty in the mining regions, elegant people crowding into the country clubs. I had to make a decision.

My decision brought me harassments as well as moments of glory. What poet could have regretted that?

Curzio Malaparte, who interviewed me some years after what I am about to relate, stated it well in his article: "I am not a Communist, but if I were a Chilean poet, I would be one, like Pablo Neruda. You have to take sides here, with the Cadillacs or with people who have no schooling or shoes."

These people without schooling or shoes elected me senator on March 4, 1945. I shall always cherish with pride the fact that thousands of people from Chile's most inhospitable region, the great mining region of copper and nitrate, gave me their vote.

Walking over the pampa was laborious and rough. It hasn't rained for half a century there, and the desert has done its work on the faces of the miners. They are men with scorched features; their solitude and the neglect they are consigned to have been fixed in the dark intensity of their eyes. Going from the desert up to the mountains, entering any needy home, getting to know the inhuman labor these people do, and feeling that the hopes of isolated and sunken men have been entrusted to you, is not a light responsibility. But my poetry opened the way for communication, making it possible for me to walk and move among them and be accepted as a lifelong brother by my countrymen, who led such a hard life.

I don't remember whether it was in Paris or Prague that I was seized by a small doubt about the encyclopedic knowledge of my friends there. Most of them were writers, and the rest, students.

"We are talking a lot about Chile," I said to them, "and it's probably because I am Chilean. But do any of you know anything about my country, which is so far away? For example, what vehicle do we use for locomotion? Elephant, car, train, airplane, bicycle, camel, or sleigh?"

Most of them replied earnestly: elephant.

There are no elephants or camels in Chile. But I can see how puzzling a country can be that starts at the frozen South Pole and stretches upward to salt mines and deserts where it hasn't rained for eons. As senator-elect of the inhabitants of that wilderness, as representative of innumerable nitrate and copper workers who had never worn a shirt collar or a tie, I had to travel those deserts for many years.

Coming into those lowlands, facing those stretches of sand, is like visiting the moon. This region that looks like an empty planet holds my country's great wealth, but the white fertilizer and the red mineral have to be extracted from the arid earth and the mountains of rock. There are few places in the world where life is so harsh and offers so little to live for. It takes untold sacrifices to transport water, to nurse a plant that yields even the humblest flower, to raise a dog, a rabbit, a pig.

I come from the other end of the Republic. I was born in green country with huge, thickly wooded forests. I had a childhood filled with rain and snow. The mere act of facing that lunar desert was a turning point in my life. Representing those men in parliament—their isolation, their titanic land—was also a difficult task. The naked earth, without a single plant, without a drop of water, is an immense, elusive enigma. In the forests, alongside rivers, everything speaks to man. The desert, on the other hand, is uncommunicative. I couldn't understand its language: that is, its silence.

Over a period of many years the nitrate corporations established veritable principalities, dominions, or empires on the pampas. The English, the Germans, invaders of every kind, took over the productive regions and gave them company names. They imposed their own currency; they prevented any kind of assembly by the people; they banned political parties and the people's press. You could not enter the premises without special permission, which, of course, very few were able to obtain.

One afternoon I spoke to the laborers in a machine shop in the offices of the María Elena potassium nitrate mine. The floor of the huge workshop was, as always, slushy with water, oil, and acids. The union leaders and I walked on a plank that kept us off that mire. "These planks," I was told, "cost us fifteen strikes in a row, eight years of petitioning, and seven dead."

The deaths occurred when the company's private police carried off seven leaders during a strike. The guards rode horses, while the workers, bound with ropes, followed on foot over the lonely stretches of sand. It took only a few shots to murder them. Their bodies were left lying in the desert sun and cold, until they were picked up and buried by their fellow workers.

Years before that, things were much worse. In 1906, for example, the strikers went from the nitrate-mine offices down to the city of Iquique to take their demands directly to the government. Exhausted by the journey, several thousand men gathered in the town square, in front of the school, to rest. They were going to see the governor in the morning, to lay their petitions before him. But they never had the chance. Troops led by a colonel surrounded the square at daybreak and began shooting and killing, without a word. More than six thousand men fell in that massacre.

In 1945, things were better, but sometimes it seemed to me that those days when people were exterminated were coming back. Once, for instance, I was denied the right to address a gathering of workers in a union hall. I called them out of the hall and in the middle of the desert I started to explain the situation to them, to consider the possible ways out of the conflict. There were about two hundred of us. Suddenly I heard the purr of motors and saw an army tank approach to within four or five meters of where I was speaking. The turret's lid lifted and a machine gun pushed up through the opening, aimed right at me. Then, alongside the weapon, an officer stood up straight, nattily dressed but dead serious, and proceeded to stare at me while I went on with my talk. That's all it came to.

The faith of the huge working class, many of them illiterate, in the Communists was born with Luis Emilio Recabarren, who began his struggles in that desert region. From a simple worker-agitator, an old-time anarchist, Recabarren became a phantasmagoric and colossal presence. He filled the country with unions and federations. Eventually he published more than fifteen newspapers devoted exclusively to the defense of the new organizations he had created. All this without having a cent. The money was raised thanks to the new conscience awakening among the workers.

I had a chance to see Recabarren printing presses that had been through heroic service and were still doing the job forty years later. Some of those presses had been smashed up by the police and had later been carefully repaired. Huge scars could be detected under the lovingly soldered seams that had set them in motion again.

During those long tours I grew accustomed to staying in the humble houses, shacks, or huts of the men of the desert. There was almost always a group with banners waiting for me at the company gates. Then I would be shown the place where I was to be lodged. All day long, men and women filed through my quarters with complaints about working conditions, or with personal problems. Sometimes their grievances were the kind a foreigner might consider comical, capricious, or even grotesque. For instance, the shortage of tea could spark off a strike that would have serious consequences. Are typically British needs like that conceivable in such a desolate region? In fact, the Chilean people can't live without having tea several times a day. Some of the barefoot workers who asked me unhappily why the exotic but indispensable beverage was so scarce argued by way of apology: "If we don't drink it, we get a terrible headache."

Those men locked inside walls of silence, in the loneliest region and under the loneliest sky, had a healthy political curiosity. They wanted to know what was going on in Yugoslavia, in China. They were deeply interested in problems and changes in the socialist countries, the outcome of the big Italian strikes, rumors of war, revolutions breaking out in far-off lands.

At hundreds of rallies, in places remote from one another, I heard the same request: to read my poems. They were often asked for by title. Of course, I never knew if all these people understood some or many of my poems, or if they didn't. It was difficult to tell in that atmosphere of absolute silence, of reverence, in which they listened to me. But what does it matter? There are quite a few poems by Hölderlin and Mallarmé that I, who am one of the most literate of fools, have never been able to fathom. And I have read them, I confess, with the same great reverence.

Sometimes dinner took on a more festive air and there was stewed chicken, *rara avis* on the pampas. The fare that most often found its way to our plates was something I had a hard time sinking my teeth into: fricassee of guinea pig. Conditions had turned this small creature, born to die in laboratories, into a popular dish.

In the many houses where I stayed, the bed I invariably was assigned had two monastic features: snow-white sheets, so stiff they could have stood up by themselves; and a hardness comparable to the desert floor's. These people did not know what a mattress was, only some bare boards as unyielding as they were flat.

Still and all, I slept the sleep of the blessed. I had no trouble dropping off into the deep sleep I shared with a legion of comrades. The day was always dry and incandescent like a live coal, but night spread its coolness out on the desert under a crown exquisitely studded with stars.

My poetry and my life have advanced like an American river, a torrent of Chilean water born in the hidden heart of the southern mountains, endlessly steering the flow of its currents toward the sea. My poetry rejected nothing it could carry along in its course; it accepted passion, unraveled mystery, and worked its way into the hearts of the people.

I had to suffer and struggle, to love and sing; I drew my worldly share of triumphs and defeats, I tasted bread and blood. What more can a poet want? And all the choices, tears or kisses, loneliness or the fraternity of man, survive in my poetry and are an essential part of it, because I have lived for my poetry and my poetry has nourished everything I have striven for. And if I have received many awards, awards fleeting as butterflies, fragile as pollen, I have attained a greater prize, one that some people may deride but not many can attain. I have gone through a difficult apprenticeship and a long search, and also through the labyrinths of the written word, to become the poet of my people. That is my reward, not the books and the poems that have been translated, or the books written to explicate or to dissect my words. My reward is the momentous occasion when, from the depths of the Lota coal mine, a man came up out of the tunnel into the full sunlight on the fiery nitrate field, as if rising out of hell, his face disfigured by his terrible work, his eyes inflamed by the dust, and stretching his rough hand out to me, a hand whose calluses and lines trace the map of the pampas, he said to me, his eyes shining: "I have known you for a long time, my brother." That is the laurel crown for my poetry, that opening in the bleak pampa from which a worker emerges who has been told often by the wind and the night and the stars of Chile: "You're not alone; there's a poet whose thoughts are with you in your suffering."

I became a member of Chile's Communist Party on July 15, 1945.

GONZÁLEZ VIDELA

The bitter wrongs my comrades and I sought to bring before the senate had a tough time reaching the senate floor. The comfortable parliamentary room seemed padded to keep out the cries of the wretched masses. My colleagues in the opposition were true experts in the art of eloquent patriotic address, and I felt smothered under the tapestry of bogus silks they rolled out.

Our hopes rose suddenly; one of the presidential candidates, González Videla, swore to see that justice was carried out, and his lively eloquence won him great popularity. I was made his campaign manager and carried the good news to all parts of the country.

The people elected him President by a landslide.

But, in our creole America, presidents often go through an extraordinary metamorphosis. In the instance I am speaking of, the new chief of state quickly changed his friends, he married his family into the "aristocracy," and was gradually transformed from a mere demagogue into a potentate.

But González Videla does not fit the pattern of the typical South American dictator. Bolivia's Melgarejo and General López of Venezuela have recognizable grass roots. These men show some glimmer of greatness and seem to be driven by a compulsion both desolate and implacable. At least, they were leaders who braved battles and bullets. González Videla, however, was the product of smoke-filled backroom politics, an irresponsible and frivolous clown, a weakling who put on a tough front.

In the fauna of our America, the great dictators have been giant saurians, survivors of a colossal feudalism in prehistoric lands. The Chilean Judas was just an amateur tyrant and on the saurian scale would never be anything but a poisonous lizard. Yet he did enough damage to seriously scar Chile, setting the country back hundreds of years. Chileans looked at one another in embarrassment, not quite understanding how it had all happened.

The man was an equilibrist, an acrobat who played to all sides. He managed to work his way into a spectacular left-wing role, and in this comedy of lies was the undisputed champion. No one questions that. In a country where politicians tend to be or seemingly are overly serious, people welcomed the advent of frivolity, and when this conga dancer changed course in midstream, it was much too late: the prisons were crammed full of political victims, and concentration camps were even set up, such as the one at Pisagua. A police state was then established, as a national novelty. The only course left open was to bide one's time and go underground to fight for the return of decency.

Many of González Videla's friends, persons who had stuck by him right to the end of his electoral campaign, were hustled off to prisons on the high cordillera or in the desert, because they could not accept his metamorphosis. In fact, the upper class around him, with its economic power, had once more swallowed our country's government, as it had done so often before. This time, however, the digestion was not pleasant and Chile went through a malaise that wavered between shocked daze and agony.

With the protection of the United States, the President our votes had elected turned into a vile, bloodthirsty vampire. His conscience surely made him lose sleep, though he set up, near the presidential palace, private garçonnières and whorehouses, complete with carpets and mirrors, for his carnal pleasures. The contemptible creature had an insignificant but twisted mind. The same evening he launched his great anti-Communist repression, he invited two or three workers' leaders to dinner. When the meal was over, he went down the palace stairs with them and embraced them, wiping away a few tears as he said, "I am weeping because I've ordered your detention. You'll be arrested as you go out the door, and I don't know if I'll ever see you again."

PORTRAIT OF AN ARRIVISTE

Gabriela Mistral reproached me in Naples for González Videla's election as President of the Republic of Chile. In her singsongy little voice—not, for all that, less implacable—the poetess rubbed it in my face, as if it had been my doing, as if the Communists and I bore the blame. Blame for what? For not knowing the future?

Gabriela, why didn't you speak up at the time? These bits of advice always come too late, and they're no better than the stick you use to beat a dead mule. No matter how political we Communists may seem, we don't have the power of divination.

As she listened to me with those big serene eyes that everything sank into, like those stones one sometimes hurls into the water and that the water swallows while remaining unmoved, I traced out certain of the events for Gabriela. In the timid, tepid atmosphere of

Social-Democratic Chile, González Videla was the one person who seemed brave and fit for battle. He was elected president of the anti-Francoists, the anti-Peronists, the Jews who wanted a nation of their own, the associations chanting the slogans of the popular struggle at the time. No one else from the ranks of his party showed the least bit of interest in the people's causes, in agrarian reform, in concessions to the workers, in the struggle against the North American empire. Naturally, once in power, he put the brakes on the anti-Francoists and the working-class leaders, betrayed the Zionists he'd presided over, closed the unions' newspapers, broke the miners' strikes with blood and fire. But this was the culmination of a slower process. All this has come to light now that the State Department has published the reports of Claude Bowers, the U.S. ambassador at the time.

This innocent man was apprised of all that González Videla was going to do, and well before the fact. He always knew what would happen, and he put it all into his reports: what the traitor would betray, what the seller would sell, how much the renegade was on the take for.

I was working in Paris when I met him. My job was to gather and ship off to Chile the defeated Spanish Republicans. A new ambassador showed up one day to the closet they'd assigned me at the Chilean Embassy: the very same man who would become President. I didn't know him.

He was short and dressed with ostentatious vulgarity. He concealed his thoughts by showing off his two rows of newly purchased large teeth.

When he introduced himself, he represented an ideal suited to my own sentiments, told me he wanted to enter the Sorbonne, that he wanted to study, that he knew little, that his education had been hurried and incomplete. He was going to be that strange specimen: an ambassador-student.

"Magnificent," I responded.

He never made it into the Sorbonne, only to the cocktail parties.

A BODY DIVIDED

My speeches became virulent and the senate was always filled to listen to me. My ouster was soon demanded and obtained, and the police were given orders to arrest me. But we poets have in us a large proportion of fire and smoke.

The smoke went into the writing. The historical parallel to all that was happening to me was dramatically close to our ancient American themes. In that year of hiding and danger, I finished my most important book, *Canto general*.

I moved from house to house, every day. Doors opened to receive me everywhere. It was always people I didn't know, who had somehow expressed their wish to put me up for a few days. They wanted to offer me asylum even if only for a few hours, or for weeks. I passed through fields, ports, cities, camps, and was in the homes of peasants, engineers, lawyers, seamen, doctors, miners.

There's an old theme, a "body divided," that recurs in the folk poetry of all our countries. The popular singer imagines his feet in one place, his kidneys somewhere else, and goes on to describe his whole body, which he has left behind, scattered in countrysides and cities. That's how I felt in those days.

Among the heartwarming places where I stayed, I recall a two-room house hidden away on one of the poorer hills of Valparaíso. I had to keep to a part of one room, and a small section of window from which I could observe the life of the port. From that humble watchtower, my eyes took in only a fragment of the street. At night I would see people bustling past. It was a poor area, and the narrow street, a hundred meters below my window, monopolized all the light in the neighborhood. Dumpy little stores and junk shops lined it.

Trapped as I was in my corner, my curiosity knew no bounds. Private speculations and conjectures. Sometimes I would find myself in a quandary. Why, for example, would passers-by, whether indifferent or in a hurry, always pause at one store? What fascinating merchandise was displayed in that window? Whole families would stop for long minutes, with children on their shoulders. I couldn't see the rapt look on their faces as they gazed into the magic window, but I could imagine it.

Six months later I learned that it was just a shoe-store window. Shoes are man's greatest interest, I concluded. I vowed to study, investigate, and put this matter down in writing. I have never had the time to carry out this intention, this vow made in such odd circumstances. Yet quite a few shoes have gone into my poetry. They tap their way through many of my lines, although I never set out deliberately to put shoes in my poems.

Visitors would suddenly drop in at the house and carry on long conversations; it never entered their minds that close by, separated by a flimsy partition of cardboard and old newspaper, was a poet, with God knows how many professional man-hunters on his trail.

Saturday afternoons, and Sunday mornings as well, the sweetheart of one of the girls in the family would come to the house. He was not in on the secret. He was a young worker, the girl's heart was his, but he hadn't won their full confidence yet. From my peephole I would watch him get off the bicycle he used on his egg route in the huge working-class neighborhood. Not long after, I would hear him enter the house humming a tune. He was a threat to my tranquility. I call him a threat because he insisted on courting the girl a few centimeters from my ear. She would invite him to go make platonic love in some park or at the movies, but he resisted heroically. And I cursed under my breath at the innocent egg man for being such a stay-at-home.

The rest of the people in the house were in on the secret: the widowed mother, the two delightful daughters, and the sons, who were seamen. They unloaded bananas in the harbor and were sometimes fit to be tied because no ship would hire them. From them I heard that an old ship was being scrapped. With me directing the operation from my hidden corner, they removed the lovely figure from the ship's prow and hid it in a storehouse down in the port. I got to know her years later, when my escape and exile were a thing of the past. As I write these memoirs here beside the sea, that handsome woman carved in wood, who has a Greek face like all the figureheads on old sailing ships, gazes at me with her wistful beauty.

The plan was to ship me out with one of the boys, in his cabin, and put me ashore with the bananas when we reached Guayaquil. The seaman explained to me that when the ship dropped anchor at this port in Ecuador I was to appear on deck suddenly, like a well-dressed passenger, smoking a cigar, although I have never been able to smoke one. Since I was on the verge of departure, the family decided it was time I had the right kind of suit made—elegant and tropical—and I was duly fitted.

My suit was ready in less than no time. I've never had so much fun as I had when I received it. The women of the house took their notions of style from a celebrated film of the day: *Gone with the Wind*. What the boys, on the other hand, considered the last word in elegance was something they had picked up from the dance halls of Harlem and the bars and cheap dance joints of the Caribbean world. The double-breasted jacket was fitted with a belt and came down to my knees. The trousers hugged me at the ankles.

I put away this picturesque attire, styled by such kindly people, and never had the opportunity to wear it. I never came out of hiding on any ship, and I never went ashore with the bananas in Guayaquil, dressed like a phony Clark Gable. On the contrary, I chose the cold way out. I departed for Chile's far south, the far south of the Americas, intending to cross the mountains.

A ROAD IN THE JUNGLE

Ricardo Fonseca had been the secretary general of my party until this time. He was a strong-minded man with a smile, a southerner like me, from the cold climate of Carahue. My life underground, my hideouts, my clandestine excursions, the publication of my pamphlets had been entrusted to Fonseca; most important of all, he had carefully kept secret the places where I had stopped. During my year and a half in hiding, the only one who always knew where I would eat or sleep each night was my young and radiant leader and secretary general, Ricardo Fonseca. But his health gradually wasted away until the only thing remaining was the green flame that peered out of his eyes; his smile dimmed gradually, and one day our good comrade left us forever.

While the party was underground, a new leader was elected, a husky man, a longshoreman from Valparaíso, Galo González, a complex man with a deceptive and deadly earnest face. I should mention that there was never a personality cult in our party, although it was an old organization that had survived all the proverbial ideological weaknesses. The Chilean conscience, the conscience of a people that has accomplished everything with its own hands, always rose above these. We have had very few caudillos in the history of Chile, and our party mirrored this.

Yet, aided by the banning of the party, the pyramidal politics of the Stalin era also produced a somewhat rarefied atmosphere in Chile. Galo González could not stay in touch with the bulk of the party. The persecution was being stepped up. There were thousands of prisoners and there was a special concentration camp on Pisagua's desert coast. Galo González led an outlaw's life filled with revolutionary activity, but the lack of contact between the leaders and the general body of the party became more and more pronounced. He was a great man, a wise man of the people, and a courageous fighter.

Instructions for the next step in my flight reached him and were carried out to the letter this time. I was to be taken somewhere a thousand kilometers from the capital and would go on from there across the cordillera on horseback. Argentine comrades would be waiting for me along the way.

We left at sundown in the safety of an automobile we were lucky enough to get. My friend Dr. Raúl Bulnes, then a doctor in the mounted police, took me in his automobile, which was above suspicion, to the outskirts of Santiago, where the party's organization took over. In another car, specially equipped for a long trip, an old party friend, the chauffeur Escobar, was waiting for me.

We stayed on the road day and night. In the daytime, I bundled up in blankets to increase the effect of my disguise of beard and glasses, especially when we went through towns and cities, or when we stopped for gas.

I passed through Temuco at noon. I didn't stop anywhere; no one recognized me. As luck would have it, my old Temuco was my exit route. We crossed the bridge and the village of Padre Las Casas. We halted a fair distance from the city and sat down on a rock to have a bite to eat. There was a creek far down the slope, and the sound of its waters came up to me. It was my childhood saying goodbye. I grew up in this town, my poetry was born between the hill and the river, it took its voice from the rain, and like the timber, it steeped itself in the forests. And now, on the road to freedom, I was pausing for a moment near Temuco and could hear the voice of the water that had taught me to sing.

We set out again. Only once did we go through a moment of anxiety. From the middle of the highway, a determined-looking carabinero officer flagged down our car. I was struck dumb, but the scare turned out to be groundless. The officer asked us to drive him a hundred kilometers along the road. He sat beside the driver, Comrade Escobar, and carried on a friendly chat with him. I made believe I was sleeping, so as not to speak. Even the stones of Chile knew my poet's voice.

Without any untoward incidents, we arrived at our destination, a timber estate that looked uninhabited. Water lapped at it on all sides.

First you crossed vast Lake Ranco to land among thickets and giant trees. From there you proceeded on horseback for a stretch, until you came to a place where you caught another boat, on Lake Maihue this time. One could barely make out the owner's house, camouflaged by the hilly countryside, by the giant vegetation, by nature's unfathomable hum. I've heard people say that Chile is the last corner of the world. That place overgrown with jungle, hemmed in by snow and lakes, was indeed one of the last habitable spots on this planet.

The house in which I was given a room was makeshift, like everything in the area. A cast iron stove, filled with firewood that looked as if it had just been cut from the forest, burned day and night. Heavy rain from the south pelted the windows without respite, as if it were fighting to break into the house. The rain dominated the sunless forest, the lakes, the volcanoes, the night, and turned savagely on that human shelter for obeying different laws and not accepting its victory.

I barely knew Jorge Bellet, the friend who was waiting for me. An ex-flier, a cross between a practical man and a prospector, in boots and a short heavy combat jacket, he had the air of a born leader, a military man's cocky attitude that somehow fitted into the surroundings, although the colossal trees of the forest were the only troops in formation there.

The lady of the house was a very frail, whining woman afflicted with neurosis. The humdrum solitude of the place, the everlasting rain, the cold all seemed a personal affront to her. She spent a good part of the day whimpering, yet the house was run like clockwork and the food was wholesome, fresh from the forest and the water.

Bellet managed the lumber company, which specialized in railroad ties for Sweden and Denmark. The saws cutting the huge logs ground out their shrill lament all day long. First you heard the deep underground thud of the felled tree. Every five or ten minutes the ground shuddered like a drum in the dark at the hard impact of crashing rauli, mañiu, and larch trees, giant works of nature, seeded there by the wind a thousand years before. Then the saw sectioning the bodies of these giants struck up its whine. The metallic sound of the saw, grating and high-pitched like a savage violin, following the obscure drum of the earth welcoming its gods, created the tense atmosphere of a legend, a ring of mystery and cosmic terror. The forest was dying. I heard its lamentations with a heavy heart, as if I had come there to listen to the oldest voices anyone had ever heard.

The big boss, the owner of the forest, was a man from Santiago whom I hadn't met. His visit, slated for later on in the summer, was feared. His name was Pepe Rodríguez, and I was told he was a latter-day capitalist who owned looms and other mills, a busy, dynamic, electrifying man, and an out-and-out reactionary, a prominent member of Chile's most extreme right-wing party. I was passing through his domain without his knowledge, and those qualities of his were an asset to me. No one would possibly come to look for me here. The civil authorities and the police were loyal subjects of the great man whose hospitality I was enjoying, and there was little or no chance that I would ever run into him.

My departure was imminent. The snows were about to come down on the cordillera, and the Andes are no joking matter. My friends studied the road conditions every day. To say "roads" is to stretch the word. In reality, we would be venturing out over tracks the humus and the snow had blotted out long ago. The wait was becoming torture. Also, my friends on the Argentine side must be looking for me by this time.

When everything seemed to be ready, Jorge Bellet, captain general of the timberland, warned me that something had cropped up. He looked down in the mouth as he said it. The owner had sent word that he was on his way and would arrive in two days.

I was upset. We hadn't quite completed our preparations. After all the tedious work, there was now great danger that the proprietor would discover that I was staying on his land. Everyone knew he was a close friend of my persecutor, González Videla. And everyone knew González Videla had put a price on my head. What should we do?

From the outset, Bellet was all for confronting Rodríguez, the owner. "I know him very well," he told me. "He's quite a man, he will never turn you in."

I objected. The party's instructions called for absolute secrecy, and Bellet was proposing that we violate those instructions. I said so. We had a heated discussion. And after weighing the political pros and cons, we decided that I should go to an Indian cacique's house, a cabin nestled at the foot of the jungle.

I moved into the cabin and there my situation became very precarious. So much so that finally, after many objections, I agreed to meet Pepe Rodríguez, the owner of the business, the sawmills, and the forests. We settled on a neutral point, neither his house nor the cacique's cabin. At sundown I saw a jeep approaching. A man who was both mature and youngish, with graying hair and set features, got out of the jeep with my friend Bellet. The first thing he said was that, from then on, he would be responsible for my safety. Under those circumstances, no one would dare try anything against me.

We talked without much warmth, but the man gradually won me over. It was very raw out and I invited him into the cacique's house, where we continued our conversation. At a word from him, a bottle of champagne, another of whiskey, and some ice appeared.

At the fourth glass of whiskey, we were arguing in loud voices. The man was an absolutist in his convictions. He was well informed and said interesting things, but the edge of insolence in his voice infuriated me. We both banged on the cacique's table with the palms of our hands, but we finished the bottle in relative peace.

Our friendship was a lasting one. One of the best things about him was his unconditional frankness, the frankness of a man who is used to running things. But he also read my poetry in an extraordinary way, with such an intelligent and virile voice that my poems seemed to be born all over again.

Rodríguez went back to the capital, to his businesses. He made one final gesture in my behalf. He called his subordinates together around me and said to them, in his typical voice of command: "If any obstacles come up within the next week to keep Señor Legarreta from crossing into Argentina through the smugglers' pass, you will open another road so he can get to the border. Drop all work on the timber, and open that road. Those are my orders."

Legarreta was my name at the time.

Pepe Rodríguez, that domineering, feudal man, died two years later, bankrupt and persecuted. He had been accused of heading a big smuggling operation and spent many months in jail. That must have meant unbearable suffering for a man with such an arrogant nature. I have never known for certain if he was guilty or innocent of the crime he was accused of. But I did learn that our oligarchy, who years before would have lost sleep hoping for an invitation from the generous Rodríguez, deserted him as soon as they saw him on trial and broken. As for me, I still stand by him and can't put him out of my memory. Pepe Rodríguez was a small emperor who gave orders to open sixty kilometers of road in the jungle to help a poet reach freedom.

THE ANDEAN MOUNTAINS

The Andean mountains have hidden passes, used by smugglers in the old days, so hostile and difficult that the rural police no longer bother to patrol them. Rivers and precipices block the traveler's way.

My companion Jorge Bellet headed the expedition. Our five-man escort, expert horsemen and road scouts, was joined by my old friend Victor Bianchi, who had come to the region as surveyor in some land disputes. He did not recognize me. I had a heavy beard after a year and a half of living in hiding. As soon as he knew about my plan to cross the jungle, he offered us his invaluable services as veteran

explorer. He had once climbed Aconcagua on a tragic expedition in
which he had been one of the only survivors.

We traveled single-file, protected by the solemn hour of dawn. I
had not ridden a horse in many years, not since childhood, but here
we were, on our way to the pass. The southern Andean forest is populated by huge trees set apart from one another: giant larches and
mayten trees, as well as tepa and coniferous trees. The rauli trees have
an amazing girth. I stopped to measure one. It had the diameter of a
horse. The sky overhead can't be seen. Below, leaves have been falling
for centuries, forming a layer of humus the hoofs of the mounts sink
down into. We were passing through one of primitive nature's great
cathedrals.

Our way took us through hidden and forbidden territory, and we
accepted even the flimsiest indications we could follow. There were
no tracks, no trails; my four mounted companions and I wove in and
out, overcoming such obstacles as powerful trees, impassable rivers,
enormous crags, desolate snows, guessing more often than not, looking for the road to my freedom. My companions were sure of their
bearings, the best way between the thick clumps of vegetation, but, to
be on the safe side, they notched the bark of the huge trees here and
there with a machete, blazing a trail to guide them back, once they
had left me to my fate.

Each one moved along, absorbed in that solitude without boundary lines, in the green and white silence: the trees, the long vines, the
humus deposited by hundreds of years, the partly fallen trees suddenly becoming another roadblock. It was all the dazzling and secretive work of nature and at the same time a growing threat of cold,
snow, and pursuit. It all came into play: solitude, danger, silence, and
the urgency of my mission.

Sometimes we followed a dim trail left by smugglers perhaps or by
common outlaws fleeing from justice; we wondered how many had
perished, surprised by winter's icy hand, in the heavy snowstorms

that break loose in the Andes and surround the traveler, burying him under seven stories of snow.

On either side of the trail in that wild desolation, I saw something that looked like the work of human hands. Broken branches piled together, they had endured many winters; a vegetable offering from hundreds of travelers, tall wooden tombs to remember the fallen, to remind us of those who had not been able to go on and had been left there forever, under the snows. With their machetes, my companions also lopped off those branches that touched our heads, diving at us from the tops of the huge conifers, from the oaks whose last leaves were fluttering before the coming of the winter storms. And on each grave mound I, too, left a memento, a wooden calling card, a branch from the forest to adorn the tomb of some unknown traveler.

We had to cross a river. Those small springs born on the Andean peaks plummet down, unload their vertiginous, crushing power, turn into waterfalls, tear up land and rocks with the energy and speed gathered in those staggering altitudes. But this time we came upon a pool, a huge mirror of water, a ford. The horses went in, lost their footing, and swam to the other side. My mount was soon almost totally covered by the water, I began to sway unsteadily, my drifting feet thrashed about, while the animal struggled to keep its head above water. So we went across. And no sooner had we reached the other shore than my guides, the peasants who accompanied me, grinned and asked: "Were you very scared?"

"Very. I thought my end had come," I replied.

"We were behind you with a rope ready in our hands," they said.

"My father fell in right there," one of them added, "and the current dragged him away. We weren't about to let the same thing happen to you."

We went on, eventually entering a natural tunnel opened in the impressive rock perhaps by a powerful river that has since disappeared or by a spasm of the earth that created this formation in the mountains, dug this canal in the hinterlands, excavated from the rock, the granite which we were now entering. A little farther on, the mounts kept slipping, they would try to get a footing in the rocky depressions, their legs buckled, sparks flew from their shoes. I was thrown from my horse and sprawled out on the rocks more than once. My horse was bleeding at the nose and legs, but we stubbornly continued on our vast, magnificent, grueling way.

There was something waiting for us in that wild forest. Suddenly we came out into a neat little meadow, an unbelievable vision, nestled in the mountain's lap: crystalline water, green grass, wildflowers, the murmur of streams, and a blue sky over us, a generous light unbroken by foliage.

We stopped inside this magic circle, like guests in a holy place: and even holier was the ceremony in which I took part. The cowboys dismounted. A bull's skull had been set down in the center of the hollow, as if for some ritual. My companions approached it in silence, one by one, and left a few coins and some food in its bone sockets. I joined them in that offering intended for rough-mannered men who had strayed away like Ulysses, for fugitives of every breed, who would find bread and assistance in the dead bull's eyepits.

But the unforgettable ceremony did not end here. My rustic friends shed their hats and started a strange dance, hopping around the abandoned skull on one foot, retracing the circles of tracks left by the dances of so many others who had passed that way before. There with my inscrutable companions I came to understand then, in some only vaguely defined way, that communication existed between people who did not know one another, that there was solicitude, pleas and answers to those pleas, even in the most far-flung and out-of-the-way places in the world.

Farther along, that night, just before we were to cross the frontier that would separate me from my country for many years, we came to the last mountain gorges. Suddenly we saw a burning light, a sure sign of human life, and coming closer, we found several ramshackle sheds that looked empty. We entered one of them and saw, by the firelight, huge logs burning in the center of the room, bodies of giant trees that burned there day and night, releasing, through cracks in the roof, smoke that drifted in the dark like a heavy blue veil. We saw piles of cheeses, stacked there by those who had curdled them at that altitude. Several men, huddled together like sacks, were lying next to the fire. In the silence, we heard the strings of a guitar and the words of a song, born of the live coals and the darkness, bringing us the first human voice we had met on our trip. It was a song of love and faraway places, a lament of love and yearning addressed to spring, which was still far off, to the cities from which we came, to life's infinite spaces. They didn't know who we were, they knew nothing about the fugitive, they didn't know my poetry or my name. Or did they know it, did they know us? Anyway, we sang and ate next to that fire, and later we walked through the dark into some crude rooms. A thermal spring passed through them, volcanic water we plunged into, a warmth that broke from the mountains and drew us close to itself.

We splashed around happily, washing, cleansing off the heaviness of our long ride. We felt refreshed, born again, baptized, when we set out at dawn on the final kilometers that would take me away from the shadows hovering over my country. We left on our horses, singing, with a new air filling our lungs, a breath that drove us on to the great highway of the world waiting for me. When we tried—this is still fresh in my mind—to give the mountaineers some money to pay for the songs, the food, the thermal waters, the bed and the roof, that is, for the unexpected welcome we had met, they refused our offer without even considering it. They had done what they could for us, that's all. And "that's all," the silent "that's all," implied many things, perhaps recognition, perhaps our common dreams.

SAN MARTÍN DE LOS ANDES

An abandoned shack marked out the frontier for us. I was now a free man. On the cabin's wall I wrote: "Goodbye, my country. I am leaving, but I take you with me."

A Chilean friend was supposed to be waiting for us in San Martín de los Andes. This little mountain village in Argentina is so tiny that all I had been told, by way of instructions, was: "Go to the best hotel. Pedrito Ramírez will be waiting for you there." But such is life: There wasn't one best hotel in San Martín de los Andes; there were two. Which one should we pick? We decided on the more expensive one, located on the edge of town, after discounting the first, which we had seen on the lovely town square.

It so happened that the hotel we chose was so posh that they wouldn't take us in. The effects of several days' journey on horseback, the sacks on our shoulders, our bearded and dusty faces, drew hostile looks. Anyone would have been afraid to let us in. And more so the manager of a hotel whose customers were British aristocrats from Scotland, who came to Argentina for salmon fishing. There was nothing aristocratic about us. The manager gave us the *vade retro*, alleging, with theatrical glances and gestures, that the last available room had been taken ten minutes before.

Just then an elegant man, obviously an army officer, appeared in the doorway, accompanied by a blonde who looked like a movie star. He roared in a thundering voice: "Hold it. No one kicks Chileans out! They're staying right here!" And we stayed. Our protector looked so much like Perón, and his lady so like Evita, that we all thought: It's them! But later, after we had washed and dressed, and were sitting at a table enjoying a bottle of suspect champagne, we found out that the man was the commander of the local garrison and she an actress from Buenos Aires who was paying him a visit.

We passed ourselves off as lumbermen raring to make a good

deal. The commander called me the "Mountain Man." Victor Bianchi, whose friendship and love of adventure had made him come that far with me, got hold of a guitar and charmed the Argentine men and ladies with his suggestive Chilean songs. But three days and their nights went by, and Pedrito Ramírez had not come for me. I was beside myself. We didn't have a clean shirt left, or any money for new ones. A good lumberman, Victor Bianchi said, should at least have clean shirts.

Meanwhile, the commander gave a lunch for us at his garrison. We became better friends and he confessed to us that, for all his physical likeness to Perón, he was anti-Perón. We spent long hours arguing about who had the worse President, Chile or Argentina.

One morning, Pedrito Ramírez burst into my room. "You bastard!" I shouted at him. "What's kept you so long?" The inevitable had occurred. He had been patiently waiting for me to come to the other hotel, the one on the square.

Ten minutes later, we were rolling over the pampa. And we rolled day and night. Once in a while, the Argentines would stop the car to sip some maté tea, and then we would set off again across that interminably monotonous land.

IN PARIS WITH PASSPORT

Naturally, my biggest headache in Buenos Aires was to get myself a new identity. The false papers I had used to cross the Argentine border would be no good to me for a transatlantic trip or to move around in Europe. How was I going to get new ones? Alerted by the government of Chile, the Argentine police were looking high and low for me.

In this tight spot, I recalled something that lay hidden in my memory. Miguel Angel Asturias, the novelist, my old Central American friend, was, I thought, in Buenos Aires, on a diplomatic mission for his country, Guatemala. Our faces had a vague likeness. By common consent, we had classed ourselves as *chompipe*, an Indian word for "turkey" in Guatemala and part of Mexico. Long-nosed, with plenty to spare in face and body, we shared a resemblance to the succulent bird.

He came to see me in my hideout.

"Friend chompipe," I said to him, "lend me your passport. Allow me the pleasure of arriving in Europe as Miguel Angel Asturias."

Let me say that Asturias has always been a liberal but has stayed out of activist politics. Yet he didn't think about it twice. A few days later, between "Señor Asturias this" and "Señor Asturias that," I crossed the wide river separating Argentina and Uruguay. I went into Montevideo, got past airports and police lookouts, and finally reached Paris, disguised as the eminent Guatemalan novelist.

But in France my identity posed a problem once more. My brand-new passport would never get me past the implacable close scrutiny of the Sûreté. I would have to give up being Miguel Angel Asturias and turn back into Pablo Neruda. But how could I, when Pablo Neruda had never arrived in France? Miguel Angel Asturias had.

My advisers made me check in at the George V Hotel. "There, among international celebrities, no one is going to ask you for your papers," they said. So I stayed there for several days, without giving much thought to my mountain clothes, which struck a discordant note in that rich and elegant world.

And then Picasso showed up, whose kindness matched his genius. He was as thrilled as a little boy, because he had just given the first speech of his life. Its theme had been my poetry, my persecution, my absence. Now, with brotherly feeling, the inspired minotaur of modern painting got me out of my predicament, taking care of all the details this involved. He spoke to the authorities; he called up a good many people. I don't know how many marvelous paintings he failed to paint on account of me. I felt very badly that he was losing time so precious to him.

A congress for peace was meeting in Paris at this time. I showed up at the congress at the last minute, just to read one of my poems. All the delegates applauded and embraced me. Many had thought me dead. They couldn't imagine how I had dodged the relentless persecution of the Chilean police.

On the following day Alderete, a veteran newspaperman for France-Presse, dropped in at my hotel. "When the press gave out the news that you were in Paris," he said, "the Chilean government roundly denied it. Your double had showed up here; Pablo Neruda was in Chile, they were hot on his trail, it was only a matter of hours till his arrest. What should we answer back?"

I recalled that during an argument about whether Shakespeare had or had not written his works, a preposterous and fine-spun discussion, Mark Twain had chipped in: "It wasn't William Shakespeare who really wrote those plays, but another Englishman who was born on the same day at the same hour as he, and who died on the same day, and, to carry the coincidences still further, was also named William Shakespeare."

"Say that I am not Pablo Neruda," I told the newspaperman, "but another Chilean who writes poetry, fights for freedom, and is also called Pablo Neruda."

Getting my papers straightened out was not easy. Aragon and Paul Eluard were helping me. In the meantime, I had to lead a semi-clandestine life.

One of the places where I took shelter was Mme Françoise Giroux's home. I shall never forget this highly original and intelligent lady. Her apartment was in the Palais-Royal, next door to Colette's. She had adopted a little Vietnamese boy. The French army was doing

the work the North Americans would take over later on: killing innocent people in far-off Vietnam. So she adopted the child.

I remember that one of the most beautiful Picassos I have ever
seen was in this house. It was a very large painting, from his pre-
cubist period. It showed a pair of red plush drapes, falling, coming
together like the two halves of a window, above a table. A loaf of long
French bread spanned the table from end to end. The painting inspired reverence. The enormous loaf of bread on the table was like
the central figure in an ancient icon, or like El Greco's *St. Maurice*
in El Escorial. I gave the painting my own title: *The Ascension of the
Holy Bread*.

One day Picasso himself came to visit me in my hideout. I led him
over to the painting he'd done so many years before. He had forgotten it completely. He started going over it very earnestly, sinking into
an extraordinary and rather sad absorption very seldom seen in him.
He spent more than ten minutes in silence, stepping up close to the
forgotten work and then back.

"I like it more all the time," I said to him when he ended his contemplation. "I am going to suggest that my country's national museum buy it. Madame Giroux is prepared to sell it to us."

Picasso turned his head toward the painting once more, his eyes
piercing the magnificent loaf, and his only comment was: "It's not
bad at all."

I found a house for rent that seemed an extravagance to me. It was on
Pierre-Mille Street, in the fifteenth *arrondissement*, that is, to hell and
gone. It was a neighborhood of workers and poor people. You had to
travel for hours on the Métro to get there. What attracted me to the
house was that it looked like a cage. It had three floors, tiny hallways
and rooms. It was a tall bird cage defying description.

The ground floor, which was the largest and had a wood-burning stove, I made into a library and a room for entertaining, which I did from time to time. Some friends, almost all Chileans, moved into the upper floors. José Venturelli and Nemesio Antúnez, painters both, and others I can't remember, stayed there.

About this time, I received a visit from three outstanding figures in Soviet literature: the poet Nikolai Tikhonov, the playwright Alexander Korneichuk (who was also a government official in the Ukraine), and the novelist Konstantin Simonov. I had never seen them before. They embraced me like a long-lost brother. And, besides a hug, each gave me a resounding kiss, one of those Slavic kisses between men that are a sign of friendship and respect, and which I had a hard time getting used to. Years later, when I understood the meaning of those brotherly, masculine kisses, I had occasion once to begin an anecdote with these words: "The first man who ever kissed me was a Czechoslovakian consul..."

The Chilean government did not want me. Did not want me at home or abroad. Wherever I went, I was preceded by notes and telephone calls asking other governments to make things difficult for me.

I found out that there was a file on me at the Quai d'Orsay which said, roughly: "Neruda and his wife, Delia del Carril, make frequent trips to Spain, carrying Soviet instructions back and forth. They receive these instructions from the Russian writer Ilya Ehrenburg, with whom Neruda also makes clandestine trips to Spain. In order to keep closer contact with Ehrenburg, Neruda has rented and moved into an apartment in the same building where the Soviet writer lives."

It was a string of lies. Jean-Richard Bloch gave me a letter for a friend of his who was an important official in the Ministry of Foreign Relations. I explained to the functionary that they were trying to get me deported from France on the basis of the wildest assumptions. I told him that I was very eager to meet Ehrenburg but, unfortunately, had not yet had the honor. The important functionary threw me a look of pity and promised to investigate. This was never done, however, and the absurd charges were allowed to stand.

So I decided to introduce myself to Ehrenburg. I knew he went to La Coupole every day, where he lunched at a Russian hour, that is, around sundown. "I'm Pablo Neruda, the poet, from Chile," I said to him. "According to the police, we're close friends. They claim that I live in the same building as you. Since they're going to throw me out of France because of you, I wish to meet you, at least, and shake hands."

I don't believe Ehrenburg ever blinked at any phenomenon in the world. And yet I saw something very much like a look of stupefaction emerging from his shaggy brows, from under his angry mop of gray hair. "I also wanted to meet you, Neruda," he said. "I like your poetry. But, to begin with, have some of this *choucroute à l'Alsacienne.*"

From then on, we became great friends. I believe he began to translate my *España en el corazón* that same day. I must admit that the French police unintentionally provided me with one of the most gratifying friendships I have ever had, and also presented me with the most eminent of my Russian translators.

One day, Jules Supervielle came to see me. By then I had a legal Chilean passport in my own name. The aging and noble Uruguayan poet very seldom went out any more. I was touched and surprised by his visit.

"I've brought you an important message. My son-in-law, Bertaux, wants to see you. I don't know what it's about."

Bertaux was the chief of police. We went to his office. The old poet and I sat down facing the officer across his desk. I have never seen more telephones on one table. How many were there? No fewer than twenty, I believe. His intelligent and shrewd face looked at me across the forest of telephones. I was sure every line to Paris's underground life was there on that overloaded spot. I thought of Fantômas and Inspector Maigret.

The chief of police had read my books and knew my poetry surprisingly well.

"I've received a request from the Chilean ambassador to take away your passport. The ambassador claims that you are using a diplomatic passport, and that would be illegal. Is this information correct?"

"I don't have a diplomatic passport," I replied. "This is simply an official passport. I am a senator in my country, and as such, I have a right to this document. What's more, here it is. You may examine but not take it away, because it is my private property."

"Is it up-to-date? Who renewed it?" Monsieur Bertaux asked me, taking my passport.

"It's up-to-date, of course," I said to him. "As for saying who renewed it, that's something I can't do. The Chilean government would remove that official."

The chief of police examined my papers slowly. Then he picked up one of his numberless telephones and asked to be put through to the Chilean ambassador. The telephone conversation took place in my presence.

"No, Mr. Ambassador, I cannot do it. His passport is in order. I don't know who renewed it. I repeat, it would be wrong to take away his papers. I cannot, Mr. Ambassador. I am very sorry."

The ambassador's insistence was plain, and a slight note of irritation was also evident in Bertaux's voice. He finally put down the receiver and said to me: "He seems to be your determined enemy. But you can stay in France as long as you wish."

I left with Supervielle. The old poet couldn't quite understand what was going on. For my part, a feeling of triumph mingled with revulsion went through me. The ambassador who was harassing me, collaborating with my persecutor in Chile, was the same Joaquín Fernández who boasted of his friendship with me and who never passed up a chance to play up to me, who that same morning had sent me a little affectionate message via the Guatemalan ambassador.

ROOTS

Ehrenburg, who was reading and translating my poems, scolded me: Too much *root*, too many *roots* in your poems. Why so many?

It's true. The frontier regions sank their roots into my poetry and these roots have never been able to wrench themselves out. My life is a long pilgrimage that is always turning on itself, always returning to the woods in the south, to the forest lost to me.

There the huge trees were sometimes felled by their seven hundred years of powerful life, uprooted by storms, blighted by the snow, or destroyed by fire. I have heard titanic trees crashing deep in the forest: the oak tree plunging down with the sound of a muffled cataclysm, as if pounding with a giant hand on the earth's doors, asking for burial.

But the roots are left out in the open, exposed to their enemy, time, to the dampness, to the lichens, to one destruction after the other.

Nothing more beautiful than those huge, open hands, wounded or burned, that tell us, when we come across them on a forest path, the secret of the buried tree, the mystery that nourished the leaves, the deep-reaching muscles of the vegetable kingdom. Tragic and shaggy, they show us a new beauty: they are sculptures molded by the depths of the earth: nature's secret masterpieces.

Once, Rafael Alberti and I were walking together, with waterfalls, thickets, and woods all around us, near Osorno, and he pointed out that each branch was different from the next, the leaves seemed to be competing for an infinite variety of style. "They look as if they had been selected by a landscape gardener for a magnificent park," he said. Years later, in Rome, Rafael remembered that walk and the natural abundance of our forests.

That is what it was like. It isn't, not any more. I grow sad, thinking of my wanderings as a boy and as a young man, between Boroa and Carahue, or around Toltén in the hills along the coast. How many discoveries! The graceful bearing and the fragrance of the cinnamon tree after the rain, the mosses whose winter beard hangs from the forest's innumerable faces!

I pushed aside the fallen leaves, trying to uncover the lightning streak of some beetles: the golden carabus, who dresses in iridescence to dance a minuscule ballet under the roots.

Or later, when I rode across the mountains to the Argentine side, under the green domes of the giant trees, an obstacle loomed up ahead: the root of one of them, taller than our mounts, blocking our way. Strenuous work and the ax made the crossing possible. Those roots were like overturned cathedrals: greatness laid bare to overwhelm us with its grandeur.

Beginning and End of Exile

IN THE SOVIET UNION

In 1949, my exile just over, I was invited for the first time to the Soviet Union, to the celebration of Pushkin's sesquicentennial. The twilight and I came at the same time to my appointment with the cold pearl of the Baltic, the ancient, new, noble, heroic Leningrad. The city of Peter the Great and Lenin the Great has "angel," like Paris. A gray angel: steel-colored avenues, lead-colored stone palaces, and a steel-green sea. The most magnificent museums in the world, the treasures of the Tsars, their paintings, their uniforms, their dazzling jewels, their ceremonial dress, their weapons, their tableware, were all before my eyes. And the new, immortal mementos: the cruiser *Aurora*, whose cannons backed Lenin's thought, knocked down the walls of the past, and opened history's doors.

I was there for an appointment with a poet dead over a hundred years, Alexander Pushkin, author of imperishable legends and novels. This prince of poets of the people holds the heart of the great Soviet Union. To celebrate his sesquicentennial, the Russians had reconstructed the palace of the Tsars, stone by stone. Each wall had been rebuilt exactly as it had existed in the past, rising again from the dusty rubble to which it had been reduced by Nazi artillery. The old

blueprints of the palace, the documents of the times, were consulted
to reconstruct the luminous windows, the embroidered cornices, the
flowery capitals. To build a museum in honor of an extraordinary
poet of another era.

What first impressed me in the U.S.S.R. was the feeling of immensity it gives, of unity within that vast country's population, the movements of the birches on the plains, the huge forests so miraculously
unspoiled, the great rivers, the horses running like waves across the
wheat fields.

I loved the Soviet land at first sight, and I realized that not only
does it offer a moral lesson for every corner of the globe where human life exists, a way of comparing possibilities, an ever-increasing
progress in working together and sharing, but I sensed, too, that an
extraordinary flight would begin from this land of steppes, which
preserved so much natural purity. The entire human race knows that
a colossal truth is being worked out there, and the whole world awaits
eagerly to see what will happen. Some wait in terror, others simply
wait, still others believe they can see what is coming.

I was in the middle of a forest where thousands of peasants in
traditional festive costumes were listening to Pushkin's poems. Everything hummed with life: men, leaves, vast stretches of land where
the new wheat was beginning to show its first signs of life. Nature
seemed to form a triumphant union with man. Out of those poems of
Pushkin's in the Mikhailovsky forest, the man who would fly to other
planets must inevitably rise.

A heavy rain came down while the peasants were at the celebration. A lightning bolt struck close to us, charring a man and the tree
sheltering him. It all seemed a part of the torrential natural scene.
What's more, that poetry accompanied by rain was already in my
books, it concerned me.

The Soviet countryside is steadily changing. Huge cities and canals are under construction; the geography itself is altering. But even on that first visit I recognized the affinities that linked me to them, and also everything that seemed beyond my grasp or furthest from my spirit.

In Moscow, writers live in constant ferment, a continual exchange of ideas. There, long before the scandalmongering West discovered it, I learned that Pasternak and Mayakovsky were the best Soviet poets. Mayakovsky was the public poet, with a thundering voice and a countenance like bronze, a magnanimous heart that revolutionized language and met head-on the most difficult problems in political poetry. Pasternak was a great poet of evening shadows, of metaphysical inwardness, and politically an honest reactionary who in the transformation of his country saw no further than an enlightened deacon. Yet the severest critics of his static political views often recited Pasternak's poems to me by heart.

The existence of a Soviet dogmatism in the arts for long periods of time cannot be denied, but it should also be mentioned that this dogmatism was always considered a defect and combated openly. With the critical essays of Zhdanov, a brilliant dogmatist, the personality cult produced a serious hardening in attitude toward the development of Soviet culture. But there were rebuttals from every quarter, and we know that life is stronger and more obstinate than precepts. The revolution is life; precepts prepare their own grave.

Ehrenburg is advanced in age but is still one of the most genuine and ebullient of the great agitators of Soviet culture. I often visited my good friend at his apartment on Gorky Street, where Picasso paintings and lithographs lined the walls, or at his dacha near

Moscow. Ehrenburg has a passion for plants and is almost always in his garden pulling weeds and conclusions out of everything that grows around him.

Later the poet Kirsanov, who translated my poetry into Russian so admirably, became a good friend of mine. Like all Soviet poets, Kirsanov is an ardent patriot. In his poetry there are brilliant flashes and the rich music of the beautiful Russian language, which his pen releases into the air in cascades.

Another poet I frequently visited in Moscow and in the country was a Turk, Nazim Hikmet, a legendary writer kept in prison for eighteen years by his country's bizarre governments. Accused of attempting to incite the Turkish navy into rebellion, Nazim was condemned to the punishments of hell. The trial was held on a warship. He told me he was forced to walk on the ship's bridge until he was too weak to stay on his feet, then they stuck him into a section of the latrines where the excrement rose half a meter above the floor. My brother poet felt his strength failing him. The stench made him reel. Then the thought struck him: My tormentors are keeping an eye on me, they want to see me drop, they want to watch me suffer. His strength came back with pride. He began to sing, low at first, then louder, and finally at the top of his lungs. He sang all the songs, all the love poems he could remember, his own poems, the ballads of the peasants, the people's battle hymns. He sang everything he knew. And so he vanquished the filth and his torturers. When he told me those things I said to him: "You sang for all of us, my brother. We need have no doubts any longer, or wonder what to do. We know now that we must begin to sing."

He also told me of the sufferings of his people. The peasants are brutally persecuted by feudal lords in Turkey. Nazim would see them arrive in prison; he would watch them swapping for tobacco the crust of bread doled out to them as their daily ration. Eventually, they would begin looking at the grass distractedly. Then with closer attention, almost avidly. And one day they would stuff a few blades of grass into their mouths. Later they would pull up fistfuls and gulp them down. In the end, they would eat the grass on all fours, like horses.

Passionately anti-dogmatic, Nazim has lived many long years of exile in the U.S.S.R. His love for this country, which took him in, comes tumbling out in his words: "I believe in the future of poetry. I believe, because I am living in the country where the soul craves poetry more than anything else." Many secrets that people have to see for themselves vibrate in these words. The Soviet man, with doors open to him in all the libraries, all the classrooms, all the theaters, is at the center of the writers' thoughts. This is something that should not be forgotten when the objectives of literary action come under discussion. On the one hand, the new forms, the urgent renewal of all that exists, must transcend and break down literary molds. On the other, how can one fail to fall in step with such a profound and far-flung revolution? How can one exclude from one's central themes the victories, conflicts, human problems, abundances, progress, growth of an immense country facing a total change in political, economic, and social systems? How can one not make common cause with a people battered by ferocious invasions, hemmed in by implacable colonialists, obscurantists of every stripe and color? Can literature or the arts assume an air of ethereal independence before events of such vital significance?

The sky is white. By four in the afternoon it is black. From that hour on, night blankets the city.

Moscow is a winter city. It is a beautiful city of winter. The snow has settled on the infinitely repeated roofs. The pavements shine, invariably clean. The air is hard transparent glass. A soft steel color, the tiny feathers of the snow swirling about, the coming and going of thousands of passers-by as if they didn't feel the cold, all of it suggests a dream in which Moscow becomes a huge winter palace with extraordinary ornamentations, ghostly as well as living ones.

It is thirty degrees below zero in this Moscow set like a star of fire and snow, a burning heart, in the earth's breast.

I look out the window. There's an honor guard in the streets. What is happening? Even the snow is motionless where it has fallen. It is the great Vishinsky's funeral. The streets clear solemnly to let the procession pass. A profound silence settles down, a peacefulness in the heart of winter, for the great soldier. Vishinsky's fire returns to the roots of the Soviet mother country.

The soldiers who presented arms as the procession went past remain in formation. From time to time, one of them performs a little jig, raising his gloved hands and stomping his high boots for a second. Other than this, they seem immutable.

A Spanish friend told me that during World War II, immediately after a bombing, on the most intensely cold days, the Muscovites could be seen eating ice cream in the streets. "I knew then that they would win the war," my friend said, "when I saw them eating ice cream so calmly in the middle of a horrifying war and in below-zero weather."

The trees in the park, white with snow, are frosted over. Nothing can match these crystallized petals in the parks, during the Moscow winter. The sun makes them translucent, drawing white flames from them, but not one drop melts from their flower patterns. This is an arborescent world that lets us glimpse, through its spring garden of snow, the Kremlin's ancient towers, the thousand-year-old slender spires, the golden domes of St. Basil's.

After leaving the outskirts of Moscow, on the way to another city, I see broad white highways. They are frozen rivers. On those still riverbeds the silhouetted figure of a fisherman absorbed in himself appears, from time to time, like a fly on a glossy tablecloth. The fisherman halts at that long frozen sheet, picks out a spot, and drills the ice until he has an opening through which the buried current can be seen. He can't catch anything right away because the fish have fled, frightened by the iron that made the hole. Then the fisherman sprinkles a little food to lure the runaways back. He drops his hook and waits. He waits for hours on end in that hellish cold.

The work of writers, I say, has much in common with the work of these Arctic fishermen. The writer has to look for the river, and if he finds it frozen over, he has to drill a hole in the ice. He must have a good deal of patience, weather the cold and the adverse criticism, stand up to ridicule, look for the deep water, cast the proper hook, and after all that work, he pulls out a tiny little fish. So he must fish again, facing the cold, the water, the critic, eventually landing a bigger fish, and another and another.

I was invited to a writers' congress. In the seats of honor were the great fishermen, the great writers of the Soviet Union. Fadeyev with his white smile and his silver hair; Fedin with the face of an English fisherman, thin and sharp; Ehrenburg with his turbulent shock of hair and his suit which, even when worn for the first time, gives the impression of having been slept in; Tikhonov.

Also on the dais, with Mongolian features and their recently printed books, were the spokesmen of the farthest Soviet republics, peoples I had never even heard mentioned by name before, nomad countries with no alphabets.

TO PUSHKIN

Dear Friend:

One hundred fifty years after your birth, the writers invited me to celebrate you. And so I came to know the Soviet Union for the first time. I don't know why, but I felt as if it was you who invited me, who invited us, and since then I have felt that I have some connection to your tormented life—that I am your friend. The celebration was so beautiful, amid the settings and landscapes of your life and your poetry. Spring was suffused with Pushkin. Your growing, crystal-line work ran like a river beside us. Your verses blossomed in the trees.

There are masters of what we call literature who transcend it, changing not only the language of books, but language as it is spoken in daily life; changing the combinations of words, giving them new velocities and space to move. A national poet throws open the windows and lets inside the silence and the sound of the earth, the passionate movement of history, the thundering of the sea and the song of birds. That was your grandeur, and it is your legacy.

I wish now to attest in this solemn congress that this legacy has been defended through fifty years of Soviet literature. These authors were profoundly national and at the same time immensely generous toward foreign cultures. These writers the revolution gave your fatherland, hand in hand with the Soviet people, created buildings, paper, printing presses, until the book was loved and respected, until it became the center of a new society. This was far from easy in that era of transformations and struggle of a kind never before seen on the face of the earth. The Soviet writers were heroes not only of their people, but of human hope.

And when the terrible war reached the feet of the statues, when the invaders tried to destroy these people and this culture, the Soviet Union's authors fought and fell, fought and won, spilled their blood and their words, their love and their rage, to defend your legacy of crystal and the high humanism of the October Revolution.

Books have grown stronger, have invaded cities, fields, villages, populated libraries, streets, houses, hospitals, factories; have reached remote and obscure regions; all over, Soviet man has labored with book in hand. And he will reach the moon holding a book.

Your luminous heritage was defended and multiplied. A poet tells you this from remote terrains, from austral America. If you were here among us, I would say to you right now, "Comrade Pushkin, you may be happy."

INDIA REVISITED

In 1950 I had to make a sudden visit to India. In Paris, Joliot-Curie sent for me to ask me to go on a mission. I was to travel to New Delhi, get in touch with people of different political views, gauge on the spot the chances of strengthening the Indian movement for peace.

Joliot-Curie was the world President of the Partisans for Peace. We had a long talk. He was worried because pacifist opinion carried so little weight in India, although India had always been widely known as the pacifist country par excellence. The Prime Minister himself, Nehru, was generally recognized as a leading advocate of peace, a time-honored and deep-rooted cause in that country.

Joliot-Curie handed me two letters: one for a scientist in Bombay, and the other to be delivered personally to the Prime Minister. It seemed strange to me that I should be the one picked for such a long trip and a task apparently so simple. Perhaps my enduring love for that country, where I had spent some years in my youth, had something to do with it. Or else the fact that I had received the Peace Prize that same year for *Que despierte el leñador*, a distinction accorded Pablo Picasso and Nazim Hikmet also.

I boarded the plane for Bombay. I was going back to India thirty years later. It was no longer a colony fighting for its emancipation, but a sovereign republic: the dream of Gandhi, whose first congresses I had attended in 1928. Perhaps none of my friends from those days were alive, revolutionary students who had confided their stories of struggle to me, like brothers.

I got off the plane and headed straight for customs. From there I would go to some hotel, deliver the letter to the physicist Raman, and go on to New Delhi. I hadn't counted on my hosts. My suitcases were taking forever to get out of the place. A number of people I thought were customs inspectors were going through my baggage with a fine-tooth comb. I had seen many inspections, but never one like this. My luggage did not amount to much, only a medium-sized suitcase with my clothes, and a small leather bag containing my toilet articles. But my trousers, my shorts, my shoes were lifted out and checked over by five pairs of eyes. Pockets and seams were explored with meticulous attention. In Rome I had wrapped my shoes, so as not to soil my clothes, in a wrinkled newspaper I had found in my hotel room. I believe it was the *Osservatore Romano*. They spread the page on a table, held it up to the light, folded it as carefully as if it were a secret document, and finally put it aside with some of my papers. My shoes were also studied inside and out, like unique samples of fabulous fossils.

This incredible search lasted two hours. They made an elaborate bundle with my papers (passport, address book, the letter I was to hand the head of state, and the page from the *Osservatore Romano*) and ceremoniously secured it with sealing wax before my eyes. Then I was told I could go on to a hotel.

Using all my willpower so as not to lose our proverbial Chilean patience, I remarked that no hotel would allow me to register without identification papers and that the object of my trip to India was to hand the Prime Minister a letter, which I could not deliver because they had confiscated it.

"We'll talk to the hotel and they will take you in. As for the papers, we'll return them to you in due time."

This was the country whose struggle for independence was part of my experience as a young man, I thought. I shut my suitcase and my mouth simultaneously. A single word crossed my mind: Shit!

At the hotel I ran into Professor Baera and told him of my mishaps. He was a good-natured Hindu. He passed these incidents off lightly. He had a tolerant attitude toward his country, which he considered still in the process of formation. I, on the other hand, saw something perverse in that chaos, something very far from the welcome I had expected from a newly independent country.

Joliot-Curie's friend, to whom I had brought a letter of introduction, was the director of nuclear-physics studies in India. He invited me to visit their installations, adding that we had been asked to lunch that same day by the Prime Minister's sister. Such has been my luck, and such it continues to be, all my life: one hand rams me in the ribs with a club, and the other offers me a bouquet of flowers to make up for it.

The Institute for Nuclear Research was one of those clean, bright, luminous places where men and women dressed in gauzy white circulate like running water, crossing corridors, steering their way around instruments, blackboards, and trays. I understood only a small part of the scientific explanations, but the visit was a purifying bath that washed off the stains of humiliation suffered at the hands of the police. I have a dim memory of seeing what looked like a bowl with some mercury in it. Nothing more surprising than this metal, which displays its energy like some form of animal life. Its mobility, its capacity for liquid, spherical, magical transformation, has always caught my imagination. I have forgotten the name of Nehru's sister, with whom we had lunch that day. My ill humor dissipated in her presence. She was a woman of great beauty, made up and dressed like an exotic actress. Her sari flashed with color. Gold and pearls heightened her air of opulence. I took to her immediately. It was quite a contrast to see such a refined woman eating with her hand, sticking her long, jeweled fingers into the rice and curry sauce. I told her I was on my way to New Delhi to see her brother and the friends of world peace. She replied that, in her opinion, all the people of India should join the movement.

At the hotel that afternoon I was given the packet with my papers. The double-faced police had broken the sealing wax they themselves had affixed to it after packing up the documents in front of me. They must have photographed them all, including my laundry bills. I eventually found out that the people whose addresses were in my book had all been visited and interrogated by the police. Among them was Ricardo Güiraldes's widow, who was my sister-in-law then. This shallow woman was a theosophist, and her one passion was the Asian philosophies; she lived in a remote Indian village. She was subjected to a good deal of harassment because her name was in my address book.

In New Delhi I met with six or seven of the Indian capital's leading personalities the very day of my arrival, sitting under a sunshade for protection from the celestial fire. They were writers, philosophers, Hindu or Buddhist priests, the kind of Indians who are so adorably simple, so stripped of all pretension. Everyone agreed that the supporters of the peace movement were acting in the spirit of their ancient country, with its unbroken tradition of goodness and understanding. They wisely added that they thought any sectarian or hegemonic leanings should be corrected: neither the Communists nor the Buddhists nor the middle class should arrogate the movement. The important thing, the crux of the matter, was that all factions should contribute. I agreed with them.

The Chilean ambassador, Dr. Juan Marín, writer and physician, and an old friend of mine, came to see me at dinnertime. After many circumlocutions, he explained that he had had an interview with the chief of police. With the typical calmness the authorities adopt when talking to diplomats, the head of the Indian police had told him that my activities worried the Indian government and that he hoped I would leave the country soon. I told the ambassador that my sole activity had been to speak, in the hotel's garden, with six or seven eminent persons whose ideas, I assumed, were common knowledge. As for me, I said, the minute I deliver Joliot-Curie's message to the Prime Minister, I'll no longer be interested in staying in a country that, in spite of my proven sympathy for its cause, treats me so discourteously, without any reason whatever.

My ambassador had been one of the founders of the Socialist Party in Chile, but he had softened up, possibly because of the years and his diplomatic privileges. He did not resent the Indian government's stupid attitude, and I did not ask him for his support. We parted amiably—he relieved of the heavy responsibility my visit placed on him, and I with all my illusions about his sensibility and his friendship lost forever.

Nehru had granted me an appointment for the following morning in his office. He rose and shook my hand without any trace of a welcoming smile. His face has been photographed so often that it's not worth the trouble of describing. Dark, cold eyes looked at me without feeling. Thirty years before, he and his father had been introduced to me at a huge rally for independence. I mentioned this to him, but it produced no change in his face. He replied in monosyllables to everything I said, scrutinizing me with his steady, cold eyes.

I handed him the letter from his friend Joliot-Curie. He told me he had great respect for the French scientist, and took his time reading the letter. In it Joliot-Curie spoke of me and asked Nehru to assist me in my mission. He finished, put the letter back into its envelope, and looked at me without a word. It suddenly struck me that my presence provoked an involuntary dislike in him. It also crossed my mind that this man with a bilious complexion must be going through a bad physical, political, or emotional experience. There was something high and mighty about him, something stiff, as if he was accustomed to giving orders but lacked the strength of a leader. I recalled that his father, Pandit Motilal, zamindar or landowner of the old breed of feudal lords, had been Gandhi's grand treasurer and had helped the Congress movement not only with his political wisdom but also with his large fortune. I thought perhaps the silent man before me had in some subtle way reverted to a "zamindar" and was staring at me with the same indifference and contempt he would have shown one of his barefoot peasants.

"What shall I tell Professor Joliot-Curie when I return to Paris?"

"I shall answer his letter," he said dryly.

I was silent for a few minutes that seemed an eternity. Apparently Nehru did not feel at all like saying anything more to me, yet he didn't show the slightest sign of restlessness, as if it would have been all right for me to remain there without any reason whatever, squelched by the feeling that I was wasting the time of such an important man.

I felt that I had to say a few words about my mission. The cold war threatened to turn red-hot at any moment now. A new cataclysm could swallow humanity. I mentioned the terrible danger of nuclear weapons. And how important it was for those who want to avoid war to stick together.

He continued buried in his thoughts, as if he hadn't heard me. After a few moments he said, "As a matter of fact, both sides are pelting each other with arguments about peace."

"Personally," I said, "I think all those who talk of peace or want to contribute something to it can belong to the same side, to the same movement. We don't want to exclude anyone, except those who preach revenge and war."

There was more silence. I realized that the conversation was over. I rose to my feet and put out my hand to take my leave. He shook my hand silently. As I walked to the door, he asked, with some friendliness, "Can I do anything for you? Is there anything you would like?"

I am very slow to react, and unfortunately for me, I am not malicious. However, for once in my life, I took the offensive: "Oh, yes! I almost forgot. I lived in India once, but I have never had a chance to visit the Taj Mahal, which is so close to New Delhi. This would have been a good time to see that magnificent monument, if the police had not notified me that I can't leave the city limits and must return to Europe as soon as possible. I am going back tomorrow."

Pleased with myself at getting in my little thrust, I said goodbye quickly and left the office. The hotel manager was waiting for me at the reception desk. "I have a message for you. They've just called from the government offices to tell me that you may visit the Taj Mahal whenever you wish."

"Get my bill ready," I said. "I'm sorry I have to pass up that visit. I'm going to the airport right now, I'm taking the first plane to Paris."

Five years later, in Moscow, I had occasion to sit on the annual Lenin Peace Prize committee, an international assembly of which I was a part. When the moment came to present and vote on the year's candidates, the Indian delegate proposed Prime Minister Nehru's name. The shadow of a smile crossed my face, but none of the others on the jury understood it, and I voted affirmatively. The international prize consecrated Nehru as one of the champions of world peace.

MY FIRST VISIT TO CHINA

I visited China twice after the revolution. The first time was in 1951, the year I was one of those commissioned to take the Lenin Peace Prize to Madam Soong Ch'ing-ling, Sun Yat-sen's widow.

She was receiving the gold medal for which she had been proposed by Kuo Mo-jo, vice premier of China and a writer. Kuo Mo-jo was also vice chairman of the prize committee, together with Aragon. Anna Seghers, the filmmaker Alexandrov, several others I don't remember, Ehrenburg, and I were also on the jury. There was a secret alliance between Aragon, Ehrenburg, and me which had enabled us to see that the prize was given, in other years, to Picasso, Bertolt Brecht, and Rafael Alberti. It had not been easy, of course.

We left for China on the Trans-Siberian Railroad. Getting into that legendary train was like boarding a ship that sailed on land into infinite and mysterious distances. Everything around me was yellow, for leagues and leagues, on either side of the window. It was mid-autumn and all we could see were silver birches with their yellow petals. And then, farther than the eye could see, the prairie, tundra, or taiga. From time to time, the stations of new cities. Ehrenburg and I would get out to stretch our legs. At the stations, peasants crowded in the waiting rooms with their bundles and suitcases, waiting for the train.

We barely had time to walk around a little in those places. They were all the same; each had a statue of Stalin, made of cement. Sometimes it was painted silver, and sometimes gold. Of the dozens we saw, all exactly alike, I don't know which was uglier, the silver or the gilt. Back on the train, Ehrenburg entertained me for a whole week with his skeptical and witty conversation. He was a deeply patriotic Russian, but he discussed many aspects of life in that era, smiling sardonically.

He had arrived in Berlin with the Red Army. He was undoubtedly the most brilliant war correspondent there has ever been. The Red soldiers loved this eccentric, shy man. Not long before, in Moscow, he had shown me two presents those soldiers had given him, after unearthing them from the German ruins. They were a rifle made by Belgian gunsmiths for Napoleon Bonaparte, and two minuscule volumes of the works of Ronsard, printed in France in 1650. The little volumes were singed, and stained with rain or blood.

Ehrenburg donated Napoleon's beautiful rifle to the French museums. "What do I want it for?" he said to me, stroking the tooled cannon and the burnished gunstock. But Ronsard's tiny books he lovingly kept for himself.

Ehrenburg was an ardent Francophile. On the train he recited one of his clandestine poems for me. It was a short love song to France, addressing her as the woman he loved.

I call the poem clandestine because this was the era when accusations of cosmopolitanism were rife in Russia. Newspapers often carried charges of obscurantism; all modern art seemed cosmopolitan to them. Such and such a writer or painter would fall into disgrace and suddenly have his name obliterated, under such a charge. Thus, like a hidden flower, Ehrenburg's Francophile poem had to keep its tenderness to itself.

Much of what Ehrenburg showed me would soon disappear forever during Stalin's dark night, disappearances I tended to blame on their dissident and contradictory character.

With his unruly locks, deep wrinkles, nicotine-stained teeth, cold gray eyes, and melancholy smile, Ehrenburg was the old skeptic, the great disillusioned man. I had recently opened my eyes to the great revolution and was blind to sinister details. I found little to quarrel with in the general poor taste of the time or in those statues smeared with gold and silver. Time would prove that I was not right, but I don't think even Ehrenburg fully realized the immensity of the tragedy. Its magnitude would be revealed to us all by the Twentieth Congress.

The train seemed to move over the yellow stretches at a snail's pace, day after day, birch after birch. We had passed the Ural Mountains and were crossing Siberia.

We were having lunch in the dining car one day, when a table occupied by a soldier caught my eye. He was very drunk. He was a smiling young fellow whose cheeks bloomed with health. He kept ordering raw eggs from the waiter which he would break and drop on his plate with glee. Then he would immediately ask for a couple more. Judging by his ecstatic grin and his childish blue eyes, he was feeling mellower all the time. And he must have been at it for quite some time, because the yolks and whites were beginning to slide dangerously over the side of his plate, falling onto the floor of the car. "Tovarich!" the soldier called out to the waiter with enthusiasm and ordered new eggs to increase his treasure.

My eyes were fastened eagerly on this surrealist scene, so innocent and so unexpected in that Siberian emptiness, an oceanic setting.

The alarmed waiter finally called a military policeman. The guard, who was heavily armed, looked down at the soldier sternly, towering over him. But the soldier took no notice and went on busily breaking more and more eggs. I fully expected the policeman to jolt the wastrel out of his daydream. But I couldn't believe my eyes. The herculean guard sat down next to the boy, stroked his blond head tenderly, and began talking to him quietly, smiling, convincing him. Then he suddenly lifted him gently from his seat and led him away by the arm, like an older brother, through the car door to the station and into the streets of the town.

I thought bitterly of what would have happened to a poor drunken Indian if he had started breaking eggs on a trans-equatorial train.

During those trans-Siberian days, Ehrenburg could be heard energetically hammering away, morning and afternoon, at his typewriter keys. There he finished *The Ninth Wave*, his last novel before *The Thaw*. For my part, I wrote, only sporadically, some of *Los versos del capitán*, love poems for Matilde, published anonymously later in Naples.

We left the train in Irkutsk. Before catching the plane for Mongolia, we went down for a stroll by the lake, celebrated Lake Baikal, at the border of Siberia, the door to freedom in the rime of the Tsars. The thoughts and dreams of prisoners and exiles wandered off toward that lake. It was the only possible way of escape. Baikal! Baikal! Low-pitched Russian voices still repeat it now, singing the old ballads.

The Institute for the Study of Lakes invited us to lunch. The scientists let us in on their secrets. No one has ever been able to determine the exact depth of this lake, son and eye of the Ural Mountains. Some unusual fish are taken from two thousand feet down, blind fish pulled out of its night-black depths. My appetite was whetted immediately and I asked the scientists if I could try a couple of those exotic fish at table. I am one of the few persons in the world who has eaten fish from those abysses, washed down with good Siberian vodka.

From there we flew to Mongolia. I have a hazy memory of that lunar landscape whose inhabitants still live in nomad's tents, while they establish their first printing presses, their first universities. On all sides of Ulan Bator a circular, infinite wasteland opens out, like the Atacama Desert in my country, interrupted only by clusters of

camels that make the solitude more archaic. Incidentally, I tasted
Mongolian whiskey, in magnificently wrought silver cups. Every
people makes its alcoholic beverages from what they can. This one
was made of fermented camel's milk. Shivers still run up and down
my spine when I recall its taste. But how wonderful to have been in
Ulan Bator! More so for someone like me who lives in all beautiful
names. I live in them as in dream mansions intended just for me.
And so I have lived, relishing every syllable, in Singapore's, in Samarkand's names. When I die, I want to be buried in a name, some
especially chosen, beautiful-sounding name, so that its syllables will
sing over my bones, near the sea.

The Chinese are among the people in the world who smile the most.
They smile through implacable colonialism, revolutions, famines,
massacres, as no other people can. The smile of Chinese children
is the most beautiful harvest of rice ever threshed by this immense
populace.

But there are two kinds of Chinese smiles. There is a natural one
that lights up the wheat-colored faces. This is the smile of the peasants and the vast majority of people. The other is a detachable, false
smile that can be pasted on below the nose, and taken off. It's the
smile of the officials.

When Ehrenburg and I landed for the first time at the Peking
airport, it was hard for us to tell the two kinds of smiles apart. The
real, the best ones, went around with us for many days. These were
the smiles of our Chinese fellow writers, novelists and poets who
welcomed us with noble hospitality. So we met Ting Ling, novelist, Stalin Prize winner, chairman of the Writers' Union; Mao Tung,
Siao Emi, and charming Ai Ch'ing, old Communist and prince of
Chinese poets. They spoke French or English. They were all dragged
under by the Cultural Revolution years later. But at the time of our
visit they were the flower of Chinese literature.

The next day, after the award-giving ceremony for the Lenin Prize, called the Stalin Prize then, we dined at the Soviet Embassy. In addition to the lady being honored, there was Chou En-lai, old Marshal Chu Teh, and several others. The ambassador had been a hero of Stalingrad, a typical Soviet soldier, who sang and called for one toast after another. I was seated next to Soong Ch'ing-ling, very dignified and still quite beautiful. She was the most respected female personality of the day.

Each of us had a small crystal decanter filled with vodka all to himself. There were frequent calls of *"Kanpai,"* a Chinese toast that obliges you to drain your glass at one gulp, without leaving a drop. Old Marshal Chu Teh, across from me, never stopped filling his glass and, with his wide peasant's grin, egged me on to a new toast every few minutes. At the end of the meal, I chose a moment when the old strategist's attention was diverted to try a drink from his bottle of vodka. My suspicions were confirmed. I discovered that the Marshal had been drinking just water with his meal, while I was gulping down large quantities of liquid fire.

At coffee time, my neighbor at table, Soong Ch'ing-ling, the marvelous woman we had come to honor, drew a cigarette out of her case. Then, with an exquisite smile, she held it out to me. "No, I don't smoke, thank you," I said to her. I admired her cigarette case, and she said, "I keep it as a memento of something very important in my life." It was a stunning object, solid gold, studded with diamonds and rubies. After examining it with great care and praising it once again, I returned it to its owner.

She forgot very quickly that I had given it back to her, because as we rose from the table she turned to me with a piercing look and said, "My cigarette case, please?"

I was positive I had returned it to her, but looked for it, anyway, on the table, then under it, without success. Sun Yat-sen's widow's smile had vanished and two black eyes pierced through me like implacable rays of light. The sacred object could not be found anywhere, and I was starting to feel absurdly responsible for its loss. Those two black rays were about to convince me that I was a jewel thief.

Fortunately, when I could bear it no longer, I saw the cigarette case reappear in her hands. She had simply found it in her bag, of course. She recovered her smile, but I did not smile again for ages. Now I have an idea that the Cultural Revolution probably relieved her of the lovely gold cigarette case for good.

At that time of year the Chinese wore blue, blue mechanics' coveralls that clothed men and women alike, giving them a unanimous, sky-blue look. No ragged clothing. But no automobiles either. Thick crowds packed every place, flowed in from everywhere.

It was the second year of the revolution. There must have been shortages and difficulties in many places, but these were not noticeable in our tours of Peking. What particularly bothered Ehrenburg and me were small details, small tics in the system. When we wanted to buy a pair of socks and a handkerchief, it turned into a problem of state. Our Chinese comrades discussed it among themselves. After nervous deliberation on their part, we left the hotel in a caravan. Our car was in the lead, with those of the guards, the police, the interpreters bringing up the rear. The flock of cars roared off, opening its way through the crowd, which was always dense. We rolled like an avalanche down the narrow channel opened by the people. When we reached the store, our Chinese friends jumped out, quickly herded all customers out of the store, halted traffic, formed a barrier with their bodies, a human passageway Ehrenburg and I went through with our heads down, to come out fifteen minutes later, our heads down once more, each with a little package in his hands, firmly determined never to buy another pair of socks in China.

These things used to infuriate Ehrenburg. Take the case of a restaurant, which I'm going to relate now. At the hotel they would serve us the awful English food China inherited from its colonial rulers. I

am a great admirer of Chinese cooking and I told my young interpreter that I was dying to try Peking's famous cuisine. He replied that
he would check into it.

I don't know whether he really did, but we had to go on chomping
on the hotel's dull roast beef. I spoke to him about it again. He looked
thoughtful and said to me, "Our comrades have met together several
times to look into the situation. The problem is about to be solved."

On the following day an important member of the welcoming
committee came to see us. After putting his smile on right, he asked if
we really wanted to eat Chinese food. Ehrenburg said yes, definitely.
I added that I had been familiar with Cantonese food since boyhood
and was eager to taste the truly famous Peking condiments.

"This is somewhat of a problem," the Chinese comrade said, with
a worried air. Silence. A shake of his head. Then he went on: "Almost
impossible."

Ehrenburg smiled his confirmed skeptic's wry smile. I, on the
other hand, was fit to be tied. "Comrade," I said to him, "please prepare my papers for my return to Paris. If I can't have Chinese food
in China, I'll have it in the Latin Quarter, where it is not a problem."

My violent response got results. Four hours later, with our numerous committee leading the way, we arrived at a famous restaurant
where they had prepared glazed duck for five hundred years. An exquisite, memorable dish.

Open day and night, the restaurant was a short three hundred
meters from our hotel.

THE CAPTAIN'S VERSES

In the course of these wanderings from place to place as an exile, I
came to a country I had never visited, and I learned to love it deeply:
Italy. Everything in that country seemed fabulous to me. Especially the Italian simplicity: the olive oil, the bread and the wine of

spontaneity. Even the police . . . The police, who never mistreated me but hounded me without respite. It was a police force I found everywhere, even in my sleep and in my soup.

Writers invited me to read my poems. I read them, in good faith, everywhere, in universities, in amphitheaters, to the dockworkers of Genoa, in Florence at the Palazzo dell' Arte della Lana, in Turin, in Venice.

I read to capacity crowds with infinite pleasure. Someone next to me would repeat each poem after me in the sublime Italian tongue, and I liked to hear my poems with the added splendor of that magnificent language. The police, however, did not like it very much. In Castilian, fine, but the Italian version was full of ellipses. Lines in praise of peace, a word already proscribed by the "Western" world, and especially my poetry's slant in favor of the people's struggles, were dangerous.

In the municipal elections, the town council seats had gone to the people's parties and I was received as guest of honor at the stately town halls. Often, I was made an honorary citizen of the city. This was the case in Milan, Florence, and Genoa. The councilmen conferred their distinctions on me before or after my readings. Notables, aristocrats, and bishops would gather in the hall. We would drink a glass of champagne, which I accepted in behalf of my remote country. Between embraces and hand kissing I would finally make it down the front steps of the city hall. The police, who never gave me a moment's rest, would be waiting for me in the street.

What happened in Venice was a slapstick comedy. I gave my reading in the lecture hall. I was once more made an honorary citizen. But the police wanted me out of the city where Desdemona was born and suffered; they were stationed at the doors of my hotel, day and night.

My old friend Vittorio Vidali, Commandant Carlos, had come from Trieste to hear my poems. He shared with me the infinite pleasure of riding over the canals and seeing from the gondola the ash-gray palaces going past. As for the police, they were pestering me more than ever, always at our heels, a couple of paces behind us. I decided to make my escape, like Casanova, from a Venice that was trying to bottle me up. I put on a burst of speed, with Vittorio Vidali and the Costa Rican writer Joaquín Gutiérrez, who happened to be with us. Two Venetian policemen charged after us. We managed to jump quickly into the only gondola in Venice with a motor, the Communist mayor's. The municipal authority's gondola cut swiftly through the canal waters, while the representatives of the other authority scurried about like deer, looking for a boat. They took one of the many romantic vessels, painted black and with gold decorations, used by lovers in Venice. It followed us far off, hopelessly, like a duck chasing a sea dolphin.

All this persecution came to a head one morning in Naples. The police came to my hotel, not very early, because in Naples no one goes to work early, not even the police. Using an alleged error in my passport as a pretext, they asked me to accompany them to the prefecture. There they offered me an espresso and informed me that I must leave Italian soil that same day.

My love for Italy did not help me any.

"I am sure there's some misunderstanding," I said.

"Not at all. We think very highly of you, but you have to leave the country."

And then, in a roundabout way, as obliquely as possible, they let it be known that the Chilean Embassy was asking for my expulsion.

The train was leaving that afternoon. My friends were already at the station to say goodbye. Kisses. Flowers. Shouts. Paolo Ricci. The Alicattas. Many, many others. *Arrivederci. Adiós. Adiós.*

During my train ride to Rome, my police guards spared no efforts to be nice to me. They carried my suitcases aboard and stowed them away. They bought me *L'unità* and *Paese sera*, but by no means the rightist newspapers. They asked me for autographs, some for themselves and others for their relatives. I have never seen such well-mannered policemen: "We are sorry, *Eccellenza*. We are poor, we have families to think of. We must obey orders. We hate to . . ."

At the station in Rome, where I had to get off to change trains to go on to the border, I was able to make out an enormous crowd from my window. I heard shouting. I saw great commotion and confusion. Armfuls of flowers advanced toward the train, raised over a river of heads. "Pablo! Pablo!"

When I went down the car's steps, elegantly guarded, I became the center of a swirling melee. In a matter of seconds, men and women writers, newsmen, deputies, perhaps close to a thousand persons, snatched me away from the hands of the police. The police, in turn, moved in and rescued me from the arms of my friends. During those dramatic moments I made out a few famous faces. Alberto Moravia and his wife, Elsa Morante, like him a novelist. The eminent painter Renato Guttuso. Other poets. Other painters. Carlo Levi, the celebrated author of *Christ Stopped at Eboli*, was holding out a bouquet of roses. In the midst of all this, flowers were spilling to the ground, hats and umbrellas flew, fist blows sounded like explosions. The police were getting the worst of it, and I was once more recovered by my friends. During the scuffle I had a glimpse of gentle Elsa Morante striking a policeman on the head with a silk parasol. Suddenly the luggage hand trucks were going by and I saw one of the porters, a corpulent *facchino*, bring a club down on a policeman's back. These were the Roman people backing me up. The fray became so confused that the police pulled me aside and appealed to me: "Talk to your friends. Tell them to calm down . . ."

The crowd was shouting: "Neruda stays in Rome. Neruda is not leaving Italy! Let the poet stay! Let the Chilean stay! Throw the Austrian out!" (The "Austrian" was De Gasperi, the Italian Prime Minister.)

After half an hour of the fracas, a superior order arrived, granting me permission to remain in Italy. My friends hugged and kissed me, and I left the station, sad to be walking on the flowers the battle had scattered everywhere.

I woke up the next morning in the house of a senator with parliamentary immunity; I had been taken there by the painter Renato Guttuso, who still didn't have much faith in the word of the government authorities. I received a telegram from the island of Capri. It had been sent by the eminent historian Edwin Cerio, whom I did not know personally. He expressed indignation at what he considered an outrage, a desecration of Italian tradition and culture. He ended by offering me a villa where I could stay on Capri.

It all seemed a dream. And when I got to Capri, with Matilde Urrutia, my Matilde, the unreal sensation of dreaming increased.

We came to the marvelous island on a winter night. The coast loomed through the shadows, whitish and tall, unfamiliar and silent. What would happen? What would happen to us? A little horse carriage was waiting. Up and up the deserted nighttime streets the carriage climbed. White, mute houses, narrow vertical lanes. It finally pulled up and the coachman took our bags into the house, which was also white and apparently empty.

We went in and saw a fire blazing in the huge hearth. Standing in the glow of the burning candelabra was a tall man, with hair, beard, and suit equally white. He was Signore Edwin Cerio, historian and naturalist, who owned half of Capri. He stood out in the shadows like the image of *Taita* God in children's stories. He was almost ninety years old and he was the most distinguished man on the island.

"Make yourselves at home, no one will bother you here."

And he left us, thoughtfully contenting himself with sending short messages with news or advice, notes written in an exquisite hand, accompanied by a single leaf or a flower from his garden. For us, Edwin Cerio was the embodiment of the large, generous, and perfumed heart of Italy.

Afterward, I got to know his work, books that are more genuine than Axel Munthe's, though not as famous. Noble old Cerio repeated with roguish humor: "Capri's town square is God's masterpiece."

Matilde and I took refuge in our love. We went for long walks through Anacapri. The small island, divided into a thousand tiny orchards, has a natural splendor, too much commented on but strictly true. Among the rocks, wherever the sun and the wind beat down most, in the arid earth, diminutive plants and flowers burst out, grown in precise and exquisite patterns. This hidden Capri that you enter only after a long pilgrimage, after the tourist label has peeled off from your clothes, this popular Capri of rocks and minuscule vineyards, of humble people, hard-working and natural people, has an absorbing charm. By now you have assimilated things and people; coachmen and fishwives know you; you are part of the hidden Capri of the poor; and you know where to find the good wine and where to buy the olives that the natives of Capri eat.

All those depraved things we read about in novels may take place behind high palace walls. But I shared a happy life in great solitude or among the simplest people in the world. Unforgettable time! I worked all morning at my poems and Matilde typed them in the afternoon. It was the first time we had lived together in the same house. In that place whose beauty was intoxicating, our love grew steadily. We could never again live apart. There I finished *Los versos del capitán*, a book of love, passionate but also painful, which was published later in Naples anonymously.

And now I am going to relate the story of this book, one of my most controversial works. It remained a secret for a long time, for a long time it did not carry my name on its cover, as if I were disowning it or as if the book itself did not know who its father was. There are natural children, offspring of natural love, and, in that sense, *Los versos del capitán* was a natural book.

The poems in it were written here and there, during my exile in Europe. They were published anonymously in Naples, in 1952. My love for Matilde, homesickness for Chile, the passions of social consciousness fill the pages of this book that went through many editions without its author's name.

For its first printing, the artist Paolo Ricci obtained some fine paper, antique Bodoni printing types, and engravings copied from Pompeian urns. Paolo also made up the list of subscribers, with brotherly devotion. The lovely volume was soon out, an edition of only fifty copies. We had a long celebration for this, with a table full of flowers, *frutti di mare*, wine as transparent as water, a unique offspring of the vines of Capri. And also with the cheer of friends who loved our love.

A few suspicious critics suggested political motives for the appearance of this book without a signature. "The party is against it, the party doesn't approve," they said. But it wasn't true. Fortunately, my party is not against expressions of beauty.

The real truth is that I did not want those poems to wound Delia, whom I was leaving. Delia del Carril, sweetest of consorts, thread of steel and honey tied to me during the years when my poetry sang most, was my perfect mate for eighteen years. This book, filled with sudden and burning love, would have reached her like a rock hurled against her gentleness. That, only that, was the profound, personal, respectable reason for my anonymity.

Later, still without a first and last name, the book reached adulthood, a natural and courageous adulthood. It made its own way through life and I had to acknowledge it, at last. Now the "captain's verses," signed by the genuine captain, tramp the roads, that is, bookstores and libraries.

END OF EXILE

My exile was nearing its end. It was the year 1952. We crossed Switzerland en route to Cannes to catch an Italian ship that would take us to Montevideo. This time we didn't want to see anyone in France. Alice Gascar, my loyal translator and long-time friend, was the only one I notified that we were passing through. In Cannes, however, something unexpected awaited us.

On the street, near the shipping line, I met Paul Eluard and his wife, Dominique. They had heard I was coming and were waiting to invite me to lunch. Picasso would also be there. Then we ran into the Chilean painter Nemesio Antúnez and his wife, Inés Figueroa; both would also be at the lunch.

It was the last time I would see Paul Eluard. I picture him in the Cannes sunlight wearing a blue pajama-like suit. I shall never forget his tanned, ruddy face, his intense blue eyes, his infinitely boyish smile, under the African light of the glaring streets in Cannes. Eluard had come from Saint-Tropez to say goodbye to me; he had brought Picasso along and had arranged the lunch. The party was all set.

A stupid, unforeseen incident ruined my day. Matilde did not have a visa for Uruguay. We had to hurry over to that country's consulate. We took a taxi and I waited at the door. Matilde smiled optimistically when the consul came out to receive her. He looked like a nice boy. He was humming a melody from *Madame Butterfly* and wasn't dressed much like a consul: an undershirt and walking shorts; and it never occurred to her that during their conversation the fellow would turn into a common extortioner. With his Pinkerton looks, he wanted to charge for overtime and raised all sorts of obstacles. He had us chasing around all morning. At lunch the bouillabaisse tasted like bitter gall to me. It took Matilde several hours to get her visa. Pinkerton dug up more and more red tape by the second: she had to have her photograph taken, to change dollars into francs, to pay for a long-distance call to Bordeaux. The fee for a transit visa that should have been free came to more than $120. I even started thinking that Matilde would miss the boat, and I wasn't going to leave either. For a long time I recalled this as one of the bitterest days in my life.

RANDOM OCEANOGRAPHY

I am an amateur of the sea. For years I have been collecting information that is of little use because I usually navigate on land.

Now I am returning to Chile, to my oceanic country, and my ship is approaching the coasts of Africa. It has now passed the ancient Pillars of Hercules, armed today to serve one of the last bulwarks of imperialism.

I observe the sea with the complete detachment of a true oceanographer, who knows its surface and its depth, without literary pleasure, but with a connoisseur's relish, a cetacean's palate.

I have always enjoyed sea stories and I have a fishnet in my library. The books I like to look up the most are William Beebe's or a good monograph on the Volutidae of the Antarctic Ocean.

Plankton interests me—the nutritious waters, molecular and electrified, that stain the sea like violet lightning. Thus I came to know that whales feed almost exclusively on these infinitely proliferating sea creatures. The tiniest plants and unreal Infusoria overrun our shaky continent. Whales open their enormous mouths as they shift from place to place, raising their tongues to their palates to let these living and visceral waters fill and nourish them. That is the feeding method of the glaucus whale (*Rhachianectes glaucus*), which goes past my Isla Negra windows on its way to the South Pacific and the tropical islands.

That is also the migratory route of the sperm or toothed whale, the most Chilean of hunted whales. Chilean sailors used them to illustrate the folkloric world of the sea. On their teeth the knives of the sailors scrimshawed hearts and arrows, tiny memorials to love, childish drawings of their ships or their sweethearts. But our whalers, the boldest in the watery hemisphere, did not traverse the Strait of Magellan and Cape Horn, the Antarctic and its furies, simply to unstring the teeth of the menacing sperm whale, but to seize its treasure of blubber and, especially, the tiny sac of ambergris this monster hides in its mountainous abdomen.

I am coming from somewhere else now. I have left behind me the last blue sanctuary of the Mediterranean, the grottoes, the marine and submarine contours of the island of Capri, where the sirens climbed on the rocks to comb out their blue hair, for the churning of the sea had dyed and drenched their wild tresses.

In the Naples aquarium I was able to see the electrical molecules of primeval organisms and a jellyfish soaring and falling, made of silver and vapor, fluttering in its solemn blue dance, girdled below by the only electric belt any lady of the deep has ever worn.

Many years ago in Madras, in the gloomy India of my youth, I paid a visit to a marvelous aquarium. I can still see the shiny fish, the poisonous morays, the schools of fish dressed in fire and rainbow, and, more than that, the super-serious octopuses with their measured strides, metallic computers with innumerable eyes, legs, suckers, and stored-up information.

Of the giant octopus we all encountered for the first time in Victor Hugo's *The Toilers of the Sea* (Victor Hugo is also a tentacled and polymorphous octopus of poetry), of that species I only got to see the fragment of an arm in Copenhagen's Museum of Natural History. This was indeed the legendary kraken, terror of the ancient seas, who would seize a sailing vessel and drag it down, covering it, entangling itself around it. The fragment I saw, preserved in alcohol, indicated that the creature was more than thirty meters long.

But what I was really after was the trail, or rather the body, of the narwhal. Since my friends knew next to nothing about the giant sea unicorn of the North Seas, I came to feel that I was the narwhal's exclusive spokesman and to believe that I, too, was a narwhal.

Does the narwhal exist? Can such an extraordinarily pacific sea creature with an ivory lance four or five meters long on its brow striated from tip to tip in the style of Solomon, and ending in a needle, can it and its legend, its marvelous name, go unnoticed by millions of human beings?

Of its name—narwhal or narwal—I can only say that it is the most beautiful of undersea names, the name of a sea goblet that sings, the name of a crystal spur. Then why doesn't anyone know its name? Why isn't there anyone with Narwal for a last name, or a beautiful Narwal building, even a Narwal Ramírez or a Narwala Carvajal?

There aren't any. The sea unicorn is shrouded in mystery, in its currents and transmarine shadows, with its long ivory sword submerged in unexplored oceans. In the Middle Ages, hunting unicorns was a mystical, an aesthetic sport. The land unicorn lives on forever in tapestries, a dazzling creature surrounded by alabastrine ladies with high coiffures, aureoled in its majesty by birds that trill or flash their brilliant plumage. As for the narwhal, medieval monarchs considered it a magnificent gift and sent one another fragments of its fabulous body. From it, one scraped a powder which, diluted in liqueurs, bestowed—O eternal dream of man!—health, youth, and virility.

Wandering around one day somewhere in Denmark, I entered an old shop where objects of natural history were for sale—a business, unknown in our America, that holds great fascination for me. There, in a corner, I discovered three or four narwhal horns. The largest was five meters long. I thrust and parried with them and stroked them for a long while.

The old man who owned the shop watched me tilting, with an ivory lance in my hands, at imaginary windmills, invisible windmills of the sea. Then I replaced each one in its corner. All I could buy myself was a tiny one, from a baby narwhal, one of those which go out to explore the cold Arctic waters with their innocent spur.

I put it away in my suitcase, but in a small *pension* facing Lake Leman in Switzerland I had a craving to see and touch the sea unicorn's magic treasure. And I took it out of my suitcase.

I can't find it now.

Did I leave it lying somewhere in the Vésenaz *pension*, or did it roll under the bed at the last minute? Or could it have returned in some unaccountable way to the polar circle one night?

I look at the small waves of a new day on the Atlantic.

On either side of its bow, the ship leaves a white, blue, and sulphuric gash of water, foam, and churned-up depths.

The portals of the ocean are trembling.

Over them soar diminutive flying fish, silver and translucent.

I am on my way back from exile.

I gaze at the waters a long time. I am sailing over them to other waters: the tormented waves of my country.

The sky of a long day covers all the ocean.

Night will come once more to hide the huge green palace of mystery with its shadow.

Voyage and Homecoming

A LAMB IN MY HOUSE

I had a relative, a senator who, having triumphed in some recent elections, came to spend a few days at my house in Isla Negra. That's how the story of the lamb begins.

Well, the senator's most enthusiastic supporters came to throw a feast for him. On the first afternoon of the feasting, a lamb was cooked in the Chilean country style, with a huge fire outdoors and the animal's body stuck on a wooden spit. This is called "roast on the stick" and is enjoyed with lots of wine and plaintive creole guitars.

Another lamb was being kept for the following day's festivities. While his fate hung in the balance, he was tethered outside my window. All night long, he moaned and cried, bleating and complaining of his loneliness. It was heartbreaking to listen to the lamb's modulations, so much so that I decided to get up at dawn and abduct him.

I put him in a car and drove a hundred and fifty kilometers to my house in Santiago, where the knives would not get him. He had no sooner arrived than he set to munching greedily on the choicest things in my garden. He loved the tulips and didn't spare a single one. He didn't take liberties with the rosebushes, for thorny reasons, but he gobbled down the gillyflowers and the lilies with uncanny delight. There was nothing I could do but tether him again. And he set to bleating at once, obviously trying to move my heart as he had done before. I was desperate.

Now the story of Juanito and the story of the lamb will join. At about that time there had been a farm laborers' strike in the south. The landowners in the area, who paid the tenant farmers only twenty cents a day, ended the strike with sticks and jail sentences. One country boy was so scared that he hopped a moving train. The boy's name was Juanito; he was a devout Catholic and knew nothing of the things of this world. When the conductor on the train came by to check the tickets, the boy said he didn't have one, he was going to Santiago, he thought trains were for people to get on and travel whenever they had to. Naturally, they were going to put him off. But the third-class passengers—country people, as always big-hearted—took up a collection and paid the fare.

Juanito walked the streets and squares of the capital with a parcel of clothes under his arm. He didn't know anyone and so did not talk to anyone. In the country it was said that in Santiago the thieves outnumbered the other people, and the boy was afraid they would take the shirt and espadrilles he carried wrapped in newspaper under his arm. In the daytime he roamed the busiest streets, where people were always in a hurry and jostled out of their way this Kaspar Hauser fallen from another star. At night he also sought the most crowded neighborhoods, but these were the avenues with cabarets and night life, and he looked even more outlandish there, a pale shepherd lost among sinners. Without a cent to his name, he couldn't eat, and one day he collapsed on the ground in a dead faint.

A crowd of curious people gathered around the boy lying on the street. He had fallen in front of a small restaurant. He was carried inside and set down on the floor. It's his heart, some said. It's his liver, others said. The restaurant owner came over, took one look, and said, "It's an empty stomach." The corpse revived as soon as it had had a few mouthfuls. The proprietor set him to washing dishes and took a great liking to him. He had reason; the country boy washed mountains of dishes and was always smiling. Everything was going well; he had a lot more to eat than in the country.

The city wove its spell in a strange way to make the shepherd and the sheep meet one day in my house.

The shepherd felt like seeing the city and ventured a little beyond the mountains of dishes. He went down one street eagerly, crossed a square, and found everything fascinating. But when he tried to go back, he couldn't. He hadn't taken down the address of the hospitable premises that had taken him in, because he didn't know how to write, and he searched for them in vain. He never found them again.

Touched by his predicament, someone told him to come to me, Pablo Neruda, the poet. I don't know why the fellow suggested this. Probably because in Chile people are in the habit of passing on to me any strange thing that wanders through their heads, and of blaming me, moreover, for whatever happens afterward. These are strange national customs.

Anyhow, the boy came to my house one day and made the acquaintance of the captive animal. Having taken charge of a lamb I didn't need, I found it easy to take the next step—taking the shepherd under my wing. I gave him the job of seeing to it that the gourmet lamb did not devour my flowers exclusively but from time to time also sated its appetite on the grass in my garden.

They took to each other on the spot. During the first days, as a formality, the boy tied a string around the animal's neck, like a ribbon, and led him from place to place. The lamb ate incessantly, and his personal shepherd, too; both roamed all over the house, even into my rooms. It was a perfect kinship; they were linked by mother earth's umbilical cord, by the natural law of man. Many months went by. Shepherd and lamb rounded their anatomies with fat, especially the ruminant, who blew up to such proportions that he could barely follow his master around. Sometimes he came cautiously into my room, regarded me with indifference, and went out, dropping a small rosary of dark beads on the floor.

It all came to an end when the peasant started to pine for the provinces and told me he was returning to his remote corner of the world. It was a last-minute decision, he had to keep a vow he had made to the Virgin who was patroness of his home town, and he couldn't very well take the sheep. It was a tender parting. The shepherd took the train, with his ticket in hand this time. It was all very sad.

What was left in my garden was not a lamb but a serious, or rather, a fat problem. What was I to do with the creature? Who would look after him now? I had too many political commitments.

My house was a wreck after the persecutions my militant poetry had brought down on me. The lamb took up his plaintive tune once more.

I looked the other way and told my sister to take him with her. Alas! This time I was sure he would not escape the roasting stick.

AUGUST 1952 TO APRIL 1957

The years between August 1952 and April 1957 will not be detailed in my memoirs, since I spent almost all this time in Chile and nothing out of the ordinary happened to me, no adventures that would amuse my readers. But I ought to mention some important things that occurred during those years. I published *Las uvas y el viento*, which had been written earlier. I worked intensely on *Odas elementales, Nuevas odas elementales*, and *Tercer libro de las odas*. I organized a Continental Congress of Culture, held in Santiago and attended by outstanding personalities from all the Americas. I also celebrated my fiftieth birthday in Santiago, and prominent writers came from all over the world: Ai Ch'ing and Siao Emi came from China; Ilya Ehrenburg flew in from the Soviet Union; Drda and Kutvalek from Czechoslovakia; and among the Latin Americans present were Miguel Angel Asturias, Oliverio Girondo, Norah Lange, Elvio Romero, María Rosa Oliver, Raúl Larra, and many others. I donated my library and other property to the University of Chile. I made a trip to the Soviet Union, as juror for the Lenin Peace Prize, which I myself had received during this period, when it was still called the Stalin Prize. Delia del Carril and I separated for good. I built my house La Chascona and moved into it with Matilde Urrutia. I started the magazine *Gaceta de Chile* and edited several issues. I took part in the electoral campaigns and other activities of Chile's Communist Party. The Losada publishing house in Buenos Aires brought out my collected works on Bible paper.

THE YOUNG POET BARQUERO

When the twenty-year-old poet Efraín Barquero comes to my house, he reminds me of myself when I arrived in my country's capital thirty years back with a book of homespun verses under my arm. I went from one publisher to the next and met no one who would publish my first poems.

Nonetheless, in 1922 there was a certain romanticism among publishers, none of which exists today. I don't know how Barquero's verses will get printed. Paper costs more now, inflation has made printing costs astronomical, editors don't want to hear a word about young writers, they barely dare to bring out established authors' books.

But readers keep growing in Latin America. An indisputable cultural evolution, a never-before-seen turbulence, fills her streets with ideas, polemics, paintings, stories, and poetry. The road is open for the peoples frustrated by betrayal and greed, who have struggled to regain their independence; and the doors are now open, too, and fresh air blows in from the world with books of knowledge old and new arrived from every shore.

During our colonial past, we disguised the writings of the French Encyclopedists as religious texts, and read them to one another in secret. Today, in large parts of Latin America, in Guatemala, in Chile, in Peru, in Colombia, the modern inquisition, North American in character, hunts down, condemns, burns, and prohibits books and magazines. But truth, liberty, and culture germinate powerfully in Latin America today, and the fruits are evident in all her martyred nations.

When Barquero published his first book, with the greatest effort, I said a few things about his future as a poet in the prologue: "Efraín Barquero's poetry has body. It is a rich material, a reconstruction according to the rules of life, with words, with phrases that seemed pointless and yet at his beckoning shine like swords, gleam like wine, turn to stone, hoist aloft, once more, the dignity of song."

For all that I said about him in his first book, the publication of his new work worries me.

The years of my youth are over, and the paths of the young have not grown clearer, instead they find more and more obstacles in their way.

Social life in Western countries is not proceeding toward the solution of these problems, which are manifest in a number of painful ways. The talent of the Chilean Barquero seemed to guarantee his fate. And yet here he is now, in 1956, thin, pallid, newly arrived on the river running from the perfumed province of his birth, lost in the capital amid two million inhabitants, with a new bouquet of poems in hand.

When I see him pass through the streets of Santiago, gilded by the early autumn, it seems I am seeing myself, thirty years ago, passing over those same cold streets.

The hard hands of struggle did not snuff out the light of my poetry, they lit it up deep in my blood.

I think of Barquero and of so many young Latin American poets:

May the gift of song live on in them, and the stamp of light, despite their helplessness.

Again, their struggle will salvage honor and poetry.

JAILED IN BUENOS AIRES

At the end of this period I was invited to a Congress for Peace which was to meet in Colombo, on the island of Ceylon, where I had lived so many years ago. It was April 1957.

An encounter with the secret police may not seem dangerous, but if it's the secret police of Argentina, that is something else again—not without humor, but with unpredictable consequences. This particular night, just in from Chile and en route to far-off lands, I fell into bed exhausted. I was just starting to doze off when several policemen burst into the house. They ransacked the place: they picked up books and magazines, they rummaged in closets, and went through the underwear. And they had already taken away the Argentine friend in whose house I was staying, when they discovered me in my room at the back of the house.

"Who is this man?" they asked.

"My name is Pablo Neruda," I said.

"Is he sick?" they questioned my wife.

"Yes, he is sick and very tired after his trip. We got here today and we're flying to Europe tomorrow."

"Well, well," they said, and left the room.

They were back an hour later with an ambulance. Matilde protested, but this had no effect on them. They had their orders. They were to take me in, weary or fresh, healthy or sick, dead or alive.

It was raining that night. Thick drops came down from the heavy Buenos Aires skies. I couldn't understand it. Perón had already been ousted. In the name of democracy, General Aramburu had overthrown tyranny. Yet, without knowing how or when, whither or wherefore, whether for this or that, for nothing or everything, dead tired and ill, I was on my way to prison. The stretcher on which the four policemen were carrying me became a knotty problem as we descended stairways, entered elevators, crossed hallways. The four litter-bearers suffered and puffed. To make their distress even greater, Matilde told them in a honeyed voice that I weighed 110 kilos. And I really looked it, in sweater and overcoat, with blankets pulled up over my head—bulging like a huge mass, like Mt. Osorno the volcano, on the stretcher Argentine democracy had proffered me. I imagined, and this eased my phlebitis symptoms, that the poor devils sweating and puffing under my weight were General Aramburu himself carrying the stretcher.

We followed prison routine, and I was booked and my personal effects confiscated. I was not even allowed to hang on to the juicy detective story I had with me to keep from being bored. But I really didn't have time to get bored. Bars clanged open and closed. The stretcher went through courtyards and iron doors, penetrating deeper and deeper, past banging noises and locks. Suddenly I found myself in the middle of a crowd, the rest of the night's prisoners, more than two thousand of them. I was to be held incommunicado; no one was allowed near me. Yet hands reached under the blankets to shake mine, and one soldier put down his gun and held out a sheet of paper for my autograph.

Finally they deposited me upstairs, in the farthest cell, with a tiny, very high window. I wanted to rest, to get some sleep, sleep, sleep. I couldn't. Day had broken and the Argentine prisoners were making an ear-splitting racket, a deafening uproar, as if they were watching a soccer match between the River and the Boca teams.

Some hours later, the community of writers and friends had gone into action in Argentina, Chile, and several other countries. They took me from my cell, carried me to the infirmary, returned my belongings, and set me free. I was about to leave the prison, when one of the uniformed guards came up to me and put a sheet of paper in my hands. It was a poem he had dedicated to me, written in crude verse, filled with careless slips, innocent like all popular art. I imagine few poets have received a poetic homage from the men assigned to guard them.

POETRY AND POLICE

One day on Isla Negra the servant girl told us: Ma'am, Don Pablo, I'm pregnant. Soon after that, she had a baby boy. We never knew who the father was. She didn't care. What she did care about was that Matilde and I should be the baby's godparents. But it was not to be. We couldn't do it. The nearest church is in El Tabo, a cheerful little village where we fill up the station wagon with gas. The priest bristled like a hedgehog. "A Communist godfather? Never. Neruda will not come in that door, not even if he carries your child in his arms." The girl went back home to her brooms, crestfallen. She did not understand.

Another time, I watched Don Asterio suffer. He is an old watchmaker, well on in years, the best maker of chronometers in Valparaíso. He repairs the navy's instruments. His wife was dying—his old companion. Fifty years of matrimony. I thought I ought to write something about him. Something that would help him a little in his bitter moment. Something he could read to his dying wife. So I thought. I don't know if I was right. I wrote the poem. In it I put my admiration and my feelings for the craftsman and his craft. For that life, so pure among the ticktocks of old clocks. Sarita Vial took the poem to a newspaper. The newspaper, *La unión*, was run by Señor Pascal, a priest. He would not publish the poem; it wouldn't be published. Neruda, its author, was an excommunicated Communist.

He would not. The woman died—Don Asterio's old companion. The priest would not publish the poem.

I want to live in a world where no one is excommunicated. I will not excommunicate anybody. I would not tell that priest tomorrow: "You can't baptize So-and-So, because you are an anti-Communist." I would not tell another priest: "I will not publish your poem, your creation, because you're an anti-Communist." I want to live in a world where beings are only human, with no other title but that, without worrying their heads about a rule, a word, a label. I want people to be able to go into all the churches, to all the printing presses. I don't want anyone to ever again wait at the mayor's office door to arrest and deport someone else. I want everyone to go in and come out of City Hall smiling. I don't want anyone to flee in a gondola or be chased on a motorcycle. I want the great majority, the only majority, everyone, to be able to speak out, read, listen, thrive. I have never understood the struggle except as something to end all struggle. I have never understood hard measures except as something to end hard measures. I have taken a road because I believe that road leads us all to lasting brotherhood. I am fighting for that ubiquitous, widespread, inexhaustible goodness. After all the run-ins between my poetry and the police, after all these episodes and others I will not mention because they would sound repetitious, and in spite of other things that did not happen to me but to many who cannot tell them any more, I still have absolute faith in human destiny, a clearer and clearer conviction that we are approaching a great common tenderness. I write knowing that the danger of the bomb hangs over all our heads, a nuclear catastrophe that would leave no one, nothing on this earth. Well, that does not alter my hope. At this critical moment, in this flicker of anguish, we know that the true light will enter those eyes that are vigilant. We shall all understand one another. We shall advance together. And this hope cannot be crushed.

NEW ENCOUNTER WITH CEYLON

A universal cause, the fight against atomic death, was taking me back to Colombo. We crossed the Soviet Union en route to India in the Tu-104, a marvelous jet making the flight just to carry our huge delegation. Our only stop was Tashkent, near Samarkand. The airplane would set us down in the heart of India two days later.

We were flying at ten thousand meters. To cross the Himalayas, the giant bird soared even higher, close to fifteen thousand meters. From that altitude, an almost motionless landscape can be seen. The first barriers come into view, blue and white spurs of the Himalayas. Somewhere below, the awesome Abominable Snowman walks around in his terrifying solitude. Then, on the left, Mt. Everest's mass looms like one more small irregularity in the diadems of snow. The sun beats down on the entire strange landscape; its light cuts out profiles, jagged rocks, the commanding sight of the snowy silence.

The American Andes, which I have crossed so many times, come to mind. The disorder, the Cyclopean fury, the raging desert of our mountains do not prevail here. The Asian mountains appear more classical to me, more well-ordered. Their domes have shapes like monasteries and pagodas in the infinite vastness. The solitude reaches farther out. The shadows do not rise like walls of awe-inspiring stone but spread out like the enigmatic blue gardens of a colossal monastery.

I remind myself that I am breathing the most rarefied air in the world and watching from the skies the tallest peaks on earth. It's a unique sensation in which are mingled clarity and pride, speed and snow.

We are flying to Ceylon. Now we are losing altitude over the hot regions of India. We left the Soviet craft in New Delhi to take this Indian airplane. Its wings quiver and creak in violent storm clouds. In the middle of this seesawing motion, my thoughts go down to the flowering island. At twenty-two I lived a lonely life in Ceylon, writing my bitterest poetry there, surrounded by the beauty of nature's paradise.

I am returning, a long time afterward, for this impressive reunion in behalf of peace, whose cause the government has espoused. I see great numbers, perhaps hundreds, of Buddhist monks, in groups, dressed in their saffron tunics, immersed deep in the meditation that marks Buddha's disciples. By fighting against war, destruction, and death, these priests reaffirm the ancient sentiments of peace and harmony preached by Prince Siddhārtha Gautama, known as Buddha. How far from this—I think—is the church of our American countries, a church like Spain's, official and belligerent. How comforting it would be to true Christians if they saw Catholic priests fighting from their pulpits against the gravest and most terrifying of crimes: atomic death, which slaughters millions of innocent people and leaves its biological maculae in the human race for all time.

I went off, guessing my way through the narrow streets, to look for the house where I had lived, in the suburb of Wellawatte. I had a hard time finding it. The trees had grown. The face of the street had changed.

The old place where I had written so many painful poems was going to be torn down soon. Its doors were worm-eaten, the tropical dampness had damaged its walls, but it had stood there waiting for this final moment of parting.

I found none of my old friends. And yet the island knocked on the door of my heart again with its sharp sound, with its immense scintillation of light. The sea was still humming the same old tune under the palms, over against the reefs. I followed the forest tracks again, I saw the elephants again, with their majestic walk, blocking the paths, again I felt the headiness produced by overpowering perfumes, and I heard the sound of green things growing and the life of the forest. I reached the rock of Sigiriya, where a mad king had built his fortress. As in other days, I paid homage to the huge statues of Buddha in whose shadow men walk like tiny insects.

And I went away once more, knowing that this time I was never to return.

SECOND VISIT TO CHINA

From this peace congress in Colombo I flew across India with Jorge Amado and Zelia, his wife. The Indian planes were always crammed with turbaned passengers, covered with colors and loaded with baskets. It seemed impossible to squeeze so many people into an airplane. A crowd got off at the first airport, and another piled in to take its place. We had to go on beyond Madras, to Calcutta. The plane shuddered under the tropical storms. A day like night, darker than true night, suddenly covered us, and then left to make room for a glaring sky. The plane began staggering again; lightning and thunder illuminated the sudden darkness. I watched Jorge Amado's face go from white to yellow and from yellow to green. And he saw the same mutation of color produced in my own face by the terror that gripped our throats. It started to rain inside the plane. The water came in in heavy drops that reminded me of my house in Temuco in winter. But ten thousand meters up, those leaks did not amuse me. The amusing thing, though, was a monk sitting behind us. He opened an umbrella and with Oriental serenity went on reading his texts of ancient wisdom.

We arrived uneventfully in Rangoon, Burma. The thirtieth anniversary of my residence on earth fell just about then, my residence in Burma, where I, a complete unknown, had written my poems. In 1927, to be exact, at the age of twenty-three, I landed in this same Rangoon. It was delirious with color, a torrid and fascinating place, and its languages were impenetrable. The colony was being exploited and preyed on by its English rulers, but the city was clean and luminous, its streets sparkled with life, the shop windows displayed their colonial temptations.

It was a half-empty city now, with bare shop windows, and filth piled up in the streets. A people's struggle for independence is not an easy road. After the people's uprising and the flags of freedom, we must open our way through hardships and storms. To date, I don't know the story of independent Burma, so cloistered is it beside the powerful Irrawaddy River, at the foot of its golden pagodas, but— over and beyond the garbage in its streets and the sadness rippling past—I was able to imagine all those dark dramas that shake up new republics. It was as if the past still oppressed them.

Not a trace of Josie Bliss, my pursuer, the heroine of my "Tango del viudo." No one could supply me with information about her life or her death. The neighborhood where we had lived together no longer even existed.

Now we are flying away from Burma, crossing over the mountain spurs that separate it from China. An austere landscape, with an idyllic serenity. From Mandalay the plane soared over the rice paddies, over the baroque pagodas, over millions of palm trees, over Burma's fratricidal war, and entered the serene, linear calm of the Chinese landscape.

In Kunming, the first Chinese city across the border, our old friend the poet Ai Ch'ing was waiting for us. His broad, dark features, his large eyes brimming with mischief and kindness, his quick intelligence were once more a promise of pleasure during this long journey.

Like Ho Chi Minh, Ai Ch'ing belonged to the old Oriental stock of poets conditioned by colonialist oppression in the Orient and a hard life in Paris. Coming from prisons in their native land, these poets, whose voices were natural and lyrical, became needy students or waiters in restaurants abroad. They never lost confidence in the revolution. Very gentle in their poetry but iron-jawed in politics, they had come home in time to carry out their destinies.

In Kunming, the trees in the park had undergone plastic surgery. They had taken on unnatural forms, and sometimes one could make out an amputation packed in mud or a contorted limb still in bandages, like an injured arm. We were taken to see the gardener, the evil genius who reigned over such an unusual garden. Stumpy old firs had not grown beyond thirty centimeters, and we even saw midget orange trees covered with miniature oranges like golden rice grains.

We also visited a bizarre stone forest. Each rock was elongated like a monolithic needle or bristled like a wave in a still sea. We discovered that this taste for rocks with strange forms was centuries old. Many huge rocks with puzzling shapes decorate the squares in ancient Chinese cities. In bygone days, when governors wanted to give the emperor the best present they could find, they sent him some of these colossal stones. The presents took years to reach Peking, the huge bulks pushed for thousands of kilometers by dozens of slaves.

China does not seem enigmatic to me. On the contrary, even in the middle of its formidable revolutionary drive, I couldn't help looking at it as a country built thousands of years ago, constantly solidifying, stratifying itself. An immense pagoda: men and myths, warriors, peasants, and gods go in and out of its ancient structure. There is nothing spontaneous here, not even a smile. One looks everywhere in vain for the small, rough-hewn objects of popular art, made with errors in perspective, art that so often borders on the marvelous. Chinese dolls, pottery, wrought stone, and wood reproduce models that are thousands of years old. Everything has the seal of the object perfected and then repeated.

I had my most pleasant surprise in a village market where I found some cicada cages made of very fine bamboo. They were magnificent, one room superimposed on another with architectonic precision, each with its own captive cicada, forming castles almost three feet high. As I looked at the knots holding the bamboo strips together, and the tender green color of the stems, it seemed to me that the hand of the people, the innocence that can work miracles, had sprung back to life. Seeing my admiration, the peasants would not sell me that castle filled with sound. They gave it to me. And so the ritual song of the cicadas accompanied me for weeks, deep into Chinese territory. Only back in my childhood do I remember having received gifts as memorable and rustic as this.

We start our travels on a ship carrying a thousand passengers, peasants, workers, fishermen, a vigorous throng of people, up the Yangtze. Headed for Nanking, for several days we follow the broad river filled with vessels and work projects, crossed and furrowed by thousands of lives, everyday concerns and dreams. This river is China's main street. Very wide and tranquil, the Yangtze sometimes narrows and the ship has a difficult time passing through its tyrannical gorges. The extremely high walls on either side seem to meet overhead in the sky, where from time to time a tiny cloud can be glimpsed, sketched with the mastery of an Oriental brush, or a small house among the scars in the rock.

Few landscapes on earth have such overwhelming beauty. Perhaps the violent mountain passes of the Caucasus or our solitary and forbidding Strait of Magellan is comparable.

I observe that a noticeable change has taken place during the five years I have been away from China, and it is more pronounced as I travel deep into the country this time.

This impression is confused at first. What do I notice, what has changed in the streets, in the people? Ah, I miss the color blue. Five years ago at this same time of year I visited the streets of China, always overflowing, always throbbing with human lives. But everyone was dressed in proletarian blue then, some kind of twill or light workingman's tweed. Men, women, and children wore it. I liked this simplified dress with its varying shades of blue. It was a beautiful thing to see innumerable blue specks crossing streets and roads.

This has changed. What has happened?

The textile industry has simply grown big enough in these five years to clothe millions of Chinese women in all colors, in flowers, stripes, and polka dots, in all varieties of silk; and enough also for millions of Chinese men to wear other colors and better fabrics.

Now each street is a delicate rainbow of China's exquisite taste, of this race that doesn't know how to make anything ugly, this country where the most primitive sandal looks like a straw flower.

Sailing on the Yangtze, I was struck by how faithful the old Chinese paintings are. Up there on the mountain pass, a twisted pine tree like a minuscule pagoda brings to mind the old imaginative prints. There are few places more unreal, more fantastic and surprising than these mountain passes that rise above the great river to incredible heights and display, in any fissure in the rock, age-old signs of this wonderful people: five or six meters of newly planted vegetables, or a small temple with a five-tiered roof, for contemplation and meditation. Farther up on the bald crags we seem to make out the tunics or the vaporous wisps of the ancient myths; they're just clouds and an occasional flight of birds, painted so often by the oldest and wisest miniaturists on earth. A profound poem comes out of this magnificent world of nature, a poem as brief and bare as the flight of a bird or the silver lightning streak of water that flows, almost without stirring, between walls of rock.

But what is definitely extraordinary about this landscape is to see man working in tiny rectangles, on some little green dab on the rocks. All the way up, on the tip of the vertical walls, wherever there is a recess that holds a little bit of cultivable ground, there is a Chinese farming it. The Chinese mother earth is vast and hard. She has disciplined and shaped man, making him an instrument of work, tireless, subtle, and dogged. The combination of vast land, extraordinary human labor, and the gradual elimination of all injustice will make the people of this beautiful, far-flung, and profound China thrive.

During this voyage on the Yangtze, Jorge Amado seemed edgy and depressed. Many aspects of life aboard the ship irritated him and

Zelia, his wife. Zelia, however, has a calm temperament that can carry her through fire without getting burned.

One of these irritants was the fact that, against our wishes, we were being treated as privileged persons on the trip. With our special cabins and private dining room, we felt uncomfortable in the middle of hundreds of Chinese squeezed together everywhere on the boat. The Brazilian novelist looked at me with sarcastic eyes and dropped one of his witty, biting remarks.

In truth, the revelations about the Stalin era had snapped a coiled spring deep within Jorge Amado. We are old friends, we have shared years of exile, we had always been united by a common conviction and hope. But I believe I have been less sectarian than he; my nature and my Chilean temperament inclined me toward an understanding of others. Jorge, on the other hand, had always been inflexible. His mentor, Luis Carlos Prestes, spent nearly fifteen years of his life in prison. These are things that cannot be forgotten, they harden the spirit. I justified Jorge's sectarianism to myself, without sharing it.

The report of the Twentieth Congress was a tidal wave that drove all of us revolutionaries to take new stands and draw new conclusions. Many of us had the feeling that, from the anguish produced by those painful revelations, we were being born all over again. We were reborn cleansed of darkness and terror, ready to continue the journey with a firm grip on the truth.

Jorge, on the other hand, seems to have started a different stage in his life on board that ship, between the marvelous cliffs of the Yangtze. From then on, he became quieter, more moderate in his attitudes and declarations. I don't believe he lost faith in the revolution, but he fell back more on his work and divested it of the direct political character that had marked it until then. As if the epicure in him had suddenly come out into the open, he threw himself into writing his best books, beginning with *Gabriela, Clove and Cinnamon*, a masterpiece brimming with sensuality and joy.

Ai Ch'ing, the poet, was head of the delegation that guided us.

Every night Jorge Amado, Zelia, Matilde, Ai Ch'ing, and I ate in our private dining room. The table was covered with golden and green vegetables, sweet-and-sour fish, duck and chicken cooked in unusual ways and always delicious. After several days this exotic fare stuck in our throats, no matter how much we liked it. At last we found an opportunity to get away from such tasty dishes, but our road was rough, and took a turn that became more and more twisted, like a branch on one of those contorted trees.

My birthday happened to come along around this time. Matilde and Zelia made plans to treat me to one of our own Occidental dinners that would break our diet. It was to be a very modest treat: a chicken we would roast our way, with a tomato-and-onion salad fixed Chilean style, to go with it. The women made a big mystery of this surprise. They went secretly to our good friend Ai Ch'ing. The poet said a bit uneasily that he would have to talk to the others on the committee before giving an answer.

Their decision surprised us. The whole country was going through a wave of austerity. Mao Tse-tung had passed up his birthday celebration. Considering these severe precedents, how could mine be celebrated? Zelia and Matilde replied that what we had in mind was just the opposite: in place of that table covered with rich food—chickens, ducks, fishes that often went untouched—we would have one single chicken, a very modest chicken, prepared, however, our own way, in an oven. A new meeting between Ai Ch'ing and the invisible committee in charge of austerity measures concluded with the answer, on the following day, that there was no oven on the ship we were traveling on. Zelia and Matilde, who had already spoken to the cook, told Ai Ch'ing that there was a mistake, a magnificent oven was warming up, waiting for our possible chicken. Ai Ch'ing squinted and his eyes gazed into the Yangtze's waters.

On that July 12, my birthday, we had our roasted chicken on the table, the golden booty of the controversy. A couple of tomatoes and slices of onion brightened a small dish. The huge table stretched on beyond it, embellished, as it was every day, with dishes gleaming with luscious Chinese food.

In 1928 I had passed through Hong Kong and Shanghai. That China was a colony ruled with an iron hand—a paradise of gamblers, opium smokers, brothels, nighttime muggers, phony Russian duchesses, sea and land pirates. In contrast to the great banking institutions in those huge cities, the presence of eight or more gray battleships revealed the insecurity and the fear, the colonial extortion, the death throes of a world beginning to smell like a corpse. With the sanction of contemptible consuls, the flags of many countries waved over the privateers of Chinese and Malay criminals. The bordellos were financed by international companies. I have already told elsewhere in these memoirs how I was attacked on one occasion, stripped of clothes and money, and abandoned on a Chinese street.

All these memories came back to me when I arrived in the China of the revolution. This was a new country; I was struck by its ethical cleanliness. The defects, the small conflicts and misunderstandings, a good deal of what I am recounting, are just minor details. My predominant impression has been that of watching a triumphant change in the vast land of the oldest culture in the world. Countless experiments were underway everywhere. Feudal agriculture was about to undergo a change. The moral air was as clear as after the passing of a cyclone.

What has estranged me from the Chinese revolutionary process has not been Mao Tse-tung but Mao Tse-tungism. I mean Mao-Stalinism, the repetition of a cult to a socialist deity. Who can deny Mao the political personality of a great organizer, of the great liberator of a people? How could I fail to be impressed by his epic halo, his simplicity which is so poetic, so melancholy, and so ancient?

Yet during my trip I saw hundreds of poor peasants, returning from their labors, prostrate themselves, before putting away their tools, to salute the portrait of the modest guerrilla fighter from Yün-nan, transformed into a god now. I saw hundreds of persons waving a little red book, the universal panacea for winning at Ping-Pong, cur-ing appendicitis, and solving political problems. This adulation flows from every mouth, and every day, from every newspaper and every magazine, from every notebook and every other kind of book, from every almanac and every theater, from every sculpture and every painting.

In Stalin's case, I had contributed my share to the personality cult. But in those days Stalin seemed to us the conqueror who had crushed Hitler's armies, the savior of all humanity. The deterioration of his character was a mysterious process, still an enigma for many of us.

And now, here in plain sight, in the vast expanse of the new Chi-na's land and skies, once more a man was turning into a myth right before my eyes. A myth destined to lord it over the revolutionary conscience, to put in one man's grip the creation of a world that must belong to all. I could not swallow that bitter pill a second time.

In Chungking my Chinese friends took me to the city's famous bridge. I have loved bridges all my life. My father, the railroad man, instilled in me a great respect for them. He never called them bridges. That would have been a desecration. He called them works of art, a distinction he never conceded to paintings, sculptures, or poems, of course. Only to bridges. My father took me many times to con-template the marvelous Malleco Viaduct in the south of Chile. Until now, I had believed that the bridge stretching between the green of the southern mountains, tall and slender and pure, like a steel violin with taut strings ready to be played by the wind of Collipulli, was the most beautiful bridge in the world. The monumental bridge that spans the Yangtze is something else again. It is China's most magnifi-cent feat of engineering, carried out with help from Soviet engineers.

And in addition, it represents the end of an age-old struggle. For centuries, the city of Chungking was divided by the river, which kept it behind the times, slow, and isolated.

The enthusiasm of the Chinese friends who are showing me the bridge is too much for my poor legs. They make me go up towers and climb down to great depths to look at the water, which has been running its course for thousands of years, crossed today by this ironwork several kilometers long. Over these rails trains will run; these are bicycle paths; this enormous avenue will be for pedestrians. All this grandeur overwhelms me.

In the evening, Ai Ch'ing takes us to dinner in an old restaurant, home of the most traditional kind of cooking: a shower of cherry blossoms, a rainbow of bamboo salad, hundred-year-old eggs, lips of a young she-shark. Words can't do justice to this Chinese cooking in all its complexity, its fabulous variety, its extravagant inventiveness, its incredible formality. Ai Ch'ing gives us some pointers. The three supreme precepts for a good dinner are: first of all, flavor; second, aroma; third, color. These three elements of a meal must be respected to the letter. The flavor must be exquisite. The aroma must be delicious. And the color must be appetizing and harmonious. In this restaurant where we are going to eat—Ai Ch'ing said—another virtuoso element comes into play: sound. To the huge porcelain dish surrounded by delicacies is added, at the last minute, a small cascade of shrimp tails; falling onto a red-hot metal griddle, they produce a flute-like melody, a musical phrase that is always repeated the same way.

In Peking we were received by Ting Ling, who headed the writers' committee chosen to welcome Jorge Amado and me. Our old friend Siao Emi, the poet, was also there with his German wife, a photographer. Everything was pleasant and merry. We took a boat ride among the lotus flowers on the huge artificial lake built for the amusement of the last empress. We visited factories, publishing houses, museums, and pagodas. We ate in the most exclusive restaurant in the world (so exclusive that it has only one table), catered by the descendants of the Imperial House. We, the two South American couples, met in the home of the Chinese writers to drink, smoke, and have a good time, as we would have done anywhere on our own continent.

I would hand the daily newspaper to my young interpreter, whose name was Li. Pointing to the impenetrable column of Chinese characters with my finger, I would say: "Translate for me."

He would start right in in his newly acquired Spanish. He read me editorials on agriculture, accounts of Mao Tse-tung's swimming feats, Mao-Marxist apologies, military news that bored me the moment he began.

"Stop," I would say. "Maybe you'd better read to me from this column."

And so I got the surprise of my life one day when I put my finger in a sore. It was a reference to a political trial in which the accused were the very friends we were seeing every day. They were still part of our "welcoming committee." The trial seemed to have been underway for some time, but they had never said a word about being under investigation, nor had they mentioned that their futures hung by a thread.

Times had changed. All the flowers were wilting. When these flowers bloomed, on orders from Mao Tse-tung, innumerable slips of paper had appeared in factories and workshops, in universities and offices, on farms and in hamlets, denouncing injustices, extortions, dishonest actions by leaders and bureaucrats. And just as the war against the flies and the sparrows had been called to a halt by order of the supreme commander, when it was disclosed that their destruction would bring unexpected consequences, so the period that had come in with the opening of the corollas also ended drastically. A new order came from above: hunt out the rightists. And immediately, in every organization, on every job, in every home, the

Chinese began to force confessions out of their neighbors or to confess their own rightism.

My friend the novelist Ting Ling was accused of having had a love affair with one of Chiang Kai-shek's soldiers. It was true, but it had happened before the great revolutionary movement. She gave up her lover for the revolution, and from Yenan, with her baby in her arms, she made the long march of those heroic years. But this did not help her. She was stripped of her position as President of the Writers' Union and sentenced to wait on tables at the restaurant of the same Writers' Union she had headed for so many years. However, she did her work as a waitress with so much pride and dignity that she was soon transferred to the kitchen in a remote peasants' commune. This is the last news I had of this great Communist writer, one of the most important figures of Chinese letters.

I don't know what became of Siao Emi. As for Ai Ch'ing, the poet who accompanied us everywhere, his fate was very sad. First he was sent off to the Gobi Desert. Later he was allowed to write, as long as he never signed his writings with his own name, a name already famous in and outside China. So he was condemned to literary suicide.

Jorge Amado had left for Brazil. I would take my leave a little later with a bitter taste in my mouth. I still have it.

THE MONKEYS OF SUKHUMI

I have returned to the Soviet Union and have been invited to make a trip to the south. When I get out of the airplane, after crossing vast territories, I have left behind me the great steppes, the factories and the highways, the large Soviet cities and the smaller towns. I have come to the imposing Caucasus Mountains populated by firs and wild animals. At my feet, the Black Sea has dressed up in blue to receive us. An overpowering scent of blossoming orange trees comes from everywhere.

We are in Sukhumi, capital of Abkhazia, a small Soviet republic. This is legendary Colchis, the land of the Golden Fleece, which, six centuries before Christ, Jason had come to steal—the Greek country of the Dioscuri. Later, in a museum, I will see an enormous bas-relief in Greek marble, recently dredged out of the waters of the Black Sea. On these shores the Hellenic gods celebrated their mysteries. Today the mystery has been replaced by the simple, hard-working life of the Soviet people. These are not the same people you see in Leningrad. This land of sunlight, wheat, and huge vineyards has another tone, a Mediterranean accent. These men walk differently, these women have the eyes and hands of Italian or Greek women.

I am living in the home of the novelist Simonov for a few days and we go swimming in the Black Sea's warm waters. Simonov shows me the beautiful trees in his orchard. I recognize them and at each name he gives me I repeat like a patriotic peasant: "We have it in Chile. We also have this kind in Chile. And that one, too."

Simonov looks at me with a waggish smile. I tell him: "I'm really sorry that you'll probably never see the wild grapevine at my home in Santiago, or the poplars gilded by the Chilean autumn. There's no other gold like it. If only you could see the cherries blossom in spring and know the scent of Chile's boldo tree. If you could see how the peasants set the golden ears of corn on the roofs along the Melipilla road. If you could dip your feet in the pure, cold waters of Isla Negra. But, my dear Simonov, countries put up barriers, they play at being enemies, they exchange fire in cold wars, and we humans are cut off from one another. We reach the sky in fantastic rockets, but we don't reach our hands out in brotherly love."

"Perhaps things will change," Simonov says, smiling, and he flings a white stone at the gods submerged in the Black Sea.

The pride of Sukhumi is its fine collection of monkeys. Taking advantage of its subtropical climate, the Institute of Experimental

Medicine has bred every kind of monkey in the world there. Let's go in. In huge cages we shall see fidgety and stolid monkeys, enormous and minuscule ones, hairless and hairy ones, monkeys with thoughtful faces or with a spark in their eyes. There are also sullen monkeys, and despotic ones.

There are gray monkeys and white monkeys; apes with tricolored rumps; thickset, serious ones; and others that are polygamous and won't let their females eat without permission, which they concede only after solemnly devouring their own food.

The most advanced biological studies are conducted at this institute. The monkey is used for the study of the nervous system, of heredity, and for delicate investigations into the mystery of life and its prolongation.

A small she-monkey with two babies catches our eye. One follows her around constantly, and she carries the other in her arms with human tenderness. The director tells us that the small monkey she babies so much is not hers but an adoptive child. She had recently given birth when another female, who had also just had a baby, died. This mother promptly adopted the orphan. From then on, her mother love, her every minute of sweetness, was given to the adopted child even more than to her own. The scientists believed that such intense maternal calling would lead her to adopt other babies that were not hers, but she has rejected one after the other. Her attitude obeyed not simply a life principle but an awareness of the solidarity of mothers.

ARMENIA

Now we are flying toward a hard-working and legendary country. We are in Armenia. Far off, to the south, Mt. Ararat's snowy peak towers over Armenia's history. This, according to the Bible, is where Noah's ark came aground to repopulate the earth. A hard undertaking, because Armenia is rocky and volcanic. The Armenians farmed this land with untold sacrifice and raised their national culture to the highest place in the ancient world. The socialist society has brought extraordinary development and flowering to this noble, martyred nation. For centuries, Turkish invaders massacred the Armenians or made them their slaves. Every rock on the plateaus, every tile in the monasteries has a drop of Armenian blood. This country's socialist renaissance has been a miracle and gives the lie to those who speak, in bad faith, of Soviet imperialism. In Armenia I visited spinning mills that employ five thousand workers; immense irrigation and power works; and other powerful industries. I covered the cities and rural areas from end to end and I saw only Armenians, Armenian men and women. I met only one Russian, a blue-eyed engineer among the thousands of black eyes of this dark-skinned people. The Russian was running a hydroelectric plant on Lake Sevan. The surface area of the lake, whose waters empty out through just one channel, is too large. The precious water evaporates and parched Armenia is unable to gather its riches and put them to use. To beat the evaporation, the river has been widened. Thus the lake's level will be lowered, and at the same time, with the added water in the river, eight hydroelectric stations, new industries, gigantic aluminum plants, electric power and irrigation for the whole country, will be created. I shall never forget my visit to that hydroelectric plant overlooking the lake, whose pure waters mirror Armenia's unforgettable blue sky. When the journalists asked me for my impressions of Armenia's ancient churches and monasteries, I answered them, stretching things a little: "The church I like best is the hydroelectric plant, the temple beside the lake."

I saw many things in Armenia. I think Erivan is one of the most beautiful cities I have seen; built of volcanic tuff, it has the harmony of a pink rose. I shall never forget my visit to the astronomical observatory of Binakan, where I saw the writing of the stars for the first time. The trembling light of the stars was picked up; very fine mechanisms were taking down the palpitation of the stars in space, like an electrocardiogram of the sky. In those graphics I observed that each star has its own distinct way of writing, tremulous and fascinating, but unintelligible to the eyes of an earth-bound poet.

At the zoo in Erivan I went straight to the condor's cage, but my countryman did not recognize me. There he stood in a corner of his cage, bald-pated, with the skeptical eyes of a condor without illusions, a great bird homesick for our cordilleras. I looked at him sadly, because I was going back to my country and he would remain behind bars forever.

My experience with the tapir was something different. Erivan's zoo is one of the few that own a tapir from the Amazon, the remarkable animal with an ox's body, a long-nosed face, and beady eyes. I must confess that tapirs look like me. This is no secret.

Erivan's tapir was drowsing in his pen, near the pond. When he saw me his eyes lit up; perhaps we had met in Brazil once. The zoo keeper asked me if I would like to see him swim and I answered that I would go around the world just for the pleasure of watching a tapir swim. They opened a small door for him. He threw me a happy look and plunged into the water, puffing like some fabled seahorse, like a hairy triton. He rose up, lifting his whole body out of the water; he dived under, stirring up a stormy rush of waves; he surfaced, drunk with joyfulness, he huffed and puffed, and then he went on with his incredible acrobatics at top speed.

"We've never seen him so happy," the zoo keeper said to me.

At noon, during the lunch given for me by the Society of Writers, I told, in my speech of thanks, about the feats of the Amazonian tapir and I spoke about my passion for animals. I never skip a visit to the zoo.

In his answering speech, the president of the Armenian writers said: "Why did Neruda have to go visit our zoo? This visit to the Society of Writers would have been enough for him to find all the animal species. Here we have lions and tigers, foxes and seals, eagles and serpents, camels and macaws."

WINE AND WAR

I stopped off in Moscow on the way back. For me, this city is the seat of so many accomplished dreams, and also the residence of some of my dearest friends. For me, Moscow is a feast. As soon as I get there, I go out alone into the streets, happy to breathe, whistling cuecas. I look at the faces of the Russian men, the eyes and the braids of the Russian women, the ice cream sold on street corners, the popular paper flowers, the shop windows, in search of new things, little things that make life important.

Once again I went to visit Ehrenburg. The first thing my good friend showed me was a bottle of Norwegian liquor, aqua vitae. The label had a great painted sailing ship. Somewhere else were the departure and return dates of the ship that had taken this bottle to Australia and brought it back to its native Scandinavia.

We began to talk about wines. I recalled my young days, when the wines of our country traveled abroad, in great demand because of their excellence. They were always too expensive for those of us who wore railwayman's clothing and lived a stormy Bohemian life.

In every country I would take an interest in tracking down the wine, from the time its life began at the "feet of the people" until it was bottled in green glass or cut crystal. In Galicia, Spain, I enjoyed drinking Ribeiro wine, which is sipped from a cup and leaves a thick stain like blood on the porcelain. I remember a full-bodied wine in Hungary, called bull's blood, whose onslaughts make the violins of the gypsies tremble.

My great-great-grandparents owned vineyards. Parral, the town where I was born, is the cradle of the crude musts. From my father and uncles Don José Angel, Don Joel, Don Oseas, and Don Amós I learned to tell the difference between new wine and filtered wine. It was hard for me to follow their liking for the unrefined wine that runs out of the cask, with its original and irreducible heart. As in all things, it was difficult for me to return to the primitive, the early lustiness, after having learned the subtle distinctions of taste, having relished the epicurean bouquet. The same thing occurs in art: you wake up one morning with Praxiteles' *Aphrodite* and end up living with the savage statuary of Oceania.

It was in Paris that I tasted a noble wine in the noblest of homes. The wine was Mouton-Rothschild, with an impeccable body, undescribable aroma, perfect smoothness. It was at the home of Aragon and Elsa Triolet.

"I've just received these bottles and I am opening them especially for you," Aragon said.

And he told me the story.

The German armies were gaining ground in French territory. France's most intelligent soldier, poet and officer Louis Aragon, reached an advance post. He commanded a detachment of male nurses. His orders were to go beyond this post to a building located three hundred meters ahead. The captain in charge there stopped him. He was Count Alphonse de Rothschild, younger than Aragon and as quick-blooded as he.

"You can't pass beyond this point," he said. "The German fire is too close."

"My instructions are to get to that building," Aragon replied pertly.

"My orders are that you are not to go on, you must stay right here," the captain replied.

Knowing Aragon as well as I do, I am sure that during the argument sparks flew like hand grenades, answers like sword thrusts. But it didn't even last ten minutes. Suddenly, before the startled eyes of Rothschild and Aragon, a grenade from a German mortar struck the building, converting it instantly to smoke, rubble, and smoldering ashes.

And so France's first poet was saved, thanks to the stubbornness of a Rothschild.

Ever since then, on the anniversary of this incident, Aragon receives several *bonnes bouteilles* of Mouton-Rothschild from the vineyards of the count who was his captain during the last war.

Now I am in Moscow, at Ilya Ehrenburg's home. This great guerrilla of literature, as dangerous to Nazism as a division of forty thousand men, was also a refined epicure. I could never tell if he knew more about Stendhal or about *foie gras*. He relished Jorge Manrique's verses with as much gusto as he showed when he tasted Pommery et Greno. He was in love with everything French, with the body and soul of delicious and fragrant France.

Anyway, after the war, the rumor spread through Moscow that some mysterious bottles of French wine would go on sale. On its march toward Berlin, the Red Army had taken a fortress-cave filled with Goebbels's insane propaganda and also with the wines he had appropriated from the cellars of noble France. Papers and bottles were shipped to the general headquarters of the victorious army, the Red Army, which took the documents in for study but didn't know what to do with the bottles.

They were splendid glass bottles that flashed their dates of birth on very special labels. All were of illustrious origin and celebrated vintage. Romanée, Beaune, Châteauneuf-du-Pape rubbed elbows with blond Pouilly, amberescent Vouvray, velvety Chambertin. The entire collection was distinguished by chronological indications of the most excellent vintages.

Socialism's egalitarian attitude saw to it that these sublime trophies from the French wine presses were distributed in the liquor stores at the same prices as Russian wines. As a restrictive measure, it was decided that each buyer could purchase only a limited, specified number of bottles. Socialism's intentions are the best, but we poets are the same everywhere. Each of my comrades-in-letters sent relatives, neighbors, friends to buy, at incredibly low prices, bottles of incredibly high lineage. They were sold out in one day.

A quantity I will not disclose reached the home of Ehrenburg, Nazism's unconditional enemy. And that's why I find myself in his company now, talking of wines and drinking with him a part of Goebbels's cellar, in honor of poetry and victory.

PALACES RETAKEN

Magnates have never invited me to their big mansions and, truthfully, I was never very curious about them. In Chile the national pastime is the closing sale. People crowd to the weekly auctions that are so typical of my country. Each of these lordly homes is doomed. When the time comes, to the highest bidder goes the grating that wouldn't let me pass—me or the common people of whom I am one—and with the grating, armchairs, bleeding Christs, old-fashioned portraits, dishes, spoons, and the sheets between which so many useless lives were procreated, all change hands. The Chilean loves to walk in, touch, and look. Few of them buy anything, in the end. Then the building is pulled down and fragments of the house are put up for sale. The buyers carry off the eyes (the windows), the intestines (the staircases); the floors are the feet; and finally, even the potted palms are divided up.

In Europe, on the other hand, the huge houses are maintained. We can sometimes get a glimpse of the portraits of dukes and duchesses whom only some lucky painter saw in the buff, to the delight of those of us who still enjoy painting and those curves. We can also pry into the secrets, the curious crimes, the wigs, and those astounding files, the tapestried walls, which absorbed so many conversations destined for the electronic entertainments of the future.

I was invited to Rumania and arrived as planned. The writers took me to their collective country house, in the middle of the beautiful Transylvanian forests, to get some rest. The Rumanian writers' residence had once been the palace of Carol, the madcap monarch whose extra-regal loves became the talk of the world. The palace, with its modern furniture and its marble baths, was now at the service of Rumanian thought and poetry. I had a very good night's sleep in Her Majesty the Queen's bed, and the next day was dedicated to visiting other castles converted into museums and houses for rest and vacationing. I was accompanied by the poets Jebeleanu, Beniuc, and Radu Boureanu. In the verdant morning, deep into the fir groves of the ancient royal parks, we sang out of tune, laughed at the top of our lungs, shouted out poems in every language. Rumanian poets, with their long history of suffering during the monarchic-Fascist regimes, are at once the most courageous and the most cheerful poets in the world. That band of troubadours, as Rumanian as the birds in their forest lands, so unshakable in their patriotism, so entrenched in their revolution, and so intoxicatingly in love with life, opened my eyes. In few places have I acquired so many brothers so quickly.

I told the Rumanians about my previous visit to another noble palace, to their great delight. It was the Liria Palace, in wartime Madrid. While Franco marched with his Italians, his Moors, and his swastikas, dedicated to the holy work of killing Spaniards, the militiamen occupied this palace, which I had so often seen—every time I went down Argüelles Street—in 1934 and 1935. I would give it a glance of respect, not from a feeling of servitude toward the new Duke and Duchess of Alba, who had no power over me, a hopeless American, and a half-savage poet, but fascinated by the majesty that silent, white sarcophagi possess.

When war broke out, the Duke stayed in England; after all, his last name is really Berwick. He remained there with his best paintings and his richest treasures. With the Duke's flight in mind, I told the Rumanians that after China's liberation, Confucius's last descendant, who had made a fortune from a temple and the bones of the dead philosopher, also went away, to Formosa, with paintings, table linens, and dinnerware. And with the bones, too. He must have settled there comfortably, charging visitors a fee to view the relics.

From Spain in those days the appalling news went out to the rest of the world: HISTORIC PALACE OF THE DUKE OF ALBA LOOTED BY THE REDS, LEWD SCENES OF DESTRUCTION, LET'S SAVE THIS HISTORIC JEWEL.

I went to see the palace, since I would be allowed in now. The purported looters were at the door in blue overalls, guns in hand. The first bombs were being dropped on Madrid by the German army's planes. I asked the militiamen to let me pass. They went over my papers carefully. I was all set to take my first steps into the opulent halls when they stopped me, horrified: I hadn't wiped my shoes on the huge mat at the entrance. The floors literally gleamed like mirrors. I wiped my shoes and went in. The empty rectangles on the walls showed where the absent paintings had been. The militiamen knew everything. They told me that for years the Duke had been keeping the paintings in a London bank, in a good, strong safe. The only things of any importance in the great hall were trophies of the hunt, innumerable antlered heads and snouts of a variety of small beasts. The most striking trophy was an immense white bear standing on two legs in the center of the room, with its two polar arms open wide and a stuffed head that was laughing, with all its teeth bared. It was the militiamen's favorite, they brushed it every morning.

Naturally, I was interested in the bedrooms where so many Albas had slept, with their nightmares brought on by the Flemish ghosts who came to tickle their feet at night. Those feet were gone, but the largest collection of shoes I have ever seen was conspicuously there. The last duke had not increased his art collection, but his collection of shoes was unbelievable and incalculable. Long, glassed-in shelves that reached the ceiling held thousands of shoes. There were special ladders, like those in libraries, so one could take the shoes down, daintily by the heels, perhaps. I looked closely. There were hundreds of pairs of very fine riding boots, yellow ones and black ones. There were also some of those high shoes, with little plush vests and mother-of-pearl buttons. And scores of overshoes, pumps, and gaiters, all with their shoe trees inside, making them look as if they had solid legs and feet at their beck and call. If the glass case were opened, they would all run off to London in search of the Duke! One could have a wonderful time with these shoes, which ranged the length of three or four rooms. A wonderful time with one's eyes, and only with one's eyes, because the militiamen, shouldering arms, wouldn't let a fly touch those shoes. "Culture," they said. "History," they said. And I thought of the poor boys in espadrilles, holding off Fascism on the terrible summits of Somosierra, buried in snow and mud.

Beside the Duke's bed was a little print in a gold frame whose Gothic characters caught my eye. *Caramba!* I thought, it must be the Albas' family tree. I was wrong. It was Rudyard Kipling's "If—," that uninspired, sanctimonious poetry, precursor of the *Reader's Digest*, whose intellectual level, in my opinion, was no higher than that of the Duke of Alba's shoes. May the British Empire forgive me!

The Duchess's bathroom will be exciting, I thought. It evoked so many things. Above all, that madonna reclining in the Prado Museum, whose nipples Goya set so far apart that one thinks how the revolutionary painter must have measured the distance kiss by kiss until he had left her an invisible necklace reaching from breast to breast. But I was wrong again. The bear, the musical-comedy boot shop, "If—," and, finally, instead of a goddess's bath I found a circular room, fake Pompeii, with a step-down tub, vulgar little alabaster swans, tacky *lampadaires*; in short, a bathroom for an odalisque in a Hollywood film.

I was leaving the place with the glum feeling that I had been cheated, when I had my reward. The militiamen invited me to lunch. I went down to the kitchens with them. Forty or fifty of the Duke's household servants and attendants, cooks and gardeners, continued to cook for themselves and the militiamen who guarded the mansion.

They considered me a distinguished visitor. After some whispering, much coming and going, and receipts being signed, they brought out a dusty bottle. It was a hundred-year-old Lachryma Christi, from which I was barely allowed to take a few sips. It was a molten wine, made of honey and fire, severe and impalpable at the same time. Those tears of the Duke of Alba's will not be easy for me to forget.

A week later the German bombers dropped four incendiary bombs on the Liria Palace. From the terrace of my house I saw the two birds of omen flying over. A red glare told me immediately that I was watching the palace's final minutes.

"That same afternoon I went past the smoldering ruins," I tell the Rumanian writers, to end my story. "There I discovered a touching detail. With fire falling from the sky, with explosions shaking the earth, and the bonfire growing, the noble militiamen managed to save the white bear only. They were almost killed in the attempt. Beams were crashing down, everything was ablaze, and the huge well-preserved animal refused to pass through windows or doors. I saw it again, for the last time, with its white arms open wide, dying of laughter, on the palace garden's lawn."

ERA OF COSMONAUTS

Moscow again. On the morning of November 7, I watched the people's parade, its athletes, its glowing Soviet youth. They marched with sure and firm step through Red Square. They were being observed by the sharp eyes of a man dead many years, the founder of this security, this joy, and this strength: Vladimir Ilyich Ulyanov, immortal Lenin.

This time there were few weapons in the parade. But for the first time the enormous intercontinental missiles were rolled out. I could almost have touched those huge cigars with my hand—so innocent-looking, yet capable of carrying atomic destruction to any point on the planet.

The two Russians who had come back from the sky were being decorated that day. I felt as if I, too, had wings. The poet's job is, in great measure, like a bird's. It was precisely in the streets of Moscow, along the shores of the Black Sea, among the mountain passes of the Soviet Caucasus, that I was tempted to write a book on the birds of Chile. The poet from Temuco had every intention of investigating birds, of writing about the birds of his remote land, about sparrows and chercanas, mockingbirds and finches, condors and queltehues, while two human birds, two Soviet cosmonauts, soared into space and left the whole world dumbfounded with admiration. Feeling them over our heads, seeing with our own eyes the cosmic flight of the two men, we all held our breaths.

They were decorated that day. Next to them were their relatives— their origins, their earthly roots, roots of the people. The old men had huge peasant moustaches, the old women's heads were covered with the large shawl that is so typical of the villages and the countryside. The cosmonauts were just like us, people from the country, the village, the factory, the office. In Red Square, Nikita Khrushchev welcomed them in the name of the Soviet nation. Later we saw them in St. George's Hall. Gherman Titov, the number two astronaut, a nice boy, with big radiant eyes, was introduced to me.

"Tell me. Commander, as you flew through the cosmos and looked at our planet, could you make out Chile clearly?" It was like saying to him: "You understand, don't you, that the important thing about your trip was to see little Chile from up there."

He did not smile as I expected him to, but thought it over for a few seconds and said to me: "I do remember some yellow mountain ranges in South America. You could tell that they were very high. Maybe that was Chile."

Of course it was Chile, Comrade.

On the fortieth anniversary of the socialist revolution, I left Moscow by train, for Finland. As I crossed the city on my way to the station, fireworks, huge sheaves of skyrockets—luminous, phosphorescent, blue, red, violet, green, yellow, orange—soared very high, like volleys of cheers, like signals of mutual understanding and friendship going out from this night of victory toward all the countries in the world.

In Finland I bought a narwhal's tooth and we continued our journey. In Gothenburg we boarded the ship that would take us back to America. America and my country also keep step with life and with the times. Well, when we passed through Venezuela en route to Valparaíso, Pérez Jiménez, the tyrant, the U.S. State Department's pet baby, bastard son of Trujillo and Somoza, sent enough soldiers for a war, to stop me and my wife from getting off the ship. But by the time I reached Valparaíso, freedom had already kicked out the Venezuelan despot; the majestic satrap had hightailed it to Miami like a rabbit running in its sleep. The world has been moving fast since the first sputnik's flight. Who would have believed that the first person to knock on my cabin door in Valparaíso to welcome us would be Simonov, the novelist I had left swimming in the Black Sea?

Poetry Is an Occupation

THE POWER OF POETRY

It has been the privilege of our time—with its wars, revolutions, and tremendous social upheavals—to cultivate more ground for poetry than anyone had ever imagined. The common man has had to confront it, attacking or attacked, in solitude or with an enormous mass of people at public rallies.

When I wrote my first lonely books, it never entered my mind that, with the passing years, I would find myself in squares, streets, factories, lecture halls, theaters, and gardens, reading my poems. I have gone into practically every corner of Chile, scattering my poetry like seed among the people of my country.

I am going to recount what happened to me in Vega Central, the largest and most popular market in Santiago, Chile. An endless line of pushcarts, horse wagons, oxcarts, and trucks comes in at dawn, bringing vegetables, fruits, edibles from all the track farms surrounding the voracious capital. The market men—a huge union whose members are badly paid and often go barefoot—swarm through the coffee shops, flophouses, and cheap eating places of the neighborhoods near the Vega.

One day someone came to fetch me in a car, which I climbed into without knowing exactly where or why I was going. I had a copy of my book *España en el corazón* in my pocket. In the car they explained to me that I was invited to give a lecture at the union hall of the Vega market loaders.

When I entered the ramshackle hall, a chill like that in José Asunción Silva's poem "Nocturno" ran through me, not only because winter was so far along but because the atmosphere in the place gave me quite a shock. About fifty men sat waiting for me on crates or improvised wooden benches. Some had a sack tied around their waist like an apron, others covered their bodies with old patched undershirts, and still others braved Chile's cold July bare from the waist up. I sat down behind a small table that separated me from that unusual audience. They all looked at me with the fixed, coal-black eyes of the people of my country.

I remembered old Lafertte. He had given such impassive spectators, who don't move a facial muscle but fasten their eyes on you, a name that made me chuckle. Once, on the nitrate pampa, he had said to me: "Look, there at the back of the hall, leaning against that column, two Mohammedans are watching us. All they need is the burnoose to look like the fearless believers of the desert."

How should I handle this audience? What could I speak to them about? What things in my life would hold their interest? I could not make up my mind, but disguising my desire to run out of there, I took the book I was carrying with me and said to them: "I was in Spain a short time back. A lot of fighting and a lot of shooting were going on there. Listen to what I've written about it."

I should explain that my book *España en el corazón* has never seemed to me an easy book to understand. It tries to be clear, but it is steeped in the torrent of overwhelming and painful events.

Well, I thought I would just read a handful of poems, add a few words, and say goodbye. But it didn't work out that way. Reading poem after poem, hearing the deep well of silence into which my words were falling, watching those eyes and dark eyebrows following

my verses so intently, I realized that my book was hitting its mark. I
went on reading and reading, affected by the sound of my own poetry, shaken by the magnetic power that linked my poems and those
forsaken souls.

The reading lasted more than an hour. As I was about to leave,
one of the men rose to his feet. He was one of those who had a sack
knotted around his waist. "I want to thank you for all of us," he spoke
out. "I want to tell you, too, that nothing has ever moved us so much."

When he finished talking, he couldn't hold back a sob. Several
others were also weeping. I walked out into the street between moist
eyes and rough handclasps.

Can a poet still be the same after going through these trials of
fire and ice?

When I want to remember Tina Modotti, I have to work as hard as if
I were trying to scoop up a handful of mist. Fragile, almost invisible.
Had I or had I not known her?

She was still very lovely then: a pale oval framed by two black
wings of hair, gathered at the back, and huge velvety eyes that go on
watching across the years. Diego Rivera put her face into one of his
murals, glorified with crowns of plants and spears of corn.

This Italian revolutionary, an extraordinary artist with a camera,
went to the Soviet Union a long time ago to take photographs of its
people and monuments. But she was caught up in the uncontainable
rhythm of socialism in full progress and flung her camera into the
Moscow River, vowing to consecrate her life to the most menial work
of the Communist Party. I met her while she was carrying out this
vow in Mexico, where I was deeply moved by her death one night.

This was in 1941, and Vittorio Vidali, Commandant Carlos, was
her husband. Tina Modotti died of a heart attack in a taxi, on her way
home. She knew that she had a bad heart, but she never mentioned
it, so that they wouldn't make her cut down on her revolutionary

work. She was always ready to do whatever no one else wanted to do: sweeping offices, going long distances on foot, sitting up nights to write letters and translate articles. She nursed the Republican wounded during the Spanish war.

She had gone through a tragic experience while living with the remarkable Cuban youth leader Julio Antonio Mella, exiled in Mexico at the time. Gerardo Machado, the tyrant, sent several gunmen from Havana to kill the revolutionary leader. They were coming out of the movies one afternoon, Tina leaning on Mella's arm, when he collapsed under a burst of machine-gun fire. They toppled to the ground together, she with the blood of her dead companion all over her, while the assassins fled, protected by the police. To crown it all, the same authorities who protected the criminals tried to pin the murder on Tina Modotti.

Twelve years later, Tina Modotti's strength quietly ebbed away. The Mexican reactionaries tried to expose her to infamy again by surrounding her death with scandal, as they had once tried to involve her in Mella's death. Carlos and I stood watch over the tiny corpse. Seeing such a tough and courageous man suffer is not easy. That lion bled when they rubbed the caustic poison of slander into his wound by reviling Tina Modotti again, now that she was dead. Red-eyed from weeping, Commandant Carlos let out a roar of pain; in her small exile's coffin, Tina seemed to be made of wax. I was helplessly silent before the grief that filled the room.

The newspapers covered whole pages with sensational filth. They called her the "mystery woman from Moscow." Some added: "She died because she knew too much." Deeply moved by Carlos's savage grief, I decided to do something, and I wrote a poem challenging those who were smearing our dead friend's good name. I sent it to all the newspapers, without any hope that it would be published. Wonder of wonders! On the following day, instead of the new and juicy exposés promised the evening before, it was my outraged and insolent poem that made the front pages of all the newspapers.

The poem's title was "Tina Modotti ha muerto" (Tina Modotti Is Dead). I read it that morning at the cemetery in Mexico where we left her body to lie forever under a slab of Mexican granite. My lines are engraved on that stone.

The Mexican press did not write another line against her.

It was in Lota, many years ago. Ten thousand miners had shown up for the meeting. The coal-mining district, in constant agitation over its traditional poverty, had filled the Lota town square with miners. The political speakers talked on and on. An odor of coal and sea brine floated in the sultry noon air. The ocean was close by; under its waters the dark tunnels, where these men dug out the coal, stretched for more than ten kilometers.

Now, at high noon, they listened. The speakers' platform was very high and from it I could make out that sea of blackened hats and miners' helmets. I was the last speaker. When my name and my poem "Nuevo canto de amor a Stalingrado" (New Love Song to Stalingrad) were announced, something extraordinary occurred, a ceremony I can never forget.

As soon as they heard my name and the title of the poem, the huge mass of people uncovered their heads. They bared their heads because, after all the categorical and political words that had been spouted, my poetry, poetry itself, was about to speak. From the raised platform I saw that immense movement of hats and helmets: ten thousand hands went down in unison, in a groundswell impossible to describe, a huge soundless wave, a black foam of quiet reverence.

Then my poem outdid itself. It took on, as it never had before, a tone of combat and liberation.

This other incident happened when I was still quite young. I was the student poet wearing a dark cape, thin and underfed like any poet in those days. I had just published *Crepusculario* and I weighed less than a black feather.

I went into a run-down cabaret with some friends. This was in the heyday of tangos and troublemaking gangs of toughs. Suddenly the dancing stopped and the tango broke up like a glass smashed against a wall.

Two notorious thugs were gesturing animatedly and insulting each other in the middle of the dance floor. Whenever one stepped forward to get in a blow, the other backed away, and with him the crowd of music lovers huddling for protection behind the barrier of tables also retreated. They looked like two primitive beasts dancing in a clearing in a primordial forest.

Without thinking, I stepped forward and lashed out from behind my scrawny impotence: "You miserable bullies, fat-brained apes, you despicable scum, stop annoying people who're here to dance, not to watch a two-bit farce!"

They exchanged looks of surprise, they couldn't believe their ears. The shorter one, who had been a boxer before becoming a thug, stepped in my direction, ready to murder me. And the gorilla would have done it, if a well-aimed fist had not floored him. His opponent had finally decided to hit him.

While the fallen champion was being dragged out like a sack, and people at the tables were holding bottles out to us, and the dance girls beamed at us eagerly, the giant who had landed the knock-out blow tried, understandably, to join the victory celebration. But I turned on him like a firebrand: "Get away from here! You're no better than he is!"

A little later, my moment of glory was over. My friends and I had gone down a narrow corridor, when we made out a kind of mountain, with the waist of a panther, blocking the exit. It was the other pugilist from the underworld, the winner I had whipped with my words, who barred our way, waiting to get even.

"I've been waiting for you," he said to me.

He headed me toward another door, with a light shove, while my friends took to their heels like scared rabbits. I stood there helplessly, face-to-face with my nemesis. I glanced around quickly to see what I could grab to defend myself. Nothing. There was nothing. Only the heavy marble tops of the tables and the wrought-iron chairs, which I couldn't possibly lift. Not a flowerpot or a bottle or even a measly walking stick someone might have forgotten there.

"Let's have a little talk," the man said.

I realized how useless it was to try anything, and I thought he just wanted to size me up before devouring me, like a tiger facing a little fawn. I sensed that my only defense lay in not showing how scared I was. I returned the shove he had given me, but I couldn't budge him an inch. He was a brick wall.

Suddenly he threw back his head and the look of a wild animal left his eyes. "Are you Pablo Neruda, the poet?" he said.

"Yes, I am."

He hung his head. "What a bastard I am! Here I am, face-to-face with the poet I truly admire, and he has to tell me what a no-good bum I am!" And he went on wailing, with his head in his hands: "I'm just a hood, the other guy I had the fight with is a cocaine pusher. We're the scum of the earth. But there's one clean thing in my life. It's my girl, my girl's love for me. Look at her, Don Pablito. Look at her picture. I'll tell her sometime that you actually held it in your hands. It'll make her so happy."

He handed me the photograph of a smiling girl. "She loves me because of you, Don Pablito, because of your poems, which we've learned together by heart."

And right then and there he started reciting: "Deep inside you, a sad boy like me kneels, with his eyes on us . . ."

Just then the door burst open. It was my friends coming back with armed reinforcements. I saw their shocked faces crowding the doorway.

I walked out slowly. The man stayed behind alone, without

moving an inch, reciting: "For that life burning in her veins they would have to murder my hands"—defeated by poetry.

The airplane piloted by Powers on a spying mission over Soviet territory fell from an unbelievable altitude. Two fantastic missiles had hit it and brought it down from the clouds. Newsmen rushed to the secluded mountain spot from which the rockets had left the ground.

The marksmen were two solitary boys. In that vast world of fir trees, rivers, and snows, they munched apples, played chess and the accordion, read books, and stood watch. They had aimed upward, to defend their Russian motherland's wide sky.

They were plied with questions: "What kind of food do you eat? Who are your parents? Do you like to dance? What books do you read?"

Answering this last question, one of the young men responded that they read poems and that Pushkin, the classic Russian writer, and the Chilean Neruda were two of their favorite poets.

I felt infinitely happy when I heard about this. The missile, which had gone up so high and forced pride to plunge so low, had somehow carried an atom of my impassioned poetry.

THE PERSISTENT INFLUENCE OF TREES

Poetry should be organic in every poet, fluid of his blood, pulse and pal-pitation of his entire being. It's a matter so intimate it doesn't yield to examination, and yet, it must weather storms.

I started writing very young. Perhaps I've done nothing good or bad except write my poems. The big trees, the untamed nature of my country, which is also the southern tip of the world, always had a deep influence on me. This is a region of great solitude, barely inhabited, where it rains the better part of the year.

I wrote a melancholic poetry derived from those dark, deserted climes.

In those days I had lots of far-flung friends. Many came from Russia. They were characters, incidents, intensities of pain, strong joys, the entire extraordinary essence of a great literature that peopled my adolescent solitudes with wrenching lives. I will never forget those nights of fevered readings, when Prince Myshkin's sentiments or Foma Gordeyev's adversities mingled in my heart with the crashing of waves on the austral archipelagos.

I have written many love poems, many verses about death and life, I have dedicated much of my poetry to the intense, extreme struggles of the American peoples. Every inch of the immensity of the continent is marked by blood, agony, victory, pain. There is no American geography, there is no American poetry, if the martyred heart of the American people is forgotten. Ravenous parasites came from all over, fanning over the territory like birds of prey, and someone must tell, must sing this story.

And yet, I do not believe poetry should be political, not entirely. Poets must have their senses open to every horizon. These horizons may be unknown. Some of the greatest poems have been a kind of dialogue with darkness. Two of them: Jorge Manrique's "Coplas on the Death of His Father" and Gray's "Elegy" are thuds of the knocker against the sealed door of death. We still hear their blows, and they shall be heard so long as man exists.

In my poems, I have wished to speak of simpler, more common, more elemental things. I have made poems about wood, air, stone, the clock, the sea, tomatoes, plums, the onion. They are poems of overwhelming joy, and in them I have tried to sing again all that has ever been sung, so that everything may live again. And just as I believed the poet had a duty to relive the tragic history of blood and exploitation in Indian America, so I believed the poet had a duty to wash and cleanse ordinary things, to put down a new tablecloth for all lives.

It's strange, but I haven't been especially well understood by those who ought best to have understood me. A newspaper run by young people in one of the world's capitals begged me insistently for a few poems. I sent them one about corn and another about plums. They are two simple poems, with the clarity and joy characteristic of that part of my work. They didn't publish them. They didn't like them. But they did give me, as an extraordinary gift, the feeling that those young people perhaps were older than I.

POETRY

... How many works of art ... There's not enough room in the world for them any more ... They have to hang outside the rooms ... How many books ... How many little books ... Who can read them all ...? If they were food ... If, during a wave of great hunger, we tossed a salad, cut them up, poured some dressing on them ... We've had it ... We're fed up ... The world is drowning in a flood tide of books ... Reverdy said to me: "I notified the post office not to deliver them. I couldn't open them. I had no more space. They were climbing up the walls, I was afraid of a disaster, they were going to cave in on my head ..." Everybody knows Eliot ... Before becoming an illustrator and a playwright, and writing brilliant criticism, he used to read my poems ... I was flattered ... No one understood them better ... Then one day he started to read me his own, and I ran off selfishly, protesting: "Don't read them to me, don't read them to me" ... I locked myself in the bathroom, but Eliot read them to me through the shut door ... I was depressed ... Fraser, the Scottish poet, was there ... He blasted me: "Why do you treat Eliot like that?" ... I replied: "I don't want to lose my reader. I have cultivated him carefully. He has become familiar even with the wrinkles in my poetry ... Eliot has so much talent ... He can draw ... He writes essays ... But I want to keep this reader, to preserve

him, to water him like an exotic plant ... You understand me, Fraser ..."
Because, actually, if this continues, poets will publish only for other po-
ets ... Each will pull out his little book and put it in the other's pocket ...
his poem ... and he will leave it on the other's plate ... One day Quevedo
left his under a king's napkin ... that was truly worthwhile ... Like poetry
in a town square at high noon ... Or letting the books wear out, fall in
shreds between the fingers of mankind ... Well, this thing, where one poet
publishes for other poets, doesn't tempt me, doesn't lure me, only drives
me to bury myself deep in nature's woods, before a rock or a wave, far
from the publishing houses, from the printed page ... Poetry has lost its
ties with the reader, he's out of reach ... It has to get him back ... It has to
walk in the darkness and encounter the heart of man, the eyes of woman,
the strangers in the streets, those who at twilight or in the middle of the
starry night feel the need for at least one line of poetry ... This visit to the
unexpected is worth all the distance covered, everything read, everything
learned ... We have to disappear into the midst of those we don't know,
so they will suddenly pick up something of ours from the street, from the
sand, from the leaves that have fallen for a thousand years in the same
forest ... and will take up gently the object we made ... Only then will we
truly be poets ... In that object, poetry will live ...

LIVING WITH THE LANGUAGE

I was born in 1904. In 1921 one of my poems came out in a magazine. In 1923 my first book, *Crepusculario*, was published. I am writing these recollections in 1973. Fifty years have gone by since that
exciting moment when the poet hears the first cries of the printed
infant, alive, kicking, and doing its best, like any other newborn, to
call attention to itself.

    You can't live an entire lifetime with a language, stretching it
lengthwise, exploring it, poking around in its hair and its belly, without having this intimacy become second nature to you. That's what

happened to me with Spanish. The spoken language has other dimensions: the written language acquires unexpected elasticity. Using language like clothes or the skin on your body, with its sleeves, its patches, its transpirations, and its blood and sweat stains, that's what shows a writer's mettle. This is style. I found that my time was in a ferment over the revolutionary trends in French culture. These always attracted me, but somehow they were not the right fit of clothes for my body. Huidobro, a Chilean poet, took charge of the French innovations, adapting them admirably to his way of life and expression. At times, it seemed to me, he outdid his models. Something of the kind happened, on a larger scale, when Darío burst in upon the scene of Hispanic poetry. But Darío was a huge elephant, a music-maker who shattered all the glass windows in the Spanish language of his time to let in the air of the world. And it came in.

Our language sometimes separates us Latin Americans from the Spaniards. However, it is the ideology of the language, more than anything else, that causes the split. Góngora's frozen beauty is not made for our latitudes, but there is no poetry from Spain, not even the most recent, without an aftertaste of Góngora, without his richness. Our American stratum is dusty rock, crushed lava, clay mixed with blood. We don't know how to work in crystal. Our elegant poets sound hollow. A single drop of Martín Fierro's wine or of Gabriela Mistral's turbid honey is enough to put them in their place: standing stiffly in the parlor like vases with flowers from someone else's garden.

Spanish became a gilded language after Cervantes, it took on a courtly elegance, it lost the wild power it had brought in from Gonzalo de Berceo and the Archpriest of Hita, it lost the genital fire that still burned in Quevedo. The same thing happened in England, in France, in Italy. Chaucer's extravagances, as well as Rabelais's, were castrated; the precious style inherited from Petrarch made emeralds and diamonds glitter, but the source of greatness began to burn itself out.

This earlier wellspring had everything to do with the whole man, his freedom, his prolific nature, his excesses.

At least that was my problem, although I didn't put it in those terms, not even to myself. If my poetry has any meaning at all, it is this tendency to stretch out in space, without restrictions, and not be happy to stay in a room. I had to break out of my limited world by myself, not having traced it out within the framework of a distant culture. I had to be myself, striving to branch out like the very land where I was born. Another poet of this same hemisphere helped me along this road, Walt Whitman, my comrade from Manhattan.

CRITICS MUST SUFFER

The Songs of Maldoror, basically, form part of a great serial story. Don't forget that Isidore Ducasse took his pseudonym from a novel by the feuilletonist Eugène Sue: *Latréaumont*, written in Châtenay in 1837. But Lautréamont, we know, went much further than Latréaumont. He went much lower, he wanted to be Satanic. And much higher, a fallen archangel. At the height of his unhappiness, Maldoror celebrates the marriage of heaven and hell. Fury, dithyrambs, and agony make up the irresistible waves of Ducasse's rhetoric. Maldoror: Maldolor.

Lautréamont planned a new phase; he repudiated his gloomy side and did the prologue to a new optimistic poetry he never had the chance to write. The young Uruguayan was carried off by death in Paris. But the promised change in his poetry, the swing toward goodness and health, which he did not fulfill, has stirred up much criticism. He is venerated for his sorrow and condemned for his move toward joy. The poet must torment himself and suffer, he must live in despair, he must go on writing his song of despair. This has been the opinion on one social level, the opinion of one class. This cut-and-dried formula was followed by many who succumbed to the suffering imposed by unwritten, but still cut-and-dried, laws. These invisible laws condemned the poet to the hovel, worn shoes, the hospital, the morgue. That made everyone happy: everybody had a good time and few tears were shed.

Things changed because the world changed. And we poets suddenly led the rebellion toward joy. The unhappy writer, the crucified writer are part of the ritual of happiness in the twilight of capitalism. Taste was skillfully channeled toward the buildup of misery as a catalyst for great creativity. Decadent living and suffering were prescribed for writing poetry. Hölderlin, mad and unhappy; Rimbaud, embittered, perpetually wandering; Gérard de Nerval, hanging himself from a lamppost in a small, run-down side street; they gave the last years of the century not only the paroxysm of beauty but the road of suffering. Dogma made this road of thorns the poet's inbred prerequisite for the creations of the spirit.

Dylan Thomas was the last of those steered to his martyrdom.

Oddly, these ideas of the old surly bourgeoisie still hold true in the minds of some. Minds that don't take the world's pulse through its nose, which is where it should be taken, because the world's nose smells what is in the future.

There are critics like creeping gourd plants whose guide shoots and tendrils seek out the latest sigh in fashionable trends, terrified that they will miss out on something. But their roots remain steeped in the past.

We poets have the right to be happy, as long as we are close to the people of our country and in the thick of the fight for their happiness.

"Pablo is one of the few happy men I have known," Ilya Ehrenburg says somewhere in his writings. I am that Pablo, and Ehrenburg is not wrong.

That's why I am amazed that magazine reviewers, who should know better, worry about my material well-being, although my personal affairs should not be part of the critic's concern. I realize that the chance that I may be happy offends many. But the fact is, I am happy inside. I have a clear conscience and a restless intelligence.

To those critics who seem to begrudge poets a better standard of living, I suggest that they should be proud that books of poetry are printed, sold, and fulfill their mission of giving critics something to think about; they should be happy that writers are remunerated and that some, at least, are able to make a living from their honest labor. The critics should proclaim their pride in this, instead of always trying to spoil things.

That's why a short time ago, when I read the paragraphs devoted to me by a young critic, a brilliant ecclesiastic, I didn't think his brilliance prevented him from blundering badly.

According to him, my poetry was weakened by the happiness in it. He prescribed suffering for me. According to this theory, appendicitis should produce excellent prose, and peritonitis might possibly produce some sublime poems.

I continue to work with the materials I have, the materials I am made of. With feelings, beings, books, events, and battles, I am omnivorous. I would like to swallow the whole earth. I would like to drink the whole sea.

SHORT AND LONG LINES

As an active poet, I fought against my own self-absorption and so was able to settle the debate between the real and the subjective deep within myself. I'm not trying to hand out advice, but my experiences may possibly help others. Let's take a quick look at the results.

It is natural for my poetry to be subjected to serious criticism as well as exposed to the vicious attacks of slander. It's part of the game. I have no voice in this part of it, but I do have a vote. For the critic who gets down to essentials, my vote is in my books, in all my poetry. For the unfriendly slanderer, I also have a vote, and it, too, consists of my unbroken creative activity.

If what I am saying sounds vain, you are right. Mine is the vanity of the craftsman who has practiced his craft for a good many years with a love that has never faltered.

And if I am satisfied about one thing, it is that one way or another, at least in my own country, I have made people respect the occupation of poet, the profession of poetry.

At the time I began to write, there were two kinds of poets. Some belonged to the upper crust and earned respect because of their money, which helped them reach legitimate or illegitimate standing. The other family of poets were the militant wanderers of poetry, bar lions, fascinating madmen, tormented sleepwalkers. And let's not overlook those writers tied down, like the galley slave to his oar, to the little stool in government offices. Their dreams were almost always smothered by mountains of official stamped paper and by terrible fear of their superiors or of being laughed at.

I started life more naked than Adam but with my mind made up to maintain the integrity of my poetry. This ingrained attitude was not only valuable in itself but also stopped fools from laughing at me. And afterward, the fools who had a heart and conscience accepted, like the good people they were, the grim realities stirred up by my poetry. And those who were ill-willed gradually became afraid of me.

And so Poetry, with a capital *P*, was shown respect. Not only poetry but poets as well. All poetry and all poets.

I am keenly aware of this service to the people, and I won't let anyone snatch this merit from me, because I like to wear it like a medal. They can question everything else, but what I am telling now is solid history.

The poet's die-hard enemies will put forward many arguments that are no longer valid. They called me a hungry bum when I was young. Now they attack me by making people think I am Mr. Big, owner of a fabulous fortune, which I don't own but would love to own, among other things to upset them even more.

Others measure the length of my lines to prove that I chop them up into small fragments or stretch them out too far. It doesn't matter.

Who sets up the rules about shorter or longer, narrower or wider, yellower or redder lines? The poet who writes them is the one who determines what's what. He determines it with his breath and his blood, with his wisdom and his ignorance, because all this goes into the making of the bread of poetry.

The poet who is not a realist is dead. And the poet who is only a realist is also dead. The poet who is only irrational will only be understood by himself and his beloved, and this is very sad. The poet who is all reason will even be understood by jackasses, and this is also terribly sad. There are no hard and fast rules, there are no ingredients prescribed by God or the Devil, but these two very important gentlemen wage a steady battle in the realm of poetry, and in this battle first one wins and then the other, but poetry itself cannot be defeated.

It's obvious that the poet's occupation is abused to some extent. So many new men and women poets keep cropping up that soon we'll all look like poets, and readers will disappear. We'll have to go looking for readers on expeditions that will cross the desert sands on camels or circle the sky on spaceships.

Poetry is a deep inner calling in man; from it came liturgy, the psalms, and also the content of religions. The poet confronted nature's phenomena and in the early ages called himself a priest, to safeguard his vocation. In the same way, to defend his poetry, the poet of the modern age accepts the investiture earned in the street, among the masses. Today's social poet is still a member of the earliest order of priests. In the old days he made his pact with the darkness, and now he must interpret the light.

ORIGINALITY

I don't believe in originality. It is just one more fetish made up in our time, which is speeding dizzily to its collapse. I believe in personality reached through any language, any form, any creative means used by the artist. But out-and-out originality is a modern invention and an electoral fraud. There are some who want to be elected Poet Laureate in their country, in their language, or in the world. So they run in search of electors, they fling insults at those who seem close enough to compete for the scepter, and poetry turns into a farce.

Still, it is essential to keep one's interior bearings, to stay in control of the additional material that nature, culture, and a socially committed life contribute to bringing out the best in the poet.

In the past, the most noble, the consummate poets, like Quevedo, for example, wrote poems headed with this warning signal: "Imitation of Horace," "Imitation of Ovid," "Imitation of Lucretius."

For my part, I keep up my own tone, which gathered strength by its own nature as time went along, like all living things. There is no doubt that feelings are a major part of my earliest books, and so much the worse for the poet who does not respond with song to the tender and furious summons of the heart! Yet, after forty years of experience, I believe that the poet can take a firmer grip on his emotions in his work. I believe in guided spontaneity. For this, the poet must always have some reserves, in his pocket, let's say, in case of emergency. First, a reserve of mental notes on established poetic forms, of words, sounds, or images, the ones that buzz right past us like bees. They must be caught quickly and put away in one's pocket. I am lazy in this respect, but I know I am passing on some good advice. Mayakovsky had a little notebook he was constantly going into. There is also the reserve of feelings. How can these be preserved? By being conscious of them when they come up. Then, when we face the paper, this consciousness will come back to us more vividly than the emotion itself.

In a substantial part of my work I have tried to prove that the poet can write about any given subject, about something needed by a community as a whole. Almost all the great works of antiquity were done strictly on request. The *Georgics* are propaganda for the farming of the Roman countryside. A poet can write for a university or a labor union, for skilled workers and professionals. Freedom was never lost simply because of this. Magical inspiration and the poet's communication with God are inventions dictated by self-interest. At the moments of greatest creative intensity, the product can be partially someone else's, influenced by readings and external pressures.

Suddenly I interrupt these observations, which are a bit on the theoretic side, and I start remembering the literary life in Santiago when I was a young man. Painters and writers worked in a creative ferment, without public response. An autumnal lyricism hovered over painting and poetry. Each artist tried to be more anarchic, more demoralizing, more disorderly than the others. There were deep and troubled stirrings among Chile's social classes. Alessandri made subversive speeches. On the nitrate pampas the workers, who would create the most important people's movement on the continent, were organizing. Those were the holy days of the struggle. Carlos Vicuña, Juan Gandulfo. I quickly joined the student anarcho-syndicalist movement. My favorite book was Andreyev's *Sacha Yegulev*. Others read Artsybashev's pornographic novels and attributed an ideological thrust to them, exactly as people do today with existentialist pornography. Intellectuals made themselves at home in bars. The good old wine gave poverty a glittering golden aura that lasted till the next morning. Juan Egaña, an extraordinarily gifted poet, was going to pieces, headed for the grave. A story was making the rounds that he had inherited a fortune and had left all his money in bills on a table in an abandoned house. His drinking companions, who slept by day, went out at night to fetch wine by the keg. But Juan Egaña's poetry is a beam of moonlight that has never sent the slightest shudder through our "lyric forest." This was the romantic title of the wonderful modernist anthology put out by Molina Núñez and O. Segura Castro, a very complete book, filled with greatness and generosity. It is the Summa Poetica of a chaotic era, marked by huge gaps as well as pure, resplendent poems. The personality who made the greatest impression on me was Aliro Oyarzún, the dictator of the new literature.

No one remembers him now. He was an emaciated Baudelairean, a remarkable decadent, Chile's Barba Jacob, tormented, cadaverous, handsome, and mad. He spoke with a cavernous voice from the top of his tall stature. He invented a hieroglyphic style of stating aesthetic problems which is peculiar to a certain segment of our literary world. His voice soared; his forehead was a yellow dome of the temple of intelligence. He would say, for example: "the circle's circularity," "the Dionysian in Dionysius," "the obscurity of the obscure." Yet Aliro Oyarzún was no fool. In him were combined the paradisiacal and the infernal sides of a culture. He was a cosmopolite who gradually killed his real nature with his theories. They say he wrote his only poem in order to win a bet, and I can't understand why that poem is not in all the anthologies of Chilean poetry.

BOTTLES AND FIGUREHEADS

Christmas is approaching. Each Christmas takes us closer to the year 2000. We poets of today have been struggling and singing for happiness in the future, for the peace of tomorrow, for universal justice, for the bells of the year 2000.

Back in the thirties, Sócrates Aguirre, the subtle and excellent man who was my superior at the consulate in Buenos Aires, asked me, one December 24, to play Santa Claus, or Old Saint Nick, at his house. I have bungled many things in my life, but nothing had ever turned out as badly as my Old Saint Nick. The wads of cotton in my beard kept slipping off, and I got things all mixed up when I passed the toys around. And how could I disguise the voice that the climate of southern Chile had turned into a twang, nasal and unmistakable, from my earliest years? I had to use a trick: I spoke to the children in English, but the children pierced me with several pairs of black or blue eyes and showed more suspicion than seemed proper in well-brought-up youngsters.

Who would have guessed that among those children was one destined to become a dearest friend, an important writer, the author of one of the best biographies written about me? I am speaking of Margarita Aguirre.

In my house I have put together a collection of small and large toys I can't live without. The child who doesn't play is not a child, but the man who doesn't play has lost forever the child who lived in him and he will certainly miss him. I have also built my house like a toy house and I play in it from morning till night.

These are my own toys. I have collected them all my life for the scientific purpose of amusing myself alone. I shall describe them for small children and for others of all ages.

I have a sailboat inside a bottle. In fact, I have more than one. It's a whole fleet. They have their written names, masts, sails, prows, and anchors. Some come from far away, from other tiny little seas. One of the most beautiful was sent to me from Spain, in payment for the rights to a book of my odes. Above, on the mainmast, is our flag, with its tiny lone star. Almost all the others, however, are the work of Señor Carlos Hollander. Señor Hollander is an old seaman and he has reproduced for me many of the famous and majestic ships that came from Hamburg, Salem, or the Breton coast to load nitrate or hunt whales in the South Seas.

When I go down Chile's long highway to find the old sailor in Coronel, and into the southern city's smell of coal and rain, I actually enter the finest shipyard in the world. In the small parlor, the dining room, the kitchen, the garden, are accumulated, all in order, the parts that will be inserted into the clear bottles which the pisco has vacated. Don Carlos's whistle is a magic wand touching prows and sails, foresails and topsails. Even the tiniest puff of smoke from the port passes through his hands and is re-created to rise from a new bottled ship, gleaming and fresh, ready to set out for some chimerical sea.

In my collection the ships that have come out of the modest hands of the navigator from Coronel stand out from the others bought in Antwerp or Marseilles. For not only did he give them life, he also embellished them with his knowledge, pasting a label on each that tells the name and number of the ship's feats, the voyages it saw through wind and tide, the cargoes it distributed, fluttering across the Pacific with sails we shall never see again.

In bottles I have famous ships like the powerful *Potosí*, and the grand *Prussia*, from Hamburg, wrecked in the English Channel in 1910. Captain Hollander also delighted me by making me two versions of the *María Celeste*, which in 1882 was converted into a star, into a mystery of mysteries.

I am not about to reveal the navigational secret that lives on in its own translucence. I mean, how the tiny ships got into their loving bottles. Being a professional deceiver, and in order to mystify, I gave a detailed description, in an ode, of the long-drawn-out and minutely detailed work of the mysterious shipbuilders and recounted how they went in and out of their sea bottles. But the secret still stands.

The figureheads are my largest toys. Like so many of my things, these figureheads have been photographed for newspapers and magazines and have been discussed in a friendly light or with spite. Those who are well disposed toward them laugh understandingly and say, "What a crazy guy! Look at the kind of thing he's decided to collect!"

The mean ones see things differently. Soured by my collections and by the blue flag with a white fish which I hoist at my home in Isla Negra, one of them said, "I don't run up my own flag. I don't have figureheads."

The poor man was whining like a little kid who is jealous because other kids have tops. All this time, my figureheads from the sea smiled, flattered by the envy they aroused.

One should really refer to them as prow figureheads. They are figures with a bosom, sea statues, effigies from lost oceans. When he built his ships, man was trying to endow the prows with a higher meaning. In ancient days he placed on his ships the figures of birds, totem birds, mythical birds cut in wood. Then in the nineteenth century the whaling ships had symbolic figures carved for them: half-nude goddesses, or republican matrons with Phrygian caps.

I own both male and female figureheads. The smallest and most delightful, which Salvador Allende has often tried to take from me, is the *María Celeste*. She belonged to one of the smaller French vessels and may possibly have sailed only in the Seine's waters. She is dark-ish, carved in oak; many years and voyages have given her a dusky complexion for all time. She is a small woman who looks like she's flying, with signs of a wind carved into her lovely Second Empire clothes. Her porcelain eyes look out over the dimples in her cheeks, into the horizon. And strange as it seems, these eyes shed tears every winter. No one can explain it. The brown wood may possibly have pores that collect the humidity. But the fact is that those French eyes weep in wintertime and I see *María Celeste*'s precious tears roll down her small face every year.

RELIGION AND POETRY

One of those figureheads from a prow, representing a colossal woman with large, round breasts, rested after her navigations in my garden beside the sea.

She is my most beloved ornament. She brings me memories of a van-ished era: great clippers slicing the seven seas.

Some time ago I saw the wives of the farmhands kneeling and light-ing candles by that robust pagan sculpture. I had a hard time convincing the women that she was neither a virgin nor a goddess. That she was only a goddess for me, a goddess of sea and of distance. But however much that tall, solemn figurehead may resemble Gabriela Mistral, we had to dispel the illusions of the believers so they would not go on adorning so innocently that icon of a woman from the seas who has sailed through the most corrupt waters of our corrupt planet.

Later, I took her from the garden, and now she is closer to me, beside the fireplace.

I believe this episode represents the kernel of all religions. There is the idol, there are the believers, and there I am, and if I had fewer scruples, I could well have been a priest, a necromancer, an exploiter of fears, of the primitive idolatry that one way or another the backward and aggrieved of humankind inevitably seek out.

Then the church is built, the mystery embellished with art and craft, then dogma arrives, and no one can raise a voice against it.

It's an easy business.

For centuries, priests, in different rites and languages, have sold a slice of heaven with all the comforts included: running water, electric light, television above all, a satisfied conscience, etc. The curious thing is that this domain, where there lives a terrible being by the name of God, has never been seen by anyone. Yet they go on selling it, and the price per cubic meter of heavenly air or divine land keeps rising higher and higher.

Since I was a boy, I have rebelled against this always invisible kingdom and against the strange proceedings of the assorted gods.

There are often natural disasters in the Americas. Here, geology has yet to finish its work. The volcanoes keep spewing flames from their huge maws, the sea swells past the shore and irrupts into inhabited lands, destroying villages, human beings, and animals. Earthquakes shake our countries and entire cities are wiped out. The rivers do what they can to avoid man's dominion, and in my country, only two of them are navigable.

Great fires devour the mountains and reduce the fragrant forest to ash.

In all these catastrophes, only the poor, the forgotten, the helpless, men, women, and children, are victims. These are the people Christ preached for. And yet the God of the Christians won't have much to do with them. He lives somewhere else. In homes not destroyed by earthquakes, not annihilated by fire, not swept away by floods. Apparently God lives in the homes of the rich.

Since I was a boy, I've been unable to understand these practical aspects of religion. Nor could I grasp the theological mysteries. Nor did I comprehend why God lashed out against his own fervent followers. My country was stirred by a fire at a church a hundred years ago in the very center of the capital. The heat made the doors swell, and they refused to open, even when the faithful trampled one another to reach them. God didn't open them either, though the whole thing took place during Mass. More than a thousand devout Catholics died there.

Church fires like this have occurred many times across the face of America. Mostly in little churches built of wood. No one is saved, not even the priest giving his sermon. How are we to understand this?

I also never made sense of the constant obligation to believe avec la foi du charbonnier, *as Pascal says. The church hangs a sword of Damocles over your head. Hell is the punishment for nonbelievers. But why? Logically, understanding must have a divine origin, according to the systems of religion, and it is impossible that someone should be obliged to believe in what he doesn't understand; moreover, rightness or wrongness in this matter cannot be the grounds for reward or punishment. It is obvious that the inscrutability of divine intentions is a system of deceit and contempt for human reason.*

Regardless, it's impossible to imagine that the continuous praise of divinities, deliberate humiliation, everything that constitutes the meaning of prayer, could have an influence on divine decisions. These things are inexplicable, whereas prayers are repeated mechanically. They have become mere formulas devoid of truth. In their degeneration, certain religious systems have substituted for these prayers already lacking in meaning mechanisms that require neither thought nor words: little wheels that spin or rosary beads that glide softly between the fingers.

In the America of before, five centuries ago, something took place that gave rise to incalculable consequences. In the name of the Catholic religion, the Spanish conquistadors felled the millenary statues of the ancient gods of America, which had served the indigenous, theocratic hierarchies to exploit the primitive inhabitants. The invaders, aided by priests from the Spanish religion, destroyed temples, burned libraries that held treasures, manuscripts of inestimable value, and cruelly spilled the blood of the populations they overtook. The conquest was draped in the guise of a holy war. With cross and sword completely united, they attacked and destroyed the ancient empires, pastoral tribes, luminous cultures. Only one priest, the extraordinary Father de Las Casas, protested the butchery, thanks to the humanism that many times reached even to the convents. But he, too, was persecuted and defeated by the power of arms and the church.

The church, in its long road, had one undeniable value: with the sacrifice of the people, it raised temples that are often great artworks of undying splendor. It was superior to the political power of our time because it called not on the worst painters and sculptors but on the greatest and most creative to execute its artworks. Even today, Henri Matisse, though progressive in his values, has carried out a commission for the church in France, the exquisite decorations for the chapel in Vence. To my mind, the old Russian icons are the most interesting artworks humanity has produced.

But that is another question, and another relation of values, and possibly a subtle way of attracting a vast number of people to the various creeds. The church has also relied on the best music of former times.

In my poem "The Ship," I have tried to show a panorama of humanity in the present capitalist state. It is a small poem that protests the way social injustice seems to be accepted as something immovable.

Religion, religions have helped maintain this ship, this vessel where

*inequality and agony are so evident, to keep things as they are, to keep it
from sinking.*

*I cannot argue or enter into the philosophical or historical depths of
the entire process of religion.*

*My task as a poet is to denounce what contributes to backwardness
and lift up the hopes, open the possibilities, increase the joy of the human
race.*

BOOKS AND SEASHELLS

A bibliophile of little means is likely to suffer often. Books don't slip
from his hands but fly past him through the air, high as birds, high
as prices.

And yet, after many tries, out comes the pearl.

I remember the bookseller García Rico's surprise, in Madrid
in 1934, when I offered to buy an old set of Góngora's works that
cost only a hundred pesetas, in monthly payments of twenty. It
was very little money, but I didn't have it. I paid punctually, in
five months. It was the Foppens edition. This seventeenth-century
Flemish publisher printed, in peerless type, the work of the masters of Spain's Golden Age. I only enjoy reading Quevedo in editions where the sonnets are bravely deployed for battle, like tough
fighting ships.

Later I lost myself in the forest of bookshops, in the suburban
nooks and crannies of secondhand bookstalls and the cathedral
naves of the marvelous bookstores of France and England. My hands
came out covered with dust, but from time to time I obtained a treasure, or at least the thrill of thinking that I had.

Ready cash from literary prizes helped me to buy some editions
at outlandish prices. My library grew to a considerable size. Antique
books of poetry brightened it, and my bent for natural history filled it

with magnificent books on botany, illustrated in full color, and books on birds, insects, and fish. I found wonderful travel books in various parts of the world; incredible *Don Quixotes*, printed by Ibarra; Dante folios in exquisite Bodoni type; even a Molière from a very limited edition prepared, "Ad usum Delphini," for the son of the King of France.

But, actually, the loveliest things I ever collected were my seashells. They gave me the pleasure of their extraordinary structure: a mysterious porcelain with the purity of moonlight combined with numerous tactile, Gothic, functional forms.

Thousands of tiny undersea doors opened for me to dip into, from the day Don Carlos de la Torre, the noted Cuban malacologist, gave me the best specimens from his collection. Since then I have crossed the seven seas, wherever my travels took me, stalking and hunting down shells. But I must confess that it was the sea of Paris that, wave after wave, washed ashore most of my shells for me. Paris had transported all the mother-of-pearl of Oceania to its naturalist shops, to its flea markets.

Finding the exquisite contours of the *Oliva textilina* under the city's sargasso, among broken lamps and old shoes, was easier than plunging my hands in among the rocks of Vera Cruz or Baja California. Or catching the spear of quartz that tapers off, like a sea poem, into *Rostellaria fusus*. No one can take away the thrill I felt when I pulled out of that sea the *Spondylus roseo*, a large oyster studded with coral spines. Or when, farther on, I opened the white *Spondylus* with its snowy barbs like stalagmites in a Góngoran grotto.

Some of these trophies may have had a historic past. I remember that in the Peking Museum the most sacred box of mollusks from the China Sea was opened to give me the second of the only two specimens of the *Thatcheria mirabilis* in existence. And thus I was able to own that remarkable work of art in which the ocean

gave China the style for temples and pagodas that still survives
in those latitudes.

It took me thirty years to collect a large library. My shelves held
incunabula and other books I treasured: first editions of Quevedo, Cervantes, Góngora, as well as Laforgue, Rimbaud, and
Lautréamont. I felt as if these pages still preserved the touch of
the poets I loved. I had manuscripts by Rimbaud. In Paris, Paul
Eluard gave me, as a birthday present, Isabelle Rimbaud's two
letters to her mother, written in the hospital at Marseilles where
the wanderer had one leg amputated. These were treasures coveted by the Bibliothèque nationale in Paris and by Chicago's voracious book collectors.

I covered so many parts of the world that my library grew much
too large, beyond the normal bounds of a private library. One day I
gave away the wonderful collection of shells it had taken me twenty
years to put together and the five thousand volumes I had selected
with so much love from so many countries. I gave them to my country's university. And they were accepted by the rector, with beautiful
words, as a dazzling gift.

Any genuine person will imagine the rejoicing with which this
gift of mine must have been received. But there are also people with
twisted minds. An official critic wrote some furious articles protesting vehemently. "When will it be possible to stop international
Communism?" he raved. Another gentleman made a fiery speech in
parliament attacking the university for having accepted my marvelous cunabula and incunabula, and threatened to cut off the subsidies
the national institute receives. Between them, the writer of the articles and the parliamentarian launched an icy wave over the small
world of Chile. The rector of the university paced up and down the
halls of Congress, looking sick.

Incidentally, twenty years have gone by and no one has ever seen my books or my shells again. It's as if they had slipped back into the bookstores and the ocean.

BROKEN GLASS

Three days ago I came back to my home in Valparaíso, after being away a long time. Huge cracks in the walls were just like wounds. Disheartening rugs of shattered glass covered the floors of the rooms. The clocks, also on the floor, grimly recorded the time of the earthquake. How many lovely things Matilde's broom was now sweeping up from the floor; how many rare objects the earth's tremors had turned into trash.

We have to clean up, to put things back, and start all over again. Paper is hard to find in the middle of the mess; and then, it's hard to collect one's thoughts.

My last work was a translation of *Romeo and Juliet* and a long love poem in archaic meter, a poem that was never completed.

Come on, love poem, get up from among the broken glass, the time to sing has come.

Help me, love poem, to make things whole again, to sing in spite of pain.

It's true that the world does not cleanse itself of wars, does not wash off the blood, does not get over its hate. It's true.

Yet it is equally true that we are moving toward a realization: the violent ones are reflected in the mirror of the world, and their faces are not pleasant to look at, not even to themselves.

And I go on believing in the possibility of love. I am convinced that there will be mutual understanding among human beings, achieved in spite of all the suffering, the blood, the broken glass.

MATILDE URRUTIA, MY WIFE

My wife is from the provinces, like me. She was born in a southern city, Chillán, fortunately famous for its peasant-made pottery, unfortunately notorious for its disastrous earthquakes.

Speaking to her in my *Cien sonetos de amor*, I have told her all I feel. Perhaps these poems make clear how much she means to me. Life and the land brought us together.

It may interest no one else, but we are happy. We share the time we have together in long sojourns on Chile's lonely coast. Not in summer, when the coast, dried up by the sun, is yellow and desert-like. But in winter, yes; when the rains and the cold dress it up in an extraordinary flowering of green and yellow, blue and purple. Sometimes we go up from the wild and solitary ocean to the nervous city of Santiago, where together we weather the complicated existence of others.

Matilde sings my songs in a powerful voice.

Everything I write and everything I have is dedicated to her. It's not much, but it makes her happy.

Now I'm watching her sink her tiny shoes into the mud in the garden, and then she also sinks her tiny hands as deep as the plant has gone down.

From the earth—with her feet and hands and eyes and voice— she brought me all the roots, all the flowers, all the sweet-smelling fruits of happiness.

AN INVENTOR OF STARS

A man was asleep in his room in a Paris hotel. Since he was an incurable night owl, don't be surprised when I tell you it was twelve noon and the man was still sleeping.

He had to wake up. The wall on his left suddenly collapsed, demolished. Then the one in front of him crashed down. It wasn't a bombing. From the freshly opened pits, moustachioed workers emerged, picks in hand, and taunted the sleeper: *"Eh, lève-toi, bourgeois!* Have a drink with us!"

The champagne was uncorked. The mayor came in, with a tricolor sash across his chest. Music burst out, the notes of the Marseillaise. What was behind such strange goings-on? Well, two lines of the Paris Métro, then under construction, had met underground, just below the floor of the dreamer's hotel room.

From the moment that man told me his story, I decided to become his friend, or rather his devotee, his disciple. Since such extraordinary things happened to him, and I didn't want to miss any of them, I followed him across several countries. Captivated by this phenomenon's wild imagination, Federico García Lorca adopted a position similar to mine.

Federico and I were sitting in the Correos Café, across from Madrid's Cibeles Fountain, when the sleeper from Paris burst in upon our tête-à-tête. Though he was strapping and round as a globe, he looked sick. Once again, something words failed to describe had occurred to him. He had been in his truly modest Madrid hideaway, trying to set his music sheets in order. For I have forgotten to mention that our hero was a wonderful composer. And what happened?

"A car pulled up at the door of my hotel. Then I heard footsteps come up the stairs and go into the room next to mine. Later the newcomer began to snore. It started off as a whisper. Then the air shuddered. The closets, the walls moved under the rhythmic impact of the tremendous snores."

It had to be some wild animal. When the snoring broke into a torrent, our friend no longer had any doubts: it was the Horned Boar. In other countries his uproar had shaken basilicas, blocked highways, stirred up angry seas. What was this planetary menace up to, this abominable monster that threatened the peace of all Europe?

Every day he told new and chilling episodes about the Horned Boar. Federico, I, Rafael Alberti, the sculptor Alberto, Fulgencio Díaz Pastor, and Miguel Hernández—we welcomed him eagerly, and bade him goodbye anxiously.

Then one day he arrived with his old round-bellied laughter. And he told us: "The terrifying problem has been solved. The German Graf Zeppelin has agreed to transport the Horned Boar. It will drop him in the Brazilian jungle. He will live off the giant trees. There's no danger that he will drink up the Amazon at one sitting. There he will go on deafening the earth with his thunderous snoring."

Listening to him, Federico exploded with laughter till he had to shut his eyes. Then our friend mentioned the time he went to send off a telegram and the telegraph operator persuaded him never to send any more telegrams, only letters, because people were scared out of their wits when they received those winged messages, some even died of shock before opening them. He also told us about the time he went to look in on an interesting auction of thoroughbred horses in London. He raised his hand to greet a friend, and the auctioneer gave him, for £10,000, a mare for which the Aga Khan had bid £9,500. "I had to take the mare to my hotel and return it the next day," he said.

Now the fabulist can't tell the story of the Horned Boar, or any other story. He died here in Chile. In life, Acario Cotapos was the name of this spherical Chilean, a composer through and through and a prodigal source of unparalleled stories. I had the honor of speaking at the funeral of this man whose memory it was impossible to bury. All I said was: "Today we deliver into the shadows a splendid human being who gave us a star every day."

ELUARD THE MAGNIFICENT

My comrade Paul Eluard died a short time ago. He was so wholesome, so solid, that I found it painful and difficult to accept his loss. He was a blue and rosy Norman, tough-looking but delicate. The war of 1914, in which he was gassed twice, left him with shaky hands for the rest of his life. Yet Eluard always made me think of a sky-blue color, of deep, still water, of a gentleness aware of its own strength. Paul Eluard's poetry was so clear, transparent like drops of spring rain against a windowpane, that he may have seemed an apolitical man, a poet who would have nothing to do with politics. He was not. He had strong ties with the people of France, its causes, and its struggles.

Paul Eluard was firm. A kind of French tower with a passionate lucidity that is not the same as passionate stupidity, which is so common.

In Mexico, where we had gone together, I saw him for the first time on the verge of a dark pit—he who always kept a quiet place for sadness, a place as ready as the one reserved for wisdom.

He was worn out. I had convinced him, had dragged him, a Frenchman to the core, to that distant land, and there, the same day we buried José Clemente Orozco, I came down with a dangerous case of phlebitis that tied me to my bed for four months. Paul Eluard felt lonely, lonely and in darkness, as helpless as a blind explorer. He didn't know anyone, no doors were thrown open to him. The loss of his wife weighed heavily on him; he felt all alone here, without love. He would say to me: "We have to see life together with someone, to share every fragment of life with someone. My solitude is unreal, my solitude is killing me."

I called up friends and we made him go out. They took him off, grumbling, to ride over Mexico's roads, and at some bend in one of those roads he came across love again, his last love: Dominique.

It's very hard for me to write about Paul Eluard. I shall go on seeing him near me, alive, with the electric blue deepness, that could see so much and so far, burning in his eyes.

He had left French soil, where laurels and roots are woven together in a fragrant heritage. His tall stature was all water and stone, with ancient vines climbing up on it, bearing flowers and flashes of light, nests and transparent songs.

"Transparence," that's the word. His poetry was crystal hard as rock, water standing still in its singing stream.

Poet of the highest kind of love, fire pure as noon, in France's disastrous days he planted his heart in the center of his country and out of it came fire that was decisive in battle.

And so it was natural for him to join the ranks of the Communist Party. Being a Communist, for Eluard, meant reasserting the values of humanity and humanism with his poetry and his life.

Let no one believe that Eluard was less political than poet. His clear-sightedness and his formidable dialectical reasoning often astonished me. Together we examined many things, men and problems of our time, and his lucidity has always been of great help to me.

He did not lose himself in surrealist irrationalism, because he was not an imitator but a creator, and as such he pumped bullets of clarity and intelligence into the dead body of surrealism.

He was my friend in everyday life and now I have lost his affection, which was part of my daily bread. No one will be able to give me what he has taken with him, because his active brotherly spirit was one of my life's treasured luxuries.

Tower of France, brother! I lean over your closed eyes, they will go on giving me the light and the greatness, the simplicity and the honesty, the goodness and the naturalness you sowed on earth.

PIERRE REVERDY

I would never call Pierre Reverdy's poetry magical. This word, catchword of an era, is like the hat of a fake magician at a fair: no wild pigeon will emerge from it and fly away.

Reverdy was a physical poet, he named and touched numberless aspects of earth and sky. He named the things and the splendor of the world.

His own poetry was like a vein of quartz, subterranean but filled with light, inexhaustible. Sometimes it threw off a hard glitter, like the sheen of some black mineral torn with difficulty from its thick covering of earth. Suddenly it flew out like a spark from a match, or hid in the gallery of its mine, far from the light of day, but faithful to its own truth. Perhaps this truth, which identified the substance of his poetry with nature, this Reverdian tranquility, this unflagging honesty, gradually paved his way to oblivion. He was eventually taken for granted by others, like a natural phenomenon, a house, a river, or a familiar street that would never change its outward appearance or its place.

Now that he has gone away, now that a tremendous silence, greater than his own noble and proud silence, has carried him off, we realize that he is no longer here, that this unique light is gone, buried in earth and sky.

I say that someday his name, like an angel coming back to life, will knock down the unjust doors of oblivion.

Without trumpets, with the lyrical silence of his magnificent and enduring poetry around him like a halo, we shall see him at the last judgment, at the Essential Judgment, dazzling us with the simple timelessness of his work.

JERZY BOREJSZA

Jerzy Borejsza is no longer waiting for me in Poland. Fate reserved for this old émigré the chance to rebuild his country. When he went back to it as a soldier, after being away for many years, Warsaw was just a pile of rubble. There were no streets, no trees. No one was waiting for him. Borejsza, a dynamic wonder, worked with his people. Colossal plans sprang from his head, and then a tremendous initiative: the

House of the Printed Word. One by one its stories were built; the biggest rotary printing presses in the world arrived; and now thousands upon thousands of books and magazines are printed there. Borejsza was a tireless, down-to-earth man who converted dreams into action. His daring plans materialized, like the castles in dreams, in the new Poland with its incredible vitality.

I hadn't met him. I went to see him at the vacation camp where he was waiting for me, in northern Poland, in the Masurian Lakes region.

When I got out of the car, I saw an ungainly man in need of a shave, wearing only a pair of nondescript shorts. With the energy of a wild man, in a Spanish learned from books, he shouted: "Pablo, non habras fatiga. Debes tomar reposo." (Which in English would sound something like this: "Pablo, no have tired. You must take repose.") As a matter of fact, he did not let me "take repose" at all. His conversation was profuse, multiform, surprising, and punctuated by exclamation points. He described seven different construction plans to me in the same breath, with an analysis of several books that contributed new interpretations of history and life thrown in for good measure. "The true hero was Sancho Panza, not Don Quixote, Pablo." For him, Sancho was the voice of popular realism, the true center of his world and his time. "When Sancho runs things, he does it well, because it is the people running things."

He used to pull me out of bed early, always shouting at me: "You must take repose," and he would lead me through fir and pine forests to show me the convent of a religious sect that had migrated from Russia a hundred years before and still clung to its old rites. The nuns received him with a blessing. Borejsza was all tact and respect with those religious women.

He was gentle and active. The war years had been terrible. One day he showed me the revolver used to execute a war criminal, after a summary trial. A notebook had been found where he had painstakingly written down all his crimes. Old people and children strangled by his hands, little girls raped. They had surprised him in the very village where he had committed his atrocities. Witnesses filed past. His incriminating notebook was read to him, and the insolent assassin had only this to say for himself: "I would do it again if I could start all over." In my hands I had the notebook, and the revolver that had extinguished the life of a heartless criminal.

They catch eels in the Masurian Lakes, which multiply until you lose track of their number. We set out to go fishing very early, and we were soon watching the eels, quivering and wet, like black belts.

I became familiar with those waters, their fishermen, and the scenery around them. From morning till night, my friend got me to go up and come down, to run and to row, to meet people and learn all about trees. All this to the shout of: "Here you must take repose. There is no place like this for resting."

When I left the Masurian Lakes, he gave me a smoked eel, the longest I have ever seen.

This strange walking stick complicated my life. I wanted to eat it, because I am very partial to smoked eels, and this one, having come straight from its native lake, without a store or any other go-between, was above suspicion. But during that time there was eel on my hotel menu noon and night, and I didn't have a chance to serve myself my private eel. It started to prey on my mind.

At night I would put it out on the balcony to get some fresh air. Sometimes, in the middle of an absorbing conversation, I remembered that it was noon and my eel was still outdoors, in the full sunlight. Then I would lose all interest in the subject under discussion and would dash out to put my eel in a cool place in my room, in a closet, for instance.

I finally met an eel lover and gave him, not without qualms, the longest, tenderest, and best smoked eel that ever existed.

Now the great Borejsza, a scrawny, dynamic Quixote, an admirer of Sancho Panza like the other Quixote, sensitive and wise, builder and dreamer, is resting for the first time. He rests in the darkness he loved so much. Near his resting place, a world he gave his volcanic energy and his inexhaustible fire to is still being created.

GYÖRGY SOMLYÓ

In Hungary, I love the way life and poetry, history and poetry, time and the poet, intertwine. In other countries this matter is discussed more or less naively or one-sidedly. In Hungary every poet is committed before he is born. Attila József, Endre Ady, Gyulla Illyés are natural products of a great interchange between duty and music, between mother country and darkness, between love and pain.

György Somlyó is a poet I have seen grow in confidence and strength over a span of twenty years. A poet with fine tones that soar like a violin's, a poet who concerns himself with his own life and with other lives, a Hungarian poet down to his bone marrow—Hungarian in his generous readiness to share the reality and the dreams of a people. A poet of faithful love and active commitment, his universality bears the unique stamp of the great poetry of his country.

A poet, young but mature, who deserves to be heard by our time. A quiet poetry, transparent and intoxicating like the wine from our golden sands.

QUASIMODO

Italy's earth holds the voices of its ancient poets deep within itself, where it is purest. Walking on the soil of its fields, passing through parks where the water sparkles, going over the sands of its small blue ocean, I felt as if I were stepping on diamond-like substances, hidden accumulations of crystal, all the luster stored up by the centuries. Italy gave European poetry form, sound, grace, and rapture; she pulled it out of its early formlessness, out of its coarseness dressed up in sackcloth and armor. Italy's light transformed the rags of the medieval minstrels and the iron trappings of the chansons de geste into an abundant flow of cut diamonds.

For poets like us, recent arrivals to culture from countries where anthologies begin with poets of 1880, it was amazing to find in Italian anthologies poems dating back to the 1230s or 1310 or 1450, and between these dates the dazzling tercets, the passionate artistry, the depth and the gem-like surface of Dante, Cavalcanti, Petrarch, Poliziano.

These names and these men gave their Florentine light to our sweet-toned and powerful Garcilaso de la Vega, to good-natured Boscán; they lighted Góngora's way and shaded Quevedo's melancholy with a thrust of their own darkness; they molded the sonnets of England's Shakespeare and threw light on the essences of France, making the roses of Ronsard and du Bellay burst into bloom.

So a poet born in Italy has a difficult road cut out for him, a starlit road that demands living up to a brilliant heritage.

I have known Salvatore Quasimodo for years and I can say that his poetry has a conscience that seems phantasmagorical to us because of its profound and fiery burden. Quasimodo is a European who makes the most of his learning, his sense of balance, and all the weapons of his intelligence. Yet his position at the center of Italian poetry, as the outstanding contemporary poet of an intermittent but inexhaustible classicism, has not turned him into a warrior locked up in his tower. Quasimodo is a perfect example of the universal man, who does not get up in arms to split the world into West and East; instead, he considers it his obligation, as a man of his time, to knock down cultural barriers and show that poetry, truth, freedom, peace, and happiness are gifts that belong to all alike.

The colors and sounds of a world that is sad but orderly are combined in Quasimodo. His sadness is not Leopardi's hopeless uncertainty but represents the earth settling down to let things grow in the evening; the feeling of reverence given off by that time of day when scents, voices, colors, and bells watch over the work of the seeds that are deep in the ground. I love the poet's tight language, his classicism and his romanticism, and most of all I admire the way he has steeped himself in the tradition of beauty, as well as his power to transform everything into a language that is true and moving.

I lift a fragrant crown of Araucanian leaves over the sea and the distance and release it into the air so that life and the wind will carry it off and lay it on Salvatore Quasimodo's brow. It is not the Apollonian laurel crown we have so often seen in the portraits of Francesco Petrarca. It is a crown from our unexplored forests, made of leaves that have no name yet, leaves soaked in the dew of southern dawns.

VALLEJO LIVES ON

Vallejo was a different kind of man. I shall never forget his great yellow head, like those one still sees in old windows in Peru.

Vallejo was serious and pure in heart. He died in Paris; he was killed by the polluted Paris air, by the polluted river from which so many dead people have been fished. Vallejo died of hunger and asphyxia. If we had brought him back to his Peru, if we had let him breathe Peruvian air, maybe he would still be alive and writing poetry. I have written two poems, on different occasions, about my dear friend, my good comrade. I believe they tell the story of our friendship, which was never interrupted by time or distance. The first, "Oda a César Vallejo" ("Ode to César Vallejo"), is in the first volume of *Odas elementales*.

In the last few years, during the small literary war kept alive by little soldiers with ferocious teeth, Vallejo, César Vallejo's ghost, César Vallejo's absence, César Vallejo's poetry have been thrown into the fight against me and my poetry. This can happen anywhere. The idea is to wound those who have worked hard, to say, "This one is no good; but Vallejo was good." If Neruda were dead, they would throw him in against Vallejo alive.

The second poem, whose title is a single letter, the letter *V.*, is in *Estravagario*.

In seeking the ineffable, the tendril or thread that ties a man to his work, I speak of those who had something, or a great deal, to do with me. We shared some part of our lives and now I have survived them. I have no other way of fathoming what some people have taken to calling the mystery of poetry; I would call it the clarity of poetry. There must be some connection between a man's hands and his work, between the eyes, the viscera, the blood of man and his work. But I have no theory. I don't go around with some dogma under my arm ready to drop it on somebody's head. I am like almost everyone else: everything looks bright to me on Monday, everything looks dark on Tuesday, and I believe this is going to be a bright-and-dark year. The coming years will be a lovely blue.

LEÓN FELIPE

"Are you happy?" León Felipe would ask any and everybody, at the same time scratching his messianic little beard.

For me, it is not the inhumane but the super-humane who are supermen: it is in them that degrees of grandeur reside. And León Felipe was superhuman, extra-human, made of the mortar of the whole of humanity. It was a pleasure to hear him, to feel him, to see him.

Moreover, I read him, León Felipe himself, rather than read his poems I often read that vast, amiable man himself.

He was made of many pages. He was a young and yellow folio in which every versicle, all he'd learned, his references, his wisdom, and his tenderness were perceptibly inscribed in his gestures.

Noble poet! Beloved good man!

Ay, how much we have lost in him! How much we will go on losing!

I acquiesce, because he was for me a great example of meditative valor. Many times, he taught us how to lose. And now, when his absence begins to grow transparent, I acquiesce to his benign and hopeless teachings.

Few men like him. Few poets like that wandering Spaniard León Felipe Camino.

GABRIELA MISTRAL

I have already mentioned that I met Gabriela Mistral in my home town of Temuco. But later she broke with that town forever. Gabriela was midway through her difficult, hard-working life, and she looked monastic, like the Mother Superior of a straitlaced school.

It was around this time that she wrote her poems of the mother and child, poems worked in flawless prose, polished and graceful; for her prose was often her most penetrating poetry. She describes pregnancy, birth, and growth in these poems, and some confused gossip went around in Temuco, some vague word, unintentionally ugly, coarse talk that hurt her feelings as a maiden lady, some rumor spread by those railroad and lumber people whom I know so well, rough-mannered and impetuous people who call a spade a spade.

Gabriela felt offended, and was offended until the day of her death.

Years later, in the first edition of her great book, she inserted a long, useless note protesting the things that had been whispered about her in those mountains at the end of the world.

At the time of her memorable triumph, of her Nobel Prize, she had to pass through Temuco on her way to receive the honor. The schoolchildren waited for her at the railroad station every day. The schoolgirls came, spattered by the rain and quivering with copihues. The copihue is the southern flower, the lovely, wild corolla of

Araucanía. A useless wait. Gabriela Mistral managed to pass through at night, she took a night train so as not to accept Temuco's copihues.

Well, does this speak ill of Gabriela? It simply says that the wounds were still raw, deep within her soul, and would not heal easily. It merely shows that love and rancor struggled in the soul of this writer of such magnificent poetry, as they do in any human being's soul.

For me she always had the open smile of a good friend, a smile like flour sprinkled on the dark bread of her face.

But what were the prime elements that went into the oven of her work? What was the secret ingredient of her poetry, which was always filled with pain?

I'm not going to investigate this, and I'm sure I would not find it out, and if I do find out, I am not going to tell.

The wild mustard blooms this month of September; the countryside is a rippling yellow carpet. Here on the coast the south wind has been thrashing about with magnificent fury for the past four days. The night is filled with its resonant stir. The ocean is at once an open green crystal and a vast whiteness.

You come here, Gabriela, beloved daughter of these wild mustard blossoms, these rocks, this giant wind. We all welcome you joyously. No one will forget your songs to the hawthorns, to the snows of Chile. You are Chilean. You belong to the people. No one will forget your lines to the naked feet of our children. No one has forgotten your "cursed word." You are a moving friend of peace. For those and other reasons, we love you.

You come, Gabriela, to the wild mustard plants and the hawthorns of Chile. It is only right that I give you the true welcome of the blossoms and the thorns, in keeping with your greatness and our unbreakable friendship. September's doors, made of rock and of springtime, swing open for you. Nothing makes my heart happier than to see your wide smile enter this sacred land made to blossom and sing by the people of Chile.

It's my good luck to share with you the essence and the truth which, because of our voices and our words, will be honored. May your magnificent heart rest, live, fight, sing, and have offspring, in the Andean and ocean solitudes of our country. I kiss your noble forehead and render homage to your universal poetry.

VICENTE HUIDOBRO

The great poet Vicente Huidobro, who looked at everything through mischievous eyes, harassed me with numberless pranks, sending me childish anonymous letters attacking me, and constantly accusing me of plagiarism. Huidobro is typical of a long line of incurable egocentrics. This way of defending one's ground in the dog-eat-dog life of the times, which conceded no importance to the writer, was characteristic of the years immediately before the First World War. In America, this aggressive narcissism re-echoed D'Annunzio's arrogant effrontery in Europe. This Italian writer, who threw out or violated the canons of the petite bourgeoisie, left a volcanic wake of messianism in America. His most scandalous and revolutionary disciple was Vargas Vila.

It's difficult for me to speak ill of Huidobro, who honored me, throughout his life, with a spectacular ink-slinging war. He crowned himself the "God of Poetry" and did not think it was right that I, so much younger than he, should be part of his Olympus. I never quite understood what that Olympus was all about. Huidobro's group creationized, surrealized, and devoured the latest fashions from Paris. I was infinitely inferior, a hopeless country boy from the backwoods, a hayseed.

Huidobro was not content to be the extraordinarily gifted poet he really was. He also wanted to be Superman. There was something childishly attractive about his pranks. If he were alive today, he would have offered his services as the only qualified volunteer for the first voyage to the moon. I envision him proving to the scientists that his cranium is the only one on earth genuinely endowed with the form and flexibility to adapt itself to space travel.

Anecdotes give a good picture of him. For instance, when he returned to Chile after the last war, old by then and nearing his end, he used to show everyone a rusty telephone and say, "I myself took it from Hitler. It was the Führer's favorite telephone."

One time he was shown a bad academic sculpture, and he said, "How awful! It's even worse than Michelangelo."

A wonderful story in which he played the leading role in 1919, in Paris, is also worth telling. Huidobro published a pamphlet called *Finis Britanniae*, in which he predicted the immediate collapse of the British Empire. When no one paid attention to his prophecy, the poet decided to disappear. The press took up the case: "Chilean diplomat mysteriously kidnapped."

A few days later he was found lying outside the door of his home. "Some English Boy Scouts kidnapped me," he declared to the police. "They had me tied to a column in a basement and forced me to shout a thousand times: 'Long live the British Empire!'" Then he passed out again. The police, however, examined a package he had under his arm. It was a new pair of pajamas bought by Huidobro himself three days before in one of the better Paris shops.

The whole story came out. And the poet lost a friend, the painter Juan Gris. He had steadfastly believed in the kidnapping and had suffered greatly because of the imperialist outrage against the Chilean poet. And he never forgave him that lie.

Huidobro is a crystalline poet. Every facet of his work glitters and gives off a contagious joy. Throughout his poetry there is a European brilliance, which he crystallizes and radiates in a play of light filled with grace and intelligence.

What surprises me most about his work when I reread it is its diaphanous quality. This literary poet, who followed all the trends of a complicated era and decided to ignore nature's solemnity, lets a steady flow of singing water run through his poems, a rustle of air and leaves, and a grave humanness that completely takes over his later and his last poems.

From the delightful workmanship of his Frenchified poetry to the powerful forces in his most important writing, there is in Huidobro a struggle between playfulness and fire, escapism and immolation. This struggle makes for quite a show, taking place in plain view, with a dazzling clarity, and almost always deliberately.

There is no doubt that a prejudice in favor of seriousness has kept us away from his work. We agree that Vicente Huidobro's worst enemy was Vicente Huidobro. Death snuffed out his contradictory and impossibly playful life. Death brought a curtain down over his perishable life but raised another to leave the dazzling aspect of him in full view forever. I have proposed a monument for him next to Rubén Darío. But our governments are penny pinchers when it comes to putting up statues for artists, just as they are free spenders with senseless monuments.

We couldn't possibly think of Huidobro as a political figure, in spite of his swift incursions into revolutionary territory. He was as irresponsible toward ideas as a spoiled brat. But that's water under the bridge, and we ourselves would be irresponsible if we set to jabbing pins into him at the risk of damaging his wings. Let's say, instead, that the poems to the October Revolution and in memory of Lenin's death are Huidobro's fundamental contribution to the awakening of mankind.

Huidobro died in 1948, in Cartagena, near Isla Negra, not before writing some of the most heartbreaking and profound poems

I have read in all my life. Shortly before his death, Huidobro visited my home in Isla Negra with my good friend and publisher, Gonzalo Losada. Huidobro and I talked together as poets, as Chileans, as friends.

LITERARY ENEMIES

I suppose major and minor conflicts have always existed, and will go on existing, between writers in all parts of the world.

The number of great suicides in the literature of our American continent is considerable. In revolutionary Russia, envious persons drove Mayakovsky into a corner and he finally pulled the trigger.

Petty grudges are exacerbated in Latin America. Envy sometimes even becomes a profession. It is said that we inherited this trait from a colonial Spain that had hit rock bottom. It's true that in Quevedo, Lope de Vega, and Góngora we often come across the wounds they inflicted on one another. For all its fabulous intellectual brilliance, the Spanish Golden Age was an unhappy age, with hunger prowling outside the palaces.

In the past few years the novel has taken on a new dimension in our countries. The names of García Márquez, Juan Rulfo, Vargas Llosa, Sábato, Cortázar, Carlos Fuentes, and the Chilean Donoso are heard and their writings read everywhere. Some of them were christened together as the "boom"; it's also common talk that they are a group who blow one another's horns.

I have met most of them and find them remarkably wholesome and generous. I understand, more clearly every day, why some of them have had to leave their countries to look for a more tranquil atmosphere to work in, far from the reach of political animosity and ever-increasing envy. Their reasons for voluntary exile are irrefutable: their books have become more and more essential to the truth and the dream of our Americas.

I've had qualms about mentioning my personal experiences with envy in its extremes. I wouldn't want to seem egocentric, excessively taken with myself, but it has been my luck to draw the envy of such dogged and colorful persons that the story is worth telling.

These nagging shadows may have made me angry at times. And yet they were in fact performing a strange duty, against their will— building my reputation—as if they were part of a campaign whose sole objective was to sound my name abroad.

THE LITERARY ANTAGONIST

The tragic death of one of these shady adversaries has left a kind of empty place in my life. He kept up his private war against everything I did for so many years that I miss it now.

Forty years of literary persecution is something exceptional. I get a certain pleasure from looking back at this lonely battle of a man against his own shadow, for I myself was never an active participant.

Twenty-five journals were published by that one editor (it was always he) just to destroy me as a writer, to accuse me of all kinds of crimes, treacheries, poetic exhaustion, public and secret vices, plagiarism, sensational sexual aberrations. Pamphlets also appeared and were diligently distributed; newspaper articles that were sometimes humorous; and finally a whole book called *Neruda y yo* (*Neruda and I*), a fat volume packed with attacks and insults.

Though this "I" of "Neruda and I" is, and perhaps remains, unknown, for many who will read this book, it will prove worthwhile if I pause to recollect certain details that will show the nature of this character who hounded me for decades. His tragic end—he committed suicide in his old age—made me hesitate a long time before writing down these recollections. I am finally doing it, because I feel that this is the right time and place. An immense cordillera of hate runs through the Spanish-speaking countries; it eats away at the work of writers, with anxious envy. Few escape its ferocity.

The only way to end this kind of destructive viciousness is to publicly show it up when it is there.

My adversary, a Chilean poet older than I, fanatical and domineering, was more bluff and bluster than the real thing. This type of fiercely egocentric writer is common in the Americas. Their sourness and self-sufficiency may take different forms, but their D'Annunzian ancestry is tragically patent. But here, in our impoverished latitudes, we poets, for the most part in rags and starving, believed at least in the operatic velvet of the narcissus D'Annunzio. His South American imitators shared a certain pathetic kinship with the sordidness of an epoch in which the false aristocrats, descendants of the Europeans, lived entrenched in their haciendas. We poets wandered on inclement mornings, stepping around the vomit of drunks.

In those miserable environs, literature revealed thuggish figures and picaresque feats of survival, casting them, however, in a strange light. A great nihilism, a false Nietzschean cynicism, permitted many in our ranks to cover themselves with the masks of delinquents. Many turned their lives toward destruction or crime.

My precocious antagonist sprang from that background. First he tried to seduce me, to get me snarled up in the rules of his game. This went against the grain of my country-boy, petit bourgeois upbringing. I didn't have the nerve for it, and I didn't like being an opportunist. The man in question, older than I, was an expert at taking advantage of any situation. He lived in a world of continuous farce, where he cheated himself by playing the bully's role, as profession and protection.

It's time to identify this character. His name was Joe Blow. He was a strong, hairy man who tried to impress people with both his rhetoric and his physique.

One time, when I was only eighteen or nineteen years old, he proposed that he and I bring out a literary review. The review would be made up of just two sections: one where he would declare, in various tones, in prose pieces and poems, that I was a powerful and brilliant poet; and another where I would proclaim to the four winds that he possessed absolute intelligence and unlimited talent. Everything would be perfect this way.

I was very young, but I felt that this would be stretching things too far.

Yet I had a hard time dissuading him from it. He was amazing at publishing reviews, and it was incredible to watch the way he scraped up funds to keep up his eternal pamphleteering.

For his books and journals as well as for his domestic needs, Joe Blow was a systematic blackmailer. He traced out a precise line of action in the isolated, wintry provinces. The long-suffering practitioners of the liberal professions live isolated from the nation's culture, which is transformed into privilege and a mythology of the metropolis. He had already made up a long list of doctors, lawyers, dentists, agronomists, professors, engineers, top men in public office, etc. Enveloped in the aureole of his voluminous publications, reviews, complete works, epic and lyric pamphlets, our personage would arrive on the scene as the bearer of universal culture. He would solemnly offer all this to the obscure men he visited, and then he deigned to charge them a few miserable escudos. Confronted by his high-flown words, the victim gradually shrank down to the size of a fly. Blow generally departed with the escudos in his pocket and left the fly behind, completely snowed under by the greatness of universal culture.

At other times, he would brandish a picture recently executed by someone or other from his family, and though the paint was still wet, he would attribute it to some past master, from the home country or abroad.

Occasionally, when the deal was done, he would tell me on his way out: "I took that hayseed for fifty pesos. You want ten?"

Timid, and inwardly horrified, I would refuse.

When I was spending my vacations at my parents' home sometime around 1925, Joe Blow came to visit me. He brought with him a scheme for bilking the southern landowners out of their money. This time he was in the company of Rubén Azócar, novelist, poet, and companion from my youth, with immense eyebrows, a face like an Indian mask, a feeble constitution, and a heart that wouldn't quit. Joe Blow had talked him into coming along.

It was quite a show: the lunatic Joe Blow in riding breeches and policeman's boots, wrapped in a magnificent, exotic houppelande; and with him my scrawny comrade defending himself from the evening chill with a checked tweed jacket that was his one worthy possession in this world.

Joe Blow introduced himself as an expert in agrarian advertising and offered to prepare for the backcountry farmers of the south de luxe monographs on their estates, complete with photos of the owners and the cattle.

He would come and go on the ranches, dragging along my poor friend. Mingling flattery and veiled threats of unfavorable publicity, our man left the farm country with a fair number of checks. The landowners were stingy, but realistic, and would hand him a few bills to get rid of him.

Notable among the peculiarities of Joe Blow, Nietzschean philosopher and compulsive writer, was his intellectual and physical hooliganism. He was a professional bully in Chile's literary life. Throughout history, the bully has always relied on a small coterie of cowards to lavish praise on him, and so it was for our hero for a number of years. But life has a habit of taking the wind mercilessly out of the sails of these opportunists.

I remember, during the very same visit of that impostor to the country, something humiliating, a kind of debacle, occurred in my presence. Blow was treating Rubén Azócar and me to a few bottles of wine with the earnings from those agrarian monographs the farmers would never see. On the third bottle, he started playing his Fierabras role to the hilt. He shouted insults to enemies both imagined and real, not even sparing Azócar or me the brunt of his epithets. His cursing was unimaginative, with interminable scatological allusions. When I tried to retire from the table, he stood up to block me. He assured me the two of us were pillars of the intellectual life of the planet, and that he had nonetheless observed a certain reticence on my part with regard to his genius. Then he cried hot tears.

When he tried to embrace me, he collapsed over an assortment of glasses and bottles, and the barman, who was the owner of the place, approached. Unlike Rubén and me, who were a couple of underfed youngsters, the proprietor was a beaming, robust creature who extracted Joe Blow from beneath the table with ease. After standing him up, he made us a proposition: "It seems that the gentleman has overdone it with the drinking. It's cold out tonight, there's mud in the streets, and he could easily have an accident. I don't have rooms to rent, but I can offer him a bed to relax in and sleep it off, no fee required." All the while, he kept hold of our lunatic so he wouldn't plunge to the floor again. Joe Blow heard his offer and had the bad idea to respond: "If you offer me a bed with a woman in it, I'll take it."

Turning to us, the brawny barkeep remarked: "The gentleman is confused about me. I'm not a scoundrel, indeed, I consider myself a gentleman. And for that reason, I shall teach him a lesson."

Then, taking our Fierabras by the lapel, he dealt him a stupefying slap across the mouth. He spun him around as if he were a shop-window mannequin, marched him toward the door, and gave him a strategic last kick in the behind. Our titan tumbled out into the rain-swept night and lay there stretched out in the muck.

The little hotel where Blow and Rubén were staying was next to my house, and we walked there in the blackness of night, while our battered buffoon, who had yet to fully absorb the blows from the barkeep, stumbled along, vociferating against us.

We managed to calm his fury and I took my leave of Blow and my wretched friend, his sidekick, at the door to the hotel.

The next day, my father, Reyes the conductor, who always boasted of his punctuality, looked at me severely as he sat down at the table for lunch, and said: "Twelve-thirty, and your friends still haven't arrived."

I rushed out to look for Joe Blow and Rubén Azócar. Unpleasant as the previous night may have been, I was still too young to cut my ties with that abusive visitor.

When I entered his room, an unusual situation presented itself. The poet Rubén Azócar was alone in his shirtsleeves, seated on the bed. My comrade was ever the emotional type, given to outbursts of joy and depths of depression. Now, with his head in his hands, he looked like an ancient Aztec statue of desolation.

"What is it?" I asked. "I was waiting for you at lunch. My father has already sat down at the table."

"He's gone," he responded without looking up.

"Joe Blow?" I said. "All the better. Finally he'll give you some peace. Let's go eat."

"I can't," he answered.

"Why can't you?"

"He took my jacket," he said, almost in tears.

I took him away, almost shoving him. At my house, I draped my poet's cape over his shoulders, and that way he managed to have lunch, in at least superficially dignified garments, at the table of my father, who was a stickler for formalities.

I decided then to free myself from this burdensome friendship. But things aren't so simple.

This dreadful individual hounded me with his admiration, which he wished to see repaid through reciprocal literary esteem. His literary output struck me as a never-ending song and dance, a messianic falsification of the poet, replete with grandiloquent rhetorical repetitions. Then again, I was on a different path, vertically different, the path of my book *Venture of the Infinite Man*.

I began to receive ebullient love letters, very literary despite their numerous spelling errors. I delighted in the "embrases" sent along to me, spelled thus, with an *s*, and they struck me, I don't know why, as superior to normal embraces with their *c*'s. Those "embrases" were redolent of oysters, or so it seemed.

So it seemed, anyway, until Fierabras himself showed up one day, apprised of my new address. This time, eyeing me up cruelly, as if I had committed some enormity, he addressed me like an inquisitor.

"You received certain love letters, don't try to deny it."

"Yes, a few, now and again," I answered with adolescent vanity.

"I am referring to a woman, quite a looker, who's written to you. Here is her portrait."

I looked at the photo of a far from extraordinary girl. It was hard to imagine her as the author of those misspelled embraces.

"Yes," I said. "So?"

"I would like you to marry her," he replied.

There was something pleading in his tone of voice. Also a kind of providential air, as though he were inducting me into the Most Noble Order of the Garter. But then, there was a threat as well: I was to become part of his family, his clan, which was in general as aggressive as he.

I decided to change addresses again. And this time he didn't find me so easily, as I'd gone to live in India.

The sensationalist politico-literary harassment unleashed against me and my work by a shady Uruguayan with a Galician last name, something like Ribeyro, has been just as insane and grim. For several years now, this fellow has been publishing pamphlets, in Spanish and

French, in which he takes me apart. The fantastic thing about this is that not only do his anti-Neruda doings overcrowd printing paper that he himself pays for, but also he has spent money on expensive trips, with my destruction always in mind.

This strange character traveled to Oxford University when it was announced that I would be made doctor *honoris causa*. The Uruguayan versifier arrived with his fantastic charges, all set to tear my literary reputation to shreds. I was still wearing my scarlet gown, after receiving the honorary distinction, when the Oxford dons gleefully told me, over the ritual glass of port, about his charges against me.

Even more unbelievable and daring was this same Uruguayan's trip to Stockholm in 1963. There was a rumor that I would receive the Nobel Prize. Well, the fellow visited members of the Academy, gave interviews to the press, spoke over the radio to make the flat statement that I was one of Trotsky's killers, hoping to have me disqualified from the prize with these threats.

Time proved that the man always ran into bad luck, and both in Oxford and in Stockholm he lamentably lost his money and the fight.

IF THEY STRIKE IT, LET IT SING

In recent days, attacks on my ideas and my poetry have multiplied. Within and outside of Chile, more than one professional Anti-Nerudist has appeared. As concerns my poetry, no debate is possible. Not because my poetry is greater or loftier or clearer or better or worse than any other. No, not because of that. My poetry has to defend itself on its own. It came from the damp woodlands of Temuco to sing like the rain on the roofs in Cautín. Let it defend itself with its song alone. If they beat it with a club, let it sing. If they spit in its eyes, let it sing. If they drag it through the filthy street by its hair, let it sing, and let the neighbors come out on their balconies to hear the voice of my song of rain and struggle, of people and plants, of salads and onions, of rage and love. I will never be seen taking to the streets or the broadsheets to defend my poetry. I will spare neither adjectives nor blows for whoever thinks me a bad, a dreadful, an unbearable poet. We cannot fight for what we are, but only for what we believe. No one can fight morally for his nose or his feet, his teeth or hair. The born poet cannot fight for his poetry. The carpenter doesn't fight for his trusses, doesn't write to the papers to proclaim the supremacy of his crossbeams or the grandiose style of the chair he's woven out of bulrush.

It's not from modesty that I avoid polemics about my poetry. It is because I am a poet.

But the carpenter and the poet, every common man—and all of us are common men and women—has the duty to fight for what he believes in.

And that is a battle I accepted long ago.

CRITICISM AND SELF-CRITICISM

There is no denying that I have had some good critics. I am not referring to well-wishers at literary banquets, and I am not talking of the insults I unwillingly provoked.

I am referring to other people. Of the books written about my poetry, apart from those by enthusiastic young critics, I must name the one by Lev Ospovat, the Russian, as among the best. This young man went so far as to master Spanish, and saw my poetry with an eye on more than just sense and sound: he placed it in the perspective of the future, applying to it the northern lights of his world.

Emir Rodríguez Monegal, a critic of the first rank, published a book on my poetry and titled it *El viajero inmóvil* (The Motionless Traveler). You can see at a glance that this scholar is nobody's fool. He perceived at once that I like to travel without stepping out of my house or leaving my country or even going out of myself. (In a copy

I have of that marvelous mystery novel *The Moonstone*, there is an illustration I like very much. It shows an elderly English gentleman wrapped in his houppelande, or macfarlane or heavy frock coat or whatever it is, sitting in front of the fireplace, a book in one hand, his pipe in the other, and two drowsy dogs at his feet. That's how I would like to remain forever, before the fire, near the sea, with two dogs, reading the books it was such hard work to collect, smoking my pipes.)

Amado Alonso's book *Poesía y estilo de Pablo Neruda* (Poetry and Style of Pablo Neruda), is highly valued by many people. His passionate probing into the shadows, seeking diverse levels between words and slippery reality, is of great interest. Furthermore, Alonso's study reveals the first serious concern for the work of a contemporary poet in our language. And that honors me far too much.

To study and explain my poetry, many critics have come to me, among them Amado Alonso himself; he would corner me with questions and lead me to the wall of clarity, where I often could not follow him, at that time.

Some believe I am a surrealist poet, for others I am a realist, and still others do not believe I am a poet. They are all partly correct and partly incorrect.

Residencia en la tierra was written, or at least begun, like *Tentativa del hombre infinito*, before the heyday of surrealism, but we can't always trust dates. The world's air transports poetry's molecules, light as pollen or hard as lead, and those seeds land in the furrows, or on people's heads, giving everything an air of spring or of battle, producing flowers as well as missiles.

As for realism, I must say, in my own interest, that I detest realism in poetry. Moreover, poetry does not have to be surrealist or sub-realist, though it may be anti-realist. And it is anti-realist with all reason, with all unreason; that is, with all poetry.

I love books, the solid substance of the work of poetry, the forest of literature, I love all of it, even the spines of books, but not the labels of the schools. I want books without schools and without classifying, like life.

I like the "positive hero" in Walt Whitman and Mayakovsky, that is, in those who found him without a formula and brought him, not without suffering, into the intimacy of our physical life, making him share with us our bread and our dream.

Socialist society has to put an end to the mythology of an age of speed, in which poster ads are more valued than the merchandise, in which the essentials are tossed aside. But a writer's deepest need is to write good books. I like the "positive hero," but there is also room in my heart for Lautréamont's mourning-clad hero, Laforgue's sighing knight errant, and Baudelaire's negative soldier. Beware of separating these halves of the apple of creation, for we may cut open our hearts and stop living. Beware! We have to demand of the poet that he take his place in the street and in the fight, as well as in the light and in the darkness.

Perhaps the poet has always had the same obligations throughout history. It has been poetry's distinction to go out into the street, to take part in this or that combat. The poet didn't scare off when they said he was a rebel. Poetry is rebellion. The poet was not offended when he was called subversive. Life transcends all structures, and there are new rules of conduct for the soul. The seed sprouts anywhere; all ideas are exotic; we wait for enormous changes every day; we live through the mutation of human order avidly: spring is rebellious.

I have given all I had. I have thrown my poetry into the ring, and I have often bled with it, suffering the agonies and praising the moments of glory I have witnessed and lived through. I was sometimes misunderstood on one ground or another, and that's not really so bad.

A critic from Ecuador has said that there are no more than six pages of real poetry in my book *Las uvas y el viento*. The Ecuadorian happened to read my book without love because it was a political book, just as other super-political critics detested my *Residencia en la tierra* because they considered it too inward and gloomy. Even such an eminent writer as Juan Marinello condemned it in the past on moral grounds. I believe both are guilty of the same mistake, which springs from a common source.

At times I, too, have spoken harshly of *Residencia en la tierra*, but in doing so, I did not have in mind its poetry but the rigidly pessimistic air breathed by my book. I cannot forget that a few years ago a boy from Santiago killed himself at the foot of a tree and left my book open at the poem "Significa sombras" ("It Means Shadows").

I believe that both *Residencia en la tierra*, a dark and gloomy but essential book within my work, and *Las uvas y el viento*, a book of wide spaces and abundant light, have a right to exist somewhere. And I am not contradicting myself when I say this.

In fact, I have a soft spot for *Las uvas y el viento*, perhaps because it is my most misunderstood book; or because it was in its pages that I set out on my wanderings through the world. It contains the dust of roads and the water of rivers; it contains creatures, continuities, and places beyond the seas I had not known until I discovered them in my many travels. I repeat, it is one of the books I love most.

Of all my books, *Estravagario* is not the one that sings most but the one that has the best leaps. Its leaping poems skip over distinction, respect, mutual protection, establishments, and obligations to sponsor reverent irreverence. Because of its disrespect, it's my most personal book. Because of its range, it is one of the most important. For my taste, it's a terrific book, with the tang of salt that the truth always has.

In *Odas elementales* I decided to deal with things from their beginnings, starting with the primary state, from birth onward. I wanted to describe many things that had been sung and said over and over again. My intention was to start like the boy chewing on his pencil, setting to work on his composition assignment about the sun, the blackboard, the clock, or the family. Nothing was to be omitted from my field of action; walking or flying, I had to touch on everything, expressing myself as clearly and freshly as possible.

An Uruguayan critic was shocked because I compared some stones to small ducks. He had established that small ducks, and some other kinds of small animals, are not material for poetry. Literary refinement has come to this kind of flippancy. They are trying to force creative artists to deal only with sublime themes. But they are wrong. We'll even make poetry from those things most scorned by the arbiters of good taste.

The bourgeoisie demands a poetry that is more and more isolated from reality. The poet who knows how to call a spade a spade is dangerous to a capitalism on its last legs. It is more convenient for the poet to believe himself "a small god," as Vicente Huidobro said. This belief, this stand, does not upset the ruling classes. The poet basks in his own divine isolation, and there is no need to bribe or crush him. He has bribed himself by condemning himself to his heaven. Meanwhile, the earth trembles in his path, in his dazzling light.

Our Latin American countries have millions of illiterates; this cultural lag survives as a heritage and a privilege of feudalism. In the face of this stumbling block of seventy million illiterates, we can say that our readers have not yet been born. We must speed up the birth, so that we and all poets will be read. We must open America's matrix to bring out her glorious light.

Literary critics are often happy to render service to the notions of feudal promoters. In 1961, for example, three of my books appeared: *Canción de gesta*, *Las piedras de Chile*, and *Cantos ceremoniales*. Critics in my country did not even mention these titles during the entire year.

When my poem *Alturas de Macchu Picchu* was first published, no one in Chile dared mention it, either. Its publisher went to the offices of Chile's bulkiest newspaper, *El mercurio*, which has been in existence almost a hundred and fifty years; he had with him a paid announcement of the book's publication. They accepted it on condition that my name be removed.

"But Neruda is the author," Neira protested.

"That doesn't matter," they said.

Alturas de Macchu Picchu had to appear as an anonymous poem in the announcement. What good had the newspaper's hundred and fifty years of life been to it? In all that time, it had not learned to respect the truth, or the facts, or poetry.

Sometimes the negative passions turned against me are not merely a bitter reflex of the class struggle, but obey other causes. I have more than forty years of work and several literary prizes to my credit, and my books have been published in the most surprising languages, yet not a single day goes by that I do not receive a jab or a pommeling from the envious elements around me. My house is a case in point. I bought this house in Isla Negra, in a deserted spot, when there was no drinking water or electricity here. With the proceeds from my books, I repaired and refurbished it; I bought wooden statues now dear to me, old ships' figureheads that found shelter and rest in my home after long journeys.

But there are people who can't bear the thought that a poet has achieved, as the fruit of widely published work, the material comfort all writers, musicians, and painters deserve. Reactionary hacks, who are behind the times and are constantly demanding honors for Goethe, deny today's poets the right to live. For instance, my owning an automobile drives them crazy. According to them, the automobile is the exclusive right of businessmen, speculators, brothel managers, usurers, and crooks.

To gall them even more. I'll leave my house in Isla Negra to the people. Someday it will be used for union meetings and as a place where miners and peasants can go to get some rest. That will be my poetry's revenge.

ANOTHER YEAR BEGINS

A newspaperman asks me: "How do you see the world during this year that is just beginning?"

I answer: "At this precise moment, at 9:20 a.m. on January 5, to me the whole world looks absolutely rosy and blue."

This has no literary, political, or personal implications. This means that from my window my eyes are struck with wonder by huge beds of pink flowers, and that, farther out, the Pacific and the sky come together in a blue embrace.

But I realize, and we know it, that there are other colors in the landscape of the world. Who can forget the color of all the blood senselessly spilled in Vietnam every day? Who can forget the color of the villages leveled with napalm?

I answer another of the journalist's questions. As in other years, during these 365 days I'll publish a new book, I am sure of it. I caress it, I rough it up, I write it every day.

"What is it about?"

What can I answer? My books are always about the same thing; I always write the same book. I hope my friends will forgive me, because, on this new occasion and in this new year filled with new days, I have nothing to offer them except my poems, the same new poems.

The year just ended brought victories to all of us on earth: victories out in space and along its routes. During the year, all men wanted to fly. We have all traveled like cosmonauts in our dreams. The conquest of space belongs to all of us, whether it was North Americans or Soviets who were the first to draw a nimbus around the moon and eat the first New Year's grapes on the moon.

To us poets should fall the greater portion of the gifts discovered. From Jules Verne, who gave man's dream of space its first flying machine in a book, to Jules Laforgue, Heinrich Heine, and José Asunción Silva (without forgetting Baudelaire, who discovered its evil spell), the pale planet was investigated, sung, and put into print by us poets, before anyone else.

The years go by. You wear out, thrive, suffer, and enjoy life. The years take life away or restore it to you. Farewells become more frequent; friends enter or get out of jail; they go to Europe and come back, or simply die.

Those you lose when you are far away from the place where they die seem to die less; they go on living in you just as they were. A poet who outlives his friends tends to fill in his work with an anthology of mourning poems. I did not go on with mine, I was afraid that human grief in the face of death might become monotonous. You don't want to turn into a register of dead people, even if they are very dear to you. In 1928 in Ceylon, when I wrote "Ausencia de Joaquín" ("Absence of Joaquín") on the death of my friend Joaquín Cifuentes Sepúlveda the poet, and later in 1931 in Barcelona, when I wrote "Alberto Rojas Giménez viene volando," I thought no one else would die on me. Many have. Nearby, in the Argentine hills of Córdoba, lies buried my dearest Argentine friend, Rodolfo Aráoz Alfaro, who left our Chilean Margarita Aguirre a widow.

In this year that has just ended, the wind carried off the fragile frame of Ilya Ehrenburg, my very dear friend, heroic defender of the truth, a titan at crushing lies. And this same year, in Moscow, they buried the poet Ovadi Savich, who translated Gabriela Mistral's poetry as well as mine and did it not only faithfully and beautifully but with shining love. The same wind took away my brother poets Nazim Hikmet and Semyon Kirsanov. And others.

Che Guevara's official assassination, in poor Bolivia, was a bitter blow. The telegram announcing his death ran through the world like a cold shiver of reverence. Millions of elegies tried to join in tribute to his heroic and tragic life. Poems, many of which did not rise to the occasion, came pouring out all over the world. I received a telegram from Cuba, from a literary colonel, asking me for mine. I have not written it yet. I believe that such an elegy must contain not only immediate protest but also the profound echo of the painful story. I shall ponder over that poem until it ripens in my mind and in my blood.

I am deeply touched that I am the only poet quoted by the great guerrilla leader in his diary. I remember that Che told me once, in front of Sergeant Retamar, that he often read my *Canto general* to the pioneering, humble, glorious bearded guerrillas in the Sierra Maestra. In his diary, where it stares out like a premonition, he copied out a line from my "Canto para Bolívar" ("Song for Bolívar"): "Your small dead body like a brave captain's . . ."

THE NOBEL PRIZE

There's a long story behind my Nobel Prize. For many years my name was always mentioned as a candidate but nothing happened.

In 1963, things got serious. The radios said repeatedly that my name was very strong in the voting in Stockholm and I would probably be the winner of the Nobel Prize. So Matilde and I put into effect home-defense plan number 3. We laid in supplies of food and red wine and hung a huge padlock on the old gate in Isla Negra. I threw in a few mysteries by Simenon, expecting to be under siege for some time.

The newsmen got there fast, but we kept them at bay. They could not get past the gate secured with the huge bronze padlock, which was as beautiful as it was powerful. They prowled behind the outer wall like tigers. What were they trying to do, anyway?

What could I say about a debate in which only the members of the Swedish Academy on the other side of the world were taking part? Still, the journalists didn't hide their intentions of squeezing blood from a turnip.

Spring had come late to the South Pacific coast. Those solitary days helped me commune with the spring season by the sea, which, though late, had dressed up for its solitary festivities. In summer not a single drop of rain falls; the earth is marly, rough, rocky; not one green blade is to be seen. In winter, the sea wind unleashes fury, salt, foam from enormous waves, and then nature looks oppressed, a victim of these terrible forces.

Spring starts off with a widespread yellow operation. Everything is covered with innumerable tiny golden flowers. This tiny, powerful crop spreads over hillsides, circles rocks, presses on toward the sea, and springs up in the middle of our everyday paths, as if it were throwing us a challenge, proving to us that it is there. Those flowers had to endure an invisible life such a long time, the desolate denial of the barren earth kept them under such a long time, that they can't seem to find enough room for their yellow abundance now.

Then the tiny pale flowers burn out and everything is covered by an intense violet bloom. Spring has a change of heart from yellow to blue, and then, again, to red. How did the tiny, nameless, innumerable corollas replace one another? The wind shook out one color one day and another color the next day, as if spring's national colors kept changing in the lonely hills, and various republics took turns sporting their invading banners.

At this time of year the cactus flowers on the coast. Far from this region, on the ridges of the Andean cordillera, the cacti loom like giants, striated and thorny, like enemy columns. The cacti along the coast, on the other hand, are small and round. I have seen them crowned with twenty scarlet buds, as if some hand had left drops of blood there, a passionate tribute. Then they burst open. Facing the ocean's huge whitecaps are thousands of cacti lit up by their full-blown flowers.

The old century plant at home drew its suicidal bloom from deep within itself. This plant, which is blue and yellow, gigantic and fleshy, has lasted more than ten years beside my door, shooting up until it was taller than I. And now it is flowering only to die. It built up a powerful green spear that rose to a height of seven meters, interrupted by a dry inflorescence, lightly covered by a fine, gold dust. Then all the colossal leaves of *Agave americana* plummet down and die.

Here, next to the tall dying flower, another titanic blossom is being born. No one outside my country will know it; it only grows on these Antarctic shores. It is called chahual (*Puya chilensis*). This ancestral plant was worshipped by the Araucanians. The ancient Arauco no longer exists. Blood, death, time, and later the epic songs of Alonso de Ercilla closed the ancient history of a tribe made of clay, rudely awakened from a geological dream to defend its invaded country. When I see its flowers come up again, over centuries of obscure dead, over layers of bloodstained forgetfulness, I believe that the earth's past blooms in spite of what we are, in spite of what we have become. Only the earth goes on being, preserving its own nature.

But I forgot to describe this flower.

It's a Bromeliacea with sharp, saw-toothed leaves. It erupts by the roadsides like green fire, arraying its panoply of mysterious emerald swords. And suddenly one colossal flower, a cluster, is born at its waist, an immense green rose as tall as a man. This sole flower, made up of tinier flowers that assemble into a single green cathedral crowned with gold pollen, gleams in the light from the sea. It is the only green flower of its huge size I have ever seen, a solitary monument to the waves.

Peasants and fishermen in my country forgot the names of the small plants long ago, and the small flowers have no names now. They forgot them little by little, and the flowers eventually lost their pride. They became all mixed up and obscure, like stones the rivers drag down from the Andean snow to unfrequented parts of the coast. Peasants and fishermen, miners and smugglers remained true to their own rough life, to continuous death and the everlasting resurrection of their duties, their defeats. To be a hero in undiscovered territories is to be obscure; these territories and their songs are lit only by the most anonymous blood and by flowers whose name nobody knows.

Among these flowers there is one that has invaded my whole

house. It's a blue flower with a long, proud, lustrous, and tough stem. At its tip, swarms of tiny infra-blue, ultra-blue flowers sway. I don't know if all human beings have the gift of seeing the sublimest blue. Is it revealed to a select few? Does it remain hidden, invisible to others? Has some blue god denied them its contemplation? Or is it only my own joy, nursed by solitude and convened into pride, gloating because it has found this blue, this blue wave, this blue star in riotous spring?

Last, I shall mention the docas. I don't know if these plants exist anywhere else; multiplied by the million, they drag their triangular fingers over the sand. Spring filled those green hands with rare crimson jewels. The docas have a Greek name: *Aizoaceae*. Isla Negra's splendor on these late-spring days is the *Aizoaceae* that spill out like an invasion from the sea, like the emanation of the sea's green grotto, like the juice from the purple clusters stored up by Neptune far off in his wine cellar.

The radio has just announced that a good Greek poet has received the famed prize. The journalists have departed. Matilde and I are finally left in peace. We solemnly withdraw the huge padlock from the old gate, so that anyone, as usual, may come calling at my door unannounced. Like spring.

In the afternoon the Swedish ambassador and his wife came to see me. They brought me a basket filled with bottles and an assortment of delicacies. They had prepared it to celebrate the Nobel Prize which they had considered a sure thing for me. We didn't really feel sad about it and drank a toast to Seferis, the Greek poet who had won. As he was leaving, the ambassador took me aside and said, "I'm sure the press will interview me, and I don't know anything about him. Can you tell me who Seferis is?"

"I don't know who he is either," I answered in all honesty.

Every writer on this planet earth would really like to get the Nobel Prize sometime, whether he admits it or not.

In Latin America particularly, the various countries have their candidates, plan their campaigns, draw up their strategy. They have lost the prize for some writers who should have had it. Rómulo Gallegos is a case in point. His work is copious and dignified. But Venezuela is an oil country—in other words, a country with money—and it was decided to use this to get him the prize. An ambassador to Sweden was appointed whose ultimate goal was to obtain the honor for Gallegos. He was free with dinner invitations; he had the works of the members of the Swedish Academy published in Spanish by printing houses in Stockholm. All this must have appeared excessive to these sensitive and reserved men. Rómulo Gallegos never found out that the exaggerated efficiency of a Venezuelan ambassador may have deprived him of a literary honor he deserved so well.

In Paris I was once told a sad story edged with cruel humor. This time it was about Paul Valéry. His name was bandied about in France, even in print, as the strongest candidate for the Nobel Prize that year. Trying to ease the nervous tension produced by the imminent news, on the morning the verdict was under debate in Stockholm, Valéry left his country house very early, with his cane and his dog.

He returned from his outing at noon, for lunch. The minute he opened the door, he asked his secretary: "Were there any phone calls?"

"Yes, sir. You had a call from Stockholm a few minutes ago."

"What did they have to say?" he asked, obviously moved.

"It was a Swedish newspaperwoman who wanted to know your views on the women's suffragette movement."

Valéry himself used to tell this anecdote with some irony. And the truth is that this great poet, so impeccable a writer, never received the celebrated prize.

As for me, no one can say I wasn't very careful. In a book by a Chilean scholar praising Gabriela Mistral, I had read about the letters my austere countrywoman sent out in many directions, without compromising her austerity but driven by her natural desire to improve her chances for the prize. This made me more reticent. I no sooner learned that my name was being mentioned as a candidate (and I've lost track of how many times it was mentioned) than I made up my mind not to return to Sweden, a country I had been attracted to since boyhood, when Tomás Lago and I set ourselves up as true disciples of an excommunicated drunken Protestant minister by the name of Gösta Berling.

Besides, I was tired of being mentioned every year but never getting anywhere. It grated on me to see my name listed in the annual competition, as if I were a race horse. On the other hand, some literary and popular Chilean writers felt slighted by the Swedish Academy's indifference to them. It was a situation bordering dangerously on the ridiculous.

At last, as everyone knows, I was awarded the Nobel Prize. In 1971 I was in Paris, where I had just arrived to take up my post as Chilean ambassador, when my name began to appear in the news once again. Matilde and I frowned. We were used to the annual disappointment and had grown hard-skinned. One night in October of that year Jorge Edwards, our Embassy's counselor and a writer as well, came into the dining room of my home. Thrifty by nature, he offered to make a very simple bet with me. If I was given the Nobel Prize that year, I would treat him and his wife to dinner in the best restaurant in Paris. If it was not given to me, he would treat Matilde and me.

"Agreed," I said. "We'll have a splendid dinner at your expense."

A part of the secret reason for Jorge Edwards's risky bet began to leak out on the following day. I found out that a friend of his had called him from Stockholm. A writer and a journalist, she had told him that this time Pablo Neruda had every chance of winning the Nobel Prize.

The newsmen began to call long-distance. From Buenos Aires, from Mexico, and, above all, from Spain. There it was a foregone conclusion. Naturally, I refused to make any statement, but my doubts began to surface once more.

That evening Artur Lundkvist, my only Swedish friend who was a writer, came to see me. Lundkvist had been in the Academy for three or four years. He had come from Sweden to visit the South of France. After dinner I told him the fix I was in, having to reply to the long-distance questions of newsmen who had already conceded me the prize.

"I want to ask you one favor, Artur," I said. "If it is true, I would really like to know before it comes out in the papers. I want to be the first to tell Salvador Allende, with whom I have shared so many battles. It would make him very happy to have the news first."

Lundkvist, academician and poet, looked at me with his Swedish eyes, very seriously. "I can't tell you a thing. If there is anything to it, the King of Sweden will let you know by telegram, or else the Swedish ambassador in Paris will."

This was on the nineteenth or twentieth of October. On the morning of the twenty-first, the anterooms at the Embassy started to fill up with newsmen. Television crews from Sweden, Germany, France, and Latin America showed an impatience at my silence— due solely to lack of information—that threatened to turn into mutiny. At eleven-thirty the Swedish ambassador called and asked me if I would receive him, without saying what about. This did nothing to slacken the tension, since the interview would not take place until two hours later. The telephone kept on shrilling hysterically.

Then one of the Paris radio stations released a flash, a last-minute news bulletin, announcing that the Nobel Prize for 1971 had been awarded to the "poète chilien Pablo Neruda." I immediately went down to face the noisy assemblage from the news media. Fortunately, at this moment my old friends Jean Marcenac and Aragon appeared. Marcenac, a fine poet and a brother to me in France, let out shouts of joy. For his part, Aragon seemed happier at the news than I. Both helped me through the hard test of parrying the journalists.

I was just getting over an operation. Anemic and shaky on my legs, I had little desire to move about. Friends came to dine with me that evening. Matta, from Italy; García Márquez, from Barcelona; Siqueiros, from Mexico; Miguel Otero Silva, from Caracas; Arturo Camacho Ramírez, from Paris itself; Cortázar, from his hide-out. Carlos Vasallo, Chilean, traveled from Rome to go with me to Stockholm.

The telegrams grew into such mountains that I still have not been able to read or answer all of them. One of the countless letters I received was odd and a bit menacing. It was written from Holland by a husky black man; this was obvious from the newspaper clip-ping he sent along. "I represent," the letter said, more or less, "the anti-colonialist movement in Georgetown, British Guiana. I have requested a pass to attend the Nobel Prize ceremony in Stockholm. I was informed at the Swedish Embassy that evening dress is a re-quirement, absolutely necessary for this occasion. I have no money to buy a tail coat and I shall never wear a rented one, it would be humiliating for a free man from America to put on used clothing. I am therefore informing you that, with the little money I can scrape together, I shall travel to Stockholm to hold a press conference to de-nounce the imperialist and anti-popular character of this ceremony, even if it is being held to honor the most anti-imperialist and most popular of the world's poets."

In November, Matilde and I traveled to Stockholm. A few old friends went along with us. We were given rooms in the luxurious Grand Hotel and from there we could see the beautiful cold city, the Royal Palace across from our windows. Also staying at the hotel were the other laureates of that year, in physics, chemistry, medicine, etc., and several celebrities, some articulate and very fine-mannered, others as simple and rustic as mechanics whom chance had brought out of their workshops. Willy Brandt, a German, was not staying at the hotel; he would receive his Nobel Peace Prize in Norway. It was a pity, because, of all the award winners, he was the one I would have been most interested in meeting and talking to. I only managed to see him later at the receptions, where we were always separated by three or four people.

We had to have a practice session for the grand ceremony, and Swedish protocol actually made us stage it where it would be held. It was really comical to see such serious-looking people get out of bed and leave their hotel at a specific hour, go punctually to an empty building, climb several flights of stairs without missing a step, march left or right in strict order, sit on the stage in the same armchairs we would occupy on the day of the ceremony. All this, facing television cameras, and in an enormous empty hall where the seats of honor for the King and the Royal Family stood out, also forlornly empty. I have never been able to understand just what whim would make Swedish television film that rehearsal performed by such terrible actors.

The day the prize was to be awarded started off with the St. Lucia festivities. I was awakened by voices chanting sweetly in the hotel corridors. Then blond Scandinavian maidens crowned with flowers, their faces lit by burning candles, burst into my room. They brought me breakfast as well as a gift, a beautiful long painting of the sea.

A little later, something happened that stirred up the Stockholm police force. A letter for me was delivered at the hotel reception desk. It bore the signature of the wild anti-colonialist from Georgetown, British Guiana. "I have just arrived in Stockholm," it read. His attempt to call a press conference had failed, but as a revolutionary man of action, he was taking certain steps. It couldn't be possible that Pablo Neruda, the poet of the humiliated and the oppressed, would receive the Nobel Prize in tails. Consequently, he had bought a pair of green scissors which he would use to snip off the "tails of your cut-away, and any other appendages . . . So I am doing my duty and warning you. When you see a black man stand up at the rear of the hall, equipped with a huge pair of green scissors, you can guess exactly what is going to happen to you."

I handed the strange letter to the young diplomat assigned to me by Swedish protocol, who followed me around on all my errands. I told him, with a smile, that I had received another letter in Paris from the same crank and that I didn't think we should worry about him. The young Swede disagreed. "With all the dissenters around at this time, anything can happen. It is my duty to warn the Stockholm police," he said, and sped off to carry out what he considered his duty.

I should point out that Miguel Otero Silva was among those who had gone with me to Stockholm; an important novelist and a brilliant poet, he is not only a perfect representative of the American conscience but also an incomparable friend. There were just a few hours left before the ceremony. During lunch I mentioned that the Swedes had taken the incident of the letter of protest quite seriously.

Otero Silva, who was lunching with us, slapped himself on the forehead. "Why, I wrote that letter with my own hand; I was just pulling your leg, Pablo. What are we going to do now, with the police looking for a writer who doesn't exist?"

"You'll be taken off to jail. For your practical joke about the wild man from the Caribbean," I said to him, "you'll be punished instead of the man from Georgetown."

Just then, my young Swedish aide, back from warning the authorities, joined us at the table. I told him what had happened. "It was a practical joke. Its author is having lunch with us right now."

He dashed out again. The police had already gone to all the hotels in Stockholm, looking for a black man from Georgetown, or some such place. And they didn't relax their precautions. As we went in to the ceremony, and as we came out of the celebration ball, Matilde and I noticed that, instead of the usual ushers, four or five hefty young fellows rushed forward to take care of us—solid, yellow-haired, scissors-proof bodyguards.

The Nobel Prize ritual had an immense, disciplined, and calm audience, which applauded politely, in the right places. The aged monarch shook hands with each of us; gave us the diploma, the medal, and the check; and we returned to our seats on the stage, which was no longer squalid, as it had been during the rehearsal, but covered now with flowers and occupied chairs. They say (or said it to Matilde to impress her) that the King spent more time with me than with the other laureates and pressed my hand longer, treating me with obvious friendliness. Perhaps it was a reminiscence of the ancient kindliness of the palace toward the troubadours. In any case, no other king has shaken my hand, for a long or even a brief moment.

No doubt, that ceremony, carried out with such strict protocol, had the proper solemnity. Perhaps the solemnity given to important occasions will always exist in the world. Human beings seem to need it. But I found a charming similarity between the parade of eminent laureates and the handing out of school prizes in any small country town.

CHILE CHICO

I was coming from Puerto Ibáñez, still awed by the great General Carrera Lake, awed by its metallic waters, a paroxysm of nature comparable only to the turquoise-blue sea of Varadero in Cuba, or to our own Petrohué. And then the savage falls of the Ibáñez River, with the full effect of their terrifying grandeur. I was also shaken by the isolation and the poverty of the people in the neighboring towns, near the gigantic source of energy but without electricity, living among countless sheep, but dressed in cheap rags. At last I came to Chile Chico.

There at the end of the day the wide twilight was waiting for me.

The everlasting wind was cutting up the clouds like quartz. Rivers of light isolated one huge block the wind was holding up between the earth and the sky.

Cattle lands and sown fields struggling under polar pressure from the wind. The earth rose all around, turning into the hard rock towers of Roca Castillo, sharpened points, Gothic spires, nature's granite battlements. The irregular Aysén mountains, round as spheres, tall and flat as tables, intensified the rectangles and triangles of snow.

And the sky was working on its twilight with sheer silks and metals: a yellowness shimmered in the sky, like an immense bird suspended by pure space. Everything went through abrupt mutations, changing into a whale's mouth, a fiery leopard, glowing abstract forms.

I felt the immensity spreading out in formation overhead, picking me to witness the dazzling Aysén range with its cluster of hills, waterfalls, millions of dead and blighted trees accusing their ancient killers with the silence of a world about to be born, for which everything was in readiness: the ceremonies of the sky and the earth. But there was something missing—shelter, collective organization, houses, man. Those who live in such difficult solitudes need a common bond as vast as the huge spaces around them.

I left as the twilight was going dim and the night was coming on, overpowering, blue.

THE SOUTHERN COUNTRYSIDE

Amid comings and goings, fleeting and reprehensible loves of my youth, I grew conscious, not only of the land, but of the conflicts, pain, and devastation that extended over forest and field.

The Spanish conquest hit the ancient kingdoms of Mexico and Peru like a bolt of lightning: without grief or glory the two indigenous empires, divisive, parasitic, already dilapidated, succumbed ingloriously to the bearded invaders. In Chile, history took a different turn.

History there was a long mutual massacre stretching out over three centuries. The Indians, defending themselves, and the Spanish conquistadors exterminated each other in turn, but the crusaders and their families, though reduced to penury by the implacable progress of the war, left on the land a system of haciendas that would inexplicably persist. Indeed, not until Chile's first popular government, that of Salvador Allende, would the latifundias be broken up, between 1971 and these months of 1973 in which I am writing these memoirs. It is a commonplace that memoirs consist, in general, of personal recollections. But in a way my country, along with its problems, has followed me wherever I've gone. Someone in Europe, Asia, or the United States may take an interest in my poetry while thinking that Chile, this country long and slender as a comet, is barely visible from the sky, nestled among the geography of the world. But it has never been that way for me.

We Chileans come from a strange lineage, in part. In the rest of Latin America, the mestizos are the children of Indian women raped by Iberian soldiers. We Chileans, however, come also from the Spanish women stolen by the Arauco warriors. Throughout the centuries of this longest of patriotic wars, the Chilean Indians, implacable as the Spanish, would raze the cities and fortresses and would not leave a single Spaniard alive. But curiously, they never killed the women.

I don't know the origin of this war custom of theirs, of those Araucanians whose blood I inherited: they remain as mysterious, remote, and inscrutable to me as those who stepped forth in the sixteenth century, half-nude and armed with primitive arrows, opposing the invincible conquistadors.

The Spanish captives gave children to their Indian captors. These were the Chileans. We come from unusual circumstances. Since 1810, when the Spanish monarchy was expelled, Chile has had a national government, and my more recent compatriots felt at ease in this anachronistic system. They invented titles, called themselves nobles and scions, and went on living from the work of others. To extend their domains, they, too, killed Indians. This bloody stage of Chile's independence is called by bourgeois history, with re- pulsive hypocrisy, "The pacification of the Araucanians."

The pacifying army decimated the Araucanians and their posses- sions. Once they'd established themselves in the virgin territories, they instituted laws and installed judges, lawyers, and police. And thus, with bullets and truncheons to the head, the Spanish made their mark on the land—the bloody land I used to ride through on horseback.

The working people, like the Hernándezes up in the mountains with their threshers, were like the first soldiers of a new war. Then came the indifferent landholders. The Santiago oligarchy, which had already de- voured the extensive wine-growing provinces, spread out through the south. Life was divvied up among a scarce few landed nobles and an in- credible multitude of poor farmhands, no less Chilean than the new own- ers, but underfed, unshod, ignorant, and in tatters.

This is the social organization in which I spent my youth. Consumed by love and melancholy, we learned slowly, with dread, of the hidden his- tory of the country.

I began to look for people who would tell me of the past and present, and feverishly, I looked for books that would reveal the truth.

I learned of the existence of a small, heroic book that told of the atroci- ties committed in these years. The story of the genocide of the last races of Patagonia, which was taking place when I, an apprentice poet, navigated the rivers in my boat, moved by the melody of an accordion or by the legs of one of those untamed girls.

I looked for the book, but didn't find it: the murderous landlords had chased down, bought, or destroyed every copy.

It was called Tragic Patagonia, *and only thirty-five years later did I manage to obtain a copy of this suppressed document.*

It recounted the brutal history of the elimination from the earth of the very last of the Ona people. That pastoral race was the only one left on the planet that conserved the customs and traditions of the Stone Age. But no one cares. They were poor fishing tribes that survived on the harsh- est terrain in the entire world.

But they didn't survive the Menéndez, the Montes, the Echelarte families, who felt it endangered the raising of their sheep to have those squalid Patagonians as neighbors, and who hunted them down to a man and killed them, woman by woman, child by child, paying a pound sterling for the head of every southern native the hunters brought them. In the evenings, the new owners counted the harvest of heads as if they were counting melons and paying their minions.

And thus, in the Tierra del Fuego, the Menéndez family, whose descendants are now directors of the Union Club in Santiago and the Jockey Club in Buenos Aires, raised their flocks of sheep.

And there remained three or four survivors of those races lost in the confines of the world of my fatherland.

And so, the Chilean-Argentine Menéndez family came to own, only a few years back, more than a million sheep.

SEPTEMBER FLAGS

In the southern part of the Latin American continent, September is a wide open, flowering month. This month is also decked in flags.

At the beginning of the last century, in 1810, in the month of September, insurrections against Spanish dominion broke out or consolidated in many territories of South America. In September we South Americans commemorate the emancipation, honor our heroes, and welcome spring, spreading out so far and wide that it reaches across the Strait of Magellan to blossom as far down as southern Patagonia and Cape Horn.

The regular chain of revolutions that sprouted from Mexico to Argentina and Chile was very important for the world.

The leaders were dissimilar. Bolívar, warrior and courtier, gifted with the brilliance of a prophet; San Martín, inspired organizer of an army that crossed the tallest and most hostile mountain ranges of the planet to fight the decisive battles of Chile's liberation; José Miguel

Carrera and Bernardo O'Higgins, who established the first Chilean armies as well as the first printing presses and the first laws against slavery, abolished in Chile many years before it was abolished in the United States.

Like Bolívar and some of the other liberators, José Miguel Carrera came from the aristocratic creole class. The interests of this class clashed sharply with those of the Spaniards in America. The people were not an organized entity but an enormous mass of bondsmen at the service of Spanish rule. Men like Bolívar and Carrera, readers of the Encyclopedists, students from the military academies in Spain, had to break through walls of isolation and ignorance to stir up a national spirit.

Carrera's life was brief and resplendent as lightning. *El húsar des-dichado* (The Unfortunate Hussar) is the title I gave to a book about him I put together and published some years ago. His fascinating personality drew antagonisms down on his head the way a lightning rod draws sparks during a storm. He was finally shot in Mendoza by the rulers of the newly declared Argentine Republic. His desperate desire to overthrow the Spanish yoke had put him at the head of the wild Indians of the Argentine pampas. He besieged Buenos Aires and came very close to taking it. But he really wanted to free Chile and his heart was so set on it that he started premature civil and guerrilla wars that led him to his death. During those turbulent years, the revolution devoured one of its most brilliant and courageous sons. History has pinned the blame for this bloody deed on O'Higgins and San Martín. However, the history of the month of September, month of spring and banners, covers with its wings the memory of the three heroes of the combats waged in the vast setting of the wide pampas and the eternal snows.

O'Higgins, another of Chile's liberators, was a man of humble beginnings. His would have been an obscure, peaceful life if he had not met in London, when he was only seventeen, an old revolutionary who was making the rounds of all the courts of Europe, seeking assistance for the cause of American liberation. His name was Don Francisco de Miranda and he had the powerful affection of Empress Catherine of Russia, one of many friends. He arrived in Paris with a Russian passport, and the doors of all the chancelleries of Europe were open to him.

It's a romantic story, with such a "period" air that it sounds like an opera. O'Higgins was the natural son of a Spanish viceroy, a soldier of fortune of Irish descent, who had been governor of Chile. Miranda made it a point to look into O'Higgins's family background when he realized that the young man could be very useful to the insurrection of Spain's American colonies. Someone has told the story of the exact moment when Miranda told the young O'Higgins the secret of his birth and plunged him into insurgent action. The young revolutionary fell to his knees and, throwing his arms around Miranda, sobbed out the promise to leave immediately for his country, Chile, and lead the rebellions against Spanish power there. O'Higgins was the one who won the final battles against colonial rule and is considered the founder of our republic.

Miranda was taken prisoner by the Spaniards and died in the horrible La Carraca prison, in Cádiz. The body of this former general of the French Revolution and teacher of revolutionaries was bundled into a sack and thrown into the sea from the top of the prison wall.

Exiled by his countrymen, San Martín died a lonely old man in Boulogne-sur-Mer, France.

O'Higgins, Chile's liberator, died in Peru, far from everything he loved, banished by the creole landowning class, which quickly took over the revolution.

On my way through Lima a short time ago, in Peru's Museum of History, I discovered some paintings done by General O'Higgins in his final years. All those paintings have Chile as their theme. He painted spring in Chile, the leaves and the flowers in September.

This September I have sat down to remember the names, the events, the loves, and the sorrows of that age of insurrections. A century later the peoples are stirring again, and a turbulent current of wind and fury is waving the flags. Everything has changed since those far-off years, but history goes on its way and a new spring fills out the interminable spaces of our America.

ANDRÉS BELLO

We came from the tempestuous sea to the north. The sky turned blue, the air soft and warm.

The ship that would take me to my fatherland would touch American soil. Guayra, in Venezuela, would be our first port of call.

For an American, no country can be a substitute for the continent, we know its almost always bloody history, the popular music of all its peoples lulls and enchants us. The fruits we love are here.

I was readying myself to reach Venezuela. At the doors of the university in Santiago stands the finest monument in all of Chile: a seated man with a stern face. He incarnates, for the younger generations, the timeworn ideals of liberty and independence that gave birth to the sister republics. This marble statue, darkened beautifully by the sun, rain, and Chilean weather, represents a political writer, a professor of great intelligence. His name is Andrés Bello, he was a friend of Bolívar's, Venezuelan by birth, first rector of the university of my fatherland.

As I approached Guayra I could make out, amid the ragged green coastline, the marble gaze of Andrés Bello. That gaze that accompanied my student struggles, my first verses, my first loves. That Venezuelan who founded in London the greatest literary and scientific journal of revolutionary romanticism in Spanish was for us, and continues to be for many Chileans, the unity of the two republics, separated by a vast expanse of the American continent, but unified in a single longing for liberation. The Venezuelan Bello gave deep meaning and structure to the new Chilean Republic. He wrote the laws, inspired by the ideas of the French Revolution; he founded the study of sciences and letters in this country of mine, which had only just emerged from the shadows of colonialism.

My personal story is, in a certain way, conjoined to that statue on the streets of Santiago.

Bello was not a brilliant poet. The politician, the legislator, the scientist in him predominated, but his literary works, particularly his verses, were full of love for the American soil, for our mountains and our rivers. Bello tried to give a national meaning to literature at the dawn of America's independence. This tradition was forgotten, and with the enrichment of the bourgeoisie, a cosmopolitan literature, European in outlook, came to stand in for it almost entirely. When I wrote my *Canto general*, my aim was to restore to Latin American poetry its multinational character, to return, in other words, to the path marked out by the great Venezuelan.

And now there appeared from the blue of the sea, green and brilliant like an aquamarine beryl, the coast of Venezuela, fatherland of Bolívar and Bello.

RECABARREN

Recabarren and Lafertte form part of that narrow group of Chileans who make up the nation's soul, the nationality itself. By dictating that popular struggle would strive definitively for greater dignity, well-being, and culture for the workers in Chile, these patriots helped the people gain due consideration in our history.

That was their labor, as patriots and Communists.

Even now, it is impossible to summarize the life and works of Luis Emilio Recabarren.

Any search for a fighter so powerful, of such colossal stature, in the political and social history of the American continent would be in vain. There is no other titan like Recabarren, not in North America, not in Central America, not in South America.

His figure towers like a summit over the American panorama. And yet his traits will forever leave their impress on the struggles of the Chilean people. Turbulent, grandiose warriors like Emiliano Zapata in Mexico or Sandino in Nicaragua impressed insurrection on the souls of the people to the north with gunpowder and blood. It is right that they be recalled with veneration for their deeds and daring.

Recabarren knew our fatherland like none other. He, too, is a grandiose hero: but he is a hero of organization. He is the shaper of the conscience of the masses: an indefatigable agitator. But his agitation walks toward a single point: the organized action of the people. He is the first in the Americas to bring unions and syndicates to life from nothing, to make them multiply, give them new life in this land of destruction, sacrifice, and massacre.

The bourgeois governments saw for the first time the people before them, pounding the table and demanding their rights. The social reforms of the first Alessandri are the direct consequence of the tenacious organizing, the revolutionary morality of Recabarren.

We all know that Recabarren systematically created the workers' press.

But do you know what it means to publish a newspaper dedicated to the struggle, and what it meant to do so before 1920?

To publish it is to plan it, to write it, to print it on underground presses, to publicize it, to send it out to one man at a time, to pass it from hand to hand, to finance it without resources—without sources beyond solidarity. And solidarity must be created, must be sown in the sandy soil of indifference and under the threat of implacable reprisal.

Recabarren founded dozens of newspapers in these conditions. Because he understood the power of the written word, as he understood personal contact with the great masses of workers.

In the Norte Chico, my comrades took me once to see an old printing press that was still producing a small daily for the party. It was ancient, a museum piece, but it still worked. There were tremendous dents in its rollers. I asked what had caused such damage. They told me that less than half a century before, the police had raided the place. The press was destroyed, the type cases were dumped out in the street, and the building was set alight and destroyed. But the old press was still running, still defending the cause of the people.

I passed my hand over those old wounds, and when they touched that metal, I felt I was touching Recabarren's soul and his unbreakable legacy.

LAFERTTE

For many, he was Comrade Lafertte. For others, Elías. For me he was and will always remain in my memory Don Elías.

I learned many things from him. I have the feeling that before I met him, I had learned man's virtues only halfway. I had learned rectitude halfway, simplicity halfway. I had halfway acquired a sense of dignity. Walking through the pampa with Don Elías, I was able to see a man simple through and through, to come to know a completely upright human being, to befriend a person of absolute dignity.

This is a rare lesson, a select one, that life and that the party conferred on me.

Another thing Don Elías taught me, because he was a splendid teacher without knowing it, was love for the party. During the hundreds of times we spoke, in circumstances harsh or happy, with the multitudes from the pampas, my love for the party grew, this Communist sentiment I carry inside me with pride and humility grew.

I learned from him that a man, however eminent others might think him, must bow down to the law of struggle, must take on the hopes of his fellow man, must become a living cell of the party. Our own freedom is important, but human liberation is more so.

Don Elías never believed one could be a Communist outside of the party. He was a great personality, and therefore highly disciplined.

There, on the sands of Tarapacá or the mineral heights of Antofagasta, we accompanied each other, walking and talking.

The party had been born there, on the cruel plains, and there I could see the capacity for suffering and heroism of my companions in the struggle. Sometimes we talked facing the machine guns. The strike movements spread. Bad salaries, bitter life, the marvelous children of the pampas growing up in those desolate backwaters with no possibility of culture.

I saw how he tore the saltpeter from the sandy crust, how he descended into the mine shaft, how he reemerged later like a phantom of sweat and pain. Sitting at the table in Iquique with Don Elías, I wrote the sonnet "Saltpeter," which he memorized.

Many and various are the stories and anecdotes, some of them sorrowful, others scintillating, that emerge from the agitated, agitating lives of Recabarren and Lafertte.

How can one forget the way, chased down by the police of the imperialist companies, unable to gather the workers to speak with them, Recabarren showed the inexhaustible resources of his intelligence. Immediately they gathered in the tunnels of the abandoned mines as though in solitary cemeteries. And when the English saltpeter company prohibited any workers' protests in the pampa, presuming that their concession took in the whole of the territory, Recabarren had the people there gather between the tracks of the train that crossed the pampa.

"This land, at least, doesn't belong to them, because it's the property of the state railroad," he said, and so, in the narrow space between the rails, the men listened to his words in one long line.

I don't want these evocations to give the idea that our great comrades were beings lacking in humor or personalities that only lived with their faces turned to the sublime.

Recabarren was gifted with humor and joy, with humanity and tenderness. With Lafertte, much younger, he used to crack jokes and fool around, laughing uproariously at the childish ingenuousness and outlandish ideas of his younger friend.

Don Elías told me that in his first conversations with Recabarren, the theory of the transmigration of souls came up.

"What is that, then, tell me what it's about, what's this theory consist of?" Lafertte asked.

"It's a theory from the Orient. In India they believe that after death, man's soul occupies the body of an animal, transforming into an elephant, a tortoise, a bird, or a fish." Such was Recabarren's answer.

Lafertte remained there lost in thought, not knowing if Recabarren was making fun of him.

Recabarren asked him: "So what do you want to turn into after you die? What animal would you like to become if that theory is true?"

Lafertte responded: "I'd like to turn into a donkey, then, and when I walked by you, I'd give you a kick."

Recabarren answered him sardonically: "Elías, why would you want to stay in the same family?"

PRESTES

No Communist leader in America has had such a hazardous and extraordinary life as Luis Carlos Prestes, a Brazilian political and military hero. His true life and his legend long ago hurdled ideological barriers, and he has become a living embodiment of the heroes of former times. And so, when I received an invitation in Isla Negra to visit Brazil and meet Prestes, I promptly accepted. Besides, I learned that no other foreigner had been invited, and this flattered me. I felt that I was somehow attending a resurrection from the dead.

Prestes had just been freed after more than ten years of detention. These long confinements are nothing exceptional in the "free world." My friend Nazim Hikmet the poet spent thirteen or fourteen years in a Turkish prison. As I write these memoirs, six or seven Communists have been entombed in Paraguay for twelve years, with no communication whatever with the outside world. Prestes's German-born wife was turned over to the Gestapo by the Brazilian dictatorship. The Nazis chained her up aboard the ship taking her to martyrdom. She gave birth to a girl, who lives with her father today, rescued from the teeth of the Gestapo by Doña Leocadia Prestes, the leader's indefatigable mother. Then, after giving birth in a prison yard, Luis Carlos Prestes's wife was beheaded by the Nazis. All those martyred lives would guarantee that Prestes was never forgotten during his long years in prison.

I was in Mexico when his mother died. She had traveled all over the world, demanding her son's freedom. General Lázaro Cárdenas, ex-President of the Mexican Republic, telegraphed the Brazilian dictator, requesting a few days of freedom for Prestes, to attend his mother's funeral. In his message, President Cárdenas personally guaranteed Prestes's return to jail. Getúlio Vargas's answer was negative.

I shared the world's indignation and wrote an elegy to Doña Leocadia, bringing in the memory of her absent son and vehemently denouncing the tyrant. I read it at the tomb of the noble lady who had knocked in vain at the doors of the world for her son's liberation. My poem began on a sober note:

> Señora, you have made our America greater.
> You gave it a pure river whose waters flow abundantly,
> a giant tree with infinite roots,
> a son worthy of his deeply rich country.

As the poem progressed, however, it turned on the Brazilian despot more and more violently.

I read it everywhere, and it was reproduced in leaflets and postcards that reached all parts of the continent.

During a stopover in Panama once, I included it in one of my readings, after I had finished reciting my love poems. The hall was jammed and the heat of the isthmus had me perspiring. I had just started to read my invectives against Vargas when I felt my throat drying up. I broke off and reached for a glass I had near me. At that moment, I saw someone dressed in white hurrying toward the rostrum. Thinking it was a general helper in the hall, I held out the glass to let him fill it with water. But the man in white brushed it aside indignantly and addressed the gathering, shouting excitedly: "I am the Brazilian ambassador. I want to protest: Prestes is nothing but a common criminal . . ."

At these words, the audience cut him off with ear-splitting whistles. A black student, with shoulders as broad as a wardrobe, got up in the middle of the hall and, with his hands threateningly aimed at the ambassador's throat, thrust his way toward the rostrum. I rushed in to protect the diplomat, and luckily I managed to get him out of the place without any further damage to his high office.

With such credentials, my trip from Isla Negra to Brazil to take part in the popular celebration seemed natural to the Brazilians. I was stunned when I saw the crowd packed into Pacaembú Stadium, in São Paulo. I'm told there were more than 130,000 people. Their heads looked very tiny in the vast circle of the stadium. Small of stature, Prestes, who was at my side, seemed to me a Lazarus who had just walked out of the grave, neat and dressed up for the occasion. He was lean and so white that his skin looked transparent, with that strange whiteness prisoners have. His intense look, the huge violet circles under his eyes, his extremely delicate features, his grave dignity, were all a reminder of the long sacrifice his life had been. Yet he spoke as calmly as a general after a victory.

I read a poem in his honor, written a few hours earlier. Jorge Amado changed only the Spanish word "albañiles," bricklayers, for the Portuguese "pedreiros." Contrary to my fears, the poem read in Spanish was understood by the multitude. After each line of my slow reading, there was an explosion of applause from the Brazilians. That applause had a deep resonance in my poetry. A poet who reads his poems to 130,000 people is not the same man, and cannot keep on writing in the same way, after such an experience.

At last I find myself face-to-face with legendary Luis Carlos Prestes. He is waiting for me in the home of some friends of his. All of Prestes's features—the small stature, the leanness, the whiteness of onionskin paper—take on the precision of a miniature. His words also, and perhaps his thinking, seem to match his physical make-up.

For a man of his reserve, he is very friendly with me. I believe he is giving me the kind of benevolent treatment we poets frequently receive from others, a tolerance half-tender and half-evasive, very much like that adopted by grownups toward children.

Prestes invited me to lunch one day the following week. Then one of those disasters occurred to me that can only be blamed on fate or my irresponsibility. It so happens that, although the Portuguese language has its Saturday and Sunday, it does not single out the other days of the week as Monday, Tuesday, Wednesday, etc., but with devilish names like *segunda-feira*, *têrça-feira*, *quarta-feira*, skipping, however, the first *feira*. I get all tangled up in those *feiras*, and never know which day is which.

I went to spend a few hours at the beach with a lovely Brazilian friend, ever mindful, however, that Prestes had set the luncheon date for the next day. On the *quarta-feira* I discovered that Prestes had waited for me in vain on the *têrça-feira*, with the table set, while I idled away the hours on the beach at Ipanema. He looked for me high and low, but no one knew where I was. In deference to my special tastes, the ascetic captain had ordered excellent wines that were difficult to obtain in Brazil. We were to have had lunch alone.

Every time I remember this story, I could die of shame. I have been able to learn just about everything in my life, except the names of the days of the Portuguese week.

CODOVILLA

When I was about to leave Santiago, I heard that Victorio Codovilla wanted to talk to me. I went to see him. We were always good friends, right up to his death.

Codovilla had been a member of the Third International and possessed all the faults of the time. He was authoritarian, a personalist, and always thought he was right. He imposed his judgment on others easily and cut through their will like a knife going through butter. He was always in a hurry when he came to meetings, giving the impression that he had thought out everything and had all the answers ready, and seemed to listen to the opinions of others out of politeness and with a certain impatience; then he would issue peremptory orders. His tremendous ability and his knack for summing things up were overpowering. He worked without respite, imposing that same rhythm on his fellows, and always gave me the feeling that he was one of the great political thinking machines of the day.

He always showed a very special feeling of understanding and deference toward me. This Italian—transformed and utilitarian in public life—was human to a fault, with a profound artistic sense that made him understand errors and weaknesses in men of culture. But this did not stop him from being implacable, and at times deadly, in political life.

He was worried, he told me, about Prestes's misinterpretation of Perón's dictatorship. Codovilla believed Perón and his movement were an offshoot of European Fascism. No anti-Fascist could sit back quietly and accept Perón's increasing power or his repeated repressive actions. Codovilla and the Argentine Communist Party believed, at this time, that insurrection was the only answer to Perón, and wanted me to talk with Prestes about this. "It's not a mission," he told me, but I sensed some preoccupation behind his usual cocksure front.

After the Pacaembu rally, I had a long talk with Prestes. It was impossible to find two men who were more dissimilar, more diametrically opposed. A hefty man brimming with health, the Italo-Argentine invariably seemed to take over a whole room, a whole table, everything around him. Thin and ascetic, Prestes looked frail enough for a puff of wind to sweep him out the window. Yet I discovered that, behind their appearances, the two men were equally tough.

"There's no Fascism in Argentina. Perón is a caudillo but not a Fascist," Prestes said, answering my questions. "Where are the brown shirts? The Fascist militias?

"Besides, Codovilla is wrong. Lenin says that insurrection is not something to play with. And you can't always be declaring war without soldiers, with only volunteers to count on."

Deep down, these two men, so different from each other, were inflexible. One of them, probably Prestes, was right about these things, but the dogmatism of both these admirable revolutionaries often built up an atmosphere around them that I found impossible to breathe.

I should also add that Codovilla was a man of vitality. I was very much in favor of his fight against the hypocrisy and puritanism of the Communist era. Our great Chilean of the old-time party days, Lafertte, was an obsessively militant teetotaler. Old Lafertte also growled constantly against love affairs and flirtations, outside the pale of the Civil Registry, between men and women of the party. Codovilla defeated our limited teacher with his own limitless vital capacity.

MAYAKOVSKY

In my youth, I read with goose bumps that story by Chamisso about the man who sold his shadow. For me, the most dreadful part was when, the transaction complete, the Devil knelt down and carefully rolled up the shadow the man had sold him.

I have always had the feeling that a number of great poets, in one way or another, have sold the shadow that accompanied them; that it was cut from the floor, rolled up, compressed, torn from its proprietor by various devils, among them passing fads, lethargy and lack of vision, the literary salon, even, at times, slow, steady bribery on the part of the bourgeoisie.

From Mayakovksy we have inherited his incomplete poetry and his extremely vast shadow.

His is the image of the poet who will not sell his shadow, who will make use of it his whole life long, wrapping himself in it like a cape and sleeping in the shelter of that personal shadow that made his every act and dream stand out in black and white with the dramatic light and darkness of his irreplaceable personality.

His poetry, from without, strikes us as incomplete, because death cut it short with its dreadful shears. In the meantime, the Soviet Union grew prodigiously. We need Mayakovsky's poem about Valentina, the cosmonaut, the woman who went further than all other women in humanity's history. Only Mayakovsky would achieve those tones like gunshots to celebrate the spaceship. No one will write the poems he never managed to write himself, because he had the imperious elegance of a cosmonaut and even his poems of love and combat possess cosmic substances. He snatched from his era so many new materials, with the craving of a conquistador and that eloquence which is his great attribute, and it blew through poetry and altered it like the passing over of a storm.

If more than one poet corresponds to each revolution, because poetry is electrified in human movement, still, not all revolutions have their body, blood, and soul in a single poet, as was the case with Mayakovsky. The great human palpitation of the October Revolution remained alive in his poetry, and his songs are events, memorable occurrences that support us. In earlier revolutions, a poet offered a song, many others gave more or less accomplished sonorous support. Mayakovksy confided his turbulent soul, which was consumed from top to bottom, sacrificing his poetry like a shimmering material for the construction of socialism.

That is why Mayakovksy's shadow is so incalculable and doesn't diminish, but grows.

His shadow passes the equator and arrives like the tail of a comet to the lost outskirts of Latin America, illuminating the conscience of the young writer. This shadow emerges from the library, noisily casting down countless volumes of dogmatic words. It bursts into the streetfights and enters like a subtle influence into the conduct of beings. This shadow is at times like a sword and at others like an orange, it has the color of summer.

The poets of my generation tried to leave Mayakovsky on the shelf like a good classic, assigned to his proper place. But his bad manners make him step out every day, joining with us in the combats and victories of our time. For Mayakovsky was, above all, a good companion.

A great companion for all latitudes, for all races, for all people, for all poets.

And a teacher for the poets of all latitudes, of all races, of all peoples.

STALIN

Many people have thought that I am or have been an important politician. I don't know where this famous legend got started. One day I was frankly surprised to see my picture, as tiny as a stamp, included in a two-page spread in *Life* magazine in which it had put on display the leaders of world Communism, for the benefit of its readers. My likeness, stuck in somewhere between Prestes and Mao Tse-tung, seemed a funny joke to me, but I did not disabuse anyone, because I have always detested letters of rectification. Aside from this, it was amusing to have the C.I.A. fall into this error despite the five million agents it has throughout the world.

The longest contact I have maintained with any of the key figures of world socialism was during our visit to Peking. It consisted of a toast I drank with Mao Tse-tung during a ceremony. As our glasses touched, he looked at me with smiling eyes and a broad grin that was half friendly and half ironic. He held my hand in his, squeezing it a few seconds longer than customary. Then he returned to the table he had left.

On my many visits to the U.S.S.R. I saw neither Molotov nor Vishinsky nor Beria; not even Mikoyan or Litvinov, more sociable and less mysterious than the others.

I saw Stalin at a distance, more than once, always in the same spot: the platform which stands high over Red Square and is crowded with high-level leaders every year on May 1 and November 7. I spent long hours in the Kremlin, as part of the jury for the prizes that bore Stalin's name, without ever meeting him even in a hallway. He never came to see us during our voting sessions or lunches, and he never had us called in even for a word of greeting. The prizes were always awarded unanimously, but there were times when the debate for the selection of the winning candidate was hard fought. I always had the feeling that, before the final decision was made, someone on the jury panel rushed the possible outcome of the voting to the great man to see if it had his blessing. But I really can't recall a single time when we had any objection from him, and although he was obviously close by, I don't recall that he ever acknowledged our presence there. Without doubt, Stalin cultivated his mysteriousness systematically; or else he was extremely timid, a man who was his own prisoner. It is possible that this trait had much to do with the strong influence Beria had over him. Beria was the only one who went in and out of Stalin's rooms unannounced.

However, on one occasion I did have an unexpected encounter, which even now seems remarkable to me, with the Kremlin's mystery man. The Aragons—Louis and Elsa—and I were on our way to the Kremlin to take part in the meeting that would decide the Stalin Prizes that year. Heavy snowstorms held us up in Warsaw. We would not make our appointment on time. One of the Russians with us radioed ahead to Moscow, in Russian, the names of the candidates Aragon and I favored—who, by the way, were approved at the meeting. But the strange thing about this is that the Russian, who received a reply over the telephone, called me aside and surprised me by saying, "I congratulate you, Comrade Neruda. When the list of possible winners of the prize was submitted to Comrade Stalin, he exclaimed: 'And why isn't Neruda's name among them?'"

The following year, I received the Stalin Prize for Peace and Friendship Among Peoples. I may have deserved it, but I still ask myself how that withdrawn man ever found out that I existed.

Around that time I heard of other similar interventions by Stalin. When the campaign against cosmopolitanism was growing more intense and the starched-collar sectarians were calling for Ehrenburg's head, the telephone rang one morning in the home of the author of *Julio Jurenito*. Lyuba answered. A vaguely familiar voice asked: "Is Ilya Gregorievich there?"

"That depends," Lyuba answered. "Who are you?"

"This is Stalin," the voice said.

"For you, Ilya, some joker," Lyuba told Ehrenburg.

But when he got to the telephone, the writer recognized Stalin's well-known voice: "I spent the night reading your book *The Fall of Paris*. I am calling to tell you to keep on writing books as interesting as this one, dear Ilya Gregorievich."

Maybe that unexpected call made the great Ehrenburg's long life possible.

Another case: Mayakovsky was already dead, but his obstinate reactionary enemies attacked the poet's memory tooth and nail, determined to wipe him off the map of Soviet literature. Then something happened that upset these designs. His beloved Lili Brik wrote a letter to Stalin pointing out how shameful these attacks were and passionately defending Mayakovsky's poetry. His assailants, who thought themselves invulnerable, protected by their collective mediocrity, were in for a rude jolt. On the margin of Lili Brik's letter, Stalin noted down: "Mayakovsky is the best poet of the Soviet era."

After that, museums and monuments sprang up in honor of Mayakovsky and many editions of his extraordinary poetry were published. His opponents froze, struck powerless by Jehovah's trumpet blast.

I also learned that among Stalin's papers found after his death there was a list that read: "Do not touch," in his own handwriting. That list was headed by the composer Shostakovich, followed by other eminent names: Eisenstein, Pasternak, Ehrenburg, etc.

Many have believed me a die-hard Stalinist. Fascists and reactionaries have described me as a lyric interpreter of Stalin. I am not particularly put out by this. Any judgment is possible in a diabolically confused era.

The private tragedy for us Communists was to face the fact that, in several aspects of the Stalin problem, the enemy was right.

This revelation, which was staggering, left us in a painful state of mind. Some felt that they had been deceived. Desperately, they accepted the enemy's reasoning and went over to its side. Others believed that the harrowing facts, implacably brought to light during the Twentieth Congress, proved the integrity of a Communist Party which survived, letting the world see the historical truth and accepting its own responsibility.

If it is really true that we all shared this responsibility, the act of denouncing those crimes led us back to self-criticism and analysis, elements essential to our doctrine, and gave us the weapons needed to prevent such horrible things from happening again.

This has been my stand: above the darkness, unknown to me, of the Stalin era, Stalin rose before my eyes, a good-natured man of principles, as sober as a hermit, a titanic defender of the Russian Revolution. Moreover, this small man with his huge moustache had become a giant in wartime. With his name on its lips, the Red Army attacked and demolished the power of Hitler's demons.

And yet I dedicated only one of my poems to this powerful personality. It was on the occasion of his death. Anyone can find it in my collected works. The death of the Cyclops of the Kremlin had worldwide impact. The human jungle shuddered. My poem captured the feeling of that panic on earth.

A LESSON IN SIMPLICITY

Very put out about it, Gabriel García Márquez told me how some erotic passages of his marvelous *One Hundred Years of Solitude* had been cut in Moscow.

"That's not right at all," I told the publishers.

"The book doesn't lose anything by it," they replied, and I saw that they had made the cuts without malice. Still, they did make them.

How can these things be set right? Each day, I am less and less of a sociologist. Aside from my general Marxist principles, aside from my dislike of capitalism and my faith in socialism, I understand humanity's persistent contradictions less and less.

We poets of this age have had to make a choice. The choice has not been a bed of roses. The terrible, unjust wars, the continual pressures, money's aggressiveness, all injustices have made themselves felt with greater intensity every day. The decrepit old system has baited its hooks with conditional "freedom," sex, violence, and pleasures paid for in easy monthly installments.

Today's poet has looked for a way out of his anguish. Some have escaped into mysticism, or the dream of reason. Others are fascinated by the spontaneous and destructive violence of the young; they have become immediatists without realizing that, in today's belligerent world, this experience has always led to repression and sterile agony.

In my party, Chile's Communist Party, I found a large group of simple people who had left far behind them personal vanity, despotism, and material interests. I felt happy knowing honest people who were fighting for common decency, for justice.

I have never had any difficulties with my party, which, although modest, has achieved extraordinary victories for the people of Chile, my people. What more can I say? My only hope is to be as simple as my comrades, as persistent and invincible as they. We never learn enough about humility. I was never taught anything by individualist pride, which entrenches itself in skepticism so as not to espouse the cause of human suffering.

FIDEL CASTRO

Two weeks after his victorious entry into Havana, Fidel Castro arrived in Caracas for a short visit. He had come to thank the government and the Venezuelan people publicly for the help they had given him. This help had consisted of arms for his troops, and, naturally, it was not Betancourt (recently elected President) who supplied them, but his predecessor, Admiral Wolfgang Larrazábal. Larrazábal had been a friend of the Venezuelan leftists, including the Communists, and had acceded to the act of solidarity with Cuba that they had asked of him.

I have seen few political welcomes more enthusiastic than the one the Venezuelans gave the young victor of the Cuban revolution. Fidel spoke for four uninterrupted hours in the huge square of El Silencio, the heart of Caracas. I was one of the 200,000 people who stood listening to that long speech without uttering a word. For me, and for many others, Fidel's speeches have been a revelation. Hearing him address the crowd, I realized that a new age had begun for Latin America. I liked the freshness of his language. Even the best of the workers' leaders and politicians usually harp on the same formulas, whose content may be valid, though the words have been worn thin and weakened by repetition. Fidel ignored such formulas. His language was didactic but natural. He himself appeared to be learning as he spoke and taught.

President Betancourt was not there. He dreaded the thought of facing the city of Caracas, where he had never been liked. Every time Fidel mentioned him in his speech, whistles and catcalls broke out, which Fidel's hands tried to silence. I believe a definite hostility was established that day between Betancourt and the Cuban revolutionary. Fidel was neither Marxist nor Communist at the time; his words had nothing to do with either ideology. My personal opinion is that the speech, Fidel's fiery and brilliant personality, the enthusiasm he stirred up in the multitude, the intensity of the people of Caracas listening to him, troubled Betancourt, a politician of the old school of rhetoric, committees, and secret meetings. From then on, Betancourt has persecuted with implacable brutality anything at all that smacked of Fidel Castro or the Cuban revolution.

On the day after the rally, while I was on a Sunday picnic in the country, some motorcycles came to us with an invitation to the Cuban Embassy. They had been looking for me all day and had finally discovered my whereabouts. The reception would be that same afternoon. Matilde and I went straight to the Embassy. The guests were so numerous that they overflowed the halls and gardens. Outside, there

were swarms of people, and it was difficult to get through the streets
leading to the building.

We crossed rooms packed with people, a trench of arms holding
cocktail glasses high. Someone led us down corridors and stairs to
another floor. Celia, Fidel's closest friend and secretary, was waiting
for us in an unexpected part of the house. Matilde remained with
her, and I was taken into the next room. I found myself in a kind of
servant's room, a gardener's or chauffeur's. In it there was only a bed
someone had hurried out of, leaving it all messed up, with the pillow
on the floor, and a small table in a corner; nothing more. I thought I
would be led from there to some cozy little sitting room to meet the
Commandant. Well, that's not what happened. Suddenly the door
opened and Fidel Castro's tall figure filled the frame.

He was a head taller than I. He came toward me with quick strides.
"Hello, Pablo!" he said, and smothered me in a bear hug.

His reedy, almost childish voice took me by surprise. Something
about his appearance also matched the tone of his voice. Fidel did not
give the impression of being a big man, but an overgrown boy whose
legs had suddenly shot up before he had lost his kid's face and his
scanty adolescent's beard.

Brusquely, he interrupted the embrace, and galvanized into action, made a half turn, and headed resolutely toward a corner of the
room. I had not noticed a news photographer who had sneaked in and
was aiming his camera at us from the corner. Fidel was on him with
a single rush. I saw him grab the man by the throat and start shaking
him. The camera fell to the floor. I went over to Fidel and gripped
his arm, frightened by the sight of the tiny photographer struggling
vainly. But Fidel shoved him toward the door, making him disappear.
Then he turned back to me, smiling, picked the camera off the floor,
and flung it on the bed.

We did not speak of the incident, only of the possibility of a press
agency for all of Latin America. I think Prensa Latina was born of

that conversation. Then we went back to the reception, each of us through his own door.

As I was returning from the Embassy with Matilde an hour later, the terrified face of the photographer and the instinctive speed of the guerrilla leader, who had sensed the intruder's silent entry behind his back, came into my mind.

That was my first meeting with Fidel Castro. Why did he object so savagely to being photographed? Did his objection hide some small political mystery? To this day, I can't understand why our interview had to be kept so secret.

My first meeting with Che Guevara was entirely different. It took place in Havana. It was almost 1:00 a.m. when I went to see him at his office in the Department of Finance or Economy, I don't quite remember which, where he had invited me. He had set our appointment for midnight, but I arrived late. I had attended an interminable official ceremony for which I had been seated with the presidium.

Che was wearing boots and regimentals, with pistols at his waist. His clothes struck a discordant note in the banking atmosphere of the office. Che was dark, slow-speaking, with an unmistakable Argentine accent. He was the kind of man you talk with unhurriedly on the pampas between one maté and the next. His sentences were short and rounded off with a smile, as if leaving the discussion up in the air.

I was flattered by what he told me about my book *Canto general*. He would read it to his guerrillas at night, in the Sierra Maestra. Now, years later, I shudder when I think that my poems accompanied him to his death. Through Régis Debray I learned that, till the very end in the Bolivian mountains, he kept only two books in his duffel bag: a math book and my *Canto general*.

Something that Che told me that night threw me off quite a bit but perhaps explains his fate. His look wandered from my eyes to the darkened window of the office. We were talking of a possible North

American invasion of Cuba. I had seen sandbags scattered at strategic points in the Havana streets. Suddenly he said, "War . . . War . . . We are always against war, but once we have fought in a war, we can't live without it. We want to go back to it all the time."

He was thinking out loud, for my benefit. I was frankly startled, listening to him. For me, war is a menace, not a goal.

We said goodbye and I never saw him again. Afterward, there was his fighting in the Bolivian jungle, and his tragic death. But I keep on seeing in Che Guevara the pensive man who in his heroic battles always had a place, next to his weapons, for poetry.

Latin America is very fond of the word "hope." We like to be called the "continent of hope." Candidates for deputy, senator, President call themselves "candidates of hope." This hope is really something like a promise of heaven, an I.O.U. whose payment is always being put off. It is put off until the next legislative campaign, until next year, until the next century.

When the Cuban revolution came, millions of South Americans had a rude awakening. They couldn't believe their ears. This wasn't in the cards for a continent that has lived hoping desperately against hope. Suddenly here was Fidel Castro, a Cuban no one had heard of, seizing hope by its hair, or its feet, and not letting it fly off but seating it at his table; that is, at the table and in the house of the peoples of America.

From then on, we have made great strides on this road of hope now turned into a reality. But we live with our hearts in our mouths. A neighboring country, very powerful and highly imperialist, wants to crush Cuba, hopes and all. The masses of all the Americas read the paper every day, listen to the radio every night. And they sigh with satisfaction. Cuba exists. Another day. Another year. Another five years. Our hope has not had its head chopped off. Its head will not be chopped off.

THE LETTER FROM THE CUBANS

Writers in Peru, among whom I have always had many friends, had long urged that I be given an official decoration by their country. I confess that medals of this kind have always seemed a bit silly to me. The few I had were pinned on my chest without love, for duties performed, for time put in as consul; that is, as an obligation or a routine. I passed through Lima once and Ciro Alegría, the great novelist of *The Starving Dogs*, who was then the Peruvian writers' president, insisted that his country should give me a decoration. My poem *Alturas de Macchu Picchu* had gone on to become a part of Peruvian life; perhaps in those lines I had expressed sentiments that had lain dormant like the stones of that remarkable structure. Moreover, the President of Peru at that time, the architect Belaúnde, was my friend and reader. Although the revolution that later ousted him violently gave Peru a government that was unexpectedly open to the new roads of history, I still believe that Belaúnde was a man of irreproachable honesty, whose mind was set on somewhat chimerical goals that finally turned him away from terrifying reality and separated him from the people he loved so deeply.

I accepted the decoration, this time not for consular services but for one of my poems. Besides, and this is not the least of it, there are wounds separating the people of Chile and Peru that have yet to be healed. Not only athletes, diplomats, and statesmen must take pains to stanch that blood from the past, but poets also, and with all the more reason, for their souls have fewer frontiers than the souls of other people.

Around that same time I made a trip to the United States, where an international congress of the P.E.N. club was to be held. My friends Arthur Miller, the Argentines Ernesto Sábato and Victoria Ocampo, the Uruguayan critic Emir Rodríguez Monegal, the Mexican novelist

Carlos Fuentes were among those invited. Writers from almost all the socialist countries of Europe also attended.

When I got there, I was told that the Cuban writers had also been invited. At the P.E.N. club they were surprised that Carpentier had not come, and I was asked if I could clear this up. I went to see the representative of Prensa Latina in New York, who offered to cable a message to Carpentier. The answer given through Prensa Latina was that Carpentier could not come because the invitation had arrived too late and the North American visas had not been ready in time. Someone was lying now: the visas had been issued three months before, and three months before, the Cubans had known about the invitation and had accepted. Evidently there had been a higher-up, last-minute decision against attending.

As always, I did what I had to do. I gave my first poetry reading in New York, to such a large crowd that closed-circuit television had to be set up outside the auditorium so that hundreds of people who could not get in could see and hear. I was touched by the echo my poems, violently anti-imperialist, stirred up in that North American crowd. I understood many things there, and in Washington and California, when students and ordinary people showed approval of my words against imperialism. I learned on the spot that the North American enemies of our peoples were also enemies of the North American people.

I gave several interviews. The Spanish-language edition of *Life* magazine, edited by parvenu Latin Americans, distorted and mutilated my opinions. They did not correct this when I asked them to. But it was nothing very serious. They had suppressed a paragraph in which I condemned the war in Vietnam and another about a black leader who had just been assassinated. Only years later did the newspaperwoman who edited the interview acknowledge that it had been censored.

During my visit I discovered—and this does honor to my comrades, the North American writers—that they exerted relentless pressure to see that I was granted an entry visa to the United States. I believe the P.E.N. club even threatened the State Department with an open letter of censure if it continued to deny me an entry permit. At a public gathering where she received an award, the most respected figure in North American poetry, the elderly poet Marianne Moore, took the floor to say how happy she was that my legal entry into the country had been obtained through the united action of the poets. I was told that her words, which were vibrant and moving, drew a tremendous ovation.

The outrageous fact is that I had barely returned to Chile after that tour, which was marked by my most combative political and poetic activity, a major part of which was used to defend and support the Cuban revolution, when I received the well-known slanderous letter from the Cuban writers, accusing me of little less than submission and treason. I no longer remember the words used by my public prosecutors. I can say, however, that they set themselves up as instructors in revolution, pedantic teachers of the norms by which writers of the left must be guided. With arrogance, insolence, and flattering words they hoped to reform my poetry as well as my social revolutionary work. My decoration for my Macchu Picchu poem and my attendance at the P.E.N. club congress, my statements and my readings, my acts and words condemning the North American system, spoken right in the lion's mouth—all this was called into question, falsified or maligned by those writers, many of them newly come into the revolutionary camp, and many of them justly or unjustly in the pay of the new Cuban state.

This bag of injustices bulged with signatures, requested with suspicious spontaneity from the committees of writers' and artists' associations. Delegates rushed about Havana looking for signatures from entire guilds of musicians, dancers, and artists. Artists and writers who were passing through, who had been generously invited to Cuba and filled the most fashionable hotels, were asked to sign. Some of the writers whose names were printed at the bottom of the unjust document later sent me surreptitious messages: "I never signed it; I found out what it was all about after seeing my name, which I never signed." A friend of Juan Marinello's told me that the same thing had happened to him, although I haven't been able to check on that. I have verified it in other cases.

The affair was a ball of wool or snow or ideological skulduggery that must be made to grow bigger and bigger at all costs. Special agencies were set up in Madrid, Paris, and other capitals, whose sole job was to send out copies of the lying letter, in huge batches. Thousands of those letters went out, especially from Madrid, in bunches of twenty to thirty copies for each addressee. In a gruesome way, it was amusing to receive those envelopes, decorated with stamps bearing Franco's portrait, while inside the envelopes Pablo Neruda was accused of being a counterrevolutionary.

It is not up to me to ferret out the motives for that fit of rage: political chicanery, ideological weakness, literary spite and envy—and who knows what else—were responsible for this battle of so many against one. I was told later that the enthusiastic editors, promoters, and hunters of signatures for the famous letter were the writers Roberto Fernández Retamar, Edmundo Desnoes, and Lisandro Otero. I don't recall ever reading Desnoes and Otero or meeting them personally. Retamar, yes. In Havana and Paris he tagged behind me constantly with his adulation. He used to tell me that he had published many essays and articles praising my work. I really never considered him important, just one more among the political and literary arrivistes of our time.

Perhaps they fancied that they could harm or destroy me as an active revolutionary. But when I got to Teatinos Street in Santiago to take up the matter for the first time with the party's central committee, they had already formed their opinion, at least politically. "It is the first attack against our Chilean party," I was told.

We were living through serious conflicts at the time. Venezuelan, Mexican, and other Communists were having ideological disputes with the Cubans. Later, in tragic circumstances but in silence, the Bolivians also dissented.

The Communist Party in Chile decided to award me, in a public ceremony, the Recabarren medal, which had recently been established and was to go to its best activists. It was a levelheaded response. The Chilean Communist Party endured this period of divergences intelligently, it stuck by its intention of analyzing our disagreements internally. In time, all traces of a fight have been wiped away. A clear understanding and a fraternal relationship exist between the two most important Communist Parties of Latin America.

As for me, I continue to be the same person who wrote *Canción de gesta*. It is a book I still like. I can't forget that with it I became the first poet to devote an entire book to praising the Cuban revolution.

I understand, of course, that revolutions, and particularly those who take part in them, fall into error and injustice, from time to time. The unwritten precepts of the human race affect revolutionaries and counterrevolutionaries equally. No one can escape errors. A blind spot, a tiny blind spot in a revolutionary process is not very important within the larger context of a great cause. I have continued to sing, love, and respect the Cuban revolution, its people, its noble protagonists.

But everyone has his failings. I have many. For instance, I don't like to give up the pride I feel about my inflexible stand as a fighting revolutionary. Maybe that, or some other flaw in my insignificant self, has made me refuse until now, and I will go on refusing, to shake hands with any of those who knowingly or unknowingly signed that letter which still seems ignominious to me.

12

Cruel, Beloved Homeland

EXTREMISM AND SPIES

Former anarchists—and the same thing will happen tomorrow to the anarchists of today—very often drift off toward a very comfortable position, anarcho-capitalism, the refuge of political snipers, would-be leftists, and false liberals. Repressive capitalism considers Communists its biggest enemies, and its aim seldom misses the mark. All those individualist rebels are delighted, one way or another, by the reactionary know-how, the strong-arm method that treats them as heroic defenders of sacrosanct principles. Reactionaries know that the danger of change in a society is not in individual revolts but in the organization of the masses and in a widespread class consciousness.

I saw all this clearly in Spain during the war. Some anti-Fascist groups were playing out a masked carnival before Hitler's and Franco's forces, which were advancing on Madrid. Naturally, I don't include anarchists like Durruti and his Catalans, who fought like lions in Barcelona.

Spies are a thousand times worse than extremists. From time to time, enemy agents hired by the police, reactionary parties, or foreign governments filter in among the activists of revolutionary parties. Some of them carry out special missions of provocation; others are patient observers. Azev's is a classic case. Before the fall of Tsarism, he took part in numerous terrorist acts and was jailed many times. The memoirs of the chief of the Tsar's secret police, published after the revolution, related in detail how Azev had always been an agent of the Okhrana. The terrorist and the informer coexisted in the mind of this bizarre character, whose actions were responsible for the death of a grand duke.

Another curious incident occurred in Los Angeles, San Francisco, or some other California city. During the insane wave of McCarthyism, all the activists in the Communist Party in town were arrested. There were seventy-five persons, all told, with complete files on their lives and their day-to-day movements. Well, the seventy-five turned out to be police agents. The F.B.I. had permitted itself the luxury of creating its own miniature "Communist Party," with individuals who were strangers to one another, in order to prosecute them later and claim sensational victories over non-existent enemies. This way of doing things got the F.B.I. into such grotesque predicaments as the one where some fellow called Chambers, an ex-Communist bought by police dollars, kept the most explosive international secrets hidden in a pumpkin. The F.B.I. was also implicated in horrifying acts, among them the execution, or assassination, of the Rosenbergs, which particularly outraged the world.

It was always more difficult for these agents to infiltrate Chile's Communist Party, an organization with a long history and a strictly proletarian origin. On the other hand, guerrilla methods in Latin America opened the floodgates for all kinds of squealers. The spontaneous character and the youth of these organizations made it hard to detect and unmask spies. That's why the guerrilla leaders were haunted by suspicions and had to keep an eye even on their own shadows. In a way, this cult of risk was encouraged by the romantic spirit and the wild guerrilla theories that swept Latin America. This era may have come to an end with the assassination and heroic death of Ernesto Guevara. But for a long time the supporters of this tactic saturated the continent with theses and documents that virtually allotted the popular revolutionary government of the future, not to the classes exploited by capitalism, but to all and sundry armed groups. The flaw in this line of reasoning is its political weakness: It is sometimes possible for a great guerrilla and a powerful political mind to coexist, as in the case of Che Guevara, but that is an exception and wholly dependent on chance. The survivors of a guerrilla war cannot lead a proletarian state simply because they were braver, or because they were luckier in the face of death, or better shots when facing the living.

Now I'll recount a personal experience. I was in Chile, just back from Mexico. At one of the political gatherings I attended, a man came over to say hello to me. He was a middle-aged man, the model man of today, very correctly dressed and wearing those glasses that make people look so respectable, rimless glasses that are clipped to the nose. He turned out to be a very affable person. "Don Pablo, I had never been able to build up the courage to approach you, although I owe you my life. I am one of the refugees you saved from the concentration camps and gas ovens when you put us aboard the *Winnipeg*, bound for Chile. I am a Catalan, a Freemason. I've established a place for myself here. I work as a top salesman of sanitary articles for Such and Such Co., the most important of its kind in Chile."

He told me he lived in a nice apartment in the center of Santiago. His next-door neighbor was a well-known tennis champion named Iglesias, who had been my schoolmate. They spoke of me frequently and had finally decided to invite me to the house and entertain me. That's why he had come to see me.

The Catalan's apartment had all the signs of the comfortable life of our bourgeoisie. Impeccable furniture; a golden and abundant paella. Iglesias was with us all through lunch. We laughed at the memory of the old schoolhouse in Temuco, in whose basements the bats' wings brushed our faces. At the end of lunch, the hospitable Catalan gave a little speech and made me a gift of two splendidly reproduced photographs: one of Baudelaire and the other of Edgar Allan Poe. Splendid heads of poets, which, of course, I still have in my library.

One day our Catalan had a stroke that left him immobile in bed, without the use of speech or facial expression. Only his eyes moved, filled with pain, as if trying to say something to his wife, an excellent Spanish Republican with an irreproachable past, or to his neighbor Iglesias, my friend the tennis champion. The man died without speaking or moving again.

While the house was still filled with tears, friends, and wreaths, his neighbor the tennis player received a mysterious call: "We know of your close friendship with the dead man. He never tired of praising you. If you want to do a very important service to the memory of your friend, open his strong box and take out a little steel case put away for safekeeping there. I'll call you again in three days."

The widow wouldn't hear of such a thing. Her grief was extreme, she didn't want to know about anything. She left the apartment and moved to a rooming house on Santo Domingo Street. The landlord was a Yugoslav, a member of the resistance, a man toughened by politics. The widow begged him to examine her husband's papers. The Yugoslav found the little metal case and opened it with much difficulty. Then the strangest cat was let out of the bag. The documents which had been put away there disclosed that the dead man had been a Fascist agent. Copies of his letters revealed the names of dozens of emigrants who, on returning to Spain secretly, had been thrown into prison or executed. There was even a letter in Franco's hand, thanking him for his services. Information from the Catalan also helped the Nazi navy sink freighters leaving the Chilean coast with war materials. One of these was our beautiful ship the veteran *Lautaro*, pride of Chile's navy. It was sunk during the war, with its cargo of nitrate, as it left Tocopilla. The wreck took the lives of seventeen naval cadets, drowned or burned to death.

These had been the criminal acts of a smiling Catalan who invited me to lunch one day.

THE COMMUNISTS

... Some years have passed since I became a member of the party ... I am happy ... Communists make a good family ... They have weather-beaten hides and warm hearts ... They take whacks everywhere ... Whacks exclusively for them ... Long live spiritists, royalists, deviates, criminals of every ilk ... Long live philosophy with its smoke screen but without skeletons ... Long live the dog that barks but also bites, long live lecherous astrologers, pornography , cynicism, long live the shrimp, long live everyone, except Communists ... Long live chastity belts, long live the conservatives who haven't washed their ideological feet in five hundred years ... Long live the lice of the poor, the free trip to potter's field, anarcho-capitalism, Rilke, André Gide and his sweet little Corydon, long live all kinds of mysticism ... Anything goes ... They're all heroes ... All newspapers should be brought out ... They can all be published, except the Communist papers ... Let all politicians into Santo Domingo free as birds ... Let them all celebrate the death of bloodthirsty Trujillo, except those who fought him hardest ... Long live the carnival, the last days of the carnival ... There are masks for everyone ... Christian idealist masks, extreme-left masks, good-gray-lady and charitable-matron masks ... But watch out, don't let the Communists in .. Lock the door tight ... Don't make a mistake ... They have no right to anything ... Let's worry about the subjective, man's essence, the essence of essence ... We'll all be happy that way ... We've got freedom ... Freedom is great! ... They don't respect it, they don't know what it is .. Freedom to worry about the essence ... About the essentials of essence ...

... That's how the last years passed ... Jazz went out, soul arrived, we floundered in the postulates of abstract painting, the war staggered and killed us ... Everything remained the same on this side ... Or didn't

it . . . ? *After so many speeches about the spirit and so many whacks on the head, something was going badly . . . Very badly . . . They had figured it out wrong . . . The people were organizing . . . The guerrilla wars and the strikes went on . . Cuba and Chile won their freedom . . . Countless men and women sang the Internationale . . . How odd . . . How disheartening . . . Now they sing it in Chinese, Bulgarian, in the Spanish of Latin America . . . We've got to do something about it quickly . . . We must ban it . . . We must talk about the spirit some more . . . And sing the praises of the free world some more . . . We must hand out some more whacks, some more dollars . . . This can't go on . . . Between the freedom to hand out whacks and German Arciniegas's fear . . . And now Cuba . . . In the middle of our hemisphere, in the middle of our apple, these long-beards all singing the same song . . . And what good is Christ to us . . . ? What good have the priests done us . . . ? We can't trust anybody any more . . . Not even the priests . . . They don't see eye to eye with us . . . They don't see how our stocks are plunging in the market . . .*

. . . Meanwhile, men are soaring into the solar system . . . Shoes track up the moon . . . Everything struggles to change, except the outworn systems . . . These outworn systems were spawned in the immense spiderwebs of the Middle Ages . . . Spiderwebs stronger than the steel of machinery . . . Yet there are people who believe in change, who have made changes, who have made the changes work, who have made change burst into flower . . . Caramba! . . . Nobody can hold spring back!

POETRY AND POLITICS

I have spent almost all of 1969 in Isla Negra. Starting early in the morning, the sea goes into its fantastic swelling-up routine, looking as if it were kneading an infinite loaf of bread. The spilling foam, driven up by the icy yeast of the deep, is white like flour.

Winter is solidly entrenched and foggy. Every day we add to its local charm with a fire in the hearth. The whiteness of the sands on the beach offers us a world forever solitary, as it was before there were any people or summer vacationers on earth. But don't think that I hate summer crowds. As soon as summer nears, girls come to the sea, men and children approach the waves cautiously, leaping clear of danger. It's their version of man's thousand-year-old dance, perhaps the first of all summer dances.

In winter the houses in Isla Negra are covered up by night's darkness. Only mine lights up. Sometimes I think there is someone in the house across the road. I see a light in a window. It's only an optical illusion. There is no one in the Captain's house. It's the light from my window mirrored in his.

I've gone to write every day of the year in the hideaway where I do my work. It's not easy to get there or stay there. For the moment my two dogs, Panda and Chou Tu, have something to keep them happy. It's a Bengal tiger's skin, which I use as a rug in this small room. I brought it from China a good many years ago. Its claws and hair have fallen out. And there's some danger from the moths, but Matilde and I ward them off.

My dogs like to sprawl out over the old enemy. They fall asleep instantly, like victors after a battle, drained by the fight.

They stretch across the door as if to force me to stay in, to go on with my work.

There's always something going on in this house. There's a long-distance call for me. What should the answer be? I'm not in. Someone sends another message. What should the answer be? I'm in.

I'm not in. I'm in. I'm in. I'm not in. This is the life of a poet whose remote hideaway in Isla Negra has stopped being remote.

I am always being asked, especially by journalists, what I am writing, what I am working on. This question has always surprised me because it's so superficial. For, as a matter of fact, I am always doing the same thing. I have never stopped doing the same thing. Poetry?

I had been at it a long time before I realized that I was writing something called poetry. I have never been interested in definitions or labels. Discussions of aesthetics bore me to death. I am not belittling those who have them, but I am as indifferent to the birth certificate of a literary work as I am to the post-mortem on it. "And nothing exterior shall ever take command of me," said Walt Whitman. And, for all their merits, the paraphernalia of literature should not take the place of naked creation.

I changed notebooks several times during the year. Those notebooks bound together by the green thread of my handwriting are around somewhere. I filled many that gradually turned into books, passing from one metamorphosis into another, from immobility into movement, from glowworms into fireflies.

Political life came like a thunderclap to pull me away from my work. I returned to the crowds once more.

The human crowd has been the lesson of my life. I can come to it with the born timidity of the poet, with the fear of the timid, but once I am in its midst, I feel transfigured. I am part of the essential majority, I am one more leaf on the great human tree.

Solitude and multitude will go on being the primary obligations of the poet in our time. In solitude, the battle of the surf on the Chilean coast made my life richer. I was intrigued by and have loved passionately the battling waters and the rocks they battled against, the teeming ocean life, the impeccable formation of the "wandering birds," the splendor of the sea's foam.

But I learned much more from the huge tide of lives, from the tenderness I saw in thousands of eyes watching me together. This message may not come to all poets, but anyone who has felt it will keep it in his heart, will work it into his poems.

To have embodied hope for many men, even for one minute, is something unforgettable and profoundly touching for the poet.

PRESIDENTIAL CANDIDATE

One morning in 1969 the secretary general of my party and other comrades came to my seaside hide-out, my house in Isla Negra. They came to offer me the conditional candidacy for President of the Republic, a candidacy they would propose to the six or seven parties of Popular Unity. They had everything ready: program, type of government, emergency measures for the future, etc. Up until that moment, each of those parties had a candidate and each wanted to keep him. We Communists were the only ones who did not have one. Our position was to back the one candidate designated by the leftist parties; he would become Popular Unity's candidate. But it was all up in the air, and it could not be left like that much longer. The candidates of the right were in the thick of the race and had their publicity machines going strong. Unless we united under a common electoral cause, we would suffer a crushing defeat.

The only way to achieve some sort of unity quickly was for the Communists to name their own candidate. When I accepted the party's nomination, we made the Communist position quite clear. Our support would be thrown to the candidate who had the good will of the others. If such a consensus was not reached, I would remain a candidate right through to the end.

It was a courageous way to force the others to come to an agreement. When I accepted I told Comrade Corvalán I was doing it on condition that my resignation would be accepted when I tendered it. My withdrawal was inevitable, I felt. It was far too improbable that everyone could be rallied around a Communist. In other words, all the other parties needed our support (even the Christian-Democratic candidates), but none of them had to give us theirs.

However, my candidacy, started that morning in Isla Negra, beside the sea, caught fire. I was in demand everywhere. I was moved by the hundreds and thousands of ordinary men and women who crushed me to them and kissed me and wept. Slum dwellers from the outskirts of Santiago, miners from Coquimbo, men who worked copper in the desert, peasant women who waited for me hours on end with babies in their arms, the neglected and poor from the Bío-Bío River to beyond the Strait of Magellan—I spoke or read my poems to them all in pouring rain, in the mud on streets and roads, in the south wind that sends shivers through each of us.

My enthusiasm was mounting. More and more people were attending my rallies, more and more women coming to them. Fascinated and terrified, I began to wonder what I would do if I was elected President of a republic wholly untamed, patently unable to solve its problems, deeply in debt—and probably the most ungrateful of them all. Its Presidents were acclaimed in the first month and martyred, justly or not, for the remainder of the five years and eleven months of their tenure.

ALLENDE'S CAMPAIGN

It was a happy day when the news came: Allende had emerged as the one promising candidate of the entire Popular Unity. With the approval of my party, I quickly turned in my resignation. Before a huge and happy crowd, I announced my withdrawal and Allende accepted his nomination. The enormous rally was held in a park. People filled every visible space, including the trees; legs and heads stuck out of the branches. There is nothing like these hard-bitten Chileans.

I knew the candidate. I had been with him in three previous campaigns, reading poems and making speeches all through Chile's abrupt and endless territory. Three times in succession, every six years, my persistent comrade had been a presidential contender. This would be the fourth, and the victorious time.

Arnold Bennett or Somerset Maugham (I don't remember just which of the two) tells about a time when he had to share a room with Winston Churchill. The first thing that eminent politician did on waking was to stretch out a hand to take a huge Havana from the night table, the moment he opened his eyes, and start smoking it, right then and there. Only a healthy cave man, with the iron constitution of the Stone Age, can do this.

None of those who accompanied Allende could keep up with his stamina. He had a knack worthy of Churchill himself: he could fall asleep whenever he felt like it. Sometimes we would be traveling over the infinite arid stretches of the north of Chile. Allende slept soundly in a corner of the car. Suddenly a small red speck would appear on the road, and, as we approached, it would become a group of fifteen or twenty men with their wives, their children, and their flags. The car would stop. Allende would rub his eyes to face the high sun and the small group, which was singing. He would join in and sing the national anthem. And he would speak to them—lively, swift, and eloquent. Then he would return to the car and we would continue on over Chile's long, long roads. Allende would sink back into sleep effortlessly. Every twenty-five minutes or so, the scene would be repeated: group, flags, song, speech, and back to sleep.

Facing huge crowds of thousands upon thousands of Chileans, going from car to train, from train to airplane, from airplane to ship, from ship to horse, Allende would carry out the day's heavy schedule, never holding back, during those exhausting months. Almost all the members of his group lagged behind, fatigued. Later, when he was in fact President of Chile, his implacable efficiency was the cause of four or five heart attacks among his co-workers.

AMBASSADOR IN PARIS

When I came to take over the Embassy in Paris, I found that I had to pay a heavy price for my vanity. I had accepted the post without giving it much thought, once again letting myself be swept along by the current of life. I was pleased at the idea of representing a victorious popular government, after so many years of mediocre and lying ones. Perhaps, deep down, what appealed to me most was the thought of entering with new dignity the Chilean Embassy building where I had swallowed so many humiliations when I organized the immigration of the Spanish Republicans into my country. Each of my predecessors had had a hand in my persecution, had helped to revile and hurt me. The persecuted would now sit in the persecutor's chair, eat at his table, sleep in his bed, and open the windows to let the new air of the world into the old Embassy.

The most difficult part was to let air in. The stifling showplace décor stung my nostrils and my eyes that night in March 1971 when Matilde and I came into our bedroom and got into the illustrious beds where ambassadors and ambassadors' wives had died peacefully or in torment.

It's a bedroom large enough to lodge a warrior and his horse; there's space enough for the horse to feed and the horseman to sleep. The ceilings are very high and finely decorated. The furniture consists of velvety things in a color vaguely resembling a dry leaf's, trimmed with horrible fringes, furnishings in a style that shows signs of riches and traces of decadence at the same time. The rugs may have been lovely sixty years ago. Now they have taken on the permanent color of footprints and a moth-eaten smell of conventional and defunct conversations.

In addition, the nervous personnel who had been waiting for us had thought of everything except the heat in the gigantic bedroom. Matilde and I spent our first diplomatic night in Paris numb with cold. On the second night, the heat worked. It had been in use for sixty years and its filters had become useless. The hot air of the antiquated system allowed only carbon dioxide to pass through. We couldn't complain about the cold, like the night before, but we felt palpitations and distress from the poisoning. We had to open the windows to let in the cold winter air. Maybe the old-time ambassadors were getting even with an upstart who had come to supplant them without bureaucratic merits or genealogical crests.

We decided we would have to look for a house where we could breathe with the leaves, the water, the birds, the air. Eventually this idea would turn into an obsession. Like prisoners kept awake by the idea of freedom, we searched and searched for pure air outside of Paris.

Being an ambassador was something new and uncomfortable for me. But it held a challenge. A revolution had taken place in Chile. A revolution Chilean-style, analyzed and discussed a good deal. Enemies within and without were sharpening their teeth to destroy it. For one hundred and eighty years, the same kind of rulers under different labels had succeeded one another in my country, and they all did the same thing. The rags, the disgraceful housing, the children without schools or shoes, the prisons, and the cudgeling of my poor people continued.

Now we could breathe and sing. That's what I liked about my new situation.

In Chile, diplomatic appointments require the senate's approval. The Chilean right had constantly praised me as a poet and had even honored me with speeches. Of course, it's obvious that they would have much preferred making these speeches at my funeral. In the senate vote to ratify my appointment as ambassador, I squeezed by with a majority of three votes. The rightists and some Christian-hypocrites voted against me, under the secrecy of the little white and black balls.

The previous ambassador had literally covered the walls with a tapestry of photographs of every one of his predecessors in the post, in addition to his own portrait. It was an impressive collection of vacuous people, save two or three, among whom was the distinguished Blest Gana, our small Chilean Balzac. I ordered the descent of the spectral portraits and replaced them with more solid men: five engraved likenesses of the heroes who gave Chile a flag, nationhood, and independence; and contemporary photographs of Aguirre Cerda, progressive President of the Republic; Luis Emilio Recabarren, founder of the Communist Party; and Salvador Allende. The walls now looked infinitely better.

I don't know what the secretaries in the Embassy thought, rightists almost all of them. The reactionary parties had run the country for a hundred years. Not even a doorman was appointed unless he was a conservative or a royalist. Calling themselves "revolution in freedom," the Christian-Democrats, in turn, showed a voracity parallel to that of the ancient reactionaries. Later, these parallels converged until they almost became the same line.

The bureaucracy, the archipelagos of the public buildings, everything was still overrun with employees, inspectors, and counselors from the right, as if Allende and Popular Unity had not won in Chile and the ministers in the government were not socialists and Communists now.

This state of affairs led me to request that the post of counselor at the Embassy in Paris be filled by one of my friends, a career diplomat and an outstanding writer, Jorge Edwards. Although he came from the most powerful and reactionary family in the country, he was a man of the left, without any party affiliation. What I needed more than anything was an intelligent functionary who knew his work and whom I could trust. Until then, Edwards had been chargé d'affaires in Havana. Vague rumors had reached me of some difficulties he had had in Cuba. Since I had known him for years as a man of the left, I did not consider this very important.

My new counselor arrived from Cuba in a very nervous state and told me his story. I got the impression that both sides were right and at the same time neither was, the way it sometimes happens in life. Little by little, Jorge Edwards repaired his shattered nerves, stopped chewing his nails, and helped me with evident ability, intelligence, and loyalty. During his two years of hard work at the Embassy, my counselor was my best comrade and functionary, perhaps the only one in that huge office building who was politically impeccable.

When a North American company tried to put an embargo on Chilean copper, a wave of feeling ran through the whole of Europe. Not only did the newspapers, television, and radio take up this affair with special interest, but once again the conscience of the people rallied to our defense.

Stevedores in France and Holland refused to unload the copper at their ports as a sign of protest against the aggression. That marvelous gesture stirred the world. Such stories of solidarity teach more about the history of our time than the lecture rooms at any university.

More humble but even more touching incidents also come to mind. On the second day of the embargo, a French lady of modest means, from a small country town, sent us a one-hundred-franc note from her savings to help Chile defend its copper. And a letter of warm support as well, signed by all the inhabitants of the town, including the mayor, the parish priest, workers, athletes, and students.

Messages came to me from Chile, sent by hundreds of friends, known and unknown, who congratulated me for standing up to the international pirates. I received a package by parcel post, sent to me by a working-class woman, containing a mate gourd, four avocados, and a dozen green chili peppers.

At the same time, Chile's reputation had grown remarkably. We had been transformed into a country that actually *existed*. Before this, we had gone unnoticed among the great number of underdeveloped countries. Now, for the first time, we had an identity and no one could ignore the great fight we were putting up to build a future for our country.

Everything happening in our country stirred up extraordinary interest in France and all of Europe. Popular rallies, student meetings, books in all languages studied, examined, photographed us. Every day, I had to put off journalists who wanted to know all there was to know and much more. President Allende was a world figure. The discipline and firmness of our working class were admired and praised.

Warm sympathy toward Chile grew enormously as a result of the conflicts arising from the nationalization of our copper deposits. It was clear to people everywhere that this was a giant step along the road to Chile's new independence. Without subterfuge of any kind, the popular government made our sovereignty definitive by reconquering copper for our country.

RETURN TO CHILE

When I returned to Chile I was received by new vegetation in the streets and in the parks. Our marvelous spring had been painting the forest leaves green. Our old gray capital needs green leaves the way the human heart needs love. I inhaled the freshness of this young spring. When we are far from our country, we never picture it in its winter. Distance wipes away the hardships of winter, the forsaken country towns, children barefoot in the cold. The memory only thinks of bringing us green countrysides, yellow and red flowers, the blue sky of our national anthem. This time I actually found the beautiful season which has so often been only a dream created by distance.

Another vegetation splotched the walls of the city. It was the moss of hatred covering them with its tapestries. Anti-Communist posters gushing insolence and lies; posters against Cuba; anti-Soviet posters; posters against peace and humaneness; bloodthirsty posters predicting mass murders and Jakartas. This was the new vegetation defiling the city's walls.

I knew from experience the tone and the drift of this propaganda.

I had lived with it in pre-Hitler Europe. That was exactly the spirit of Hitlerite propaganda: the extravagant use of lies, with no holds barred; the all-out campaign of threats and fear; parading all the weapons of hatred against what the future promised. I felt that they wanted to change the very essence of our life. I could not understand how there could be Chileans who insulted our national spirit like this.

When the reactionary right had to depend on terrorism, it used it unscrupulously. General Schneider, the army chief of staff, a respected and respectable man who opposed a coup d'état to prevent Allende's accession to the presidency of the Republic, was assassinated. Near his home, a motley crew of fiends machine-gunned him in the back. The operation was directed by an ex-general who had been kicked out of the army. The gang was made up of young members of the social set and professional delinquents.

When the crime was proved and the man who was the brains behind it was thrown into jail, he was sentenced to thirty years by a military court. However, the sentence was reduced to two years by the Supreme Court. In Chile, a poor devil who steals a chicken because he is hungry gets double the sentence imposed on the assassin of the commander in chief of the army. This is the class-conscious application of laws elaborated by the ruling class.

Allende's victory came as a weird shock to that ruling class. For the first time, it crossed their minds that laws so carefully fabricated by them could bounce back in their faces. They scurried off somewhere for cover, with their stocks, jewels, banknotes, gold coins. They went off to Argentina, Spain, they even got as far as Australia. Their terror of the people would have made them reach the North Pole in record time.

Later they would come back.

FREI

Blocked everywhere by diabolical and legal obstacles, the Chilean road was at all times strictly constitutional. In the meantime, the oligarchy patched up its tattered clothing and transformed itself into a Fascist faction. The North American blockade became more implacable after the nationalization of copper. In league with ex-President Frei, I.T.T. threw the Christian-Democrats into the arms of the new Fascist right.

The diametrically opposed personalities of Allende and Frei have always preoccupied Chile. Perhaps for the very reason that they are such different men, each in his own way a strong leader in a country without a tradition of strong leaders, each with his own goals and his road well marked out.

I think I knew Allende well. There was nothing enigmatic about him. As for Frei, we were in the senate at the same time. He is a strange, highly premeditative man, a far cry from Allende's spontaneity. Yet he often explodes into violent laughter, strident cackles. I like people who are given to loud outbursts of laughter (I am not gifted that way). But there are laughs and laughs. Frei's break out of a troubled, serious face, very intent on the needle and thread with which he is sewing together his political life. It's a sudden laughter that is a bit startling, like the screech of certain birds at night. Aside from this, his behavior is generally circumspect and deliberately cordial.

I often found his political zigzagging depressing, before it disillusioned me completely. I remember that one day he came to see me in my house in Santiago. At that time the possibility of an understanding between the Communists and the Christian-Democrats was in the air. They were not yet called Christian-Democrats, but Falange Nacional, a horrid name adopted while they were still deeply impressed by the young Spanish Fascist Primo de Rivera. Then, after the Spanish war, they came under the influence of Maritain, became anti-Fascists, and took a different name.

Our conversation was casual but friendly. We Communists were interested in reaching some kind of understanding with all men and all sectors of good will; we would never get anywhere by ourselves. Although he was naturally evasive, Frei let me know the leftist feelings he apparently had at that time. He made me a parting gift of one of those laughs that fall out of his mouth like stones. "We'll have another talk," he said. But, two days later, I realized that our conversation had ended for good.

After Allende's triumph, Frei, an ambitious and cold politician, believed he needed a reactionary alliance if he was to return to power. It was merely a pipe dream, the frozen dream of a political spider. His web will not hold up; the coup d'état he sponsored won't do him any good. Fascism does not put up with compromises, it demands submission. Frei's figure will become more obscure each year. And someday his memory will have to face responsibility for the crime.

TOMIC

From its beginning, from the moment it dropped the unacceptable name of Falange, the Christian-Democratic Party interested me very much. It came into being when a small group of Catholic intellectuals formed a Maritain-Thomist elite. This philosophy did not appeal to me. I harbor a natural indifference toward people who are theorists about poetry, politics, or sex. But the practical consequences of that small movement were felt in a special, unexpected way. I got several young leaders to speak out for the Spanish Republic at the huge meetings I organized on my return from Madrid, which was still in the throes of fighting then. This participation was unprecedented;

prodded by the Conservative Party, the old Church hierarchy almost broke up the new party. Only the intervention of a farsighted bishop saved it from political suicide. A statement from the Bishop of Talca saved the group that would eventually turn into Chile's biggest party. Its ideology changed completely with the years.

After Frei, the most important man among the Christian-Democrats was Radomiro Tomic. I met him in my senate days, right in the middle of strikes and election stumping in northern Chile. In those days the Christian-Democrats followed us Communists around in order to take part in our rallies. We were and still are the most popular people in the deserts of potassium nitrate and copper—I mean, among the most victimized workers on the American continent. Recabarren came from there, the workers' press and the first unions were born there. None of this would have been possible without the Communists.

At that time, Tomic was not only the most promising Christian-Democrat but their most attractive personality and most gifted speaker.

Things had changed very much in 1964 when the Christian-Democrats won the elections that carried Frei to the presidency of the Republic. The campaign of the candidate who defeated Allende was based on unprecedented anti-Communist attacks, conducted with newspaper and radio warnings intended to terrorize the people. This propaganda was enough to make anybody's hair stand on end: nuns would be shot, little boys would die run through by the bayonets of bearded men just like Fidel, little girls would be torn from their parents and shipped to Siberia. Later, from testimony given before a U.S. Senate special committee, we learned that the C.I.A. had spent twenty million dollars in that savage campaign of terror.

Once he had been anointed President, Frei gave his only big rival in the party a Greek gift: he appointed Radomiro Tomic Chilean ambassador to the United States. Frei knew that his government would renegotiate with the American copper companies. At this time, the entire country was pleading for nationalization. Like an expert sleight-of-hand artist, Frei changed this term to "Chileaniza-tion," and with new agreements, he insured the delivery of our major national wealth into the hands of the powerful consortiums, Ken-necott and Anaconda. The economic consequences were disastrous for Chile and heartbreaking for Tomic: Frei had wiped him off the map. An ambassador of Chile to the United States who collaborated in handing over the copper would not receive the support of the Chil-ean people. Of the three candidates at the next election, Tomic took a poor third place.

Shortly after resigning from his post as ambassador to the United States, at the beginning of 1968, Tomic came to see me in Isla Negra. He had recently arrived from the north and was not yet officially a candidate for the presidency. Our friendship stood firm through the political storms, and still does. But we had a hard time understanding each other this time. He wanted a wider alliance of the progressive forces to take the place of our Popular Unity, under the name of the Union of the People. This proposal was impossible; his part in the copper negotiations disqualified him with the political left. More-over, the two major parties of the popular movement, the Commu-nists and the socialists, had come of age and could carry a man of their own to the presidency.

Discouraged as he was, Tomic revealed something to me before leaving my home. Andrés Zaldívar, the Christian-Democratic sec-retary of the Treasury, had shown him documents that proved the country's economy was already bankrupt. "We're heading for a fall," Tomic told me. "The situation can't last four more months. It's disas-trous. Zaldívar has given me the details, our bankruptcy is inevitable."

A month after Allende was elected, but before he took over the presidency, the same cabinet minister, Zaldívar, publicly announced the country's imminent economic disaster, but this time he blamed it on the international repercussions of Allende's election. That's how history is written. At least that's how it is written by twisted, oppor-tunist politicians like Zaldívar.

ALLENDE

My country has been betrayed more than any other in our time. From the nitrate deserts, from the submarine coal mines, from the terrible heights where the copper lies buried and is extracted with inhuman labor by the hands of our people, a freedom movement of magnificent proportions sprang up. That movement raised a man named Allende to the presidency of Chile to carry out reforms and measures of justice that could not be postponed, and to rescue our national wealth from the claws of foreigners.

Wherever he went, in the most far-off countries, the people admired our President and praised the remarkable pluralism of our government. Never in the history of the United Nations in New York had an ovation been heard like the one given the President of Chile by delegates from all over the world. Here in Chile, in the middle of enormous difficulties, a truly just society was being erected, based on our sovereignty, our national pride, and the heroism of the best of Chile's population. On our side, on the side of the Chilean revolution, were the constitution and the law, democracy and hope.

They had everything they wanted on their side. They had harlequins and jumping jacks, lots of clowns, terrorists with pistols and chains, phony monks and degraded members of the armed services. They all rode the merry-go-round of petty spite. Jarpa the Fascist went along, hand in hand with his nephews from "Fatherland and Freedom," ready to break anyone's head or spirit, as long as they recovered for themselves the huge hacienda they called Chile. With them, livening up the show, tripped a great banker and dancer, spattered with blood, González Videla, the rumba king; rumbaing from side to side, he had long ago handed his party over to the enemies of the people. Now it was Frei who was dangling his Christian-Democratic Party before the same enemies of the people, dancing to the tune these enemies played, dancing, moreover, with ex-Colonel

Viaux, whose dirty work he had shared. These were the principal actors in the comedy. They had in readiness all the food they had hoarded, the "miguelitos,"* the clubs, and bullets like those that had inflicted mortal wounds on our people in Iquique, Ránquil, Salvador, Puerto Montt, José María Caro, Frutillar, Puente Alto, and so many other places. Hernán Mery's assassins danced with those who should have been defending his memory. They danced with a light heart, as if they could never hurt a fly. They were offended at being reproached for those "silly little details."

Chile has a long civil history with few revolutions and many stable governments, all of them conservative and mediocre. Many little Presidents and only two great ones: Balmaceda and Allende. Curiously enough, both came from the same background, the moneyed class, which calls itself the aristocracy here. As men of principles bent on making a great country out of one diminished by a mediocre oligarchy, the two were steered down the same road to death. Balmaceda was driven to suicide for refusing to deliver the nitrate riches to foreign companies.

Allende was murdered because he nationalized the other wealth of Chile's subsoil: copper. In both cases, the Chilean oligarchy set bloody revolutions in motion. In both cases, the military played the bloodhounds. The English companies in Balmaceda's time, the North Americans in Allende's time instigated and financed these military actions.

In both cases, the homes of the Presidents were sacked by orders from our distinguished "aristocrats." Balmaceda's rooms were smashed with axes. Allende's home, thanks to world progress, was bombed from the air by our heroic airmen.

---

* Probably devised by someone named Miguel, these are clusters of nails sharpened at both ends and bent into a curve. They are dropped along the road to puncture the tires of oncoming vehicles. —*Trans.*

Yet these two men were very different. Balmaceda was a captivating orator. His imperious nature drove him to rely more and more on himself. He was sure of the high purpose of his intentions. He was surrounded by enemies at all times. His superiority over those around him was so great, and his solitude so vast, that he ended by withdrawing into himself. The people, who should have gone to his aid, did not exist as a power, that is, were not organized. This President was doomed to behave like a visionary, a dreamer: his dream of greatness remained a dream. After his death, the rapacious foreign businessmen and our creole parliamentarians gained possession of the nitrate: for the foreigners, the property and the concessions; for the creoles, the bribe money. Once the thirty pieces of silver had been exchanged, everything returned to normal. The blood of a few thousand men of the people dried up quickly on the battlefields. The most exploited workers in the world, those in Chile's northern regions, never stopped producing enormous quantities of pounds sterling for London.

Allende was never a great orator. And as a statesman he never took a step without consulting his advisers. He was the anti-dictator, the democrat of principles, even in the smallest particulars. The country that fell to his lot was no longer Balmaceda's inexperienced people; he found a powerful working class that knew what it was all about. Allende was a collective leader; although not from the popular classes, he was a product of the struggle of those classes against the paralysis and corruption of their exploiters. This makes the work Allende realized in such a short time superior to Balmaceda's; going further, it is the most important achievement in the history of Chile. The nationalization of copper alone was a titanic accomplishment. As were the ending of the monopolies, the farsighted agrarian reform, and many other objectives attained under his government, whose essential nature was collective.

Allende's acts and works, whose value to the nation can never be obliterated, enraged the enemies of our liberation. The tragic symbolism of this crisis became clear in the bombing of the government palace; it brings to mind the blitzkrieg of the Nazi air force against defenseless foreign cities—Spanish, English, Russian. Now the same crime was being carried out again in Chile. Chilean pilots were dive-bombing the palace, which for centuries had been the center of the city's civic life.

I am writing these quick lines for my memoirs only three days after the unspeakable events took my great comrade President Allende to his death. His assassination was hushed up, he was buried secretly, and only his widow was allowed to accompany that immortal body. The aggressors' version is that they found clear signs of suicide on his lifeless body. The version published abroad is different. Immediately after the aerial bombardment, the tanks went into action, many tanks, fighting heroically against a single man: the President of the Republic of Chile, Salvador Allende, who was waiting for them in his office, with no other company but his great heart, surrounded by smoke and flames.

They couldn't pass up such a beautiful occasion. He had to be machine-gunned because he would never have resigned from office. That body was buried secretly, in an inconspicuous spot. That corpse, followed to its grave only by a woman who carried with her the grief of the world, that glorious dead figure, was riddled and ripped to pieces by the machine guns of Chile's soldiers, who had betrayed Chile once more.

Farewell

And with this, we end our journey around myself. While speaking, while being with you all, while submitting my poetry and my battles to your criteria and your hearts, I have wanted to wound no conscience and to snuff out none of your dreams. Hopefully in my words you've found answers to some hidden questions tucked against your breast. But I also wish for new questions, new dissatisfactions to awaken in you this evening. For the life, the joys, the heartaches of the world to enter into our house every day, knocking down the doors. Life is made of the mysterious substances of the night that dies and the dawn that will be born. May there arise, for each of you, a newborn question along with every recently discovered answer. Till tomorrow, ladies and gentlemen. Till the mystery of tomorrow.

PABLO NERUDA, "Journey Through My Poetry"

Editorial Note:
Texts Added to This Edition

1. JOURNEY THROUGH MY POETRY

This text is made up of two fragments, probably the introduction and epilogue of the lecture-recital that Neruda gave in Santiago after returning to Mexico on December 8, 1943, in the tribute to him held at the Municipal Theater. The writer Fernando Alegría, who was present at the event, conveyed to Professor Hernán Loyola a spoken version of an oft-quoted affirmation of Neruda's. "If you ask me what my poetry is, I have to tell you: I don't know. But if you ask my poetry, it will tell you who I am." We now publish, for the first time, the only known version in writing of this phrase: "What is my poetry? I don't know. It would be easier to ask my poetry who am I."

We have included both fragments, the introduction and the epilogue, as the opening and closing paragraphs of this edition of the *Memoirs*.

2. THE GIRL FROM THE JOURNEY BACK

This text is clearly the continuation of the threshing episode at the Hernándezes', which concludes "Childhood and Poetry," the first part of the *Memoirs*. The text added here describes the return of the young poet from the place where the threshing was carried out.

If the chapter "Love in the Wheat" describes the traditional threshing with a mare, the celebrations that follow the day's work, and finally the sexual initiation of the young traveler, this last part, unpublished before now, tells of his return from this adventure and has a certain ironic tone. Young Neruda is traveling on horseback with a ready and willing girl. This is the moment to show off his newly acquired manhood. But a miserable trifle comes in the way of the consummation: he can't find a place to tie up his horse.

3. THE HORSE FROM THE SADDLER'S

We add this text in the belief that it brings this part of the memoirs to a poignant close, describing the poet's return to the world of his childhood, which he finds changed and, in a certain way, destroyed. The lone vestige that allows for a proper reencounter is this wooden horse, which had been part of his life as a young student.

Matilde Urrutia, in her book *My Life with Pablo Neruda*, notes: "This horse was at a hardware store in Temuco. When Pablo was a schoolboy, he used to take this street and always saw it and stroked its muzzle. He lived with this horse, grew up with it, considered it something of his own. Every time we went to Temuco, he would ask the owner to sell it to him, but it was no use. Nor did the owner's friends have any luck, insist as they might. But one day, the hardware store caught fire; the firemen arrived, and lots of people, and of course, some of Pablo's friends were among them. Later they told us that they heard just one single shout: 'Save Pablo's horse! Don't let the horse burn!'" And that was how it was rescued, it was the first thing the firemen took out. Not long afterward, they auctioned off everything that had been salvaged from the fire. The owner, knowing of Pablo's passion for the horse, had bidders attend to raise the price. He knew Pablo wouldn't let the horse get away from him, and he wound up paying a pretty penny for it."

It is currently housed in the Sala del Caballo in the house in Isla Negra, where it is one of the items from the poet's youth on display.

4. ROAMING IN VALPARAÍSO

Parts of this chapter were written expressly for the memoirs; the rest draws from the article "Valparaíso," which Neruda wrote in 1965, and which was published in German in the Swiss journal *Du Atlantis,* Zurich, February 1966, with photographs by Sergio Larrain. The complete version appeared in Spanish for the first time in the *Obras completas* of Pablo Neruda (third edition, Buenos Aires, Losada, 1968).

For this edition of the *Memoirs*, the 1965 article was reordered and added to the original text, which we publish here in a new version, faithful to the original typescript, with handwritten corrections by Neruda himself. This text varies in a number of ways, principally stylistically, from the previous edition of the present work. There are also several paragraphs that were omitted, but that strike the editors as important, because in them, Neruda adopts the position of poet-memoirist—that is, a poet who remembers episodes from his life and writes his memoirs at a mature age from one of his life's essential backdrops: Isla Negra. Here, Neruda is contemplating nostalgically the lost Valparaíso of his youth.

5. THE *SONNETS OF DARK LOVE* AND THE LAST
LOVE OF THE POET FEDERICO

A handwritten note by Matilde Urrutia explains the motive for the non-publication of these texts. She says: "This article was written for the memoirs. Pablo and I talked many times about whether to include it or no. His precise words to me were: 'Is the public sufficiently free of prejudices to accept Federico's homosexuality without compromise to his prestige?' That was his misgiving. I had similar doubts, and I didn't include it in the memoirs. I leave it here, I don't believe I have a right to destroy it."

6. THE GIFT OF MIST

This text was written in 1962. On the occasion of Rafael Alberti's sixtieth birthday, Neruda composed these lines about one of the many nights he walked from his building in Madrid to the home of the poet from Cádiz. It has been included for its interesting atmosphere of evocation: in the middle of the fog that coats the solitary streets, Neruda is followed by a ghostly dog. He reaches Alberti's home, filled with sculptures by Alberto Sánchez, and there the dog takes up its post. Alberti tells the same story in his memoirs, *La arboleda perdida*, where he recalls that Neruda gave him "that big Irish sheepdog with the tangled hair and a wounded leg that he found one foggy night in Madrid."

7. PORTRAIT OF AN ARRIVISTE

At the bottom of the first page of this article about González Videla, Neruda's great political enemy, the following annotation in pencil appears: "This piece was written for the memoirs, and mysteriously got lost." Further, the following note is written in ink on a piece of typing paper: "This chapter/this piece was written for the memoirs, it mysteriously got lost, it was found in the search for originals of this book." The annotation is most likely Matilde's, and the book she mentions is, without a doubt, *El fin del viaje* (The End of the Journey), an anthology of Neruda's unpublished works that she prepared in 1981.

8. TO PUSHKIN

Neruda arrived to the Soviet Union for the first time on June 6, 1949, to participate in a ceremony commemorating the one hundred and fiftieth anniversary of Pushkin's birth. Amid recitals and lectures, he composed this text in the form of a letter, describing to the great national poet the experience of participating in a celebration of his sesquicentennial.

9. THE YOUNG POET BARQUERO

This text has been included as a continuation of the chapter "August 1952 to April 1957" because it is Neruda's perspective in 1956 on a young poet in whom he seems to see himself as he was when he arrived in Santiago at the beginning of the twenties. The text also refers to Neruda's literary offspring, because Efraín Barquero, as *Memoria Chilena* states, was considered in his early days "as a natural extension of the line of poetic development opened by Pablo Neruda."

10. THE PERSISTENT INFLUENCE OF TREES

In this text, Neruda speaks of his own poetry, and this makes it particularly pertinent to the eleventh section of the book, "Poetry Is an Occupation," which includes the chapters "The Power of Poetry," "Poetry," and "Living with the Language." It is part of an unfinished piece initially intended to be the introduction of *Elemental Odes*.

11. RELIGION AND POETRY

This is an interesting text in which, departing from the candles lit on Isla Negra for one of his figureheads, Neruda reflects on the origins of religion. He expands considerably on the content of the last paragraphs of the chapter "Bottles and Figureheads." In other passages of the *Memoirs*, Neruda includes reflections evoked by episodes in his life and observations of the world, for example in "The Reclining Gods," where he reflects on Christianity and Buddhism through the lens of his experiences in the Orient.

12. LEÓN FELIPE

Neruda wrote this text in July of 1972, when he had already begun to work systematically on the *Memoirs*.

13. THE LITERARY ANTAGONIST

A smaller part of the contents of this extensive text was already contained in the chapter "Literary Enemies," where Neruda offers general considerations of the behavior of his principal literary enemy, whom he refers to as Joe Blow. In the text we now include, Neruda tells in much greater detail certain facts about his legendary antagonist. The same stories appear in a highly synthetic form in the verses of the poem "Corona del archipiélago para Rubén Azócar" in the book *La barcarola*.

14. IF THEY STRIKE IT, LET IT SING

This is one of the poet's responses to attacks against his poetry.

15. THE SOUTHERN COUNTRYSIDE

This was written for the *Memoirs* in 1973, as the author says in the text. It seems to the editors that Neruda, who had extolled and described the natural world of the south in so many poems and other writings, now wished to write a historico-political text centered on the human landscape of southern Chile.

16. ANDRÉS BELLO

This text appears to consist of travel notes. For Neruda, the marble stare of Bello "accompanied my student struggles, my first verses, my first loves." Besides linking him with his life in this way, Neruda assigned to Bello a role of primary importance in the cultural emancipation of Spanish America. In one of his lectures, he said that Bello began the work Neruda continued in his *Canto general*.

17. RECABARREN

This text and the following one are part of a long lecture apparently delivered at an internal ceremony of the Communist Party in the mid-1970s. In both texts, these leaders of the workers' movement are tied to personal memories from Neruda's life. Luis Emilio Recabarren is the figure Neruda most admired from Latin America's history.

18. LAFERTTE

The workers' leader Elías Lafertte, with whom Neruda conducted his senatorial campaign for the northern provinces in 1945, is another person Neruda admired, one who was linked to an important phase in his life.

19. MAYAKOVSKY

This was written in June of 1963, possibly on the occasion of the seventieth anniversary of Mayakovsky's birth. Neruda considered Mayakovksy one of the most important authors of contemporary poetry and described him as a "poet who sank his hand into the collective heart and extracted from it the faith and fortitude required to forge his new songs."

Chronology

The present chronology was prepared especially for this edition of the *Memoirs* and attempts to follow along with its sections and their contents. Its main purpose is to orient the reader with respect to the poet's life. However, the book does not always follow a chronological order. There are sections, like the eleventh, that deal with a miscellany of themes, with texts about poetry, diverse events, people, the author's collector streak, etc., so that, in this case and in others like it, the chronology must be seen as independent of the matter of the book.

1. THE COUNTRY BOY

1903 OCTOBER 4: The teacher Rosa Neftalí Basoalto marries José del Carmen Reyes, son of José Angel Reyes Hermosilla, owner of the one-hundred-hectare Belén estate.

1904 JULY 12: At the home of the Reyes-Basoalto family in the city of Parral, Ricardo Eliecer Neftalí Reyes Basoalto is born. Later he will adopt the name Pablo Neruda.

1904 SEPTEMBER 14: Rosa Neftalí Basoalto dies of tuberculosis. José del Carmen goes to Argentina to work and leaves Neftalí Reyes child at the Belén estate.

1905 After returning from Argentina, José del Carmen finds work with the Araucanía railroad and moves with his son to Temuco. Neruda always insisted that his birth as a poet occurred in this region, where the basic elements of his poetic vision of the world were forged.

1905 NOVEMBER 11: José del Carmen marries Trinidad Candia Marverde, who already has a son, Rodolfo Reyes Candia, born in the spring of 1895. Trinidad takes as her own the young Ricardo Eliecer Neftalí.

1907 The girl Laura Reyes, offspring of a relationship between Neruda's father,

José del Carmen Reyes, and Aurelia Tolrá in Talcahuano, comes to live with the family. Rodolfo, Neftalí, and Laura are half siblings: all have the same father but different mothers. Trinidad Candia accepts them all with the same affection. For the poet, she is the paradigm of maternity and of the humble goodness of village people.

1910 Young Ricardo Neftalí enters the Liceo de Hombres in Temuco.

1917 The Temuco daily *La Mañana* publishes, in the January 18 edition, "Entusiasmo y perseverancia" (Enthusiasm and Perseverance), the first article by the young Ricardo Neftalí Reyes. Several of his early poems will appear in this paper.

1918 Between this year and 1922, Ricardo Neftalí will publish articles in *La Mañana* and *El Diario Austral* in Temuco; the *Revista Cultural* in Valdivia; *Ratos Ilustrados* in Chillán; and *Corre-Vuela* in Santiago.

1919 He participates in the Floral Games of Maule with the poem "Comunión ideal" (Ideal Communion), which he signs with the pseudonym Kundalini. He wins third prize.

1920 FEBRUARY: Summer trip from Temuco to Bajo Imperial (now known as Puerto Saavedra). Young Ricardo Neftalí's encounter with the ocean is another of the key moments for the formation of his poetic world.

1920 The young poet meets Gabriela Mistral, later the winner of the 1945 Nobel Prize in Literature, who arrives in Temuco to take over as principal of the Liceo de Niñas.

1920 JULY: Assault on the headquarters of the Federation of Students and persecution of the "antipatriots," which will lead to the imprisonment and death of the poet Domingo Gómez Rojas. Though he does not participate in the events, Neruda follows them from Temuco, where he welcomes the fleeing writer José Santos González Vera.

1920 Adopts the nom de guerre Pablo Neruda. He will later declare he took this pseudonym from the Czech author Jan Neruda. The poet Miguel Arteche has offered an alternative hypothesis: that the name Neruda may have come from *A Study in Scarlet*, in the Sherlock Holmes series, which alludes to a performance by the violinist Norman Neruda. Research carried out by the Chilean doctor Enrique Robertson has established that the violinist Norman Neruda actually existed. Robertson has also found scores in which the name of the composer Pablo Sarasate appears alongside that of Norman Neruda.

1920 NOVEMBER: Neruda receives first prize in the Spring Floral Games in Temuco for his poem "Salutación a la Reina" (Salutation to the Queen).

2. LOST IN THE CITY

1921 JANUARY 22: The journal *Claridad*, number 12, published by the Federation of Students, publishes a laudatory notice of Neruda and his poetry signed by

Fernando Ossorio, pseudonym of Raúl Silva Castro, with a brief selection of his poems.

1921 MARCH: Neruda travels by train to Santiago to begin his studies in French education at the University of Chile.

1921 APRIL 18: Neruda begins his relationship with Albertina Rosa Azócar, one of the muses of *Twenty Love Poems and a Song of Despair*. The poet never revealed the identity of the two central muses of this volume. He mentioned them only in lectures and memoirs by the names Marisol and Marisombra, and in his *Memorial de Isla Negra* (Isla Negra Memorial) as Rosaura and Terusa. Terusa was Teresa León, his great love from the provinces. This wasn't discovered until 1974, when numerous love letters Ncruda sent to her were published.

1921 JULY 2: Neruda becomes a regular contributor to *Claridad*, starting with issue 28.

1921 OCTOBER 14: Neruda receives first prize in the Prologues' Competition in the Spring Festival for the poem "La canción de la fiesta" (The Song of the Feast).

1923 JANUARY–MARCH: The poet spends his long summer vacations in Temuco and Puerto Saavedra. He will continue to pass his summer and winter vacations in the south of Chile. This is, perhaps, a way of softening the harsh poverty he lives through in his student years in Santiago.

1923 JULY: *Crepusculario* (Crepusculary) is published by Claridad, based in Santiago, with illustrations by Juan Gandulfo, Juan Francisco González, Jr., and Barak. The book will make his name as an author. In the September 2 edition of *La Nación*, the critic Alone writes a fulsome appreciation that concludes with the prophetic words: ". . . as he outranks and surpasses the rest of his generation, we may rightly presume that with time, if blind destiny does not block his path, he will be counted among the very best, and not only of this country and of his era."

1923 Neruda travels to Valparaíso with a group of friends to take leave of the artist Abelardo "Paschin" Bustamante and the poet Alberto Rojas Giménez, who are departing for Paris. Orlando Oyarzún left a record of this journey, probably the same one Neruda relates in "Roaming in Valparaíso" in these pages.

1924 JUNE: A few days before Neruda's twentieth birthday, the first edition of *Twenty Love Poems and a Song of Despair* appears. It will become one of the most widely read, published, and translated books in the world. At the end of 1924, the poet will fail to attend his final exams for his studies in French education. His abandonment of his studies leads to a break with his father, who cuts off the meager monthly allowance he had been sending from Temuco.

3. THE ROADS OF THE WORLD

1924 Neruda meets Álvaro Hinojosa, who will become one of his closest friends. Between 1925 and 1927, Neruda travels several times to Valparaíso, invited by Hinojosa.

1925 NOVEMBER: Neruda moves to Chiloé at the invitation of his friend Rubén Azócar, who has been hired as a professor in Ancud. There, at the beginning of 1926, Neruda will write his only novel, *El habitante y su esperanza* (The Resident and His Hope), at the request of the publisher Nascimento.

1926 JANUARY: The same publisher releases *Venture of the Infinite Man*, and later the book of prose poems *Anillos* (Rings), written by Neruda and his friend Tomás Lago.

1926 The letters the poet sends to his sister, Laura, describe his situation: "My clothing is in an impossible state, and I can't go out wearing it," he tells her on March 9, and on October 27, he will write: "From today forward, I no longer have board included. How do I remedy this situation . . . ? I'm too old not to be eating every day."

1927 APRIL 11: Decree 372 appoints Neruda honorary consul in Rangoon.

1927 JUNE: Neruda's voyage to the Orient begins at the Mapocho Station, in Santiago, where many friends come to say goodbye to him. From there, he catches the train to Valparaíso. After a few days at the home of Álvaro Hinojosa, they catch another train that links up with the Trans-Andean Railway. On June 15, they reach Buenos Aires, and embark two days later.

1927 JULY: Neruda and Hinojosa reach Madrid after disembarking in Lisbon. They travel to Paris by train; while there, Neruda meets César Vallejo. They continue to Marseilles, where they depart for the Orient.

1927 EARLY OCTOBER: Neruda assumes the office of consul in Rangoon, the largest city in Burma, at that time still part of the British Empire.

4. LUMINOUS SOLITUDE

1927 OCTOBER 25: Neruda sends his first letter to the Argentine writer Héctor Eandi. This is the beginning of an exchange of letters that will be fundamental for information about the poet's life in the Orient.

1927 NOVEMBER: Neruda travels to Madras, in India.

1927 DECEMBER 7: In a letter to his friend Yolando Pino, he mentions the book he is writing, *Colección nocturna*. This is the initial title of *Residence on Earth*.

1928 JANUARY: After taking care of his initial consular responsibilities, he continues his journeys with Álvaro Hinojosa. They travel to French Indochina and to the Kingdom of Siam (now Thailand).

1928 FEBRUARY: The two men reach China, where they are met by "a winter of snow, rain, and wind." In mid-February, they arrive in Japan.

1928 MARCH: Neruda meets Josie Bliss, the Burmese lover who will take him through many stages of passion, from the first flush of love to abandonment. In *Residence on Earth*, she will appear as "la bienamada" (the beloved) and "la maldita" (the damned one).

1928 AUGUST 6: In a letter to the author José Santos González Vera, Neruda writes: "I have passed over a limit I never thought myself able to cross, and the truth is, my results surprise and console me. My new book will be called *Residence on Earth*, and consists of twenty poems that will be published in Spain."

1928 NOVEMBER: Neruda travels to Calcutta, where he reunites with Álvaro Hinojosa, after having parted ways with him in March. Hinojosa tries to make his fortune in the flourishing Indian cinema industry.

1928 DECEMBER 5: Neruda is named honorary consul in Colombo, capital of Ceylon (now Sri Lanka).

1928 DECEMBER: Neruda has the opportunity to attend the Indian National Congress, which takes place in Calcutta, with such luminaries as Mahatma Gandhi and Jawaharlal Nehru.

1929 MID-JANUARY: Neruda travels from Calcutta to Colombo, where he assumes the office of consul. Álvaro Hinojosa accompanies him briefly before departing for Bombay.

1929 NOVEMBER: Intending to publish *Residence on Earth*, Neruda sends the original manuscript to Spain. It reaches the hands of the Minister-Counselor of the Chilean Embassy, Carlos Morla Lynch, who passes it along to Rafael Alberti. Despite his enthusiasm, shared by other Spanish poets, he is unable to aid in its publication.

1930 MAY: Neruda is named honorary consul of Singapore and Java, with residence in Batavia and jurisdiction over the Dutch possessions of the Sunda Islands.

1930 DECEMBER 6: The poet marries Maria Antonieta Hagenaar Vogelzang, a Javanese Dutch woman. In a letter to his father on December 15, Neruda says: "For me, she is the sum of all perfections, and we are completely happy . . . Maria has an excellent character and we understand each other marvelously." Nonetheless, the marriage is an unhappy one and in the poem "Itineraries" (*Extravagaria*, 1958) Neruda includes, among his unanswered questions: "Why did I marry in Batavia?"

5. SPAIN IN MY HEART

1932 EARLY FEBRUARY: The closure of his consulate obliges Neruda and his wife to return to Chile.

1932 APRIL 19: Neruda and his wife disembark in Puerto Montt. They will travel to Temuco by train, and from there, after a brief sojourn in the home of the poet's family, will leave for Santiago. Neruda has neither home nor employment and arrives in a country living through one of the gravest social and economic crises of its history.

1932 The Ministry of Foreign Affairs employs Neruda for two hours daily in its
      library. The salary is barely enough to cover the cost of the pension where
      he and his wife reside.

1932 JULY: Neruda is transferred to the Cultural Affairs Department of the Min-
      istry of Labor as chief librarian. With its higher pay grade, the post offers a
      measure of relief from his economic distress.

1933 JANUARY 24: Empresa Letras of Santiago de Chile publishes *El hondero en-
      tusiasta* (The Enthusiastic Slinger), a book the poet wrote ten years before.

1933 APRIL: The publisher Nascimento releases *Residence on Earth* (1925–1931)
      in a limited edition of one hundred copies.

1933 AUGUST: Neruda is named assistant consul to the Consul General in Buenos
      Aires. It is a prominent position, better paid and with more responsibilities
      than his precarious consular posts in the Orient.

1933 END OF AUGUST: Neruda and his wife arrive in Buenos Aires. They visit
      Héctor Eandi, whom Neruda finally meets in person.

1933 OCTOBER 13: At a gathering in homage to Federico García Lorca, Neruda
      and the Spanish poet meet. It is the start of a very close friendship. García
      Lorca has just arrived in Buenos Aires to prepare the Latin American debut
      of his play *Blood Wedding*. Their meeting takes place in the home of the Ar-
      gentine author Pablo Rojas Paz and his wife, Sara Tornú.

1933 NOVEMBER 10: At the Hotel Plaza in downtown Buenos Aires, there is a
      well-attended banquet for Neruda and García Lorca. They present a joint
      discourse in honor of Rubén Darío.

1933 NOVEMBER 11: The poet is given a consular post in Barcelona.

1934 MAY: Along with his pregnant wife, Neruda arrives in Barcelona to take up
      his post. In 1950, he will recollect the Spain he arrived in as the home of "a
      brilliant fraternity of talents where my work was fully known."

1934 MAY 25: The poet Alberto Rojas Giménez, one of Neruda's closest friends,
      dies in Santiago. Neruda dedicates to him the elegy "Alberto Rojas Giménez
      viene volando" ("Alberto Rojas Giménez Comes Flying").

1934 MAY 31: Neruda travels by train to Madrid, where Federico García Lorca
      waits for him at the Estación del Norte.

1934 JUNE 2: At a party given for Neruda, held in the home of Carlos Morla
      Lynch, the poet meets the Argentine painter Delia del Carril, who will be-
      come his second wife.

1934 JULY: Neruda and Miguel Hernández meet during one of the latter's trips to
      Madrid from Orihuela, the town of Hernández's birth.

1934 AUGUST 18: Malva Marina Reyes Hagenaar, the poet's only daughter, is
      born in Madrid. On the twenty-fifth of the month, Neruda writes to inform
      his father and attempts to minimize the girl's health problems, even as she
      is in danger of dying.

1934 DECEMBER 6: Neruda gives a recital at the University of Madrid. García

Lorca introduces him as "a poet closer to death than to philosophy, closer to pain than to intelligence, closer to blood than to ink."

1934 DECEMBER 19: Neruda is given a temporary commission as attaché to the Chilean Embassy in Madrid, while maintaining the functions he carries out at the consulate in Barcelona.

1935 APRIL: The pamphlet *Homenaje a Pablo Neruda de los poetas españoles/ Tres cantos materiales* (Spanish Poets Pay Homage to Pablo Neruda/Three Material Songs) is published in Madrid by Plutarco. In addition to the "Three Material Songs," it includes a tribute to Neruda by all the most important Spanish poets of the day, with the exception of Juan Ramón Jiménez and Juan Larrea.

1935 JUNE 21-25: Neruda participates in the First International Congress of Writers for the Defense of Culture, which takes place in Paris.

1935 SEPTEMBER 15: The first edition of *Residence on Earth I and II* appears in Madrid, published in two volumes by Cruz y Raya in its series Ediciones del Árbol.

1935 OCTOBER: Gabriela Mistral is transferred from Madrid to Lisbon, and Neruda takes over the role of consul in Madrid.

1935 OCTOBER: The first volume of the journal *Caballo verde para la poesía* (Green Horse for Poetry), edited by Neruda, appears. Three more volumes follow. Issues 5 and 6 are printed, bound, and delivered to the warehouse, but are lost amid the outbreak of the Spanish Civil War.

1935 NOVEMBER-DECEMBER: The prestigious French magazine *Les Mois*, which offers monthly reports on significant events in the literary world, affirms that "the most important poetry publication of the year is undoubtedly the two-volume collection *Residence on Earth* by the Chilean Pablo Neruda."

1936 JULY 18: With the military uprising led by Francisco Franco, the Spanish Civil War begins.

1936 AUGUST 18: The poet Federico García Lorca is murdered in Granada.

1936 SEPTEMBER 24: In the militant journal *El mono azul* (The Blue Monkey), the poem "Canto a las madres de los milicianos muertos" (Song to the Mothers of the Murdered Militiamen) appears. It will later form part of the collection *España en el corazón* (Spain in My Heart).

1936 EARLY NOVEMBER: Madrid is bombarded. Neruda, Delia del Carril, Luis Enrique Délano, and his wife, Lola Falcón, leave for Valencia, where Neruda will depart from to Barcelona to reunite with his wife and daughter, who arrived there in July.

1936 DECEMBER 7: The Madrid and Barcelona consulates are shuttered. Neruda is not assigned to another post. He and his family travel to Marseilles and from there to Monte Carlo, where he will leave María Antonieta Hagenaar and his daughter. The two of them travel on to Holland.

1937 JANUARY: Neruda resides in Paris with Delia del Carril.

1937 FEBRUARY 20: Neruda gives a lecture in homage to Federico García Lorca, under the auspices of the Alliance of Antifascist Intellectuals. Neruda openly declares his support for the Spanish Republic, and receives notice of the Ministry's disapproval of his political activities in Paris.

1937 In France, Neruda and Nancy Cunard edit the journal *Les poètes du monde défendent le peuple espagnol* (Poets of the World Defend the Spanish People). Six issues will be published.

1937 APRIL: Neruda works for the Association for the Defense of Culture, helping to organize the Second International Congress of Writers for the Defense of Culture.

1937 JULY 4–7: Neruda helps lead the Second International Congress of Writers for the Defense of Culture, which takes place in Valencia and Madrid. Paris is the meeting point for the foreign delegates, who will travel from there to warring Spain by train.

6. I WENT OUT TO LOOK FOR THE FALLEN

1937 AUGUST 26: Neruda, Delia del Carril, Raúl González Tuñón, and his wife, Amparo Mom, embark in Antwerp on the steamer *Arica*. On October 10, they reach Valparaíso. During the crossing, the poet completes *España en el corazón* (Spain in My Heart).

1937 OCTOBER: In Santiago two large gatherings welcome Neruda, one in the Parque Cousiño and the other in the Quinta Normal restaurant. The latter, organized by the P.E.N. club, has some two hundred guests.

1937 NOVEMBER 7: In the Honor Hall of the University of Chile, a ceremony takes place to inaugurate the Alliance of Chilean Intellectuals for the Defense of Culture. In his speech, Neruda affirms its goals of fighting fascism and of solidarity with Republican Spain.

1937 NOVEMBER 13: The publisher Ercilla, based in Santiago, publishes *España en el corazón*. The first edition, of 2,800 copies, soon sells out.

1937 DECEMBER 13: At the Municipal Theater in Santiago, the Alliance of Chilean Intellectuals for the Defense of Culture organizes its first public presentation, the centerpiece of which is a lyrical discussion entitled "Tempestad en España" (Storm in Spain) by Pablo Neruda and Raúl González Tuñón. The evening's success will lead its organizers to repeat the event on December 19 in Valparaíso.

1938 MAY 6 OR 7: José del Carmen Reyes, the poet's father, dies in Temuco.

1938 AUGUST 1: The journal *Aurora de Chile* (Daybreak in Chile) appears, edited by the Alliance of Chilean Intellectuals for the Defense of Culture and overseen by Neruda.

1938 AUGUST 18: Neruda's stepmother, Trinidad Candia Marverde, "La Mamadre," dies. The family decides to place José del Carmen and his wife in the same niche. Overwhelmed by the double loss and the exhumation of his father's remains, Neruda will write "La copa de sangre" (The Cup of Blood), an extremely important autobiographical text.

1938 OCTOBER 25: The standard bearer of the Popular Front, Pedro Aguirre Cerda, triumphs in Chile's presidential elections, defeating the socialist candidate Gustavo Ross.

1938 NOVEMBER 7: Located at the Montserrat Monastery, Catalonia, Ediciones Literarias del Comisariado del Ejército del Este, directed by Manuel Altolaguirre, publishes *España en el corazón* in an initial print run of five hundred copies.

1939 The purchase of Isla Negra and its cabin is finalized. The poet will build several new wings onto the house, and will compose the better part of his works there.

1939 At the beginning of the year, President Pedro Aguirre Cerda names Neruda consul, second class, in Paris starting on April 15. His main responsibility will be immigration from Spain.

1939 MARCH: Neruda leaves for France via Buenos Aires and Montevideo, where he participates in the International Congress of American Democracies. There he requests the aid needed to transport Spanish refugees to Chile.

1939 END OF APRIL: Neruda arrives in Paris. He begins work, struggling against the obstacles the embassy puts in his way as well as the politicians and the press opposed to the Chilean government.

1939 JUNE: In the French port of Le Havre, repair work begins on the *Winnipeg*, the ship that will transport the Spanish refugees.

1939 JULY 29: Minister of Foreign Affairs Abraham Ortega tells the Minister in Paris that "they will accept up to 1,500 able-bodied refugees along with their families, that is, their wives and children, until the ship is at capacity."

1939 AUGUST 4: The *Winnipeg* departs from the port of Trompe-loup. On board are around two thousand Spanish refugees and thirty-five Chileans who had fought for the International Brigades.

1939 AUGUST 30: The *Winnipeg* reaches Arica. After receiving offers of work, some of the refugees decide to stay there.

1939 SEPTEMBER 2: The *Winnipeg* arrives in Valparaíso at night. The passengers disembark on the third, the same day the Second World War begins.

1939 MID-NOVEMBER: Before returning to Chile, the poet travels to Holland to visit his daughter, Malva Marina, and Maruca Hagenaar.

1939 EARLY DECEMBER: Neruda begins his return voyage to Chile with Delia del Carril on the transatlantic liner *Augustus*, which reaches Valparaíso on the twenty-ninth of the month.

7. MEXICO, BLOSSOMING AND THORNY

1940 JANUARY 1: Neruda and Delia are greeted in Santiago by artists, writers, politicians, and Spanish refugees.

1940 JANUARY 18: In Spain, the poet Miguel Hernández is sentenced to death. Neruda tries to help him from Chile. Eventually, Franco will commute his sentence to the maximum of thirty years' imprisonment.

1940 JUNE 19: Neruda is officially named Chile's Consul General in Mexico.

1940 LATE JULY: Neruda leaves Valparaíso on the steamship *Yasukuni Maru* with Delia del Carril, Luis Enrique Délano, and his wife, Lola Falcón.

1940 AUGUST 17: They reach Mexico City. The poet takes up his post on the twenty-first. He and Delia rent an apartment on Calle Revillagigedo and later a house called Quinta Rosa María.

1941 APRIL: Neruda grants a Chilean entry visa to the muralist David Alfaro Siqueiros, who had been imprisoned for his role in an attempt to assassinate Trotsky. The Ministry orders the visa annulled. Siqueiros had planned to paint a mural at the Escuela México in Chillán. Finally, he is accepted into Chile, and the poet is penalized with a month's suspension from work without pay.

1941 JUNE: Neruda and Delia travel to Guatemala, where he meets Miguel Ángel Asturias. He gives a recital organized by a group of young poets with the authorization of the dictator Jorge Ubico.

1941 JULY 24: In Mexico, Neruda participates in an homage to Simón Bolívar organized by the National Autonomous University. He reads his poem "Un canto para Bolívar" (A Song for Bolívar). A fascist group interrupts the proceedings.

1941 LATE AUGUST: There is a break with Octavio Paz.

1941 After the German invasion of the U.S.S.R., Neruda plays an active role in actions and aid organizations supporting the Soviet Union in the war.

1941 DECEMBER 28: At a restaurant in Cuernavaca, Neruda, Delia, Luis Enrique Délano, his wife, and their young son, Poli Délano, are attacked by a group of German Nazis. The poet is wounded in the head. The Mexican press unilaterally condemns the violence.

1942 JANUARY 5: The photographer Tina Modotti, an active opponent of Fascism, dies in Mexico. Neruda will write the poem "Tina Modotti ha muerto" (Tina Modotti Has Died), the first verses of which are engraved on Modotti's tomb.

1942 EARLY MARCH: Neruda travels to Cuba with Delia del Carril; invited by the country's Ministry of Education. There he receives notice of the death of Miguel Hernández in a Francoist prison in Alicante.

1942 SEPTEMBER 30: At an event organized by the Friends of the Soviet Union, Neruda reads his poem "Canto de amor a Stalingrado" (Song to Stalingrad), which is later printed on posters and pasted on the walls of Mexico City.

1943 FEBRUARY: Neruda travels to the United States with Delia to participate in La Noche de las Américas (The Night of the Americas), which takes place in one of the major theaters on Broadway.

1943 MARCH 2: Malva Marina Reyes Hagenaar, the poet's only daughter, dies in German-occupied Holland.

1943 JULY 2: The poet marries Delia del Carril in Tetecala, in the state of Morelos, Mexico.

1943 JUNE: Leocadia Felizardo de Prestes, mother of the communist leader Luis Carlos Prestes, dies in Mexico. Luis Carlos is imprisoned in Brazil at the time. Pleas for Prestes's temporary release to allow him to attend the burial are rejected. At the funeral, on June 18, Neruda reads his poem "Dura elegía" (Hard Elegy), in which he levels bitter critiques at President Getulio Vargas, though without naming him. The Brazilian government protests. The Chilean Minister of Foreign Affairs considers this a grave breach of protocol. Neruda requests six months' leave to travel to Chile and initiate his retirement from the diplomatic service.

1943 AUGUST 21: Neruda receives a doctor *honoris causa* from the University of San Nicolás de Hidalgo, in Morelia, Michoacán.

1943 AUGUST 27: Mexico says goodbye to Neruda at El Frontón, a large sporting facility capable of accommodating the crowd. On this occasion, he reads his poem "En los muros de México" (On the Walls of Mexico), which he will later include in his *Canto general*.

1943 Neruda and Delia depart for Panama. Their long return voyage to Chile includes stops in many countries on the Pacific coast.

8. MY COUNTRY IN DARKNESS

1943 SEPTEMBER 3: Neruda and Delia arrive in Panama, where they remain for several days.

1943 SEPTEMBER 8: Neruda arrives in Bogotá, invited by the government of the liberal President Alfonso López Pumarejo. Conservative senator Laureano Gómez attacks him in verse, and Neruda responds with his "Tres sonetos punitivos para Laureano Gómez" (Three Punitive Sonnets for Laureano Gómez).

1943 OCTOBER 15: Neruda arrives in Lima, where the President of the Republic, Manuel Prado, invites him to lunch and arranges for him to visit the Inca ruins of Macchu Picchu.

1943 OCTOBER 31: After three days' journey by mule from Cuzco, Neruda, Delia, and the Peruvian congressman Uriel García reach Macchu Picchu.

1943 NOVEMBER 4: Neruda arrives in Santiago, where he participates in the activities of the Communist Party.

1944 MAY 21: Neruda receives the Municipal Literature Prize, awarded by the city of Santiago.

1944 DECEMBER: Though not officially a member of the Communist Party, Neruda is named its candidate to the senate for the provinces of Tarapacá and Antofagasta.

1945 JANUARY–MARCH: As part of his electoral campaign, Neruda crosses the pampa with Elías Lafertte, a former worker from the saltpeter mines,

President of the Communist Party, and a senatorial candidate himself. Both are victorious in the elections of March 4.

1945 MAY 24: Neruda is awarded Chile's National Prize for Literature.

1945 JULY 8: Neruda receives his Communist Party membership card.

1945 JULY 15: In São Paolo, Brazil, in the Pacaembú Stadium, an event honors the Communist leader Luis Carlos Prestes, recently freed through an amnesty decree. In front of more than a hundred thousand people, Neruda reads his poem "Saludo a Luis Carlos Prestes" (Greetings to Luis Carlos Prestes).

1945 SEPTEMBER: Neruda withdraws from public life to rest in Isla Negra and devote himself to the composition of a poem about Macchu Picchu.

1946 JULY 21: A center-left coalition elects Gabriel González Videla as candidate for the presidency. In August, Pablo Neruda is named propaganda chief and will accompany González Videla on his tours through the country.

1946 SEPTEMBER 1: At a ceremony in Santiago's National Stadium celebrating the close of the campaign, Neruda accepts González Videla's oath to uphold his governning program.

1946 SEPTEMBER 4: González Videla wins the presidential election.

1947 JUNE 12: A strike by Santiago's public transport workers ends with four dead and dozens wounded. González Videla publicly blames the Communist Party for these incidents. Neruda contradicts him in the senate.

1947 AUGUST 17: The coal miners declare an indefinite strike. González Videla accuses the Communist Party of provoking strikes for political ends, breaks with the party, and puts the coal-mining regions under military control.

1947 OCTOBER 14: Neruda delivers the first of three speeches in the senate that will make him President González Videla's main adversary.

1947 NOVEMBER 27: Neruda writes in the daily paper El Nacional in Caracas: "The democratic crisis in Chile is a dramatic warning for our continent." His words circulate in other countries in Latin America as "A Personal Letter to Millions of Men."

1947 DECEMBER 10: In the senate, Neruda delivers the second of his three speeches against González Videla.

1947 DECEMBER 24: The government sends a written order for the Justice Department to file a petition for the impeachment of Senator Pablo Neruda.

1948 JANUARY 6: In the senate, Neruda delivers one of his most celebrated speeches, published later under the title "Yo acuso" (I accuse).

1948 JANUARY 27: Neruda attempts to reach Argentina by car. The attempt is a failure, as is a second one, this time to reach Mendoza, and a petition for political asylum in Mexico.

1948 FEBRUARY 3: The Supreme Court strips Senator Neruda of his post. An arrest warrant is issued, and the poet goes underground, moving from house to house while finishing Canto general.

1948 FEBRUARY 26: María Hagenaar travels to Chile. The government sponsors her trip with the express purpose of causing problems for the poet. Eventually he agrees to make payments to his ex-wife.

1948 AUGUST 25–30: At the World Congress of Intellectuals in Defense of Peace in Wrocław, Poland, the celebrated painter Pablo Picasso gives the one public speech of his life, proposing a resolution in Neruda's defense.

1949 FEBRUARY: The poet reaches the town of Futrono, in the south of Chile. At a tree plantation, he makes preparations to flee to Argentina.

1949 MID-FEBRUARY: Neruda, with two friends and three mule drivers, crosses the mountains on horseback through a pass used by horse thieves and contrabandists.

1949 EARLY MARCH: Neruda reaches San Martín de los Andes in Argentina, then travels on to Buenos Aires. With the help of the writer Miguel Ángel Asturias, who lends him his passport, he manages to depart for Europe.

1949 APRIL 25: Neruda makes a surprise appearance at the closing ceremony of the First World Congress of the Partisans for Peace in Paris.

9. BEGINNING AND END OF EXILE

1949 APRIL–MAY: Neruda takes up residence in Paris with Delia del Carril.

1949 JUNE 6: Neruda and Delia travel to the Soviet Union. In Moscow and Leningrad he participates in the activities commemorating the one hundred and fiftieth anniversary of the birth of the poet Alexander Pushkin.

1949 JULY–AUGUST: Neruda travels through Eastern Europe, participating in conferences, events, and meetings in Poland, Hungary, and Czechoslovakia.

1949 AUGUST–SEPTEMBER: Neruda and Delia travel to Mexico to the Latin American Congress of the Partisans of Peace, which takes place between September 3 and 10. He again meets Matilde Urrutia, whom he first knew in 1946 in Santiago.

1949 SEPTEMBER: The poet is ill with thrombophlebitis. Matilde comes to care for him. This is a new beginning of a love affair that will remain a constant throughout the rest of the poet's life.

1950 APRIL: The first edition of Canto general is published in Mexico. The flyleaves are illustrated by the Mexican muralists Diego Rivera and David Alfaro Siqueiros. In Chile, a clandestine edition is published with engravings by José Venturelli. Canto general will become a worldwide classic. A monumental, incomparable work, it is a grandiose poetic vision of the Americas' nature, history, and culture.

1950 JUNE 24: Neruda and Delia leave for Europe.

1950 JULY: Again, he and Delia move to Paris, traveling from there to Czechoslovakia, Romania, Hungary, and the Soviet Union.

1950 OCTOBER: The physicist Frédéric Joliot-Curie, President of the World Peace Council, arranges for Neruda to visit New Delhi to interview Indian Prime Minister Pandit Nehru, who gives him a cold reception and places him under police observation. The causes of Nehru's attitudes are not clear from the poet's memoirs, but the Telangana Rebellion (1946–1951), a peasant movement supported by the Indian Communist Party and suppressed by the government, offers a possible explanation.

1950 NOVEMBER 16–22: Neruda participates in the Second World Congress of the Partisans for Peace in Warsaw. Among the winners of the International Peace Prize are two Pablos and one Paul: Picasso, Neruda, and Robeson.

1950 DECEMBER: Neruda is named a member of the International Committee of the jury for the Stalin Prize for the Strengthening of Peace Between Nations.

1951 EARLY AUGUST: Matilde Urrutia arrives in Paris. From now until his return to Chile, the poet will brave countless difficulties to be with his beloved. He travels to East Berlin to participate in the third World Festival of Youth and Students, and manages to get Matilde to accompany him and to sing there.

1951 LATE AUGUST: The poet visits Bucharest. He stays in the same house as Matilde, where he writes the first poems of what will eventually become the book *The Captain's Verses*.

1951 SEPTEMBER: Neruda travels to China on the Trans-Siberian Railroad as part of the delegation attending the World Peace Council to award the Stalin Prize to Soong Ch'ing-ling, widow of Sun Yat-sen, a fighter for democracy and the first President of the People's Republic of China, who died in 1925.

1951 LATE NOVEMBER: Neruda travels privately to Nyon, a small city on the banks of Lake Geneva, where he will spend several days with Matilde.

1951 MID-DECEMBER: Neruda travels to Prague and later to the U.S.S.R., where he will participate in meetings of the jury for the Stalin Prize.

1951 LATE DECEMBER: Neruda sees Matilde in Rome, which the two of them will leave, along with Delia and a group of friends, to go to Naples to celebrate the New Year.

1952 JANUARY 11: The Ministry of the Interior notifies Neruda that he must leave Italy. The police escort him by train to Rome, where a large group of protesters who are waiting for him get permission to take the poet to a hotel to await the results of the petitions filed on his behalf. On January 15, the deportation order is revoked.

1952 MID-JANUARY: Historian and naturalist Edwin Cerio gives the poet use of a villa in Capri. On the twenty-third, Matilde and Neruda leave to spend a long period on the island. There he will finish his book *The Captain's Verses* and move forward with the writing of *Las uvas y el viento* (The Grapes and the Wind).

1952 JANUARY 30: Delia del Carril leaves for Chile to help Neruda return to his country.

1952 JULY 8: In Naples, *The Captain's Verses* is printed in an edition of forty-four signed and numbered copies, not for sale. The book continues to be published anonymously until 1962.

1952 LATE JULY: Neruda travels to Cannes with Matilde to return to America.

Before he ships out, he is notified of his expulsion from France. During the crossing he meets the Uruguayan architect Alberto Mántaras and his wife, Olga, who will become close friends.

1952 AUGUST 10: Neruda arrives in Montevideo and takes leave of Matilde, who travels on to Buenos Aires. The poet takes a plane to Santiago. He arrives on the twelfth and is greeted with a large event in the Plaza Bulnes.

10. VOYAGE AND HOMECOMING

1952 OCTOBER 27: At midday, Neruda and Delia have a serious accident, crashing into a truck. The poet is released with his arm in a brace. Delia has to remain on bedrest in the hospital.

1952 NOVEMBER: Neruda and Matilde buy a piece of property at the foot of San Cristóbal Hill in Santiago, where they will later build La Chascona, a house named in honor of Matilde's abundant flowing hair. In the interim, Matilde moves into an apartment in the Providencia Commune, while Neruda continues to live with Delia in the Casa Michoacán.

1952 EARLY DECEMBER: Neruda travels to Europe to participate in the World Peace Council in Vienna. Later, he attends the celebrations of the thirty-eighth anniversary of the U.S.S.R. and the deliberations for the Stalin Prize.

1953 MARCH 5: During the preparations for the Continental Congress of Culture, which will be celebrated in April in Santiago, Stalin dies in the U.S.S.R. On Isla Negra, Neruda writes the poem "En su muerte" (At His Death) as an homage.

1953 APRIL: *Todo el amor* (All the Love), an anthology of Neruda's love poetry chosen by the poet himself, is published in Santiago.

1953 APRIL 26–MAY 3: The Continental Congress of Culture takes place in Santiago. Nearly two hundred delegates from various Latin American countries attend.

1953 EARLY MAY: The Mexican muralist Diego Rivera, who has traveled to Chile to participate in the Continental Congress of Culture, paints a portrait of Matilde, in front and in profile, and Neruda's features are evident in her reddish hair.

1953 AUGUST: Neruda travels through the *pampa salitrera* (the saltpeter pampa) with the Communist leaders Elías Lafertte and Salvador Ocampo.

1953 DECEMBER 21: The news arrives that Neruda is one of the winners of the Stalin Prize for the Strengthening of Peace Between Nations.

1953 DECEMBER 29: The poet composes a document donating his library and his collection of seashells to the University of Chile to create a foundation for the study of poetry that will bear his name. This is one of the ways Neruda will commemorate turning fifty.

1954 JANUARY 20–24: Neruda delivers a series of five lectures entitled "Mi poesía" (My Poetry) at the summer school of the University of Chile.

1954 MID-FEBRUARY: Neruda travels to Goiânia, Brazil, where he takes part in the First National Congress of Brazilian Intellectuals.

1954 FEBRUARY 27: Nascimento publishes the first edition of *Las uvas y el viento* in Santiago.

1954 JUNE–JULY: Neruda stays busy with the very full program of cultural activities that will celebrate his fiftieth birthday. On July 12, the festivities begin at the Honor Hall of the University of Chile.

1954 JULY 14: Losada, in Buenos Aires, publishes the first edition of *Elemental Odes*, the beginning of an ambitious literary project in which, as Saúl Yurkievich has stated, Neruda aims for a poetry "that broadens its domain to take in the entirety of the world" and "fully grasps every dimension of the real in its inexhaustible variations." Three more books will follow: *New Elemental Odes* (1956), *Third Book of Odes* (1957), and *Navigations and Returns* (1959).

1954 AUGUST 10: Neruda's friend Ilya Ehrenburg presents him with the Stalin Prize for the Strengthening of Peace Between Nations.

1954 MID-DECEMBER: Neruda, Delia del Carril, and Volodia Teitelboim travel to the Second Congress of Soviet Writers. On April 17, 1955, in Chile, Neruda will deliver an extensive lecture on this congress, which hints at a new cultural openness in the U.S.S.R.

1954 DECEMBER: Neruda participates in the meetings of the jury of the Stalin Prize in Moscow. Afterward, he travels to Stockholm for the World Peace Council. He returns to Chile on the thirtieth.

1955 FEBRUARY: Neruda breaks definitively with Delia del Carril. The poet takes up residence in the still-unfinished La Chascona, where he will live with Matilde Urrutia.

1955 NOVEMBER: Invited to the centennial of the death of the Polish national poet Adam Mickiewicz, Neruda travels with Matilde to Warsaw, Kraków, and Poznan.

1956 FEBRUARY 14–25: The Twentieth Congress of the Communist Party of the Soviet Union takes place, and the crimes of the Stalin years are revealed for the first time. Henceforward, in assorted writings and poems, Neruda will critically revise his opinion of Stalin. His poetry will change as well.

1957 LATE JANUARY: Losada, in Buenos Aires, publishes the first edition of the *Obras completas* (Complete Works) of Neruda.

1957 EARLY APRIL: Neruda travels with Matilde to Buenos Aires. The Argentine government has begun persecuting communists. On April 11, they arrest Neruda in a morning raid. He is freed the next day. They travel on to Montevideo.

1957 APRIL: Still in the Uruguayan capital, Neruda is elected President of the Chilean Writers' Society. He and Matilde continue to Brazil, where they will spend time with Jorge Amado and his wife, Zelia Gattai.

1957 JULY: Neruda and Matilde travel to Colombo, Ceylon, to the World Peace

Council, where they again meet Jorge Amado and Zelia. The poet returns to the streets and the home where he lived thirty years before.

1957 JULY: Together with Jorge and Zelia, they travel to India, then to Rangoon. They fly to China and explore the Yangtze River in celebration of the poet's fifty-third birthday.

1957 SEPTEMBER–OCTOBER: Neruda and Matilde travel through several countries in Eastern Europe before arriving in Paris, where, on October 4, they will receive news of the feats of Sputnik, the first artificial satellite to orbit Earth, and of the Soviets' entry into the space era. This chapter of contemporary history will interest Neruda greatly and will also be echoed in his poetry.

11. POETRY IS AN OCCUPATION

1958 JUNE: Neruda travels through Chile, participating in the events surrounding the announcement of Salvador Allende's presidential candidacy.

1958 AUGUST 18: Losada, in Buenos Aires, publishes the first edition of *Extravagaria*, which will inaugurate a new stage in Neruda's work, in which he leaves behind utopian certainties and opts for an ambivalent and antidogmatic vision of life.

1959 JANUARY 3: Neruda and Matilde travel by ship to Venezuela. On January 18, they reach the port of La Guaira.

1959 JANUARY 26: At the Cuban Embassy in Caracas, he meets with Fidel Castro.

1959 NOVEMBER: The University of Santiago Press publishes a private edition of *One Hundred Love Sonnets*, dedicated to Matilde Urrutia.

1960 MARCH: Neruda and Matilde depart from Montevideo for Europe on the *Louis Lumière*. Vinícius de Moraes is on the same ship. The two poets will write sonnets dedicated to each other.

1960 MAY 21 AND 22: Two successive earthquakes destroy part of the central and southern regions of Chile. In Europe, Neruda writes "Cataclismo" (Cataclysm) and plans a deluxe edition illustrated by well-known painters to raise funds for the victims in his country. He writes "Pequeña historia de los *Veinte poemas de amor*" (A Brief History of *Twenty Love Poems*) as a prologue for a special edition that Losada will publish to celebrate the book's selling a million copies.

1960 MID-NOVEMBER–DECEMBER: Neruda and Matilde leave Marseilles for Cuba, arriving on December 5. Neruda gives lectures and recitals. Casa de las Américas publishes his book *Canción de gesta* (Chanson de geste), dedicated to the Cuban Revolution, in an edition of twenty-five thousand copies. Ernesto "Che" Guevara receives the poet in the middle of the night in his office in the Central Bank.

1961 JUNE 26: Losada, in Buenos Aires, publishes *Las piedras de Chile* (The Stones of Chile), a book of poems illustrated with photos by Antonio Quintana.

1961 SEPTEMBER: On Chilean Independence Day, Neruda inaugurates "La Sebastiana," his house in Valparaíso.

1961 OCTOBER 31: Losada in Buenos Aires publishes *Cantos ceremoniales* (Ceremonial Songs).

1962 JANUARY 16: The journal *O Cruzeiro Internacional* begins publishing the series "Las vidas del poeta. Memorias y recuerdos de Pablo Neruda" (The Lives of the Poet: Memoirs and Recollections of Pablo Neruda).

1962 MARCH 30: A ceremony inducts Neruda into the Department of Philosophy and Humanities at the University of Chile. The poet Nicanor Parra gives the welcoming address.

1962 EARLY APRIL: Neruda travels with Matilde to Uruguay, then on to Italy, where he will meet Alberto Tallone, a master typesetter, who will produce various editions of Neruda's work.

1963 Neruda receives the San Valentino Prize for the Italian version of *Twenty Love Poems and a Song of Despair*.

1963 SEPTEMBER 29: Neruda speaks at a meeting of some three thousand people in Santiago's Bustamante Park, harshly criticizing the Chinese Cultural Revolution.

1964 FEBRUARY: Neruda concludes his translation of *Romeo and Juliet* for the commemoration of the fourth centenary of Shakespeare's birth at the University of Chile's theater.

1964 JULY: The poet's sixtieth birthday is celebrated with a great number of events.

1964 JUNE 2–JULY 12: Losada, in Buenos Aires, publishes *Memorial de Isla Negra* (Isla Negra Memorial), Neruda's poetic autobiography, in five separate volumes.

1964 OCTOBER 10: The Theater Institute of the University of Chile debuts Neruda's translation and adaptation of *Romeo and Juliet*, directed by Eugenio Guzmán with music by Sergio Ortega.

1964 DECEMBER: Eudeba, a university press in Buenos Aires, publishes *Genio y figura de Pablo Neruda* (Pablo Neruda, the Man and the Legend) by Margarita Aguirre. This is the first biographical book about the poet.

1965 MARCH 27: María Antonieta Hagenaar, Neruda's first wife, dies in The Hague.

1965 MARCH–APRIL: Neruda leaves for Europe with Matilde. On April 16 they arrive in Paris, traveling on to Moscow and then to Budapest at the government's invitation. There, Neruda meets Miguel Ángel Asturias again. Both have accepted assignments to write about their impressions of the country. This is the origin of the book *Comiendo en Hungría* (Eating in Hungary).

1965 MAY 19: Neruda participates in the International Writers' Conference, organized by East Germany on the occasion of the twentieth anniversary of the defeat of Nazism.

1965 JUNE 1: Neruda receives a doctor *honoris causa* in philosophy and letters from Oxford University. He is the first Latin American poet to receive this distinction.

1966 MARCH 21: The playwright Arthur Miller invites Neruda to participate as a guest of honor at the P.E.N. club conference in New York, which will be held from June 12 to 18. At the beginning of June, Neruda departs for the U.S.A. with Matilde. He will become one of the stars of the event, which hosts delegates from fifty-six countries.

1966 JUNE 18: Neruda gives a recital at the Inter-American Development Bank in Washington, D.C., and records several of his poems for the Library of Congress.

1966 JULY 4: Neruda and Matilde arrive in Peru. Neruda gives lectures in Lima and Arequipa to raise money for the victims of the recent earthquake. He has lunch with President Fernando Belaúnde and receives Peru's highest honor: the Order of the Sun.

1966 JULY 12: On his sixty-second birthday, Neruda returns to Chile with Matilde.

1966 JULY 31: An open letter to Pablo Neruda, signed by more than a hundred Cuban artists and intellectuals, is publicized worldwide. The letter criticizes Neruda's participation in the P.E.N. club congress, his lunch with the President of Peru, and his acceptance of the Order of the Sun. Professor Hernán Loyola notes that Neruda saw these as "gratuitous aggression" and "a grave offense to his revolutionary trajectory and dignity . . ." On August 1, the poet publishes a telegram responding to the Cubans.

1966 Losada, in Buenos Aires, publishes *Neruda: El viajero inmóvil* (Neruda: The Immobile Voyager) by Emir Rodríguez Monegal, a biography of the poet that includes an analysis of some of his works.

1966 SEPTEMBER: Lumen, in Barcelona, publishes *Una casa en la arena* (A House in the Sand), a book of texts and prose poems by Neruda about his home in Isla Negra, with photos by Sergio Larraín.

1966 OCTOBER 28: Neruda and Matilde are married in a civil ceremony in Isla Negra.

1966 NOVEMBER 1: *Arte de pájaros* (Art of Birds) appears in an edition published by the Society of Friends of Contemporary Art, illustrated by the painters Nemesio Antúnez, Mario Carreño, Héctor Herrera, and Mario Toral.

1967 OCTOBER 14: The Theater Institute of the University of Chile debuts Neruda's only dramatic work in Santiago: *Fulgor y muerte de Joaquín Murieta: Bandido chileno injusticiado en California el 23 de July de 1853* (Glory and Death of Joaquín Murieta: A Chilean Bandit Murdered Unjustly in California on July 23, 1853). The music is by Sergio Ortega, Pedro Orthous directs, and the choreography is by Patricio Bunster.

1967 NOVEMBER 24: Neruda travels to Parral, the city where he was born, to receive the title of Hijo ilustre (Distinguished Son), awarded by the local government.

1967 DECEMBER 4: Losada, in Buenos Aires, publishes *La barcarola* (The Barcarole).

1968 JANUARY: Soviet poet Yevgeny Yevtushenko visits Chile. He gives a recital with Neruda in Russian and Spanish at the National Stadium in Santiago. Some seven thousand people attend.

1968 APRIL 24: With "Escarabagia dispersa" (Random Beetling), Neruda begins a series of articles he will publish fortnightly for two years in the journal *Ercilla* in Santiago under the general title "Reflexiones desde Isla Negra" (Reflections from Isla Negra).

1968 JULY 12: Neruda celebrates his sixty-fourth birthday in Isla Negra. He plans to write his memoirs based on the series of articles published by the journal *O Cruzeiro Internacional* in 1962.

1968 AUGUST 22: Neruda travels to Montevideo with Matilde. They continue to Brazil. In São Paolo, Neruda inaugurates a monument to Federico García Lorca. Then he visits Salvador, Congonhas, Petrópolis, Ouro Prêto, and Brasília, where he meets the city's founder, architect Oscar Niemeyer.

1968 OCTOBER: From Brazil they travel on to Colombia, where Neruda and Miguel Ángel Asturias form part of the jury for the First Festival of University Theater in Manizales.

1968 NOVEMBER: Losada, in Buenos Aires, publishes *Las manos del día* (The Hands of the Day).

1968 Neruda tells his editor Gonzalo Losada of his plan to build Cantalao, a place where writers and artists can stay to work, on a piece of land he has purchased near Isla Negra.

12. CRUEL, BELOVED HOMELAND

1969 JANUARY AND FEBRUARY: Neruda participates in the electoral campaign for the Communist Party candidates in the March parliamentary elections.

1969 JULY: Nascimento, in Santiago, publishes *Aún* (Still).

1969 AUGUST: The Society for Contemporary Art in Santiago publishes *Fin de mundo* (End of the World) in an edition illustrated by Mario Carreño, Nemesio Antúnez, Pedro Millar, María Martner, Julio Escámez, and Oswaldo Guayasamín.

1969 AUGUST 19: The Chilean National Library in Santiago inaugurates a bibliographic exhibition of the work of Pablo Neruda.

1969 AUGUST 21: The Catholic University of Chile awards Neruda a doctor *scientiae et honoris causa*.

1969 SEPTEMBER 30: The Communist Party declares Neruda its candidate for the Presidency of the Republic in the 1970 elections. The campaign slogan will be "For Popular Unity."

1969 OCTOBER: Neruda makes a cross-country campaign trip from Arica to Lota. In December a second trip will take him to Temuco and Punta Arenas. At the beginning of 1970, a mass of people will greet him in the port of Valparaíso.

1970 JANUARY: Neruda relinquishes his candidacy to support Salvador Allende, who will become the only left-wing candidate.

1970 The Santiago publisher Lord Cochrane releases a deluxe edition of *Twenty Love Poems and a Song of Despair* illustrated with watercolors by Mario Toral.

1970 APRIL: Neruda leaves for Europe with Matilde. In Moscow he participates in the ceremonies surrounding the hundredth anniversary of Lenin's birth. He will later travel to the Westminster Poetry Festival in London.

1970 JUNE 23: In Cannes, Neruda and Matilde board a ship bound for the Americas. They pass through Barcelona on the twenty-fourth and spend their brief time there with Gabriel García Márquez.

1970 EARLY JULY: Neruda and Matilde stop in Venezuela, where Neruda participates in the Third Latin American Congress of Writers in Caracas. They continue on to Peru, where the poet will give a recital dedicated to the victims of the May 31 earthquake and will meet with President Velasco Alvarado.

1970 MID-JULY: Neruda and Matilde return to Chile. Neruda participates actively in the presidential campaign of Salvador Allende, who will win the election on September 4.

1970 Losada, in Buenos Aires, publishes *La espada encendida* (The Sword Aflame) and *Las piedras del cielo* (The Stones of the Sky).

1970 The Society for Contemporary Art in Santiago publishes *Maremoto* (Tsunami), illustrated with color engravings by Karin Oldfelt.

1971 JANUARY: Neruda travels to Easter Island, where he will remain for around ten days filming chapters of the TV series *Historia y geografía de Pablo Neruda* (History and Geography of Pablo Neruda), directed by Hugo Arévalo, for the Catholic University's Channel 13. This trip will lead to the book *La rosa separada* (The Separated Rose), which will be published in 1972.

1971 JANUARY 21: The Chilean Congress approves Neruda's nomination as ambassador to France.

1971 MARCH 20: Neruda and Matilde arrive in Paris. On the twenty-sixth, he presents his credentials to President Georges Pompidou.

1971 JULY 12: Neruda celebrates his sixty-seventh birthday.

1971 SEPTEMBER–OCTOBER: Neruda searches for a quiet place outside the city to write. In Condé-sur-Iton, in Normandy, an hour and a half from Paris, he finds an old house that had once been attached to a noble estate.

1971 OCTOBER 21: From the Swedish ambassador in Paris, Gunnar Hägglö, Neruda receives official notification that he has won the Nobel Prize in Literature. The Swedish Academy's text describes Neruda as "the poet of violated humanity," noting that he himself has been repeatedly persecuted and that the community of the oppressed from across the world found its place in his work.

1971 LATE OCTOBER: The poet undergoes an operation at Cochin Hospital in Paris. Dr. Raúl Bulnes, a friend of Neruda's and his neighbor in Isla

Negra, travels from Chile to be present during the procedure. Afterward, Neruda goes to relax in the house he has purchased, which he christens "La Manquel."

1971 EARLY DECEMBER: Neruda and Matilde travel to Stockholm. The Nobel Prize ceremony takes place on the tenth. At the official dinner, Neruda gives a brief speech in the name of this year's winners, and follows it with his acceptance speech.

1971 DECEMBER 31: Neruda celebrates New Year's with a group of friends at La Manquel.

1972 JANUARY: Neruda grants Mikis Theodorakis permission to set his *Canto general* to music. The oratorio *Canto general* will be finished after the poet's death, and will debut in Greece in 1974.

1972 FEBRUARY: Neruda participates in the meetings of the Chilean delegation with the Paris Club to renegotiate the country's external debt.

1972 APRIL 10: Neruda gives the opening address for the celebration of the fiftieth anniversary of the P.E.N. club in New York.

1972 APRIL 25: Neruda and Matilde travel to Moscow, where Neruda will be admitted to a clinic between April 26 and May 5.

1972 MAY: Losada in Buenos Aires publishes *Geografía infructuosa* (Fruitless Geography).

1972 MID-JUNE: Neruda travels to London to participate in the International Poetry Festival. He is reunited with Octavio Paz, and the two men reconcile.

1972 JUNE 28: Neruda returns to Paris, where he is hospitalized for several days.

1972 JULY 12: Neruda celebrates his sixty-eighth birthday with a dinner at the embassy. He invites a group of friends to La Manquel. Participants in the festivities include Julio Cortázar and his partner, Ugnė Karvelis, Gabriel García Márquez, Carlos Fuentes, Mario Vargas Llosa, Jorge Edwards, Poli Délano, and the Chilean Foreign Minister, Clodomiro Almeyda.

1972 MID-JULY: Neruda receives palliative surgery.

1972 JULY: Laura Reyes, the poet's sister, arrives in Paris with Homero Arce, a poet whose aid Neruda has requested in the preparation of his memoirs.

1972 OCTOBER 26: Neruda meets with French President Georges Pompidou.

1972 OCTOBER 28: Neruda is elected to a four-year term as member of UNESCO's Advisory Board.

1972 NOVEMBER 20: Neruda and Matilde return to Chile by plane.

1972 DECEMBER 5: A ceremony takes place in the National Stadium in Santiago to celebrate the poet's winning the Nobel Prize. General Carlos Prats, Vice President of the Republic, attends in place of President Allende, who is on an overseas tour.

1972 DECEMBER 31: Neruda sees in the New Year with friends at La Sebastiana, his house in Valparaíso.

1973 The Allende government agrees, through the Corporation for Urban Improvement, to carry out the Cantalao project, the poet's last dream: a residence close to the sea where writers and artists can work. The architects Raúl Bules, Carlos Martner, and Virginia Plubins are responsible for the design, with Neruda's active participation.

1973 FEBRUARY 2: President Salvador Allende and his wife arrive in Isla Negra to visit Neruda. Also in attendance is a writer from the Communist Party, Luis Corvalán, and the senator Volodia Teitelboim. On this occasion, Neruda renounces his French ambassadorship.

1973 FEBRUARY 16: Quimantú, in Santiago, publishes *Incitación al Nixonicidio y alabanza de la revolución chilena* (Incitation to Nixonicide and Praise of the Chilean Revolution) in an edition of seventy thousand copies.

1973 Despite his fragile health, Neruda continues writing. He is working on the end of his memoirs and on seven volumes of poetry. He intends to publish them to celebrate his seventieth birthday, on July 12, 1974.

1973 EARLY APRIL: At the Hotel Miramar in Viña del Mar, where the poet is recovering after a round of cobalt radiation therapy, he dictates to the journalist Luis Alberto Mansilla an homage to Pablo Picasso, who died on April 8.

1973 MID-APRIL: Matilde travels to Paris to arrange for the transport of possessions they have left at the embassy and to put La Manquel up for sale.

1973 JULY 12: Neruda celebrates his sixty-ninth birthday in Isla Negra with a small group of friends he receives from his bed.

1973 AUGUST 30: Again, Luis Alberto Mansilla visits. The poet asks him to come to Isla Negra so he can dictate a contribution to the ninetieth-birthday celebrations of Dr. Alejandro Lipschutz.

1973 SEPTEMBER 11: The poet and Matilde learn from radio and television broadcasts of the military coup, the bombardment of La Moneda Palace, and the death of President Allende.

1973 SEPTEMBER 14: Neruda dictates a text to Matilde for the close of his memoirs. The house on Isla Negra is raided by a military patrol.

1973 SEPTEMBER 19: The poet's health worsens. He is transferred to Santiago by ambulance in the company of Matilde. He is admitted with a fever to the Clínica Santa María.

1973 SEPTEMBER 23: The poet dies at 10:30 p.m. The vigil is held at his house La Chascona, which is in a ruinous state after numerous acts of vandalism.

1973 SEPTEMBER 25: Pablo Neruda is buried in Santiago's Cementerio General. Despite the intimidating military presence, a mass of people spontaneously joins the funeral procession, and the poet's burial becomes the first manifestation of popular rejection of the military government.

Index

Ady, Endre, 353
Aga Khan, 347
Aguirre, Margarita, 133, 335, 378
Aguirre, Sócrates, 334
Aguirre Cerda, Pedro, 178, 184–85,
    205, 436
Ai Ch'ing, 261, 280, 290, 294–95, 298,
    300
Alarcón, Asterio, 285–86
Alba, Duke and Duchess of, 309–12
Alberti, Rafael, 86, 88, 140, 142, 144,
    145, 151, 154, 158, 160, 163, 171–75,
    241–42, 257, 347, 453
Alderete (journalist), 236
Alegría, Ciro, 418
Alegría, Fernando, 451
Aleixandre, Vicente, 86, 142, 145
Alekseevich, Pyotr (Peter the Great),
    243
Alessandri Palma, Arturo, 68, 333,
    398
Alexandrov, Grigory, 257
Alicattas (Naples friends), 266
Allende, Salvador, 337, 385, 391,
    432–33, 436, 438, 439, 440, 441, 442,
    443, 444–47
Alone (Hernán Díaz Arrieta), 64
Alonso, Amado, 372
Altolaguirre, Manuel, 142, 144–45, 150,
    156, 157

Altolaguirre, Paloma, 145
Alvarez del Vayo, Julio, 180, 185
Amado, Jorge, 289, 293–95, 298, 300,
    404
Amado, Zelia, 289, 293–95
Andreyev, Leonid, 51, 333
Antúnez, Nemesio, 238, 271
Aparicio, Antonio, 142
Apollinaire, Guillaume, 52, 60
Aragon, Elsa, see Triolet, Elsa
Aragon, Louis, 158, 159, 162, 180, 187,
    236, 257, 306–307, 385, 410
Aramburu, Pedro Eugenio, 283–84
Aráoz Alfaro, Rodolfo, 378
Arce, Homero, 61
Arciniegas, Germán, 428
Arenales, Angélica, 197
Argensola, Bartolomé Leonardo de,
    138, 143
Argensola, Lupercio Leonardo de, 138,
    143
Arguijo, Juan del, 138
Arrau, Claudio, 121
Artsybashev, Mikhail, 333
Asterio (watchmaker), 285–86
Asturias, Miguel Angel, 197, 234–35,
    281
Auden, W. H., 160
Azev (spy), 424
Azócar, Rubén, 366–68, 454

Baera (professor in India), 252
Balmaceda, José Manuel, 445–46
Barba Jacob, Porfirio, 334
Barquero, Efraín, 281–83
Bartolomé (eccentric in Valparaíso),
     76–77
Basoalto de Reyes, Rosa, 10
Baudelaire, Charles, 28–29, 373,
     377–78, 426
Bécquer, Gustavo Adolfo, 172
Beebe, Charles William, 272
Beecham, Thomas, 161
Belaúnde, Fernando, 418
Bellay, Guillaume du, 354
Bellet, Jorge, 225–27, 228
Bello, Andrés, 396–97, 455
Beniuc, Mihai, 309
Bennett, Arnold, 432–33
Berceo, Gonzalo de, 326
Bergamín, José, 142
Beria, Lavrenti, 409, 410
Berling, Gösta, 384
Bertaux (chief of police in France),
     239–40
Betancourt, Rómulo, 413, 414
Beyle, Marie-Henri ("Stendhal"), 307
Bhrampy (houseboy), 113, 124, 125,
     128, 131, 132–33
Bianchi, Victor, 83–84, 228–29, 234
Blest Gana, 435
Bliss, Josie, 108–109, 118–19, 290
Bloch, Jean-Richard, 238
Blow, Joe, 364–69
Blum, Léon, 178
Bolívar, Simón, 379, 393, 394, 396, 397
Borejsza, Jerzy, 350–53
Boscán, Juan, 354
Bose, Subhas Chandra, 102–103
Botana, Natalio, 153
Boureanu, Radu, 309
Bowers, Claude, 219
Braganza, Duchess of, 86
Brandt, Willy, 386–87
Brecht, Bertolt, 257
Brik, Lili, 411
Brunet, Marta, 121
Buddha, 103–104, 105, 288

Buffalo Bill, 14, 24
Bulnes, Raúl, 224
Byron, George Gordon ("Lord"), 171

Caballero, José, 142
Cabezón, Isaías, 54
Calcutta Strangler (wrestler), 57
Calderón de la Barca, Pedro, 143
Camacho Ramírez, Arturo, 386
Candia Marverde, Trinidad, 12–13
Capablanca, José Raúl, 135
Cárdenas, Lázaro, 402
Carlos (commandant), see Vidali,
     Vittorio
Caro, Rodrigo, 138
Carol (Romanian monarch), 309
Carpentier, Alejo, 158, 419
Carrera, José Miguel, 393–94
Carril, Delia del (wife), 162–63, 238,
     270, 281
Carroll, Lewis, 159
Carvajal, Armando, 121
Casas, Bartolomé de las, 340
Castro, Fidel, 413–16, 417, 442
Catherine (empress of Russia), 395
Cavalcanti, Guido, 354
Céline, Louis-Ferdinand, 175
Cerio, Edwin, 268–69
Cernuda, Luis, 142, 145
Cervantes, Miguel de, 326, 343
Chambers, Whittaker, 424
Chamisso, Adelbert von, 407
Chaucer, Geoffrey, 326
Chekhov, Anton, 25
Chiang Kai-shek, 300
Chou En-lai, 262
Christ, 104, 301, 308, 339, 428
Churchill, Winston, 433
Chu Teh, 262
Cifuentes Sepúlveda, Joaquín, 378
Codovilla, Victorio, 405–406
Colette, Sidonie-Gabrielle, 236
Columbus, Christopher, 59, 149
Condon (shipping magnate), 88–89
Condon, Alfredo, 150
Condon, Carmen, 150
Confucius, 309

Corniglion-Molinier (aviator), 164
Cortázar, Julio, 362, 386
Cortés, Hernán, 207–208
Corvalán, Luis, 431
Cotapos, Acario, 142, 347
Crevel, René, 154
Cruchaga Tocornal, Miguel, 177
Crusoe, Robinson, 80
Cunard, Lady Emerald, 160–61
Cunard, Nancy, 159–62

D'Annunzio, Gabriele, 359, 364
Dante Alighieri, 342, 354
Darío, Rubén, 87, 136–39, 326, 361
Debray, Régis, 416
de Gaulle, Charles, 201, 203
Deglané, Bobby, 146
Demaría, Alfredo, 50
Desnoes, Edmundo, 421
Desnos, Robert, 154
Díaz Arrieta, Hernán ("Alone"), 64
Díaz Casanueva, Humberto, 144
Díaz Pastor, Fulgencio, 347
Diego, Gerardo, 86
Donoso, José, 362
Dostoevsky, Feodor, 25
Drda, Jan, 280
Drieu La Rochelle, Pierre, 175
Ducasse, Isidore ("Lautréamont"), 145,
    327, 343, 373
Durruti, Buenaventura, 423

Echelarte (family), 393
Edwards, Jorge, 384, 436–37
Edward VIII (Duke of Windsor), 161
Egaña, Juan, 333
Ehrenburg, Ilya, 44, 195, 238–39, 241,
    245–46, 249, 257–60, 261, 263–64,
    280, 305, 307–308, 328, 378,
    410–11
Ehrenburg, Lyuba, 410
Einstein, Albert, 176
Eisenstein, Sergei Mikhailovich, 411
El Greco, see Theotokópoulos,
    Doménikos
Eliot, T. S., 324
Eluard, Dominique, 271, 348

Eluard, Paul, 158–59, 236, 271, 343,
    347–49
Emar, Juan (Pilo Yáñez), 47–48
Ercilla, Alonso de, 9, 18, 381
Escobar (chauffeur), 224
Escobar, Zoilo, 74–76
Espinosa, Pedro de, 145

Fadeyev, Alexander, 249
Fantômas (fictional character), 240
Fauré, Gabriel, 119
Fedin, Konstantin, 249
Felipe, León, 169, 170, 201, 356–57
Fernández, Joaquín, 240–41
Fernández Retamar, Roberto, 379, 421
Fierro, Martín (fictional character), 326
Figueroa, Inés, 271
Fonseca, Ricardo, 222–23
Foppens, Jean François, 341
Franck, César, 119–21
Franco, Francisco, 145, 151–52, 157–58,
    160, 166, 167, 182–83, 219, 309, 421,
    423, 426
Fraser, G. S., 324–25
Frei, Eduardo, 440–41, 442–43, 444–45
Fuentes, Carlos, 362, 419

Gable, Clark, 222
Gallegos, Rómulo, 383
Gandhi, Mahatma, 102, 251, 255
Gandulfo, Juan, 50, 333
García Lorca, Federico, 50, 65, 86,
    135–37, 139, 140, 142, 144, 145,
    146–56, 171, 175, 346–47, 453
García Lorca, Francisco, 150
García Márquez, Gabriel, 363, 386, 412
García Rico (bookseller), 341
Garcilaso de la Vega, 172, 354
Garfias, Pedro, 183–84
Gascar, Alice, 271
Gasperi, Alcide De, 267
Gattai, Zelia, see Amado, Zelia
Gauguin, Paul, 80
Gautama, Siddhārtha, see Buddha
Gide, André, 427
Girondo, Oliverio, 281
Giroux, Françoise, 236–37

Goebbels, Joseph, 307, 308
Goethe, Johann Wolfgang von, 376
Gómez, Juan Vicente, 86
Gómez de la Serna, Ramón, 143
Gómez Rojas, Domingo, 50
Góngora, Luis de, 139, 143, 159, 172,
    326, 341, 342, 343, 354, 362
González, Galo, 223
González Cruchaga, Carlos (bishop),
    442
González Tuñón, Amparo, 163
González Tuñón, Raúl, 160
González Vera, José Santos, 51
González Videla, Gabriel, 216–19,
    226–27, 444, 453
Goya, Francisco de, 138, 194, 311
Gris, Juan, 47, 360
Guevara, Alvaro ("Chile"), 58–59
Guevara, Ernesto ("Che"), 378–79,
    416–17, 424–25
Guillén, Jorge, 144, 145, 154
Güiraldes, Ricardo, 253–54
Gustaf VI (king), 385, 387, 389
Gutiérrez, Joaquín, 266
Guttuso, Renato, 267, 268

Hagenaar, María Antonieta, 133–34
Hauser, Kaspar, 278
Heine, Heinrich, 176, 377
Hernández (family), 28, 31–33, 392, 451
Hernández, Miguel, 139–42, 145, 152,
    156, 157–58, 166, 347
Herrera (general), 182–83
Herrera Petere, José, 201
Herrera y Reissig, Julio, 145
Hertz (German consul), 134
Hikmet, Nazim, 246–47, 251, 378,
    402
Hinojosa, Álvaro, 61–63, 85, 89–90,
    91–92, 95–96
Hita, Archpriest of (Juan Ruiz), 326
Hitler, Adolf, 58, 134, 175–76, 187,
    199–200, 297, 360, 412, 423, 439
Ho Chi Minh, 290
Hölderlin, Friedrich, 214–15, 328
Hollander, Carlos, 335–36
Hugo, Víctor, 273

Huidobro, Vicente, 82, 88, 164–65, 326,
    359–62, 375
Huxley, Aldous, 161
Huxley, Julian, 203–204

Ibarra, Joaquín, 342
Ibsen, Henrik, 24
Iglesias (tennis champion), 425–26
Ilyés, Gyulla, 353
Indy, Vincent d', 119

Jammes, Francis, 53
Jarpa, Sergio Onofre, 444
Jason (in Bible), 301
Jebeleanu, Eugen, 309
Jiménez, Juan Ramón, 138, 143–44, 145
Joliot-Curie, Frédéric, 251, 253, 254,
    255
Joyce, James, 95, 144
József, Attila, 353
Juanito (Chilean peasant boy), 278–80

Khrushchev, Nikita, 313
Kipling, Rudyard, 311
Kiria (mongoose), 111–12, 123–24, 125,
    130, 131–33
Kirsanov, Semyon, 246, 378
Kisch, Egon Erwin, 200
Korneichuk, Alexander, 238
Kruzi, 125–28
Kuo Mo-jo, 257
Kutvalek, 280

Labarca, Santiago, 50
Lacasa, Luis, 142
Lafertte, Elías, 316, 397, 399–401, 406,
    455
Laforgue, Jules, 343, 373, 377
Lagerlöf, Selma, 163
Lago, Tomás, 384
Lange, Norah, 281
Larra, Raúl, 281
Larraín, Sergio, 452
Larrazábal, Wolfgang, 413
Lautréamont, see Ducasse, Isidore
Laval, Pierre, 187
Lawrence, D. H., 115

Legarreta (Neruda pseudonym), 228
Lehmbruck, Wilhelm, 134
Lenin, Vladimir Ilyich Ulyanov, 243,
    312, 361
León, María Teresa, 158, 173, 174
Leopardi, Giacomo, 354
Levi, Carlo, 267
Li (interpreter), 299
Litvinov, Maxim Maximovich, 409
López, Alfonso, 217
Lorca, see García Lorca, Federico
Losada, Gonzalo, 362
Loyola, Hernán, 451
Lucretius, 332
Luis de Granada (Fray), 138
Luis de León (Fray), 149
Lundkvist, Artur, 385

Machado, Antonio, 138, 143, 151
Machado, Gerardo, 134, 318
Machado, Manuel, 138
Maigret, Inspector Jules (fictional
    character), 240
Malaparte, Curzio, 210
Mallarmé, Stéphane, 214–15
Mallo, Maruja, 142–43, 151
Malraux, André, 164–65
Mann, Thomas, 176
Manrique, Jorge, 172, 307, 323
Mansilla (Chilean consul), 94–95, 125,
    129
Mao Tse-tung, 295, 296, 299, 409
Mao Tung, 261
Maqueira, Tulio, 139–40
Marc, Franz, 134
Marcenac, Jean, 385
Marín, Arellano, 180–82
Marín, Juan, 254–55
Marinello, Juan, 374, 421
Maritain, Jacques, 441
Mason, Carlos, 11–12
Mason, Micaela Candia, 12
Matisse, Henri, 340
Matta, Roberto, 386
Maugham, W. Somerset, 125, 432–33
Mauny, Count de, 117
Maura, Duke of, 200

Maura Gamazo, Gabriel, see Maura,
    Duke of
Mayakovsky, Vladimir, 172, 245, 332,
    362, 363, 407–408, 411, 455
Medioni, Gilbert, 201
Melgarejo, Mariano, 217
Mella, Julio Antonio, 318
Membrives, Lola, 135
Menéndez (family), 393
Mery, Hernán, 445
Meza Fuentes, Roberto, 51
Michelangelo, 360
Mikoyan, Anastas, 409
Miller, Arthur, 418
Miranda, Francisco de, 395
Mistral, Gabriela, 25, 218–19, 326, 338,
    357–59, 378, 383–84
Modotti, Tina, 317–19
Molière, 342
Molina Núñez, Julio, 333
Molotov, Vyachelav, 409
Monge (railway worker), 11
Montagnana, Mario, 201
Montes (family), 393
Moore, George, 161
Moore, Marianne, 420
Mora, Constancia de la, 200–201
Morante, Elsa, 267
Moravia, Alberto, 267
Moreno Villa, José, 201
Morla Lynch, Carlos, 157–58
Munthe, Axel, 269
Murga, Romeo, 42–43

Napoleon Bonaparte, 88, 198, 258
Negrín, Juan, 180, 185
Nehru, Jawaharlal, 102, 251, 253,
    255–57
Nehru, Motilal, 102–103, 255
Neira (publisher), 376
Neruda, Matilde (wife), see Urrutia,
    Matilde
Nerval, Gérard de, 328
Niemoeller, Martin, 176
Nixon, Richard, 58
Noah (in Bible), 302
Novoa, 72–74

Ocampo, Victoria, 57, 418
O'Higgins, Bernardo, 394–85
Oliver, María Rosa, 281
Orozco, José Clemente, 194–95, 348
Ortega, Abraham, 186
Ospovat, Lev, 371
Ossietzky, Carl von, 176
Otero, Lisandro, 421
Otero Silva, Miguel, 386, 388
Ovid, 332
Oyarzún, Aliro, 66, 333–34

Pacheco, Horacio, 18–19
Panza, Sancho (fictional character),
    351, 352
Pascal (priest), 285–86, 339
Pasternak, Boris, 245, 411
Patsy, 121
Paz, Octavio, 164
Pérez Jiménez, Marcos, 314
Pérez Rulfo (commandant), 195
Perón, Eva ("Evita"), 233
Perón, Juan, 219, 233, 234, 283–84,
    405–406
Peter the Great (Pyotr Alekseevich),
    243
Petöfi, Sándor, 171
Petrarca, Francesco ("Petrarch"), 326,
    354, 355
Picasso, Pablo, 143, 235, 237, 245, 251,
    257, 271
Poe, Edgar Allan, 426
Poliziano, Angelo, 354
Pound, Ezra, 175
Powers (Buddhist theologian),
    105–106
Powers, Francis Gary, 322
Praxiteles, 306
Prestes, Leocadia, 402–403
Prestes, Luis Carlos, 294, 401–403,
    404–405, 406, 409
Prieto, Miguel, 201
Primo de Rivera, José Antonio, 440
Primo de Rivera, Miguel, 86
Proust, Marcel, 119, 120
Pushkin, Alexander, 171, 243, 244,
    249–50, 322, 453

Quasimodo, Salvatore, 354–55
Quevedo, Francisco de, 119, 138, 143,
    149, 325, 326, 332, 341, 343, 354, 362
Quixote, Don (Alonso Quixano)
    (fictional character), 42, 351, 352

Rabelais, François, 326
Raman, Chandrasekhara, 251
Ramírez, Pedrito, 233, 234
Rango (orangutan), 99
Rapín, Rafael, 155, 156
Recabarren, Luis Emilio, 68, 213–14,
    397–99, 400–401, 422, 436, 442, 455
Redl, Alfred (colonel), 200
Rejano, Juan, 201
Retamar, see Fernández Retamar,
    Roberto
Reverdy, Pierre, 324, 349–50
Reyes, Abadías, 10
Reyes, Alfonso, 191
Reyes, Amós, 10, 305
Reyes, Joel, 10, 305
Reyes, José Angel, 10, 305
Reyes, José del Carmen (father), 10,
    368
Reyes, Laura, 17, 20
Reyes, Oseas, 10, 305
Reyes, Rodolfo, 17
Ricci, Paolo, 266, 270
Rilke, Rainer Maria, 427
Rimbaud, Arthur, 91, 119, 328, 343
Rimbaud, Isabelle, 343
Rivera, Diego, 195, 196, 317
Robeson, Paul, 118
Rocambole (fictional character), 25
Roces, Wenceslao, 200–201
Rodríguez, Pepe, 226–28
Rodríguez Luna, Antonio, 201
Rodríguez Marín, F., 147
Rodríguez Monegal, Emir, 371, 418–19
Rodríguez Rapún, Rafael, see Rapín,
    Rafael
Rojas, Manuel, 51
Rojas Giménez, Alberto, 51–55, 61,
    378
Rojas Giménez, Rosita, 53
Romero, Elvio, 281

Rommel, Erwin, 195
Ronsard, Pierre de, 186, 258, 354
Rosenberg, Ethel and Julius, 424
Rothschild, Alphonse de, 306–307
Ruiz, Juan (Archpriest of Hita), 326
Rulfo, Juan, 362

Sabat Ercasty, Carlos, 66
Sábato, Ernesto, 362, 418
Saint-Saëns, Camille, 119
Salazar, Antonio, 85
Salgari, Emilio, 14, 23
Salinas, Pedro, 144, 154
Sánchez, Alberto, 142, 174, 347, 453
Sánchez, Celia, 415
Sandino, Augusto César, 398
San Martín, José Francisco de, 393, 394, 395
Santa Cruz, Domingo, 121
Savich, Ovadi, 378
Schneider, René, 439
Schubert, Franz, 119
Schweitzer, Daniel, 50
Seferis, George, 382
Seghers, Anna, 176, 200, 257
Segura Castro, Óscar, 333
Sepúlveda, Tristan, 91
Serrano Plaja, Arturo, 142
Shakespeare, William, 236, 354
Shostakovich, Dimitri, 411
Siao Emi, 261, 280, 298, 300
Silva, José Asunción, 316, 377
Simenon, Georges, 379
Simonov, Konstantin, 238, 301, 314
Siqueiros, David Alfaro, 195, 196–97, 386
Siqueiros, Jesús, 195–96
Sitwell, Edith, 59
Sobrino, Eladio, 177
Somlyó, György, 353
Somoza, Anastasio, 314
Soong Ch'ing-ling, 257, 262–63
Soustelle, Jacques, 201, 203
Spender, Stephen, 160
Stalin, Joseph, 223, 258, 294, 296, 297, 409–12
Stendhal, 307

Streicher, Julius, 176
Sue, Eugène, 327
Sun Yat-sen, 257, 262
Supervielle, Jules, 239, 240
Swift, Jonathan, 161

Tagore, Rabindranath, 96
Talvande, Maurice, see Mauny, Count de
Tamayo, Rufino, 196
Tchaikovsky, Peter Illich, 83, 84
Theotokópoulos, Doménikos ("El Greco"), 237
Thielman, María, 13
Thomas, Dylan, 328
Tikhonov, Nikolai, 238, 249
Ting Ling, 261, 298, 300
Titov, Gherman, 313
Tolstoy, Leo, 25
Tomic, Radomiro, 442–43
Torre, Carlos de la, 342
Triolet, Elsa, 180, 306, 410
Tristan, Flora, 80
Trotsky, Leon, 195, 370
Trujillo, Rafael, 314, 427
Twain, Mark, 236

Ubico, Jorge, 198
Unamuno, Miguel de, 52, 55
Urrutia, Matilde (wife), 260, 268–70, 271–72, 281, 283–84, 285, 295, 344, 345, 379, 382, 384, 386–87, 388, 389, 414–15, 416, 429, 434, 452, 453

Valdivia, Alberto, 55–56
Valéry, Paul, 383
Valle, Rosamel del, 144
Valle-Inclán, Ramón del, 138, 143
Vallejo, César, 87–88, 164, 355–56
Vargas, Getulio, 402, 403
Vargas Llosa, Mario, 362
Vargas Vila, José María, 24–25, 359
Vasallo, Carlos, 386
Vega, Lope de, 362
Velázquez, Diego, 138
Venturelli, José, 238
Verdi, Giuseppe, 121

Verne, Jules, 377
Vial, Sarita, 285
Viaux (colonel), 444–45
Vicuña, Carlos, 333
Vidali, Vittorio ("Commandant
  Carlos"), 201, 265–66, 317–18
Vignole, Omar, 56–57
Villar, Amado, 137
Vishinsky, Andrei, 248, 409

Wagner, Richard, 119
Wendt, Lionel, 115
Whitman, Walt, 327, 373, 430
Wilson, Blanca, 14
Windsor, Duke of (Edward VIII),
  161

Winter, Augusto, 24–25
Winzer, 117–18
Woolf, Leonard, 114–15
Woolf, Virginia, 115

Yáñez, Mina, 47–48
Yáñez, Pilo (Juan Emar), 47–48
Yeats, William Butler, 163
Yegulev, Sacha (fictional character), 51,
  333
Yufu San, 93

Zaldívar, Andrés, 443
Zapata, Emiliano, 398
Zhdanov, Andrei, 245
Zweig, Arnold, 176